CLASSICAL CANONS

For Lorre,
My Belle-Lettriste

Classical Canons

Rhetoric, classicism and treaty interpretation

DAVID J. BEDERMAN
Emory University School of Law

Ashgate

Aldershot • Burlington USA • Singapore • Sydney

Published by
Ashgate Publishing Limited
Gower House
Croft Road
Aldershot
Hampshire GU11 3HR
England

Ashgate Publishing Company
131 Main Street
Burlington, VT 05401-5600 USA

Ashgate website: http://www.ashgate.com

British Library Cataloguing in Publication Data
Bederman, David J.
Classical canons : rhetoric, classicism and treaty interpretation. - (Applied legal philosophy)
1. Law - Interpretation and construction
I. Title
340.1

Library of Congress Control Number: 00-109566

ISBN 0 7546 2161 8

Printed and bound by Athenaeum Press, Ltd., Gateshead, Tyne & Wear.

Contents

Antiquity

Intermezzo

Modernity

Coda

List of Figures

Series Preface

The objective of the Dartmouth Series in Applied Legal Philosophy is to publish work which adopts a theoretical approach to the study of particular areas or aspects of law or deals with general theories of law in a way which focuses on issues of practical moral and political concern in specific legal contexts.

In recent years there has been an encouraging tendency for legal philosophers to utilize detailed knowledge of the substance and practicalities of law and a noteworthy development in the theoretical sophistication of much legal research. The series seeks to encourage these trends and to make available studies in law which are both genuinely philosophical in approach and at the same time based on appropriate legal knowledge and directed towards issues in the criticism and reform of actual laws and legal systems.

The series will include studies of all the main areas of law, presented in a manner which relates to the concerns of specialist legal academics and practitioners. Each book makes an original contribution to an area of legal study while being comprehensible to those engaged in a wide variety of disciplines. Their legal content is principally Anglo-American, but a wide-ranging comparative approach is encouraged and authors are drawn from a variety of jurisdictions.

TOM D. CAMPBELL
Series Editor
The Faculty of Law
The Australian National University

Acknowledgments

I am grateful to many colleagues for helpful insights which made this book possible. Among my Romanist and comparative law and legal history collaborators, I count Hans W. Baade, Harold J. Berman, Brian Bix, Thomas M. Franck, Edward Gordon, Herbert Hausmaninger, R.H. Helmholz, Theodor Meron, William Nelson, Charles Reid, Jr., Mortimer Sellers, Alan Watson, and John Witte, Jr. As for discussions I had on modern paradigms of statutory construction, I owe a debt to Christopher Eisgruber, William Eskridge, and Lawrence Sager. For reflections on modern treaty interpretation, I thank Maria Frankowska, Benedict Kingsbury, Rick Kirgis, John Noyes, Jordan Paust, Al Rubin, Charles Shanor, Eric Stein, Joel Trachtman, and Carlos Vázquez.

I benefitted tremendously by participating in workshops on this project at Emory University School of Law, University of Iowa College of Law, New York University School of Law, and the University of Virginia School of Law. Part of this project was also presented at the Third Meeting of the International Society for the Classical Tradition in 1995.

Thanks also go to my research assistant, John L. Mallinson, NYU Law class of 1997, who proofed the Latin quotations in the manuscript. Thanks also to Joshua K. Leader, Emory Law class of 1996, for work on Grotius' DE JURE BELLI AC PACIS. Elizabeth Snodgrass, Virginia Law class of 1997, provided superb research on the Vienna Convention on the Law of Treaties. Additional research assistance was provided by Todd Hennings, Emory class of 1993, Christine Beth Ledvinka, Emory class of 1994, and Paul A. Moore, Virginia class of 1998.

Finally, I acknowledge the superb assistance and collegiality of Professor Aldo Lupi, Professor of Latin and Greek, at Georgia State University, in Atlanta, who painstakingly checked by Latin and Attic Greek usages, as well as offering important counsel on the work.

As always, though, any errors or omissions are my responsibility alone.

* *** *

Parts of this volume have earlier appeared in print. Short segments of Chapter VII were in my article, *Reception of the Classical Tradition in International Law: Grotius'* De Jure Belli ac Pacis, 10 EMORY INTERNATIONAL LAW REVIEW 1 (1996). Chapters XI, XII and XIII formed a substantial part of my piece, *Revivalist Canons and Treaty Interpretation*, 41 UCLA LAW REVIEW 953 (1994). A few, isolated passages in Chapter III were included in my book, INTERNATIONAL LAW IN ANTIQUITY (Cambridge University Press, 2001).

* *** *

Lastly, I thank my wonderful family who helped me persevere through this project. *Vale!*

Abbreviations

AJIL	*American Journal of International Law*
AJJ	*American Journal of Jurisprudence*
AJLH	*American Journal of Legal History*
AJP	*American Journal of Philology*
CQ	*Classical Quarterly*
DJBaP	*De Jure Belli ac Pacis* (Grotius)
GRBS	*Greek, Roman and Byzantine Studies*
ICJ	*International Court of Justice*
ILM	*International Legal Materials*
Ivra	*Rivista internazionale di diritto romano e antico*
PCIJ	*Permanent Court of International Justice*
RCADI	*Recueil des Cours de l'Academie de Droit International de la Haye*
RGDIP	*Revue Générale de Droit International Public*
RIDA	*Revue internationale des droits de l'antiquité (ser. 3)*

look not to the law, but to the legislator; not to
the letter of the law but to the intention of the
legislator. . . .

Aristotle, RHETORIC,
passage i.13.17

summum ius summa iniuria

Cicero, DE OFFICIIS,
passage i.10.33

Praefatio

i. This volume examines an enduring question in law and jurisprudence: where did the special rules used to interpret legal texts come from, and why do they remain significant today? Known as "canons" of interpretation, these rules for construing legal writings (like statutes, contracts or constitutions) are at the center of one of the most contentious debates in the legal academy and courts. At stake is the balance of power between judges and legislators to make and construe laws, and thus the integrity of legal systems in representative democracies. Also at issue is the legitimacy of the written "law" itself, for if the rules for interpreting legal texts are themselves indeterminate then that casts doubt on the probity and neutrality of those writings.

This study offers an intellectual history of these canons and concludes that rules of legal interpretation originated in classical antiquity. They were derived from a unique synergy between classical rhetoric and the practice of Roman law. Canons of construction were part of the well-documented process of transmission of legal ideas from classical antiquity to medieval Europe. Moreover, this process of dissemination continued into early-Modern and Enlightenment times and culminated in their playing an important role in the creation of American constitutional culture. This volume charts the course of this extraordinary voyage.

ii. The book also tells an intellectual tale of two disciplines that have not corresponded together for quite a long time. Law and classics have had an uneasy association of late. It has not been one so much of hostility, as of indifference and aloofness. It can be neatly summarized in a classicists' skeptical question: "What can a classicist learn from a lawyer?" Here is my answer.

Although I have been much preoccupied by this challenge, I have found it impossible to answer it directly. There seemed so little common ground between law and the classics today that I despaired in writing a volume which

1

merely expressed sentiments of cheerful interdisciplinary solidarity. So, instead, what I have tried to create here is some common ground by suggesting a joint intellectual project, something that I think both classicists and legal scholars might be interested in pursuing together as intellectual partners.

iii. A number of classical scholars made this project possible. It began with an off-handed remark made over lunch at a meeting of classicists I had attended some years ago. Frankly, it was rather intimidating for me as a law professor to be presenting a paper at a conference by and for ancient historians and philologists. By the same token, I suppose it was a bit unsettling for classicists to have an academic lawyer intrude legal doctrine into their meditations, even if it was in the form of a discussion of the transmission of ideas.

The primary feeling I carried away from the meeting was that lawyers and classicists have much to say to each other. But our deliberations must be mediated by care. This caution must really be exercised, I believe, by colleagues on my side of the disciplinary fence. Classicists have much to teach legal academics about language, about texts, and about ideas. But in our attempt to learn, we must take care not to subvert the very concepts they offer. At the same time, legal academics must not in their enthusiasm rush to embrace unfamiliar ideas and declare them to be theirs. Good fences make good neighbors, and if we are to re-open a dialogue between law and the classics some intellectual distance is needed.

iv. This study hopes to achieve that happy balance. It begins with a scholarly question, asked innocently. Just as naïvely, I undertook to research it. The inquiry came in the form of a speculation. A number of classicists had been struck by that part of my presentation concerning the modern development of rules for interpreting legal texts, particularly of constitutions, statutes, and treaties — what a lawyer might call "public law" documents. They wondered whether the development of rules for interpretation, or canons of construction, may have been influenced by classical rhetorical theory.

Until that remark was made, I had been oblivious to the fact that Greek and Roman rhetoricians had much interest in juristic subjects, and certainly not in such a lawyerly task as interpreting quintessentially legal texts. From my undergraduate education, I knew a little bit about classical rhetoric. But I certainly never made any connection between rhetoric and law in antiquity.

I suppose my only defense to being considered badly educated is that I am the product of my legal training — both the one that I pursued and the one that I now profess. Lawyers seem to be uncomfortable with too closely associating with rhetoricians — or whatever we now call people whose job it is to persuade (preachers? politicians?). That is ironic, of course, because one job for the lawyer is to influence in order to achieve a client's objective, whether that be a favorable result in a business negotiation or an acquittal in a criminal proceeding. We are uneasy today with the very word "rhetoric" because it implies an art of persuasion divorced from truth. And, in order to maintain our professional equilibrium, lawyers must be both (at one and the same time) persuaders and truth-seekers.

In any event, I had come to believe that rhetoric has little to teach lawyers. The classicists' comment began a process of persuading me that I might be wrong about that. What I relate in this study is how my research proceeded in discovering whether the very current debate about the proper means and methods of interpreting legal texts (especially those having the force of public law) has deeper roots than legal scholars have previously supposed, reaching back to classical antiquity.

v. To make this study have at least the semblance of coherence, I had to choose one kind of legal text as being paradigmatic of the rest, a sort of laboratory in this clinical trial of intellectual history. I chose treaties, international agreements between sovereign nations. One reason was pure disciplinary pre-disposition: I am by training a public international lawyer. When one enters unfamiliar intellectual terrain, it is best to take some trusted things with you. And although the handling of treaty texts is neither prosaic, nor typical, for most lawyers, it is for me.

But, much more pertinently, the choice of treaties for this volume satisfied two other criterion. The first was that the kind of legal text chosen had to be one that was known to classical antiquity. Otherwise, the connection between law and classics would have been rather more attenuated, and the discussion here rather less interesting and relevant. And while comfortable in the scholarship of Roman law, I preferred to chart a course in which the materials from classical antiquity were equally accessible to both lawyers and classicists. Material on ancient statecraft and diplomacy fits that bill. Just as important, though, I found that the story captured in the material on ancient treaty-making was itself a subject of the transmission of ideas, ones that profoundly influenced the early development of international law as a modern discipline.

The second criterion to satisfy was a sense of intellectual challenge. As legal texts go, treaties are *weird*. They have a curious, multi-faceted quality about them. On the one hand, treaties appear to be just a form of contract, albeit made between sovereign States on the international plane. On the other hand, treaties and international agreements have a general, law-making character to them. They are legislative, like an act of Congress or Parliament. In the same vein, a few treaties can (say, like the Charter of the United Nations) be almost constitutional in their purpose and in the tone of their drafting. Lastly, a handful of treaties are not really reciprocal international agreements at all. They are, rather, thinly-disguised unilateral settlements or concessions in international relations. In this way, they can be much like a will disposing of an estate.

Treaties can thus reflect the full range of possibilities for any written legal instrument: reciprocal *contract*, legislative *statute*, unilateral *will*, and fundamental *constitution*. It is precisely this ambiguity in the form and function of treaties that has led to such problems in their interpretation and enforcement, especially in today's world of complex international relations.

This problem is particularly acute where one has (as today) two different kinds of institutions which can construe and enforce treaties: (1) international judicial and arbitral tribunals (such as the World Court at The Hague), applying arguably global standards and rules of construction; and (2) domestic organs (such as the Executive Branch or Supreme Court in the United States), using tools of interpretation drawn from a particular and distinctive legal and constitutional culture. This problem of discordant voices in the process and methods of treaty interpretation will form a major theme of this book. It is how I can best show that the practical business of lawyers has a bearing on the work that classicist do in studying ancient texts.

vi. Lawyers and classicists both extol and despise the texts that define our professional lives. Lawyers work daily with documents that we think are uniquely *legal* texts. Legal texts define our legal culture (documents such as the Magna Carta or the United States Constitution come to mind). They often dictate the product of our labor (drafting a contract or a will). They ritualize combat and violence (think of the pleadings filed in a court litigation). The making of legal texts (like legislation on Capitol Hill) makes news in our society and culture, and, so, whenever a legal text is fashioned it reinforces our aspirations as a profession. The fun and frustration of being a lawyer is that our universe of legal texts is constantly increasing. The work of a lawyer is, quite literally, the extension of professional power through the proliferation of legal texts.

My sense is that classical studies is about living a happy life of the mind with a finite, and very circumscribed, number of texts to play with. After all, only so many authentic and uncorrupted Latin and Attic Greek literary texts have come down to us, and the supply of inscription evidence from archaeological discoveries is limited. Classicists have, in other words, a *canon* of texts. The professional prerogative of classicists is to gloss those texts *ad infinitum*, to plumb their depths and comprehend their meaning.

What happens, then, when the imperialist lawyer makes friends with the orthodox classicist? Do we have such radically different professional attitudes towards the handling of texts that it is impossible to speak to each other on this subject? The intellectual project I have outlined here offers, I think, fruitful possibilities for inter-disciplinary collaboration.

vii. I try to proceed in this volume in a way that will promote a common enterprise.[1] I begin with what should be utterly familiar to any scholar of classical rhetoric: a basic description of the practice of declamation and public speaking in classical antiquity. Next, I try to examine the details of how Roman rhetoricians were trained to work with legal texts, the study of *stasis* and its application to questions of legal interpretation. This part of my book (chapters

---

[1] One aspect of that joint intellectual effort is sharing research. As Anthony Grafton has noted, the use of footnotes — especially in historical writing — is a "peculiar and wonderful experience. The reader hears, and even takes part in, a conversation with the author and the author's witnesses alike — a conversation more intense, more critical, and more suggestive than the reading of a bare text can ever be." Anthony Grafton, *The Death of the Footnote (Report on an Exaggeration)*, 21 WILSON QUARTERLY 72, 77 (Winter 1997).

Those notes in this book which refer to legal sources are rendered in accordance with THE BLUEBOOK: A UNIFORM SYSTEM OF CITATION (16th ed. 1996). In order to promote ease of cross-referencing, all footnotes in this volume will be numbered sequentially.

I and II) has been written so that, when the reader has finished it, they should (hopefully) have a high level of confidence of *my* understanding of classics as a discipline and mode of scholarship.

The remainder of the first part of the study (titled, appropriately enough, ANTIQUITY) brings into the conversation two new elements: a discussion of the classical literature on ancient statecraft and treaty-making (Chapter III) and a consideration of how Roman jurists dealt with issues of legal interpretation (Chapters IV and V). These chapters thread the two strands that are entwined in the remainder of this book: the intellectual debate about the utility of rhetorical tools in legal interpretation and their practical application to problems unique in interpreting agreements between States.

The next part of my volume provides the temporal connective tissue of my suggestion here that classical approaches to legal interpretation redound today. This is my INTERMEZZO, and its purpose is modest: to trace the bare outlines of the intellectual reception of this classical tradition in interpreting legal texts. The approach here is roughly chronological, with Chapter VI discussing (in very brief terms) the period culminating in the early-Modern period (about 1600), and Chapter VIII looking more closely at the Anglo-American reception of these ideas up to the early years of this century. There is one lengthy digression from this historical narrative. That is Chapter VII, which provides a vignette of the intellectual contribution made by Hugo de Groot (Grotius) to the development of canons of interpretation for treaties. His was the first systematized treatment of the subject, and he was strongly influenced by classical rhetoric and historiography.

As my study unfolds, I move not only from antiquity to modernity in this intellectual history, but also farther and farther away from the sources and methods that define classical scholarship. This transition is completed by the time one arrives at the section of my book on MODERNITY. It is here, also, that the tone shifts markedly to legal exegesis. Chapter IX tries to finish the narrative begun in previous passages by explaining how the modern debate on statutory interpretation, now raging within legal circles in the United States and elsewhere, has weird resonances with the professional battle between orators and jurists in ancient Rome.

But the major thrust of this final part of my volume is to return to my intellectual laboratory of the treaty form and to divine the canons that have been developed to practically and realistically interpret international agreements in various contexts. My exposition on this subject begins with a primer on modern approaches to treaty interpretation and how the international community has sought to systematize and codify these rules (Chapter X). This is followed by a comparison with more American approaches to the subject (Chapter XI). Chapter XII is a longish effort to examine a particular set of treaty interpretation cases, recently decided by the United States Supreme Court. These thirteen cases are, figuratively speaking, the lab mice in my clinical trial of rhetorical approaches and pathologies in modern treaty interpretation. I conclude my experiment in Chapter XIII with an attempt to formulate new canons for treaty interpretation, ones that harmonize old rhetorical forms and new values.

viii. In the process of narrating my research and conclusions on the rhetoric of legal interpretation (especially of treaty texts), it will come as no surprise that I have reached some conclusions on the uses and abuses that classical studies can have in modern legal discourse. That is the subject of my CODA. It is not enough that I prepare the ground for a disciplinary homecoming, metaphorically erecting the picnic tables, preparing the dishes, and setting the utensils so that classicists and lawyers can enjoy an intellectual feast. And although the scholarly exercise I develop here should advance that goal, there remains the question of whether the goal is worth pursuing. Why should anyone come to this banquet? Or, as has been so penetratingly put, "Can a classicist learn from a lawyer?" I believe the answer is a resounding "yes," for at stake is nothing less than the project of understanding interpretive constructs for legal texts for all ages.

Antiquity

I CLASSICAL RHETORIC AND DECLAMATION

i. Greek and Roman rhetoricians had developed a system of argumentation (known as *status* in Latin, or *stasis* (στάσις) in Greek), one branch of which concerned the proper interpretation of legal texts. *Stasis* was employed by rhetoricians as an element of forensic or judicial oratory.[2] The *stasis* is the basic issue of a dispute. The word derives from the ancient Greek expression for the stance or posture of two wrestlers or combatants.[3] In oratory, the most common context for the use of *stasis* was the court case, often (but not always) a criminal prosecution.[4]

---

[2] Other elements included (1) *progymnasmata*, elementary exercises in declamation, (2) *invention*, the theory of rhetorical composition and creativity, (3) *ideas*, or emotional aspects of rhetoric, and (4) *memory* and *delivery*. See George A. Kennedy, GREEK RHETORIC UNDER CHRISTIAN EMPERORS 54-101 (1983) [hereinafter "Kennedy, Christian"]. *See also* Donald Lemen Clark, RHETORIC IN GRECO-ROMAN EDUCATION 72 (1957); Alan Edward Douglas, *The Intellectual Background of Cicero's* Rhetorica: *A Study in Method*, in [3] 1 AUFSTIEG UND NIEDERGANG DER RÖMISCHEN WELT 95 (1973); Kathy Eden, HERMENEUTICS AND THE RHETORICAL TRADITION 8 (1997); Patrick Sinclair, *The* sententia *in* Rhetorica ad Herennium, 114 AJP 561 (1993); Wesley Trimpi, MUSES OF ONE MIND: THE LITERARY ANALYSIS OF EXPERIENCE AND ITS CONTINUITY 252-66 (1983).

[3] *See* Josef Martin, ANTIKE RHETORIK, TECHNIK UND METHODE 28-52 (1974). *See also* Kennedy, Christian, supra note 2, at 74; O.A.L. Dieter, Status, 17 SPEECH MONOGRAPHS 345 (1950). *Stases* was also a term describing civil strife. *See* W. Robert Connor, THUCYDIDES 80-81, 126 n.42 (1984).

[4] Status was used in other, non-legal contexts. As one scholar has indicated:

[Status] was helpful in exploring all material in court or out. Any student who has

Status was thus a system of organizing the arguments for each side in a forensic contest. The very basic structure of the argument was to ask three elemental questions: whether a thing is (in Latin, *an sit*), what it is (*quid sit*), and of what kind it is (*quale sit*). These are, respectively, the inquiries of fact, of definition, and of quality. A simple example was narrated in two rhetorical handbooks, the first by Marcus Tullius Cicero (the great Roman orator and politician) in the years just before the birth of Christ,[5] and by M. Fabius Quintilian (a teacher of oratory who flourished in the first century A.D.).[6] At a murder trial, the defendant was asked whether he actually committed the act

---

had constant drill in status, either in factual or fictitious themes, will develop the habit of going to the heart of any problem. He has a technic at his command for getting on the road promptly, staying on the road, and arriving at a destination. He is taught how to discover the one thing, he in relation to his material has to say.

Clark, supra note 2, at 73. *See also* Eden, supra note 2, at 1-2.

[5] *See* Marcus Tullius Cicero, 1 DE ORATORE (The Making of an Orator) 271-81 (H. Rackham transl. Loeb Classical Library ed. 1927) (passage ii. 24-26). Cicero lived from 106 - 43 BC. *See* Sonja K. Foss, CONTEMPORARY PERSPECTIVES ON RHETORIC 5 (2d ed. 1991).

I have discovered that classical studies has its own unique method of providing references. In writing this study, I try to emulate that style at the same time trying to conform to my own discipline's rules of citations. With just a handful of exceptions, all classical texts referred to in this book will be from the authoritative Loeb Classical Library editions. I will also provide a pin-point page cite to the volume of the relevant work (which is required by law review editors) and also a standard indication of the passage from which the extract is drawn. I will follow the apparent convention of referring to the specific document or fragment by name, and then including the book number (in Roman numerals), followed by the section and line (or passage) numbers.

In this book, I will follow the old form of indicating dates as BC (Before Christian Era) or AD (Christian Era).

[6] *See* 1 Quintilian, INSTITUTIO ORATORIA 451 (H.E. Butler transl. Loeb Classical Library ed. 1920) (passage iii.6.80). Quintilian lived from 35 - 95 AD. *See* Foss, supra note 5, at 5. *But see*, THE OXFORD CLASSICAL DICTIONARY 907 (2d ed. 1970) (which suggests he lived until 110 AD). The INSTITUTIO ORATORIA has been dated to 95 AD. Id. For more on the rhetorical work of both Cicero and Quintilian, read George Kennedy, THE ART OF RHETORIC IN THE ROMAN WORLD, 300 B.C. - A.D. 300, at 103-14, 149-300, 487-552 (1972) [hereinafter "Kennedy, Rome"]; James J. Murphy, *Introduction* to QUINTILIAN ON THE TEACHING OF SPEAKING AND WRITING xiv-xviii (James J. Murphy ed. 1987).

of killing another. He admitted this factual element. But the defendant denied that he had murdered the deceased, because he had acted in self-defense. This led to a definitional inquiry. In any event, there was a qualitative concern here; perhaps the deceased had been a very bad man, and the Republic was better off with him dead.[7] Cicero said this of the general rhetorical construct of *stasis*:

> Let the student first seek out the nature of the case, never obscure, whether a thing was done, what was the quality of the act, and what name it should have. Once this is ascertained, good sense at once perceives what constitutes the case, that is, without which there would be no dispute.[8]

Interpretations of legal texts were treated, under the status system, as questions of definition (*status definitivus*).[9] This was a peculiarly Latin gloss on the status system, the idea of *stasis* being itself an intellectual emigré from Greek to Roman civilizations in antiquity. Definitions in Greek philosophy (ὁρισμοί, or ὅροι) were regarded by Aristotle as statements regarding the meaning of terms, but which make no assertion as to the existence or non-existence (or the worth) of the thing defined. It was, however, Hermagoras of Temnos, writing about 150 B.C., who is generally credited with the first statement of status

---

[7] See 1 Quintilian, supra note 6, at 457 (passage iii.6.93). *See also* H.F. Jolowicz, *Academic Elements in Roman Law*, 48 L. Q. REV. 171, 181 (1932).

[8] *See* 1 Cicero, De Oratore, supra note 5, at 293-95 (passage ii.30.132). To the same effect was Cicero's remark that status

> teaches how to divide the problem into parts, to explicate what lies hidden by defining it, to explain the obscure by interpreting it, how first to see what is ambiguous, then to distinguish it, and finally to yield a rule which may be judged true or false and determine what conclusions follow from what premises and what do not.

Cicero, BRUTUS 133 (G.L. Hendrickson transl. Loeb Classical library ed. 1962) (passage xli. 152).

[9] *See* S.F. Bonner, ROMAN DECLAMATION IN THE LATE REPUBLIC AND EARLY EMPIRE 14 (1949); Eden, supra note 2, at 10 (who argues that questions of legal interpretation were handled as questions of definition, just as rhetorical manuals separated problems of proof from pointers on style).

14   *Classical Canons*

theory.[10]   Although his work has not survived, Cicero, Quintilian, and the anonymous author of another handbook on oratory, the *Rhetorica ad Herennium*,[11] all refer to Hermagoras' writing on the subject.   Hermagoras apparently conceived of a category of *quaestiones legales* (or στάσεις νομικαί) separate and distinct from concerns of fact, definition, or quality.[12]   He may have conceived this category of legal inquiries from the earlier works of Aristotle and the author of the *Rhetorica ad Alexandrum*, a Hellenistic-era manual of oratorical practice.[13]

---

[10]   *See* Antoine Braet, DE KLASSIEKE STATUSLEER IN MODERN PERSPECTIEF (1984); K. Barwick, Zur Rekonstruktion der Rehetorik des Harmagoras von Temnos, 109 PHILOLOGUS 186 (1965); Ray Nadeau, *Classical Systems of Stases in Greek: Hermagoras to Hermogenes*, 2 GRBS 53, 60-61 (1959).

[11]   *See* [Cicero], RHETORICA AD HERENNIUM vii-xv (Harry Caplan transl. 1954 Loeb Classical Library ed. 1981) (translator's introduction).   The attribution to Cicero is now known to be utterly spurious. *See* id. at vii-ix.   Likewise rejected has been the suggested authorship of Cornificius. *See* id. at ix-xiv.   The *Rhetorica ad Herennium* has been dated to around 85 B.C., which means that it was written just after Cicero's *de Inventione*. *See* Cicero, de Inventione, supra note 21, at vii-ix (translator's introduction).

[12]   *See* Nadeau, supra note 10, at 60.   Nadeau refers to this part of Hermagoras' treatment as νομικαί ζητήματα, and not as a separate *stasis*. *See* id.   *See also* Euripides' famous quip, "My tongue swore, no oath is on my soul," which is generally credited with the origination between *verba* (words) and *voluntas* (intent). 4 Euripides 211 (Arthur S. Way transl. 1912) (Loeb Classical Library rep. 1980) (*Hippolytus*, line 612).   Compare this with David Kovacs' translation of the line: "My tongue swore, but my mind is not on oath." 2 Euripides 185 (David Kovacs transl. Loeb Classical Library rep. 1995) (*Hippolytus*, line 612).
    See also Everett L. Wheeler, Sophistic Interpretations and Greek Treaties, 25 GRBS 253, 260 n.28 (1984).

[13]   *See* Bonner, supra note 9, at 15.   The authorship of the *ad Alexandrum* remains disputed. *See* [Aristotle], RHETORICA AD ALEXANDRUM 258-61 (H. Rackham transl. Loeb Classical Library ed. 1983) (editor's note).   The writings of another contemporary Greek rhetorician, Apollodorus, may have reflected a similar tendency. *See* Nadeau, supra note 10, at 64.   For the origins of rhetoric in ancient Greece, *see* John Poulakos, SOPHISTICAL REASONING IN CLASSICAL GREECE (1995).

The Romans, as reflected in their rhetorical treatises, chose to give prominence to legal questions in their oratorical discourse.[14] This may have been because of the preeminence of judicial oratory as a kind of speech-making, superior even to epideictic or deliberative forms.[15] In any event, the Romans subtly changed the definitional basis of status into a legal inquiry. As Quintilian put it, "was the [thing done] just or unjust?"[16] So it was that an inquiry into definition of a thing was transformed into a debate about legal questions. As I soon discovered, though, law and definition were two sides of the same coin for both Greek and Roman rhetoricians.

In any event, Quintilian went on to explain how the orator, once he or she determined the proper basis of the case, proceeded to use the concept of status to construct a legal argument.[17] Knowing that the basis was legal or definitional meant that the speaker could choose from a "menu" of questions which characterized the underlying dispute. These were called *constitutiones* or *quaestiones*. And once the underlying legal problem was discerned, orators were instructed in various topics (*topoi* in Greek) to address the legal case from either side. These were very specific modes of argument.[18] As an example of

---

[14] *See* George Kennedy, Rome, supra note 6, at 110-11, 117. *See also* Hanns Hohmann, *The Dynamics of Stasis: Classical Rhetorical Theory and Modern Legal Argumentation*, 34 AJJ 171, 171-72 (1989).

[15] [E]pideictic ... is devoted to the praise or censure of some particular person. [D]eliberative consists in the discussion of policy and embraces persuasion and dissuasion. The judicial is based on legal controversy, and comprises criminal prosecution or civil suit, and defence.

Rhetorica ad Herennium, supra note 11, at 5 (passage i.2.2).

[16] Quintilian, supra note 6, at 433 (passage iii.6.45).

[17] *See* id. (passage iii.6.45).

[18] *See generally*, E. Grassi, RHETORIC AS PHILOSOPHY (1980); Kathleen E. Welch, THE CONTEMPORARY RECEPTION OF CLASSICAL RHETORIC: APPROPRIATION OF ANCIENT DISCOURSE (1990); Theodor Viehweg, TOPICS AND LAW (W. Cole Durham transl. 1993). *See also* Peter Stein, REGULAE IURIS: FROM JURISTIC RULES TO LEGAL MAXIMS 39-40 (1966); Michael Frost, *Introduction to Classical Legal Rhetoric: A Lost Heritage*, 8 So.

the *status definitivus*, Cicero and Quintilian both referred[19] to the 94 B.C. trial of Norbanus, accused of treason for procuring the banishment of a rival commander. The topics would include such matters as whether there was an intention to commit treason (*intentio*), whether the defendant's political acts were ratified by the people (*ratio*), and whether one who uses force to carry out the people's will diminishes the majesty of the State (*iudicatio*).[20] These *topoi* served, in effect, as stock arguments for the advocate.[21]   Each thrust of argument was met with an opposite and equal riposte of defense and counter-argument. A weak speaker could recycle these topics without much thought or reflection. A strong orator would exercise the rhetorical skill of invention and transform these standard approaches into strong, tailor-made arguments. This was all consistent with the idea that rhetoric was a form of *civilis ratio*, political reason,[22] or, as Quintilian said, "speaking well in civil matters."[23]   To put the

---

CAL. INTERDISC. L.J. 613, 613-20 (1999) ["Frost, Introduction"]; Michael Frost, *Greco-Roman Legal Analysis: The Topics of Invention*, 66 ST. JOHN'S L. REV. 107 (1992); Peter Goodrich, *Historical Aspects of Legal Interpretation*, 61 IND. L. J. 331, 345, 351 (1986); Malcolm Heath, *The sub-structure of* stasis-theory, 44 CQ (no. 1) 114 (1994); Richard McKeon, *The Methods of Rhetoric and Philosophy: Invention and Judgment* in THE CLASSICAL TRADITION 365 (Luitpoid Wallach ed. 1966); Friedrich Solmsen, *The Aristotelian Tradition in Ancient Rhetoric*, 62 AJP 36, 169 (1941).

[19] *See* 1 Cicero, De Oratore, supra note 5, at 277 (passage ii.25.107); Quintilian, supra note 6, at 104-05 (passage vii.3.35).

[20] *See* Antoine Braet, *The Classical Doctrine of* status *and the Rhetorical Theory of Argumentation*, 20 PHILOSOPHY AND RHETORIC 79 (1987); Bonner, supra note 9, at 14.

[21] As Cicero said in his treatise, *de Inventione*, "[A]ny one in any case will . . . find all of the issues and their facts and the disputes, whatever they are, which may arise: for we shall give directions about all of them." Cicero, DE INVENTIONE 321-23 (H.M. Hubbell transl. Loeb Classical Library ed. 1949). Cicero also considered them as a form of legal maxims. *See* B. Riposati, STUDI SUI TOPICA DI CICERONE 26-30 (1947); Goodrich, supra note 18, at 351-52. For the subsequent history of this insight by Peter Abelard, *see* Stein, supra note 18, at 157-58.

[22] See Cicero, de Inventione, supra note 21, at 11-13 (passage i. 4).

[23] 1 Quintilian, supra note 6, at 441 (passage iii. 6).

point even more finely, Aristotle regarded rhetoric as "a branch of the science dealing with behavior, which it is right to call political."[24]

ii.   The difference between good and bad orators was skill — and training.   To understand the relevance of the status system to classical rhetoricians, I realized that I also had to learn something of the profession of oratory in antiquity. Rhetoric was, of course, one of the seven liberal arts (*artes liberales*) of the classical mind, along with grammar, dialectic, arithmetic, geometry, music, and astronomy.[25] If a young (invariably) man showed a familiarity with most (if not all) of these subjects, he was considered as having an *enkyklios paideia*, what we might call today a liberal education.[26]

Of course, he had to go to school for this learning, and these schools were remarkably similar in both the Greek and Roman worlds.[27] As today, education was organized on primary, secondary, and advanced levels.   The study of rhetoric was, apparently, reserved for that final stage of preparation, once a student could read and write, and had mastered grammar and dialectic, both of which taught logic and analytic reasoning.[28] Indeed, part of the study of grammar was the understanding of rules of inflection, by which one could discern the underlying structure of language and distinguish similar verbal

---

[24]   Aristotle, ART OF RHETORIC 19 (J.H. Freese transl. 1926) (Loeb Classical Library ed. 1982) (passage i.2.7; 1356a).

[25]   *See* Viehweg, supra note 18, at 17. Lawyers and doctors will be chastened to learn that their professions were not counted among the liberal arts! *See also* Eden, supra note 2, at 20-21; Robert A. Kaster, GUARDIANS OF LANGUAGE: THE GRAMMARIAN AND SOCIETY IN LATE ANTIQUITY (1988).

[26]   *See* id. *See also* Henri-Irénée Marrou, HISTOIRE DE L'ÉDUCATION DANS L'ANTIQUITÉ (1948).

[27]   *See* Clark, supra note 2, at 59-60.

[28]   *See* id. at 60-61. *See also* Aubrey Osborne Gwynn, ROMAN EDUCATION FROM CICERO TO QUINTILIAN (1926); R.H. Robbins, *Dionyisus Thrax and the Western Grammatical Tradition*, 1957 TRANSACTIONS OF THE PHILOLOGICAL SOCIETY 72; Stein, supra note 18, at 53-55.

forms. These were called canons, or κανόνες in Greek.[29] So, when classical thinkers used the word canon, it meant a technical rule of grammar in which a word's meaning or usage was ascertained.[30]

Grammatical and rhetorical training was intended not only to train court advocates, but also to

> prepar[e] young gentlemen to practice all of the arts of discourse, which, according to Isocrates, teach how to think well and live well while they teach how to speak well, for "none of the things which are done with intelligence are done without the help of speech."[31]

The fact that rhetorical study was intended as something more than training for a trial practitioner is what qualified it as a liberal study. Nevertheless, as time went on, rhetorical education did come more and more to be associated with the profession of court orator.[32]

One of the major instructional methods of rhetoric was declamation. Declamation was an elaborately structured, almost stylized, oratorical contest in which two students squared-off in debate on a selected topic. The similarities to today's moot court activities in law school or to collegiate forensic or

---

[29] There were two schools of classical grammarians — the analogists (who sought to classify and order speech and writing) and the anomalists (who embraced the inherent confusion of language). *See* F. H. Colson, *The Analogist and Anomalist Controversy*, 13 CQ 33 (1919). Canons were employed by the analogists. *See* Stein, supra note 18, at 53-56.

[30] *See* 5 Philo of Alexandria 335, 351 (F.H. Colson & G.H. Whitaker transl. 1934) (Loeb Classical Library rep. 1958) (*De somn.*, passages i. 73 & i. 102); 7 id. at 267 (*de leg. spec.*, passage i. 287) (all referring to "canons [rules] of allegory").

[31] *See* Clark, supra note 2, at 64 (quoting, 2 Isocrates 329 (George Norlin transl. Loeb Classical Library ed. 1929) (*Antidosis*, passage 257)). *See also* Richard Leo Enos, THE LITERATE MODE OF CICERO'S LEGAL RHETORIC (1988).

[32] *See* E. Patrick Parks, THE ROMAN RHETORICAL SCHOOLS AS A PREPARATION FOR THE COURTS UNDER THE EARLY EMPIRE (1945).

parliamentary debate have not gone unnoticed.[33] But I also understand that declamation was a bit of a spectator sport in ancient Rome. Seneca the Elder even likened declaimers to gladiators![34]

The epitome of declamation were the *controversiae* and the *suasoriae*. *Suasoriae* were exercises for successful epideictic or deliberative speech.[35] A handful of these survive, chiefly from Seneca's collection, and cover such military history topics as whether the Three Hundred Spartans should have fled in the face of Xerxes' host, such epic topics as whether Agamemnon should have sacrificed Iphigenia, and then-current canards like whether Cicero should have burned his books in order to save his life.[36] In these exercises the students would propound on the topic, offering the best arguments they could, and at the end of the debate they would both be subject to a withering critique by their teacher.[37] Seneca the Elder recounted these *suasoriae* exercises, and used them as a way to comment on the great orators of his time.[38] One might suppose that his volume was required reading for orators-in-training. Nevertheless, the *suasoriae* were criticized later in the Empire period (after the first century A.D.)

---

[33] *See* Clark, supra note 2, at 234.

[34] 1 The Elder Seneca, CONTROVERSIAE 423 (M. Winterbottom transl. Loeb Classical library ed. 1974) (passage iv.pr.1). Interestingly, the Greek word *palaestra* referred both to a school for wrestling and a place for debate.

[35] *See* supra note 15 and accompanying text. *See also* Clark, supra note 2, at 218-28; Trimpi, supra note 2, at 296-300.

[36] *See* 2 Seneca, supra note 34, at 507, 535 & 595 (*Suasoriae*, passages ii., iii., vii.).

[37] *See* Bonner, supra note 9, at 51-70; Clark, supra note 2, at 213-17.

[38] *See* 1 Seneca, supra note 34, at vii-xi (translator's introduction). Other declamations are extant, including those by 2 Lucian of Samosata, WORKS 173 (H.W. Fowler & F.G. Fowler 1905); 3 id. at 218.

as being utterly devoid of realistic content and practically useless, good only for the egos of schoolmasters and the amusement of adoring parents.[39]

The *controversiae* — which were styled as legal cases[40] — were also subject to the criticism of irrelevance. As recounted by Seneca, each *controversiae* began with a quotation from law, followed by a factual scenario. Each student argued the case on behalf of one of the parties. Consider this example of a *controversiae*:

> The law ordains that those who leave their ship in a storm shall lose everything; the ship and its cargo become the property of those who remain on it.

> Two men were sailing on the high seas, one the owner of the ship, the other of its cargo. They saw a shipwrecked man swimming and stretching out his hands to them; overcome by pity, they brought the ship alongside him and took him on board. Sometime afterwards they too ran into a heavy storm, with the result that the owner of the ship, who was also the helmsman, betook himself to a boat, from which he guided the ship as best he could with the tow rope, while the owner of the cargo fell on his sword. The shipwrecked man went to the helm, and did his best to save the ship. When the waves subsided and the weather changed, the ship was brought into harbor. The man who had fallen on his sword was only slightly wounded and his wound quickly healed. Each of the three claimed the ship and its cargo.[41]

Well, this example can hardly withstand a charge of absurdity. One could not offer this with a straight face in class. But teachers of rhetoric did, precisely because they were not teachers of law. The purpose of the exercise was, of course, to train in oratory, not to reach conclusions about notional legal rules.

---

[39] *See* 1 Seneca, supra note 34, at xii-xiv; Bonner, supra note 9, at 71-83 (discussing the criticisms of Asinius Pollio, Votienus Montanus, Petronius, Pliny, Juvenal, and Tacitus); Clark, supra note 2, at 250-61; M. L. Clarke, RHETORIC AT ROME: A HISTORICAL SURVEY 19 (1962).

[40] *See* 1 Seneca, supra note 34, at 13 (passage i.pr.12).

[41] This *controversiae*, and its variants, appears often in the classical rhetorical literature. *See* Cicero, supra note 21, at 321-23 (passage ii.51.153-54); Rhetorica ad Herennium, supra note 11, at 35-37 (passage i.11.19).

The recent trend of research in classical studies is to suggest that the declaimers' *controversiae* were largely modeled on extant laws. While the factual circumstances of the exercises were nutty, the laws which formed the basis of the declamation were not. S.F. Bonner's 1949 book, *Roman Declamation in the Late Republic and Early Empire*,[42] has largely been credited with originating this thesis. Bonner carefully analyzed each of the "statutes" mentioned in the Senecan declamations. Some were clearly stated or implied to be fictitious, like the one "[a]n action may lie for an offence not specified in the law."[43] Others were admittedly spurious. But the vast majority of the laws that were referred to by Seneca in his declamatory exercises were genuine, at least in the sense that they had Greek or Roman parallels.[44]

---

[42] *See* supra note 9. *See also* 1 Seneca, supra note 34, at xiii (translator's introduction).

[43] 1 Seneca, supra note 34, at 389 (passage iii.pr.17), 471 (passage v.1.1). *See* Bonner, supra note 9, at 86.

[44] *See* Bonner, supra note 9, at 108-31. *See also* Bruce W. Frier, THE RISE OF THE ROMAN JURISTS 76 (1985) (who notes a *controversiae* in the Rhetorica ad Herennium involving a conflict between two praetorian edicts, for more on which see infra notes 146-50 and accompanying text).

II *STASIS* AND QUESTIONS OF LEGAL INTERPRETATION

i. Declamation and the status system were directly linked. Many *controversiae* were designed around problems of definition. The seafaring example, rendered above, was probably so intended. So was this (rather more plausible) case:

> Some young men from the city went to Ostia in the summer season, and arriving at the shore, found some fishermen drawing in their nets. They made a bargain to give a certain sum for the haul. The money was paid, and they waited for some time until the nets were drawn ashore. When they were at last drawn out, no fish were in them, but a closed basket of gold. Then the purchasers said the haul belonged to them, the fishermen said it was theirs.[45]

The only difference is that this *controversiae* was structured around the interpretation of a contract, and not a statute. In any event, that part of *stasis* devoted to the interpretation of legal texts — what the Romans called the *constitutio legitima* — was developed to deal with all juristic writings, irrespective of form. Quintilian said as much: "what I say with reference to laws will apply equally to wills, agreements, contracts and every form of document; nay, it will apply even to verbal agreements."[46] Cicero had earlier concurred: "It is of course plain that such [legal] controversies arise no more

---

[45] The example is in Clark, supra note 2, at 239-40 (abstracting 2 Suetonius, DE GRAMMATICIS ET RHETORIBUS 439 (J.C. Rolfe transl. Loeb Classical Library ed. 1930) (*On Rhetoricians*, passage i)).

[46] 3 Quintilian, supra note 6, at 135 (passage vii.5.5).

from laws than from wills, contracts, and in any other manner which rests on a written document."[47]

Despite Quintilian's claim that *constitutio legitima* could be applied to verbal agreements, this aspect of the status system was unique in that it purported to develop modes of argument around the interpretation of legal writings. As the author of the *Rhetorica ad Herennium* put it: "[An] issue is legal when some controversy turns upon the letter of a text or arises from an implication therein."[48] By Quintilian's time in the first century A.D.,[49] legislation made by the Principate and Emperor was the chief problem of legal interpretation and Quintilian's treatise correspondingly was devoted to that issue. "Every law," he wrote, "either gives or takes away, punishes or commands, forbids or permits, and involves a dispute on its own account or on account of another law...."[50]

Every *constitutio legitima* could be classified as one of a number of types, or *quaestiones*. Hermagoras, the creator of the *stasis* system[51] identified four of these: (1) the letter of the legal writing and exceptions thereto (*ex scripto et sententia*; κατὰ ῥητὸν καὶ ὑπεξαίρεσιν); (2) contrary laws (*contrariae leges*; ἀντινομία); (3) ambiguous law (*ambiguitas*; ἀμφιβολία); and (4) inference from the laws (*collectio* or *syllogismus*; συλλογισμός).[52] Cicero's *De*

---

[47] Cicero, de Inventione, supra note 21, at 457 (*Topica*, passage xxvi.96).

[48] Rhetorica ad Herennium, supra note 11, at 35 (passage i.11.19).

[49] For more on Quintilian's time, *see* Kennedy, Roman, supra note 6, at 487-514.

[50] 3 Quintilian, supra note 6, at 135 (passage vii.5.5). For more on the political history involved in the transfer of power from the people to the Senate to the Principate and thence to the Emperor, *see* infra section III.i.

[51] *See* supra note 10 and accompanying text.

[52] Hermagoras' work is referred to in 1 Quintilian, supra note 6, at 441 (passage iii.6.61). Quintilian counts these as five *quaestiones*, however, disaggregating the "letter of the law" and "exceptions thereto." *See* id. Quintilian also refers to the work of one Albutius, who reduced the number of *quaestiones* to three, eliminating the ratiocinative

Inventione, written early in his career as an orator,[53] added another *quaestio* "about the meaning of a word, *i.e.*, on what the meaning depends, as if it were in the definitional issue."[54] This definitional question was recognized by the unknown author of the *Rhetorica ad Herennium*,[55] but was not accepted by Quintilian as a distinct category.[56] Moreover, the question of inference from existing laws was slightly transformed by Cicero to encompass "from what has been written something has been discovered which has not been written."[57] This process of inference, Cicero called "reasoning by analogy (*quartum ratiocinativum*)."[58]

Classical rhetoricians thus recognized five problems arising from the construction of legal texts: letter and spirit, ambiguity, definition, contrary laws, and syllogism. In an extended passage, Quintilian described the interrelation between these *quaestiones*:

---

basis. In a later work, Cicero seems also to adopt this tripartite approach. Cicero, De Inventione, supra note 21, at 457 (*Topica*, passage xxv. 96). *See also* Bonner, supra note 9, at 14-15; Nadeau, supra note 10, at 60-61.

[53] *See* Cicero, De Inventione, supra note 21, at vii (translator's introduction).

[54] Id. at 35 (passage i.13.17). *See also* Eden, supra note 2, at 7-8.

[55] Rhetorica ad Herennium, supra note 11, at 35 (passage i.11.19), 39 (passage i.12.21). The author of the *Rhetorica ad Herennium* added yet another *quaestio*, having to do with "transference" (*translatio*), "when the defendant maintains that there must be a postponement of time or a change of plaintiff or judges." Id. at 39 (passage i.12.22). The writer acknowledged that this "sub-type of Legal issue rarely presents itself in judicial proceedings...." Id. at 40. *See also* Cicero, de Inventione, supra note 21, at 219-25 (passage ii. 19-20).

[56] 1 Quintilian, supra note 6, at 433 (passage iii.6.46), 441 (passage iii.6.66). *See also* Clarke, supra note 39, at 28-29.

[57] Cicero, de Inventione, supra note 21, at 35 (passage i.13.17).

[58] Id. *See also* Hohmann, supra note 14, at 173-74.

There is ... a certain affinity between all of these bases. For in definition we enquire into the meaning of a term, and in syllogism, which is closely connected with definition, we consider what was the meaning of the writer.... Again, definition is a kind of ambiguity, since it brings out two meanings in the same term. The basis concerned with the letter and the intention of the law involves a legal question as regards the interpretation of words, which is identical to the question arising out of contrary laws.... But all of these bases are really distinct.... Definition, then, involves a general question as to the actual meaning of a term, a question which may conceivably have no connexion whatsoever with the content of the case in point. In investigations as to the letter and the intention, the dispute turns on the provisions contained in the law, whereas the syllogism deals with that which is not contained in the law. In disputes arising out of ambiguity we are led from the ambiguous phrase to its conflicting meanings, whereas in the case of contrary laws the fight starts from the conflict of their provisions.[59]

Modern writers have wondered whether the classical taxonomists of rhetoric went overboard in this elaborate scheme. Some have pointed out[60] that Quintilian may have been correct when he said that the five *quaestiones* were all sub-species of the first inquiry: the discrepancy between the letter and intent in legal texts.[61] But I am inclined to concur with Quintilian that there are distinct problems at work here. Moreover, I found it was useful for my project to consider them separately as I was trying to divine the classical rhetorician's approach to interpreting legal texts. That proved to be my next task.

---

[59] 3 Quintilian, supra note 6, at 163 (passage vii.10.1-3).

[60] *See* Hohmann, supra note 14, at 174-75. *See also* 4 Moriz Voigt, DAS JUS NATURALE, AEQUUM ET BONUM UND JUS GENTIUM DER RÖMER 333-76 (1871) (Appendices).

[61] *See* 3 Quintilian, supra note 6, at 163 (passage vii.10.2).

Level One. *Nature of the Problem.*

STATUS *or* BASES

whether	what	kind
an sit	*quid sit*	*quale sit*
fact	definition	quality

Level Two. *Kind of Legal Problem.*

QUAESTIONES LEGALES
or
CONSTITUTIO LEGITIMA

Definition of a Term in a Law - *Definitio*
Ambiguous Laws - *Ambiguitas*
Laws in Conflict - *Contrariae Leges*
Inference from the Laws - *Syllogismus*
Letter of the Law and Exceptions Thereto -
Ex Scripto et Sententia

Level Three. *Model Arguments to Address Problem*

TOPOI

Equitable Arguments for the Intent of the Writer,
as opposed to the Letter of the Legal Writing

Greater Good - *Comparatio*
Response to Another Actor's Harm -
Relatio Criminis
Shifting the Charge - *Remotio Criminis*
Confession and Avoidance - *Concessio*

Figure 1 - Flow Chart of *Stasis* System

ii. I decided to begin with the problems of definition and ambiguity. They are closely linked, as Quintilian said. Moroever, they were regarded by the orator as threshold problems for legal interpretation. The *Rhetorica ad Herennium* made the rather obvious point that "a text is regarded as ambiguous ... [if] it can be interpreted in two or more meanings."[62] But he also said that ambiguity was unavoidable in life.[63] Quintilian reiterated this proposition (attributed to "certain philosophers") that "there is not a single word which has not a diversity of meanings;"[64] ambiguity is inherent in all language, and legal texts were no exception.

In the same fashion, the classical rhetoricians knew that acts carrying legal consequences were not self-defining. While the *constitutio* of definition had to do with "the name by which an act should be called,"[65] orators were taught not to put too much faith in providing solutions to ambiguous words or to characterizing legal acts. They were both forms of conclusory arguments, whether for a linguistic problem or legal cause. Such arguments ("It is so,

---

[62] Rhetorica ad Herennium, supra note 11, at 85 (passage ii.11.16).

[63] The author of *ad Herennium* makes this point comically by chiding dialecticians who sought to remove all ambiguity from their speech: "And when they themselves speak, wishing to do so cautiously and deftly, they prove to be utterly inarticulate. Thus, in their fear to utter some ambiguity while speaking, they cannot even pronounce their own names." Id. at 87 (passage ii.11.16). For more on the disputation between rhetoricians and dialecticians, see id. at 87-87 n.b (editor's note).

[64] 3 Quintilian, supra note 6, at 153 (passage vii.9.1). He went on to discuss, at some length, the different ways that ambiguity can arise in single words and in combinations of words or phrases. *See* id. at 155 (passages vii.9.2-5).

As an example of the latter situation, consider the example of the *pater familias* who, in making his son his heir, says: "Let my heir give my wife thirty pounds' weight of silver, such as shall be selected." Rhetorica ad Herennium, supra note 11, at 37 (passage i.12.20). (The same example is repeated in Cicero, de Inventione, supra note 21, at 285 (passage ii.40.116)). The ambiguity arises from the pronominal subject which is not explicit, to wit, who chooses the silver, the wife or the son?

For more on this problem, *see* 1 Boaz Cohen, JEWISH AND ROMAN LAW: A COMPARATIVE STUDY 43 (1966).

[65] Rhetorica ad Herennium, supra note 11, at 39 (passage i.12.21).

because I say it is so....") were not to be favored. That is why Quintilian wrote that "it is quite unimportant how ambiguity arises or how it is remedied.... It is a perfectly futile rule which directs us to endeavour ... to turn the word in question to suit our own purpose."[66]

Quintilian's rectitude was quite mature on this point. Nevertheless, he disagreed with the great Cicero and the author of *Rhetorica ad Herennium*, both of whom (while recognizing the hopelessness of the task) sought to provide some rules for assisting orators to overcome ambiguity and to provide cogent descriptions of legal acts. An obvious strategy for an orator was to suggest that his interpretation of an ambiguous word or act was preferred because of underlying notions of law, of equity, or of morality. As Cicero wrote in *De Partitione Oratoria*, "[v]ictory is bound to go to the one who in his definition and analysis of a term has entered more deeply into the mind and ideas of the judge, and who has arrived more completely and closely at the common meaning of the term...."[67]

This advice was repeated in more specific terms elsewhere in Cicero's works. An orator could emphasize the ordinary meaning of words,[68] exploit the context the words are in, or stress an interpretation which leads to a convenient, honorable, expedient or necessary result.[69] One trick, suggested by both Cicero and the *ad Herennium* was "to show how [the text] would have been written if

---

[66]   3 Quintilian, supra note 6, at 161 (passage vii.9.14).

[67]   Cicero, de Oratore, supra note 5, at 407 (*de Partitione Oratoria*, xxxvi. 123). *See also* Cicero, de Inventione, supra note 21, at 213-19 (passage ii. 17 & 18).

[68]   Horace endorsed the current and popular usage of words "which is the final authority and is the law and rule of speech." Horace, ART OF POETRY 457 (H. Rushton Fairclough transl. 1926) (Loeb Classical Library rep. 1978) (passage 72). See also 1 Quintilian, supra note 6, at 113 (passage i.6.3) ("Custom is the greatest preceptor in speaking; and we must use phraseology, like money, which has the public stamp.").

[69]   Cicero, de Inventione, supra note 21, at 285-89 (passage ii. 50 & 51).

the writer had wished it to have the meaning" advanced by the opponent.[70] But, aside from these very general approaches to legal texts, the *constitutiones legitimae* of *ambiguitas* and of *definitio* did not provide much guidance to the orator. But it is worthy of note that classical orators had a sensible theory of ambiguity, one that informed their rhetorical judgement about the handling of other problems in legal texts.

iii. α. That brings me next to the *quaestio* of *scriptum et sententia*,[71] the letter and intent of a legal document. Problems of this sort arose whenever "the framer's intention appears to be at variance with the letter of the text."[72] The *Rhetorica ad Herennium* gave as an example of this sort of difficulty the *controversiae* of the competing claims to the shipwreck,[73] recounted in slightly fuller form above.[74] The intent of this Roman analogue of salvage was to

---

[70] Rhetorica ad Herennium, supra note 11, at 85 (passage ii.11.16). See also Cicero, de Inventione, supra note 21, at 289 (passage ii.41.120-21).

    Cicero points out, in the case of the bequest of silver, supra note 64, that the addition of the words "as desired" would have been unnecessary if the selection was vested in the heir. "Therefore in such cases it will be necessary to make use of this kind of argument: 'He would have written it in this way,' 'He would not have used that word,' 'He would not have put that word in that place'." Id.

[71] For more on the Roman understanding of the concept of sententiam, *see* Sinclair, supra note 2. Roman handling of this subject can be traced to Aristotelian origins. In his RHETORIC, Aristotle noted that in a criminal prosecution, an advocate could argue against the text of a statute by arguing for the legislator's intention (*dianoia*) over his words (*logos*). In the same way, the intention (*prohairesis*) of a contractor or testator could be affirmed. See Aristotle, Rhetoric, supra note 24, at 147 (passage i.13.17) ("look not to the law, but to the legislator; not to the letter of the law but to the intention of the legislator...."). *See also* Eden, supra note 2, at 11. For how the Greek *dianoia* was translated into the Latin *voluntas*, *see* Heinrich Lausberg, HANDBUCH DER LITERARISCHEN RHETORIK 109, 118 (1960); Trimpi, supra note 2, at 280.

[72] Rhetorica ad Herennium, supra note 11, at 35 (passage i.11.19).

[73] *See* id. at 35-37 (passage i.11.19).

[74] *See* supra note 41 and accompanying text. Harry Caplan in his translation of the *Rhetorica ad Herennium* properly traces this *controversiae* to its Greek origins. *See* id. at

reward those that remained with a vessel in peril. In both the *controversiae* recounted in *ad Herennium* and in *de Inventione*, the person who stayed on board did so either because he was too sick to move or because he had tried to commit suicide.[75] This *controversiae* set-up a dispute not only about the meaning of the word "abandoned" (*relinquerent*) in the declamatory law, but also as to whether the intent of the statute was to reward those who either (by fortuity or timidity) remained with the vessel, although not rendering valuable salvage services. This was a classic predicate of *scriptum et sententia*, the letter versus the spirit of the law.[76]

Rhetorical treatises were careful to identify different kinds of texts which raised problems of intent. It was not enough, as Cicero knew, that "a controversy over the letter and the intent occurs when one party follows the exact words that are written and the other directs his whole pleading to what he says the writer meant."[77] The intent of the drafter could have been either absolute or conditional. If absolute, the writer's intent was to be given "the same weight for every occasion and every action."[78] If conditional, that intent was "to be interpreted to fit the occasion in the light of some act or some event."[79] For example, in the drafting of a will, a testator may have always used

---

36 n.a. H.M. Hubbell called the related passage in Cicero's *de Inventione* as "smell[ing] of classical rhetoric." Cicero, Inventione, supra note 21, at 322 n.a. (editor's note).

[75] Rhetorica ad Herennium, supra note 11, at 35-37 (passage i.11.19); Cicero, de Inventione, supra note 21, at 321-23 (passage ii.51.153-54).

[76] *See also* Frier, supra note 44, at 121-22; Martin, supra note 3, at 46-48; Franz Wieacker, *The* Causa Curiana *and Contemporary Roman Jurisprudence*, 2 THE IRISH JURIST (n.s.) 151, 153 (1967). *See also* infra notes 253-54 and accompanying text.

[77] Cicero, de Inventione, supra note 21, at 291 (passage ii.42.121). *See also* Cicero, de Oratoria, supra note 5, at 395 (*de Partitiones Oratore*, passage xxxi. 108).

[78] Cicero, de Inventione, supra note 21, at 291 (passage ii.42.123). *See id.* at 287 (passage ii.40.117), where Cicero noted that the "intent of the writer must be inferred from his other writings, his deeds, words, temper and life." *See also* Eden, supra note 2, at 15-16.

[79] Id.

the word "furniture" to include his cloaks and togas.[80] This would be an absolute intention. "On the other hand," Quintilian noted, "the dispute may turn on a passage of the law which is clear in one sense and doubtful in another."[81] Imagine a law stipulating that "[a] thief shall refund four times the amount of his theft. Two thieves have jointly stolen 10,000 sesterces. 40,000 are claimed from each. They claim they are liable only to pay 20,000 each."[82] This would be situational obscurity, and so an example of conditional intent, but this time on the part of a law-maker.

β. Latin rhetoricians provided great detail to the orator who was arguing on behalf of either the text of a legal writing or the intent of its framers. Arguing for the application of the literal text of the legal instrument tended to be a straight-forward exercise. As the author of the *Rhetorica ad Herennium* noted, the primary duty of the orator in such situations was to "show the danger of departing from the letter of the text."[83] Cicero's *de Inventione* went much further than this simple observation, though. Indeed, he provided a full and complete theory for textualism. Cicero wrote that the literal interpretation of legal writings was necessary to preserve individual expectations and societal stability. Unbridled interpretation by judges would wreak havoc on legal security, "[f]or those who draw up a written document will not feel that what they have written will be fixed and unalterable, and judges will have no sure guide to follow if once they become accustomed to depart from the written word."[84] Cicero's primary *topoi*, or line of argument, in defense of the text was

---

[80] This example comes from the 3 THE DIGEST OF JUSTINIAN 140 (Theodor Mommsen & Paul Kruger ed., transl. Alan Watson 1985) (provision 33.10.7.2; Celsus, *Digest* 19) [hereinafter "Digest"]. Following legal convention, I will cite to the specific fragment in the Digest and include also the original source information on the juristic writing that the Digest quotes or abstracts.

[81] 3 Quintilian, supra note 6, at 137 (passage vii.6.3).

[82] Id. (passage vii.6.2).

[83] Rhetorica ad Herennium, supra note 11, at 81 (passage ii.9.13).

[84] Cicero, de Inventione, supra note 21, at 297 (passage ii.44.128). *See also* id. at 299-301 (passage ii.45.132) ("all principles which enable judges to give judgement and the

reminding the judge of his "duty"[85] to "comply with the law and not interpret it."[86] Cicero's overriding point was that interpretation in defiance of the legal text is unprincipled and illegitimate, "for the judges will have no rule to follow if they depart from the letter of the law, nor will they have any means of winning the approval of others to their decision which has been made contrary to the law...."[87]

Cicero was primarily concerned with textualism in statutory interpretation. Indeed, he identified three strains of textualism in legal discourse about the construction of statutes. Each of these had to do with rebutting the defense that the (typically criminal) statute would allow some deviation.[88] The most extreme of the positions is that *no* law should admit to *any* exception. In support of this proposition, Cicero said that the orator could argue that "law-makers are accustomed to make exceptions" and that "it is not hard to make an exception or excuse ... if the [lawmaker] had thought that any exception ought to be made."[89] Cicero also made a sort of constitutional argument, consonant with his theme of security of expectation. If a law needs a change it should be made by the people and Senate (later the Principate and Emperor), and not by a judge.[90]

Cicero next explored a milder version of textualism: even if one were to admit that some laws can be interpreted to embrace exceptions, the particular statute under consideration should be construed strictly. Here Cicero pointed-out that the exercise is distinguishing between different kinds of laws, and giving

---

rest of the citizens to live will be unsettled if once they depart from the law.").

[85] Id. at 295 (passage ii.43.125).

[86] Id. (passage ii.44.127).

[87] Id. at 301 (passage ii.45.132).

[88] *See* id. at 299 (passage ii.44.130).

[89] Id. at 299 (passage ii.45.131).

[90] *See* id. at 301-03 (passage ii.45.133-34).

greater textual fidelity to those dealing with "matters of the highest importance, advantage, honour and sanctity."[91] The last, and softest, form of textualist argument was that even "if it is proper to accept an excuse contrary to the letter of the law, the excuse offered by the opponents should by no means be admitted."[92] Cicero suggested some narrowly-focused arguments on the character of the criminal defendant's conduct, essentially appealing to the judge not to be lenient in the face of the law. Nevertheless, Cicero said that "this topic is indispensable because one who is speaking [for] the letter ought always to adduce some principle of equity."[93]

γ. Equity is, after all, at the heart of the argument in favor of the spirit or intent of the law, an observation that I found has been the subject of some debate between scholars of ancient rhetoric and law.[94] Attacking the text of a statute was largely an exercise in making use of what Cicero called the "assumptive branch of the equitable issue." This was a species of *quaestio* considered not under the legal or definitional basis, but under the heading concerned with whether an act, in being admitted, is right or wrong (*quale sit*).[95] There were four equitable arguments to be made in assaulting the literal application of the law: that an act was done for a greater good (comparison, *comparatio*), that it was done in justifiable response to another individual's conduct (retort of the accusation, *relatio criminis*), that legal responsibility

---

[91] Id. at 303 (passage ii.46.135).

[92] Id. at 305 (passage ii.46.135).

[93] Id. (passage ii.46.136) (emphasis added). *See also* 3 Quintilian, supra note 6, at 141 (passage vii.6.9) ("But just as the advocate who rests his case on the intention of the law must wherever possible impugn the letter of the law, so he who defends the letter of the law must also seek to gain support from the intention.").

[94] *See* infra § V.iii. *See also* Aristotle, NICOMACHAEAN ETHICS 317 (H. Rackham transl. 1926) (Loeb Classical Library ed. 1982) (passage v.10.6-7) ("This is the essential nature of the equitable: it is a rectification (*epanorthoma*) of law where law is defective because of its generality. . . ."). *See also* Eden, supra note 2, at 13-14.

[95] *See* supra notes 5-8 and accompanying text. *See also* Rhetorica ad Herennium, supra note 11, at xlvii (editor's introduction).

attached to some other person or thing (shifting the charge, *remotio criminis*), and that the act was done, but only because of ignorance, accident or necessity (confession and avoidance, *concessio*).[96]

Each of these could be used in the context of statutory interpretation. For example, if the law said that a man would be punished if he opened the city gates at night, and his defense was that he did so to admit friendly forces during a siege, that would be *comparatio*.[97]   The law might say that a Roman ambassador had to set-out on his embassy within a certain number of days after his appointment. He did not do so, however, because the Treasurer did not give him the necessary funds for the journey. That would be an excuse premised on the *topoi* surrounding *remotio criminis*.[98]

Despite the availability of these topics to challenge the letter of the law, Cicero recognized that the primary difficulty would be in persuading a tribunal that there was sufficient reason to depart from the text. Quintilian provided some rules of thumb on this point. He said that if a literal interpretation leads to an absurd result, it should be ignored, as in the case of an infant charged with violating the law that "'children shall support their parents under penalty of imprisonment'."[99] Likewise, if a literal construction leads to a manifestly unfair result, an exception should be allowed (as in the case of a foreigner who mounted the city walls in helping to repel an enemy attack).[100] Lastly, Quintilian said that the literal text of the statute should be ignored "if we find something in the actual words of the law which enables us to prove that the intention of the

---

[96] *See* Cicero, de Inventione, supra note 21, at 237-71 (passages ii. 24-33). There was also a fifth form of an assumptively equitable argument, *purgatio* or *deprecatio*, in which the defendant concedes the act and legal liability but seeks a pardon. *See* id. at 271-79 (passages ii. 34-37).

[97] *See* id. at 291-93 (passage ii.42.123).

[98] *See* id. at 293 (passage ii.42.124).

[99] 3 Quintilian, supra note 6, at 139 (passage vii.6.5).

[100] *See* id. (passage vii.6.6).

legislator was different."[101] A law, for example, which said that "anyone who is caught at night with steel in his hands shall be thrown in prison," on its face applies to someone carrying a sword, and not someone wearing a steel ring.[102]

But apart from these rules that could guide a tribunal in breaking from the statutory text, Cicero and his contemporaries felt comfortable in making direct appeals to judges (*iudices*) to exercise their power of discretion in applying the law.[103] "There is," after all, "no law which requires the performance of any inexpedient or unjust act."[104] And the Romans "value the laws not because of the words, which are but faint and feeble indications of intention, but because of the advantage of the principle which they embody...."[105] And, finally, the reason the Romans had judges was, Cicero said, to be able "not only to read [the] law, which any child could do, but to comprehend it with the mind and interpret [the lawmaker's] intentions."[106]

---

[101] Id. at 139 (passage vii.6.8).

[102] Id. at 141 (passage vii.6.8).

[103] Judges in Quintilian's time may have been more reluctant to do so in view of the fact that most laws were then handed down by the Emperor. *See* supra note 50 and accompanying text.

[104] Cicero, de Inventione, supra note 21, at 307 (passage ii.47.138).

[105] Id. at 309 (passage ii.48.141). *See also* id. at 311-13 (passage ii.48.143) ("the value of the law depends on the intention of the legislator and on the common weal, not on the words.").

[106] Id. at 307 (passage ii.47.139). Professor Baade has recently suggested that Roman rhetorical theory did not encourage recourse to the actual intent of the legislator. *See* Hans W. Baade, *The* Casus Omissus: *A Pre-History of Statutory Analogy*, 20 SYR. J. INT'L L. & COM. 45, 47 (1994).
    Professor Baade has written to me that the just-quoted extract from Cicero suggests only that an orator might speculate as to what the original drafter of the legal writing might say or do in resolving the current controversy, which is not the same thing as actually consulting "chronicles, records or reports ... or oral tradition securely traceable to contemporaries, [that is] *actual* intent." Letter from Hans W. Baade to the author, Sept. 1, 1995, at 2 (on file). Professor Baade's point is certainly supported insofar as Cicero

An additional line of argument bolstered recourse to evidence of intent: the very difficulty of the legislative task. As Xenophon generally observed, "To write all that a man ought to do is no more possible than to know everything that is going to happen."[107] And, as the elder Seneca had more pertinently noted, "Many things are understood in a law, although they are not excepted. The wording of a law is restricted, the interpretation is broad; and some things are so obvious that they need no exception."[108]

Cicero's internal debate between *scriptum et sententiam* reduced to the competing notions of legal certainty and "abstract justice" (*cum aequitatae causa abundabit*).[109] As we would expect of any rhetorical treatise, Cicero marshaled strong arguments on each side of the letter/spirit divide. But the very structure of his arguments was revealing. There were few mechanical rules for construing texts. These were largely developed later by Quintilian. Instead, Cicero's contentions are almost philosophical, concentrating on the nature of Republican government, on judicial legitimacy, and on individualized justice. The strongest argument he made for literalism was the dangers of unprincipled

---

borrowed from Aristotelian notions of rhetorically consulting the resurrected law-maker. *See* Aristotle, Nicomachaean Ethics, supra note 94, at 315-17 (passage v.10.5-6). *See also* Eden, supra note 2, at 15-16.

I would maintain, though, that Cicero and Quintilian were writing of actual intent, especially in view of their comments about analogy. *See* infra notes 115-16 and accompanying text. Further textual analysis is needed on this point. But that is for another book!

[107]   Xenophon, SCRIPTA MINORA: THE CAVALRY COMMANDER 289 (E.C. Marchant transl. 1925) (Loeb Classical Library rep. 1984) (passage ix. 1). *See* Aristotle, Nicomachaean, supra note 94, at 315 (passage v.10.4) ("Law is always a general statement, yet there are cases which it is not possible to cover in a general statement.").

[108]   Seneca, Controversiae, supra note 34, at 291 (passage ix.4.9). See also Lysias 215 (W.R.M. Lamb transl. 1930) (Loeb Classical Library rep. 1988) (xi *Against Theomnestus*, passage ii. 4) ("It would have been too much trouble for the lawgiver to have written down all the designations which have the same meaning, but what he said about one he wanted to have understood of all the others.").

[109]   Cicero, De Inventione, supra note 16, at 311 (passage ii.48.143).

discretion being vested in judges. The most powerful point he made for looking to the spirit or intent of the law was to achieve fairness.

iv. In the Roman rhetorician's mind, the question of legislative intent in statutory interpretation had a strong affinity with another *constitutio legitima*: the *question* of analogy or syllogism, what was known in Latin as *ratiocinatio* or *syllogismus*. Put simply, this question occurred whenever "a matter that arises for adjudication lacks a specifically applicable law, but an analogy is sought from other existing laws on the basis of a certain similarity to the matter in question."[110] Quintilian noted the strong relationship of this basis with *scriptum et sententiam*, but he also made a crucial distinction: "[I]n [letter and spirit] we argue against the letter, in [*syllogismus* we argue] beyond the letter."[111] Arguing "beyond the letter" of the law meant "deduc[ing] from the letter of the law that which is uncertain...,"[112] or, put another way, "infer[ring] what is doubtful from what is certain."[113]

---

[110] Rhetorica ad Herennium, supra note 11, at 41 (passage i.13.23).

For more on the origins of legal analogy in classical Greek rules of grammar, *see* Artur Steinwenter, *Prolegomena zu einer Geschichte der Analogie: Analoge Rechtsanwendung im Römischen Recht*, in 2 FESTSCHRIFT FRITZ SCHULZ 345 (1951) (pt. 1); id., 2 STUDI IN MEMORIA DI EMILIO ALBERTARIO 104 (1953) (pt. 2); id., *Das Recht der Kaiserlichen Konstitutionen*, in 2 STUDI IN ONORE DI VINCENZO ARANGIO-RUIZ 169 (1952). *See also* Peter Stein, *The Relations between Grammar and Law in the Early Principate: The Beginnings of Analogy*, in 2 ATTI DEL SECONDI CONGRESSO INTERNAZIONALE DELLA SOCIETÀ ITALIANA DI STORIA DEL DIRITTO, LA CRITICA DEL TESTO 757 (1971).

[111] 3 Quintilian, supra note 6, at 149 (passage vii.8.1). *See also* 1 id. at 113-15 (passage i.6.4), where Quintilian notes that the essence of analogy was testing what is doubtful by reference to a standard of comparison of which there is no doubt.

[112] Id. at 151 (passage vii.8.3).

[113] Id. at 153 (passage vii.8.6). *See also*, Nikolaus Benke, Exempla Contra Legem, 57 LEGAL HIST. REV. 275 (1987).

Both Cicero and the author of the *Rhetorica ad Herennium* provided the same, quite lawyerly example of a problem implicating *ratiocinatio*.[114] One Malleolous was convicted of killing his mother. Just before his execution he made an ostensibly proper will, designating certain heirs. After his death, Malleolous' younger brother (who had been one of his accusers at the trial and who had not been named an heir) challenged the testamentary heirs for his inheritance, invoking the rights of agnation.[115] No law specifically denied testamentary capacity to one condemned for matricide. The advocate for the brother would have been obliged to argue by analogy from the law which stipulated that "[i]f a man is raving mad, authority over his person and property shall belong to his agnates."[116] "Here no one specific law is adduced, and yet many laws are adduced, which form a basis for a reasoning by analogy to prove that Malleolous had or had not the right to make a will."[117]

Quintilian provided some additional archetypes of statutory analogy. Using a stock *controversia* from Seneca,[118] an unchaste priestess is, according to the law,[119] hurled from the Tarpeian rock but miraculously survived. Should the execution be attempted again? Quintilian said of this issue that "[i]f it is

---

[114] Cicero, de Inventione, supra note 21, at 319-19 (passage ii.50.148-49); Rhetorica ad Herennium, supra note 11, at 41-43 (passage i. 13). *See also* Eden, supra note 2, at 16.

[115] Agnates are near kin on the male side, the usual beneficiaries if a Roman died intestate. *See* Cicero, de Inventione, supra note 21, at 316 n.b (editor's note). *See generally* Barry Nicholas, An Introduction to Roman Law 246-64 (1962); Alan Watson, The Law of Succession in the later Roman Republic (1971).

[116] As quoted in Rhetorica ad Herennium, supra note 11, at 41 (passage i.13.23).

[117] Id. at 43 (passage i.13.23).

[118] *See* 1 Seneca, supra note 34, at 89 (passage i. 3).

[119] This was a real law and was (periodically) enforced. *See* id. at 88 n.2 (citing 4 Tacitus, Annales 185 (John Jackson transl. 1931 Loeb Classical Library rep. 1956) (passage vi. 19)) (although the historical event involved the execution of a man convicted of incest with his daughter).

right to do a thing once, is it right to do it often?"[120] Likewise, there were problems of analogy which arose when a law referred only to the whole, and a part was at issue, or vice versa.[121] Finally, recourse to analogy was required when there were intervening circumstances: "If a thing is legal before a certain occurrence, is it legal after it?"[122]

Questions of legislative intent seemed to be decisive in these problems involving analogy. The *Rhetorica ad Herennium* suggested that the process of *ratiocinatio* primarily involved looking for similar statutes and deciding "whether the absence of a text concerning the matter ... involved was intentional, because if the framer was unwilling to make any provision, or because he thought that there was provision enough thanks to the similar provisions in the other legal texts."[123] Likewise, Quintilian asked "ought we to have recourse to an analogous law? Is the point in question similar to what is contained in the letter of the law?"[124]

Cicero, as we might expect, framed the issue nicely. Speaking in favor of argument from analogy he said that "no one can include every case in one statute but that he makes the most suitable law who takes care that some things may be understood from certain others."[125] On the other side of the issue he said

---

[120] 3 Quintilian, supra note 6, at 151 (passage vii.8.3).

[121] Is that which is lawful with regard to the whole, lawful with regard to a part? Example: 'It is forbidden to accept a plough as security. He accepted a ploughshare.' Is that which is lawful with regard to a part, lawful with regard to the whole? Example: 'It is forbidden to export wool from Tarentum; he exported sheep'.

Id. (passage vii.8.4).

[122] Id.

[123] Rhetorica ad Herennium, supra note 11, at 91 (passage ii.12.18). *See also* Baade, supra note 106, at 47 & n.17.

[124] 3 Quintilian, supra note 6, at 153 (passage vii.8.7).

[125] Cicero, de Inventione, supra note 21, at 321 (passage ii.50.152).

that "inference is no better than divination, and that it is a stupid lawmaker who cannot provide for every case that he desires."[126] Arguing "beyond the letter of the law" (as Quintilian put it) was fraught with the same perils as any form of statutory interpretation.

v. These hazards were, if anything, magnified when the problem was *contrariae leges*, "when one law orders or permits a deed while another forbids it."[127] This type of *quaestio* was a perennial favorite of the declaimers. Seneca had one *controversia* involving a conflict among three laws:

> Acts motivated by force or fear shall not be valid.
> Agreements made according to the law shall stand.
> A man who acknowledges a child he has [abandoned] may
> take him back after paying for his upbringing.
>
> . . . .
>
> A man took in and educated boy twins who had been [abandoned]. When the natural father made enquiries, the foster-father promised he would reveal where they were if he was [allowed to adopt] one of them. They struck a bargain. [The natural father later sought to repudiate the deal and claim custody of both children.][128]

As one later commentator noted, the conflict of statutes is between the law that gives the natural father certain rights but also allows him to contract them away, and whether duress (what the first declamatory law called *per vim metumque gesta ne sint rata*) vitiated the bargain.[129]

---

[126] Id. (passage i.50.153).

[127] Rhetorica ad Herennium, supra note 11, at 37 (passage i.11.20).

[128] 2 Seneca, supra note 34, at 265 (passage ix. 3). For more on the phenomenon of abandoning children in antiquity, *see* Bonner, supra note 9, at 125-27.

[129] *See* Bonner, supra note 9, at 114-15. For another illustration of a conflict of laws used by the rhetoricians, *see* Cicero, de Inventione, supra note 21, at 313 (passage ii.49.144) (one law says that a tyrannicide will be rewarded; another provides that the immediate family of a tyrant will be killed after his execution; the wife kills the tyrant) and 3 Quintilian, supra note 6, at 145 (passage vii.7.5) (one act calls for a statue of a tyrannicide to be erected in the gymnasium; the other bars a statue of a woman; a woman kills the tyrant).

Quintilian was much concerned with the phenomenon of conflicting laws and sought to understand how such a clash could arise. He opined: "[I]t is clear ... that one law cannot contradict another in principle (since if there were two different principles, one law would cancel the other), and that [such] laws ... are brought into collision purely by the accidents of chance."[130] For Quintilian, most conflicts in laws were illusory. He sought, therefore, to construct an elaborate scheme which distinguished "true" from "false" conflict situations by identifying "diverse," "similar," and "dissimilar" sets of laws.[131] In cases where no reconciliation between the statutes was possible, then the task for the orator was to persuade "which of the two laws will suffer less by its contravention."[132] But Quintilian as much as admitted that this was a "problem the solution of which no general rules can be laid down."[133]

Quintilian was again being cautious, content with providing the orator with the means of identifying a problem of interpreting legal texts, and not giving definitive rules for its solution. As with the *constitutiones* of definition and ambiguity, Cicero's *de Inventione* and the *Rhetorica ad Herennium* do attempt to provide some guidance on this subject. Admittedly, the proposals in *ad Herennium* were obvious and modest: look to see if one law may have actually superseded another, and whether one might be mandatory and the other permissive.[134] In short, the instruction was to reconcile apparently discordant texts.

Cicero acknowledged, on the other hand, that true conflicts could arise. In such situations, he advised that the law enacted later should control.[135] There

---

[130] 3 Quintilian, supra note 6, at 143 (passage vii.7.2).

[131] *See* id. at 143-45 (passage vii.7.2-6).

[132] Id. at 147 (passage vii.7.8).

[133] Id.

[134] Rhetorica ad Herennium, supra note 11, at 85 (passage ii.10.15).

[135] Cicero, de Inventione, supra note 21, at 313-15 (passage ii.49.145-47). *See also* 3 Livy, *History of Rome* 415 (Frank G. Moore, Evan T. Sage & Alfred C. Schlesinger transl. 1922) (Loeb Classical Library rep. 1967) (passage vii.17.12) ("quodcumque

were other canons recognized by classical rhetoricians to govern situations of *contrariae leges*. The author of the *ad Herennium* noted that "a command is of greater force than a permission,... for that which is enjoined is necessary, and that which is allowed is optional."[136] Likewise, Cicero believed that a statute with specific provisions subsuming the dispute should prevail over a more general enactment.[137]

vi. This exposition of classical oratory, declamation practice, and the *stasis* system leads me to some conclusions about the ancient intellect which was capable of producing rules for the interpretation of legal texts. Let me summarize them here:

α. Although both judicial oratory and declamation were practiced by the ancient Greeks, they reached their practical zenith and logical rationale in the Roman Republic. The status system may have been an outgrowth of Hellenistic civilization, but it was really refined as a system of argumentation in ancient Rome. Such *rhetorica* as Cicero's *de Inventione*, the *ad Herennium*, and Quintilian's *Institutio* exhibit a very high level both of sophistication and abstraction. There is no question, moreover, that the Romans distinctively modified the Greek concept of *stasis* in order to further the development of judicial oratory. The teaching of status was clearly regarded as being an essential part of the theoretical training of a judicial orator in Rome. The stylized exercises of the *controversiae* must have been intended to reinforce the lessons for identifying different kinds of forensic issues and marshaling arguments in order to achieve a clients' objectives in a courtroom setting.

β. To the extent that the interpretation of legal texts was expected in a judicial proceeding, it was natural and obvious that the status system would provide guidance to the orator on that subject. The underlying approach of *stasis* as a system of argumentation was, however, strongly schematic. The system instructed not so much by providing rules of discourse

---

postremum populus iusisset, id ius ratumque esset"); 4 id. at 293 (passage ix.34.6) ("semper antiquae obrogat nova").

[136] Rhetorica ad Herennium, *supra* note 11, at 85 (passage ii.10.15). *See also* Quintilian, MINOR DECLAMATIONS 270 (Michael Winterbottom transl. 1984) (passage 374) ("the law which forbids is more powerful than that which permits.").

[137] See Cicero, de Inventione, *supra* note 21, at 313-15 (passage ii.49.145-47).

than it did by organizing the issues and questions for debate. That is why it was so significant that questions of definition and legal interpretation were confounded by the Romans in the same rhetorical inquiry. To ask what something was, was virtually the same inquiry as deciding the legal character of any person, event, relationship, or transaction.

That also explains the natural tension that the great rhetorical writers felt in pronouncing either rules or standards in governing the interpretation of legal texts. It seemed that as judicial oratory in Rome matured in the Principate period (the first century A.D.) there grew a great reluctance to enunciate concrete canons for such situations. Quintilian's caution in the face of the *quaestiones* of ambiguity and contrary laws was illustrative of this trend. Cicero's writings (and his practice) seven decades earlier represented the high-water mark of invention and creativity in the process of developing standards of legal construction.

All of this is not to say, of course, that general principles for interpreting statutes (or any other legal writing) were not helpful. They were. But, once again, the chief illumination of classical rhetorical theory to the problem of construing legal texts was not in content. It was in form. The rhetorical treatises of Cicero and Quintilian could certainly be criticized for being ambivalent and inconclusive. After all, every argument on one side of the case was supposed to be met by an equal and opposite contention. One can understand those who, after reading Cicero and Quintilian, feel that they really say nothing about the problems of statutory interpretation. But one must, I think, look deeper into these rhetorical writings. I find them of interest not only for the structure of arguments they provide, but also for the clues that they give to the perceived strengths and weaknesses of various topics and approaches to the meaning of legal texts.

γ. One thing certainly to be appreciated is that Roman rhetorical writers had a cogent theory for dealing with the natural ambiguities produced by language. Whether expressed as the *controversiae* of *ambiguitas* or of *definitio*, the point made by the rhetoricians was the same: any interpreter of legal texts had to be prepared for the ambiguity and vagueness of words singularly or in combination. The primary task for the orator was to accept a tolerable level of uncertainty. Understanding the intent of the legislator (or of the testator or contractor, for that matter) was *not*, according to the Roman rhetors, a simple matter of providing acceptable meanings to unclear words. Rather, their approach emphasized both factual context and abstract forms of interpretive reasoning.

δ. Classical rhetoricians thus sought to provide concrete rules for legal interpretation (again) primarily by means of taxonomy. For example, to understand the intent of a legal drafter, the rhetorician would have an orator make an argument based on whether the intent was "absolute" or "conditional."[138] Likewise, in analyzing an apparent situation of conflict of laws, the rhetorician provided rules to determine whether there was, in fact, a true clash.[139] These inquiries did not lead to answers. But they did define which appeals to public policy, morality, or sensibilities would be well-received, and which would not.

In reaching this conclusion, I had to constantly remind myself that rhetoricians were in the business of persuasion. And, even though the typical venue for such persuasion was a courtroom, the orator certainly was not limited to what we might consider today an appeal to pure legal reason. (Nor, obviously, are today's lawyers so constrained.) The insight of Cicero, Quintilian, and the author of *ad Herennium* was that certain arguments concerning legal interpretation worked better in certain circumstances. The schematic rules informed the orator when to make a particular contention.

ε. What remained for the orator was to deliver the rhetorical *coup de grace*, the final appeal which transformed a simple question of legal interpretation into a matter of great importance, clinching victory for the client. In this regard, Cicero was the master. He was apparently able to turn even a trivial dispute into a *cause célèbre*.[140] His treatise, *de Inventione*, is replete with arguments that transcend the work-a-day world of the Roman jurist. Consider these (rhetorical) questions he posed: should a judge (instead of the people, the Senate, or the Emperor) interpret a law which is vague or unclear? Are not statutes to be construed consistent with their object and purpose? Can we not

---

[138] *See* supra notes 72-76 and accompanying text.

[139] *See* supra notes 122-25 and accompanying text.

[140] Consider, for example, his oration in *pro Caecina*, which involved a disputed will and the meaning of a praetorian interdict prohibiting threats or use of force. *See generally* Frier, supra note 44.

assume that lawmakers mean what they say and say what they mean? Should not the laws be construed with conscience and reason in order to achieve justice?

These are great and enduring questions. Classical rhetoricians were the first to propound them in understanding the written law. What remains to understand is whether the construction of these questions, on top of a foundation of classical rhetoric expressed in the *stasis* system, influenced our modern ways of thinking about statutory interpretation. The most logical place to start such an inquiry into the transmission of these ideas was to ascertain the impact of *constitutio legitima* on the development of the Roman law for construing legal texts, the *ius interpretationis*.

III TREATY MAKING AND INTERPRETATION IN CLASSICAL ANTIQUITY

But the most obvious mode of narration here may not necessarily be the best way to proceed. So far in this book, I have related nothing about treaties — how ancient States made faith amongst themselves and how rules came to be developed for the proper interpretation and enforcement of written agreements. Just as I have suggested here that there was a classical tradition in the rhetorical interpretation of legal texts, so, too, was there was a classical tradition in treaty-making and treaty-construction.

Before further unwinding the skein of my story of how the classical rhetoric for interpreting legal texts was transmitted to, and received by, modernity, it is worth some pages to recount ancient practices in statecraft. The purpose of this exposition is to give one a sense of this tradition, one (I will suggest later in this work) had important influences on, and synergies with, modern treaty interpretation practices.

i. *Greek Treaty Interpretation.* α. The extent of treaty-making by Greek city-States simply was extraordinary. By one count,[141] nearly four hundred treaties are extant (through inscription evidence or literary allusions) from the period before 338 BC, when Greece came under Macedonian domination. To match this remarkable diplomatic activity, the ancient Greeks had an equally extensive lexicon for treaty instruments. These included generic terms to cover the simple act of covenant, which was similar to the Greek word

---

[141] *See* Everett L. Wheeler, *Sophistic Interpretations and Greek Treaties*, 25 GRBS 253, 255-56 (1984). *See also* 2 Coleman Phillipson, THE INTERNATIONAL LAW AND CUSTOM OF ANCIENT GREECE AND ROME 73 (1911) (who pegs the number at over 200).

for contract.[142] The Greeks also made distinctions as to kinds of treaties made upon the termination of hostilities. These could properly be considered as peace treaties, or as declarations of neutrality, or as amnesties ending periods of internal disorder.[143] Likewise, the Greeks developed terminology to cover different sorts of alliances, whether purely defensive (*epimachia*) or offensive (*symmachia*).[144] And there were a whole host of agreements establishing special individual or commercial relationships between two cities. Recognition was even given to technical instruments, treaty amendments and protocols.[145]

Perhaps the greatest tribute to the Greek practice of memorializing treaty obligations was made by a later orator, Lycortas, appearing before a Roman commission at Clitor in 184 BC. He was speaking in defense of the Greek custom to abide by treaty obligations. He said:

> What we have ratified by our oaths, what we have consecrated as inviolable to eternal remembrance, by records engraved in stone, they want to abolish, and load us with perjury. Romans, for you we have high respect; and, if such is your wish, dread also; but we respect and dread more the immortal gods.[146]

---

[142] *See* 3 Thucydides, HISTORY OF THE PELOPONNESIAN WAR 59 (C.F. Smith transl. 1919) (Loeb Classical Library rep. 1980) (passage v. 31). *See* also Aristotle, Rhetoric, supra note 24, at 151 (passage i. 15) (equating law with contract).

[143] *See* 1 Phillipson, supra note 141, at 375-76 (citing 1 Herodotus, HISTORIES 25 (A.D. Godley transl. 1920) (Loeb Classical Libary rep. 1969) (passage i. 22); and 2 Thucydides, supra note 142, at 309, 409 (passages iv. 58 & 117), and 3 id. at 49, 61 (passages v. 26 & 32); and 1 Xenophon, HELLENICA AND ANABASIS 265, 271 (Carleton L. Brownson transl. 1921) (Loeb Classical Library rep. 1932) (*Hellenica*, passage iv. 2 & 16)).

[144] *See* 1 Phillipson, supra note 141, at 376-77 (citing 3 Herodotus, supra note 143, at 67, 81 (passage v. 63 & 73); and 1 Thucydides, supra note 142, at 79 (passage i. 44)).

[145] *See* 1 Phillipson, supra note 141, at 376.

[146] *See* 11 Livy, supra note 135, at 339 (passage xxxix. 37).

The irony of this statement could not have been lost on the Romans. Many Greek city-States had notorious reputations for repudiating treaty obligations,[147] and these acts of perfidy tended to reflect badly on the faithfulness of all Greeks.

β.   Quite a few Greek international agreements contained self-consciously styled anti-deceit clauses. Writing in 1984, philologist Everett Wheeler concluded that nearly 15 percent (some 23 of 166) of all inscribed Greek treaties from the period 700 to 300 BC contained some kind of provision to avoid later fraud or trickery.[148] Most of these anti-deceit provisions were found in defensive alliances (*epimachia*), offensive alliances (*symmachia*), or peace treaties. Typical of these generic clauses were commands that the parties observe the terms of the treaty "without trick,"[149] and "not with craft nor with stratagem." One proclaimed that the cities "shall devise nothing about this oath, neither by craft nor by any false pretext."[150]

Everett Wheeler also has concluded that the use of anti-deceit provisions of ancient Greek treaties was suggestive of a concern against sophistic interpretations of these pacts. The exceptional presence of these clauses in the ratification oaths, rather than in the main texts of the treaty stipulations, raise concerns about the usually routine recitation of formulas concerning the good will of the parties to observe the treaty. Wheeler sees these provisions as part of a larger context of the specialized Greek vocabulary concerning stratagems

---

[147] The Thessalians, Parians, and Cretans were particularly targeted for their bad faith. *See* 4 Plutarch, LIVES 287 (B. Perrin transl. 1917) (Loeb Classical Library rep. 1968) (*Lysander*, passage xx); 1 Phillipson, supra note 141, at 118-19.

[148] *See* Wheeler, supra note 141, at 255-56 & n.12. The total number of Greek treaties during this period, known from both inscriptions and literary sources, is 388. *See* id. *See* also note 141.

[149] *See* id. at 256 n.15 (collecting citations to H. Bengtson, DIE STAATSVERTRÄGE DES ALTERUMS (1962) (nos. 120, 162, 163, 184, 186, 187, 260, 308, 309, 463, 551, 578, 581)).

[150] *See* id. at 256 n.18 (collecting citations to Bengtson, supra note 149 (nos. 297, 308, 481, 551)).

and deceit in war and statecraft.[151] In short, anti-deceit clauses were intended to adhere the parties to the principle of good faith in the subsequent interpretation of the treaty. It would prevent one party from employing an overly literal interpretation of a disputed clause or to play "on some ambiguity of meaning to produce an interpretation contrary to that intended and obvious."[152] A sophistic interpreter could, if unchallenged, claim fidelity to the treaty, avoid a charge of perjury and false-swearing, but still have the freedom of action under the agreement to achieve its own political ends.

One of the most famous interchanges in ancient Greek diplomacy concerning sophistic interpretations of treaties was the Athenian defensive alliance of 433 BC with Corcyra against her former parent city, Corinth. This *epimachia* was in arguable violation of the Thirty Years Peace signed in 445 BC between Athens and her allies and the Spartans.[153] After all, Athens had covenanted not to make any hostile move against Corinth. The Corcyrans and the Corinthians both made petitions to the Athenian assembly. The Corcyrans urged the conclusion of the alliance and advanced a literal reading of the treaty with Sparta.[154] The Corinthians argued that, irrespective of a technical reading of the Peace, an alliance with Corcyra (even one defensive in character) would violate the manifest object and purpose of the Thirty Years Peace. The Athenians decided that the terms of the Thirty Years Peace were ambiguous as to the conclusion of an *epimachia* with a city at virtual war with an ally of Sparta. They decided to proceed with the agreement,[155] which, with later

---

[151]   *See* Wheeler, supra note 141, at 253-54 & n.7.

[152]   Id. at 254.

[153]   *See* Sir Frank Adcock & D. J. Mosley, DIPLOMACY IN ANCIENT GREECE 191 (1975); Victor Martin, LA VIE INTERNATIONAL DANS LA GRÈCE DES CITÉS 399-400 (Paris 1940) (rep. 1979).

[154]   *See* 1 Thucydides, supra note 142, at 73 (passage i.40.2).

[155]   *See* id. at 79 (passage i. 44). *See* also Georges Ténékidès, *Droit International et Communautés Fédérales dans la Grèce des Cités*, 90 R.C.A.D.I. 469, 524-26 (1956 II) (glossing 1 Thucydides, supra note 142, at 78-79, 91 (passages i.44.1 & i. 53)).

strategems, was upgraded to an offensive alliance against Corinth and which then resulted in the resumption of hostilities against Sparta and her allies.

The Greeks were the first ancient people to develop rules of interpretation for treaties, in recognition of the certainty that any written text was capable of ambiguity and disputed meaning. The nature of ratification oaths and the development of anti-deceit clauses was illustrative of this process. Yet, the results were ambivalent. Greek treaties were not appreciably made more certain in application, nor more binding in character, because of the additions of these features.

γ. Interrelated with questions concerning the enforcement of treaty terms in ancient Greece was the problem of modifying irrelevant or onerous obligations and of prescribing the ways in which an international agreement could be unilaterally ended. Such attempts implicated the most delicate concerns of a rule of law in ancient Greek international relations. A party seeking to alone change the terms of an agreement, or to refuse subsequent performance, could rightly be charged with treaty breach and perjury for violation of its ratification oaths. To deal with these diplomatic crises, Greek city-States seemed to resort either to sophistic interpretations of treaties or to rules of Hellenic "custom" concerning specific situations.

One such situation, considered by the Greeks to be relatively innocuous and less threatening to the sanctity of treaties, was when the conclusion of a treaty directly or indirectly cast doubt on the continued validity of an earlier agreement. Obviously, if both treaties were made by the same sets of cities, this was merely a situation of treaty modification and not forced termination. Also, it was possible for one city to have a defensive alliance with two other polities at war with one another. The conclusion of two such *epimachia* would not constitute a conflicting obligation. These were, in effect, treaty recognitions of a state of neutrality.[156]

---

[156] Xenophon recounted when the Arcadians in 366 BC sought an alliance with Athens. Arcadia was at war with Sparta. Sparta and Athens had a valid peace treaty and *epimachia* in force. Athens proceeded with the treaty with Arcadia, resolving that they could remain on good terms with both the Arcadians and Spartans, despite their promise to the Spartans that they have the same friends and enemies. *See* 2 Xenophon, supra note 143, at 291 (passage vii.4.2).

Polybius recounted one possible resolution in those cases where a later treaty seemed to outright contradict an earlier agreement: the pact that was more private and less general in character would be discarded in favor of the more solemn and more general convention. The situation suggesting this resolution arose when Acarnania approached Sparta seeking assistance in a war with Aetolia, pursuant to a standing *symmachia*. Yet the Spartans also had a pre-existing *epimachia* with the Aetolians. The orator Lyciscus, the Acarnanian envoy at Sparta, was reported to have said: "Which will be the graver breach of obligation ... to neglect a private arrangement entered into with the Aetolians, or a treaty which has been inscribed on a column and solemnly consecrated in the eyes of the whole of Greece?"[157]

The first premise of Lyciscus' submission to the Spartans was surely correct: in ancient Greek practice a general treaty prevailed over a "private" arrangement. General peaces were held to cancel all outstanding networks of *symmachia*. Athens' capitulation to Sparta after the end of the Peloponnesian War resulted in the end of the Delian League. Likewise, the King's Peace of 387 BC resulted in Athens having to terminate its earlier alliance, concluded in 395, with the Boeotian League.[158] Finally, the Second Athenian Confederacy was dissolved in the aftermath of Philip of Macedon's victory at Chaeronea in 338 BC.[159]

The problem with Lyciscus' submission was that it was by no means clear that Sparta's treaty with the Aetolians was somehow more "private" and inferior to the one contemplated with the Acarnanians. Lyciscus had, therefore, an alternative argument:

> If the circumstances are the same now as at the time you made the alliance with the Aetolians, then your policy ought to remain on the same lines.... But if

---

[157]   *See* 4 Polybius, THE HISTORIES 85 (W.R. Paton transl. 1922) (Loeb Classical Library rep. 1975) (passage ix. 36).

[158]   *See* Lysias 573 (W.R.M. Lamb transl. 1930) (Loeb Classical Library rep. 1988) (xxvi *On the Scrutiny of Evandros*, passage 23).

[159]   *See* 1 Pausanias, *Description of Greece* 127-29 (W.H.S. Jones transl. 1935) (Loeb Classical Library rep. 1979) (Attica i, passage 25.3).

they have been entirely changed, then it is fair that you should now deliberate on the demands made to you as on a matter entirely new and unprejudiced.[160]

This is rightfully regarded as the first invocation of the doctrine of *rebus sic stantibus* in international law — the principle that one party may unilaterally terminate a treaty because of an intervening, fundamental change of circumstances.[161] Of course, this doctrine often was used as a pretext by ancient Greeks to allow a denunciation of a treaty on the flimsy grounds that there had been a change in government or régime in one of the cities. In 418 BC the Argives, after the expulsion of the democratic party in the city, renounced its treaty with Athens and signed one with Sparta.[162] In 353 BC, the Athenians suborned such treachery by encouraging the new government of the Arcadians to renounce their earlier treaty with Thebes.[163] It was not doubted, however, that a legitimate ground for changed circumstance could arise when one state conquered or absorbed another, thus having effects on the mutual treaty obligations of both the victor and vanquished.

Greek treaty texts thus emphasized secular, intellectual methods for ensuring compliance by the parties. And it was precisely this development of rationalistic means of treaty-making and enforcement which gave rise to the art of treaty interpretation. It also gave scope to the practices of Greek orators and politicians in offering (sometimes) sophistic or politically-calculated constructions of important international agreements. In any event, Greek and (as we shall see) Roman practices with treaty readings merged and diverged in some surprising ways.

ii. *Carthaginian Treaty Practices.* Any discussion of how the peoples of the ancient Western Mediterranean departed in their treaty practices from

---

[160]   4 Polybius, supra note 157, at 87 (passage ix. 37).

[161]   *See* A. Vamvoukos, TERMINATION OF TREATIES IN INTERNATIONAL LAW: THE DOCTRINE OF *REBUS SIC STANTIBUS* AND DESUETUDE 5-6 (1985).

[162]   *See* 3 Thucydides, supra note 142, at 144-45 (passage v. 78).

[163]   *See* 1 Demosthenes, COLLECTED WORKS 455 (A.T. Murray transl. 1939 Loeb Classical Library rep.) (*For the Liberty of the Rhodians*, passage xvi. 27).

Hellenic paradigms should start with the international relations of the former Phoenician colonies, the leading one being Carthage. The reason to begin with the Carthaginians is that they were the direct recipient of many ancient Near Eastern forms and rituals of treaty-making.[164] Yet evidence of Carthaginian treaty-making is scanty. Some sources are neutral enough about Carthaginian treaty-making. Aristotle, in *The Politics*, said simply that "Etruscans and Carthaginians, and all others with contractual obligations to each other ... certainly... have trade agreements, non-aggression pacts, and written documents governing their alliance."[165] Much of the remaining evidence we have is undoubtedly colored by narration from Latin sources, Rome being Carthage's deadly rival.

Indeed, one of the most famous treaties of antiquity — that between Carthage and Macedon, concluded in 215 BC at the height of the Second Punic War — was made under the authority of Hannibal, a Punic general in the field. This treaty, narrated by Polybius,[166] was to have sealed the fate of Rome in that great war by bringing two of its most formidable (and implacable) foes into an

---

[164]   Punic diplomatic practices were drawn from the Syrian hinterland, which, in turn, was influenced by Hittite and Babylonian ways. Polybius was adamant that Carthaginian treaty forms were distinctly eastern Mediterranean; he noted that Carthage, alone among its neighbors, swore their treaties "by the gods of their ancestors." 2 Polybius, *supra* note 157, at 61 (passage iii. 25). The Punic covenants that are extant are virtually indistinguishable in form from later Hittite parity or fealty agreements. It was routine in treaties made by Carthage that the ratification oaths would invoke the gods of both States parties, something Elias Bickerman has suggested was "alien to Greek and Roman ... practice." Elias J. Bickerman, *Hannibal's Covenant*, 73 AJP 1, 5 (1952). *See also* R. Laqueur, *Symbola*, 71 HERMES 469 (1936).

[165]   Aristotle, THE POLITICS 119 (T.A. Sinclair transl. 1969).

[166]   *See* 3 Polybius, *supra* note 157, at 421 (passage vii. 9).
Professor Bickerman makes a convincing argument that the text relied upon by Polybius was a Greek translation of a Punic document produced in Hannibal's chancellery. Bickerman speculates that the pact between Hannibal and Philip was not originally drafted in Greek. *See* Bickerman, Hannibal, *supra* note 164, at 1-3. This would mean that the version that comes to us today is a translation of a translation. This is significant since the form and content of the treaty will reflect both Hellenic and Carthaginian traditions, which is precisely Bickerman's thesis. *See* also Wheeler, *supra* note 141, at 265-66.

effective alliance.   It was an extraordinarily carefully-drafted document, reflecting the most sophisticated legal terminologies and diplomatic artifices earlier employed in Greek inter-city relations.   It also features some peculiarly Carthaginian features.   These are all worthy of some attention here.

For starters, the treaty follows ancient Near Eastern forms by opening with an announcement of the titles and authority of the individuals negotiating the treaty — Hannibal on one side, and Xenophanes (emissary of Philip V of Macedon) on the other.   The Carthaginian and Macedonian gods bearing witness to the covenant are then listed.   The individuals taking the ratification oaths are then named.   The preamble ends with the statement "Let us be friends, comrades and brethren on the following conditions."[167]   The first two operative paragraphs of the treaty reflect a form of *epimachia* undertaken by co-equal sovereigns. King Philip and his allies agreed to "support the Carthaginians."[168]   Likewise, Hannibal swore to "support" and "protect" the Macedonians and his Greek allies.[169]

This duty to "support" and "protect" was typical of the *berit* form of ancient Near Eastern parity treaties.   It was surely a more complete obligation than a Greek *epimachia*, which was triggered only when the territory of one party was invaded by a third State.   Likewise, under an *epimachia*, one city could give aid and comfort to its ally's enemy, so long as that enemy did not

---

[167]   For one English translation from Polybius, *see* Adcock & Mosley, supra note 153, at 262 [hereinafter "Carthage/Macedon Treaty"].   For another, see 2 Phillipson, supra note 141, at 81-83.   For more on the preamble in this treaty, see Bickerman, Hannibal, supra note 164, at 8-10.

The express qualification of the oath of friendship on subsequent conditions was rare in Greek practice, but more common in Roman usage. *See* 2 Polybius, supra note 157, at 55 (passage iii.22.4) (first treaty between Rome and Carthage), 5 id. at 339 (passage xxi.43.1) (treaty between Rome and Antiochus III of Syria).

See also M.L. Barré, THE GOD-LIST IN THE TREATY BETWEEN HANNIBAL AND PHILIP V OF MACEDON (1983).

[168]   *See* Carthage/Macedon Treaty, supra note 167, at ¶ 1.

[169]   *See* id. ¶ 2.

actually invade the territory of the treaty partner.[170] The treaty between Hannibal and Philip of Macedon was far more encompassing in its obligations than a typical, Hellenic defensive alliance. Yet, while not an *epimachia*, it was too heavily qualified to be a *symmachia* in Greek practice.

The care that was taken to draft these clauses was evident from the inclusion of provisions extending the pact not only to the then-current allies of the respective parties, but also to any allies and subjects each might acquire in Italy afterwards.[171] This clause was needed because, while it was clear that an alliance leader could bind its confederates to an offensive arrangement, there was some doubt whether this could be applied prospectively. This exact controversy had arisen between Rome and Carthage regarding the proper construction of the peace treaty ending the First Punic War in 241 BC. Each had agreed that "the allies of neither party should be attacked by the other."[172] Carthage had made what the Romans regarded as a sophistic interpretation of that earlier treaty by denying that it applied to subsequent allies. In other words, the Carthaginians seriously suggested that an after-acquired ally would be free to attack Rome or its confederate without engaging the international responsibility of Carthage. The Romans argued that if this had been the intent of the parties there would have been a clause in the 241 BC treaty barring either side from acquiring any new allies. Polybius reported this Roman refutation of the Punic position.[173] The force of the Roman legal argument must have persuaded the Carthaginians, because by 215 BC they had crafted a specific treaty provision to acknowledge this interpretation.

Yet, curiously enough, the covenant between Hannibal and Philip V, stipulated that military aid (normally to be provided under the terms of a *symmachia*) "does not need to be furnished against allies of one's own who

---

[170] *See*, e.g., 3 Herodotus, supra note 143, at 121 (passage v. 99) (Athenians aiding Miletus against Persia). *See also*, Bickerman, Hannibal, supra note 164, at 13 n.26.

[171] *See* id.

[172] *See* 2 Polybius, supra note 157, at 63-64 (passage iii. 27).

[173] *See* id. at 67 (passage iii. 29). *See also* 5 Livy, supra note 135, at 53-55 (passage xxi.19.4).

become enemies of the other partner."[174] This is a fair reading of the third and fourth stipulations of the compact which prescribes the duty "to be enemies to the enemies [of the other party] saving those kings, cities, and tribes with which we have sworn agreements and friendships."[175] In short, if a later confederate of Carthage or Macedon was attacked by a third party, the other party would be obliged to give it support. But, if (say) an established ally of Macedon attacked a Carthaginian ally, then Macedon was under no duty to take up arms against that confederate. This is not what one would have expected under the terms of the *symmachia*, which meant, at a minimum, that the contracting parties had the same friends and the same enemies. This sort of "savings" clause for pre-existing treaty relationships (in both *symmachiai* and *epimechiai*) had precedent in both Near Eastern[176] and Greek[177] treaty practice.

As a carefully drafted legal text, the covenant between Hannibal and Philip displays the usual panoply of anti-deceit clauses used by Greek city-States in their treaty-making. There is the (fairly) usual provision[178] that "[w]e will not make plots against, nor be in ambush for, each other; but in all sincerity and good-will, without reserve or secret design, will be [friends]."[179] Another significant provision was the limitation on Hannibal's power to conclude a separate peace with Rome. As the principal alliance partner, Carthage was free

---

[174] Bickerman, Hannibal, supra note 164, at 14.

[175] Carthage/Macedon Treaty, supra note 167, ¶¶ 3, 4 & 8.

[176] *See* Bickerman, Hannibal, supra note 164, at 14 (discussing incident where Ben Hadad of Damascus entered into a covenant with Baasha of Israel, who then proceeded to attack Hadad's ally, Asa of Judah; Ben Hadad broke his covenant with Israel).

[177] *See* 10 Diodorus Siculus, HISTORY 407 (C.H. Oldfather, C.L. Sherman, C. Bradford Welles & F.R. Walton transl. Loeb Classical Library rep. 1946) (passage xx.99.3) and 4 Polybius, supra note 157, at 87 (passage ix. 36). For example, in the *symmachia* between Miletus and Heracleia, the rights of Rhodes were reserved. *See also* Bickerman, Hannibal, supra note 164, at 14 n.27.

[178] *See* Wheeler, supra note 141, at 265-66.

[179] Carthage/Macedon Treaty, supra note 167, at ¶ 3.

to make peace with Rome, but only if certain conditions were satisfied, prerequisites detailed in the treaty at stipulation six.[180] The last provision of the treaty provided for subsequent amendment by mutual agreement.[181]

What seems significant about the 215 BC pact between Hannibal and Philip V is the extraordinary detail and complexity of its provisions, clauses which marry the strongest elements of Near Eastern and Greek treaty-making patterns. It is as if, as Professor Bickerman colorfully notes, "Abraham suddenly should become the contemporary of Polybius. This combining of new and of antique elements shows that the old-fashioned form of the 'covenant' [*berit*] was adapted in Hellenistic Carthage to the needs of a new time."[182]

Just as importantly, we have in this instrument the supple variation of traditional treaty forms in the Greek tradition, in order to deal with a very sensitive diplomatic situation. The combining of provisions common with defensive and offensive alliances was surely considered awkward and challenging. Add to that a temporal context in which the treaty was to have accommodated the changing needs of the parties over time, and one has a very significant legal document. Finally, the exquisitely-wrought provisions were self-consciously intended to deal forthrightly with subsequent problems of treaty interpretation. The fact that the alliance between Carthage and Macedon was doomed to failure does not matter. What does signify is the extraordinary union of different treaty-making modes in one instrument.

iii. *Roman treaty forms.* α. Arthur Nussbaum has written that, "The comparatively infrequent treaties of the Romans were for the most part concluded under the Republic, and they are on the whole not good examples of international law. Most of them reflect in terse technical phraseology the Roman

---

[180] *See* id. at ¶ 6, which included "(a) that the Romans may never make war on you, (b) that the Romans are not to have power over Corcyra, Apollonia, Epidamnus, Pharos, Dimale, Parthini or Atitania, (c) that the Romans also restore to Demetrius of Pharos all those of his friends now in the dominion of Rome."

[181] *See* id. ¶ 9.

[182] Bickerman, Hannibal, supra note 164, at 17.

methods of political expansion."[183] In this regard, one of the most characteristic forms of Roman treaty-making in the period of Rome's transmarine imperialism and consolidation, from 250 to 50 BC, was the unequal alliance (*foedus iniquum*).

The pattern seemed to be that Rome would first make a treaty establishing peace and friendship with a polity on its periphery. This would be characterized as an *amicitia*, which, as Matthaei noted, "was not an alliance, it was rather a state of diplomatic relations, which [could] coexist with an alliance, or exist without it."[184] In this sense, it was fully like a *philia*, or treaty of friendship, in Greek practice. The *amicitia* came, however, to be used as the form for Rome's later unequal treaties. These were instruments where all the advantages accrued to Rome: the subordinate state was under an obligation to come to Rome's aid upon request, but there was not necessarily a reciprocal duty. In contrast, the earlier form of the *foedus*, a perpetual offensive alliance contracted by Rome and a neighbor, came to be disfavored, and then nearly abandoned altogether.[185] Without question, the nature of Roman international relations, and territorial ambitions, changed during this period of legal transformation. The Romans simply had no wish to conclude *foedus* with their client states. A *foedus* was notionally perpetual; it could not have been terminated at will. Indeed, the only means for dissolving a *foedus* was the juridical "death" of the other, contracting nation. A Roman declaration of war against a *foedus* would not terminate the relationship; instead "it was merely an announcement that the other side had infringed some condition of the *foedus*, and an appeal to the arbitrament of the gods, to give victory to the side which

---

[183] *See* Arthur Nussbaum, A CONCISE HISTORY OF THE LAW OF NATIONS 11 (rev. ed. 1954); M. David, *The Treaties between Rome and Carthage and their Significance for our Knowledge of Roman International Law*, in SYMBOLAE AD JUS ET HISTORIAM PERTINENTES JULIANO CHRISTIANO VAN OWEN DEDICATAE 231, 233-34 (M. David, B.A. van Groningen, E.M. Meijers ed. 1946); H. B. Leech, AN ESSAY ON ANCIENT INTERNATIONAL LAW 29-30 (1877).

[184] Louise E. Matthaei, *On the Classification of Roman Allies*, 1 CQ 182, 191 (1907); Appian, ROMAN HISTORY 405-07 (Horace White transl. 1912) (Loeb Classical Library rep. 1982) (passage viii.1.2).

[185] *See* Matthaei, supra note 184, at 200-03.

kept the *foedus* unimpaired."[186] In contrast, an *amicitia* was terminable at will by a procedure known as *renuntiata*, with striking private law analogues.[187]

It seems, in any event, that the Romans possessed a sophisticated understanding of different treaty forms. There has been an ongoing scholarly debate[188] as to whether the Romans were able to make the recognition, that had seemed to elude the Greeks,[189] of nations living in a perpetual state of peace. Pomponius, a later jurist, noted that the true state of nature between countries was "neither war nor friendship nor *hospitium* nor an alliance."[190] The evidence suggests that this recognition may have come early in the history of the Roman Republic's relations with its neighbors. Nonetheless, there is a strong element of these relationships being legally structured along lines conveying different nuances as to the relative power of Rome and its treaty partner. More so than in Greek treaty forms, even the *hegemonic symmachia*, the Romans sought to develop treaty types which powerfully conveyed different subordinate classifications. These were clearly intended also to be an imposition of legal status, culminating in the other treaty party losing all juridical personality.[191]

β. The critical Roman institution for the enforcement and interpretation of treaties was the College of Fetials.[192] It appears that some sort of sacerdotal

---

[186]   Id. at 190.

[187]   *See* 4 Tacitus, ANNALES 203 (John Jackson transl. 1931) (Loeb Classical Library rep. 1956) (passage vi.29.3). *See also* 1 Cicero, VERRINE ORATIONS 389 (L.H.G. Greenwood transl. 1928) (Loeb Classical Library rep. 1978) (passage ii.2.36.89); and 1 Suetonius, LIVES OF THE CAESARS 407-09 (J.C. Rolfe transl. 1913) (Loeb Classical Library rep. 1989) (*Gaius Caligula*, passage iii. 3) (on the notion of *renuntiata*).

[188]   *See* Scupin, supra note 201, at 137-38.

[189]   *See* supra notes 148 - 150 and accompanying text.

[190]   4 Digest, supra note 207, at 886 (49.15.5.2; Pomponius, *Quintus Mucius* 37).

[191]   *See* 1 Phillipson, supra note 141, at 111.

[192]   *See* Matthaei, supra note 184, at 183.

college, whether called *fetiales* or something else,[193] existed in the communities close to Rome at the time of the kingship and early Republic. From Livy we know that the Alban people also had a fetial college, led by a *pater patratus*. The conclusion of many scholars is that the fetial institution was a Latin phenomenon, confined to a handful of cities in central Italy. As Rome grew in power and began to have consistent international relations with Greek and Punic outposts in southern Italy and Sicily, the rigid sacerdotal forms of the college of fetials broke down. In the period of transmarine expansion, into Greece proper and into the Near East, the forms virtually vanished. The treaty ceremonies, nonetheless, remained unchanged in form for centuries to come. The meaning and content of those forms was, however, conclusively altered.[194]

For example, the original idea of *foedera*, a perpetual peace and union, made sense when supervised by a fetial institution. After all, the fetials guaranteed the peace at the outset and also served as a neutral arbitrator in cases of dispute over whether one party had breached its duties.[195] One can even imagine a situation, as Livy narrates, of the Roman *pater patratus* consulting with his Alban counterpart in order to preserve the peace. The end of this notion of the *foedera* — and its replacement with various form of unequal alliances[196] — paralleled the end of the legal role of the fetial institution in directing the viability of Roman alliances.

Another set of scholars have adopted a different viewpoint as to the role of the fetials in Roman treaty-making in the period between 250 and 100 BC.

---

[193] *See* George E. Mendenhall, *Puppy and Lettuce in Northwest-Semitic Covenant Making*, 133 BULLETIN OF THE AMERICAN SCHOOLS OF ORIENTAL RESEARCH 26, 27 n.6 (February 1953).

[194] *See* Matthaei, supra note 184, at 182-83, 202.

[195] *See* Thomas Wiedemann, *The Fetiales: A Reconsideration*, 36 CQ 480, 488 (1987).

[196] *See* Matthaei, supra note 184, at 202. Professor Matthaei suggests that the Romans tried to use the *foedus* form in later relations with North African powers, but with mixed results. See id. (glossing Cicero, supra note 187, at 701 (*Pro Balbo*, passage xxiv)). *See also* Christiane Saulnier, *Le rôle des prêtres fetiaux et l'application de "ius fetiale" à Rome*, 58 REVUE HISTORIQUE DE DROIT FRANÇAISE ET ETRANGER 171, 182 (1980).

They concede that while the political influence of the college of fetials may have been on the wane, they have observed the extraordinary resilience of private law contract forms in the ratification ceremony presided over by the fetials.[197] Their conclusion was that while an enforcement mechanism based on the sacerdotal power of the fetials was in desuetude, a new form of obligation (based on contract and *bona fides*) was being developed.

Alan Watson, in particular, has speculated that the treaty ceremonial just described was a mutation of a *stipulatio*, bearing a strong resemblance to the oral contract used in Roman law, but with striking differences. The use of divine witnesses in treaty-making was one such distinction, and it is in this respect that the ceremony of *mancipatio* is relevant.[198] Likewise, it appears that divine witnesses may have also been considered parties to the treaty, making their role unique as both contractors and judges.[199] Another difference noted by Watson is that with the *stipulatio* it was always the person to whom the promise is being made who sets out the terms of the contract; "in the treaty it is the promisor."[200] Lastly, and most significantly, the phrasing of the *stipulatio* was always reciprocal, but with the Roman treaty form the promises being made by each country were "not technically linked."[201]

Professor Watson puts substantial emphasis on the qualifying phrase used by the Roman fetial in the treaty ratification: promising Roman

---

[197]   *See* Alan Watson, INTERNATIONAL LAW IN ARCHAIC ROME: WAR AND RELIGION 31-33 (1993).

[198]   *See* id. at 32.

[199]   Professor Watson expressed some doubts whether there was enough evidence to suggest that deities served as actual guarantors of the terms of the treaty. *See* id. at 33. See also *Semitic Influences in Early Rome*, in DAUBE NOSTER 343 (Alan Watson ed. 1974).

[200]   Watson, supra note 197, at 32. *See also* Alan Watson, ROMAN LAW AND COMPARATIVE LAW 122 (1991).

[201]   Id. *See also* id. at 61. *But see* Hans-Ulrich Scupin, *History of the Law of Nations: Ancient Times to 1648*, in 7 ENCYCLOPEDIA OF PUBLIC INTERNATIONAL LAW 132, 139 (Rudolph Bernhardt ed. 1984) (who suggests that the oaths are "corresponding").

performance for the treaty terms "as they are today most correctly understood."[202] This precautionary phrase, Watson suggests, is "unparalleled in private law."[203] Such a qualification would be inappropriate, Watson believes, for a dispute that would arise before human judges, it being impossible to know with certainty how the terms of the treaty were correctly understood when recited. His whole point is that the deities invoked in Roman treaties served neither as passive witnesses nor as putative guarantors. They were, instead, used as real judges of the *bona fides* of the parties. In cases of a charge of subsequent treaty breach, the gods would have decided whether Rome was in default and then visited punishment on the Roman people.

But there is another interpretation of the caveat uttered by the Roman fetials. It may have been a simple recognition that treaty texts were subject to variant interpretations and that both parties were under an obligation to construe it in good faith. In this sense, the fetial's utterance was no more than a form of anti-deceit clause as used by the Greeks.[204] In view of the modern perception[205] that the Romans were sticklers for treaty performance, one might wonder why the fetials felt the need for such a qualification. The truth is, of course, that substantial uncertainty exists as to whether the Romans were so scrupulous. The evidence is simply ambivalent on this point.

γ. Some have seriously suggested that the Romans regarded all treaties as *nudae pactiones* as in private law,[206] creating only moral commitments but not

---

[202]   1 Livy, supra note 135, at 85 (passage i.24.7).

[203]   Watson, supra note 197, at 32.

[204]   *See* supra notes 148 - 152 and accompanying text.

[205]   *See* Thomas A. Walker, A HISTORY OF THE LAW OF NATIONS 47 (1899) ("The infraction of formally contracted treaties was deemed by all right thinking Romans a breach of the most sacred of religious obligations and a particular cause of divine resentment.").

[206]   *See* 1 Phillipson, supra note 141, at 380-81 (ascribing this view to Mommsen).

civil, binding obligations.[207] The better view, and the one consistent with the most recent scholarship, is that treaties did have some kind of status as a binding contract. The only question was how the Romans regarded the contract to be enforced. Aside from the well-known problem of making ransom agreements with pirates or marauders,[208] the Romans tended to regard a treaty made with an enemy to be binding.[209] There are well-known instances in which the Romans made sophistic interpretations of treaties.

This arose concerning the peace treaty between Rome and the Aetolians of 197 BC.[210] This agreement had been intended to be a *foedus* between Rome and the Greeks to break Philip V of Macedon's power. The Romans promised the Aetolians all lands and conquered towns in Macedon would go to them. The Greeks, though, proved feckless and defected to Macedon in the ensuing conflict. When the Aetolians returned to alliance with Rome in the last stages of the conflict with Macedon, they claimed their right under the earlier treaty to occupy Thessaly which had surrendered to the Roman army. The Roman general Quincitius refused the Greek request, first noting that the Aetolians had breached the treaty by earlier defecting to Macedon. And, besides, because the Thesallian cities had surrendered to Rome, and had not been "conquered"

---

[207] *See* 1 DIGEST OF JUSTINIAN 63 (Theodor Mommsen & Paul Krueger eds., Alan Watson transl. 1985) (2.14.7.4; Ulpian, *Edict* 4) ("Nuda pactio obligationem non parit."). For more on this point, *see* György Diósdi, CONTRACT IN ROMAN LAW 119-35 (J. Szabó transl. 1981); Paul Girard, MANUEL ÉLÉMENTAIRE DE DROIT ROMAINE 629-41 (7th ed. 1941); Richard Hyland, Pacta Sunt Servanda: *A Meditation*, 34 VA. J. INT'L L. 406 (1994).

[208] *See* 21 Cicero, supra note 187, at 387 (*De Officiis*, passages iii. 22, 27-32), who argues that a promise to pay ransom to a pirate is unenforceable since a pirate is not to be considered a public enemy, but, rather, as an outlaw. For commentary on this, *see* Alfred P. Rubin, THE LAW OF PIRACY 5-13 (1988).

[209] *See* Henry Wheaton, HISTORY OF THE LAW OF NATIONS IN EUROPE AND AMERICA 22-23 (New York 1845).

[210] *See* 9 Livy, supra note 135, at 309 (passage xxxiii. 13).

(*captae*), as the treaty required, there was no obligation by Rome to hand them over.[211]

Quincitius' interpretive exercise was hardly necessary; surely it was legally sufficient that the Greeks had broken the 197 BC alliance with Rome. The Roman college of fetials had been consulted when the Greek's perfidy became clear. They advised that Rome could immediately terminate the state of friendship (*amicitia*) that existed between the two states. The college also advised that the Aetolians had to make an overt hostile act before the *foedus* could notionally be terminated and the war commenced.[212] This pattern[213] was repeated in the Third Macedonian War against Perseus in 172 BC[214] and the conflict with Prusias.[215] There may have also been occasions where treaty termination was allowed where there had been a fundamental change of circumstances between the parties.[216]

iv. This extended discussion of ancient statecraft and treaty practices may seem a lengthy diversion from what has been so far the thrust of this book: tracing the origins of a rhetorical view of legal texts. But, to the extent that I have chosen international agreements as being a paradigmatic form of legal text — capturing the essence of contract, legislative act, constitution, and unilateral disposition — it makes sense to explore the classical origins of the treaty, and of treaty interpretation.

What I have tried to convey here is that ancient peoples self-consciously attempted to develop rules of treaty construction. International agreements were not, in any real sense, considered self-executing or enforced by the will of some

---

[211] *See id.*

[212] *See* 10 Livy, supra note 135, at 163, 181 (passages xxxvi. 3 & 8).

[213] For more on which, *see* Matthaei, supra note 184, at 189-90.

[214] *See* 7 Livy, supra note 135, at 361 (passage xlii.25.1).

[215] *See* 6 Polybius, supra note 157, at 279 (passage xxxiii.12.5).

[216] *See* Vamvoukos, supra note 161, at 5-11.

deity or divine intervention. Men made treaties, and men kept them. Part of the act of making faith between nations was the anticipation of future dispute about the meaning of what had been agreed upon. A treaty was considered a reciprocal promise in each of the classical cultures considered here — Greek, Punic, and Roman.

I believe the essential distinction at work in the ancient act of making faith among nations was between rhetorical and legal approaches to treaty enforcement. Rhetorical approaches tended to emphasize, as I have suggested already, the persuasive aspects of international obligation. "A promise might have been made," the rhetorician declaimed, "but was it wise policy to keep it?" This mode of argument did not, in every instance, lead to a city-State or nation repudiating a treaty or terminating it. Quite the contrary. This was because the fulfillment of good faith was a value worth preserving in ancient international relations, even at the cost of some freedom of action on the part of the promising State.

I have tried to suggest here that Greek international relations exhibited strong tendencies towards rhetorical postures in treaty interpretation and compliance. When Greek city-States considered how an international agreement should be properly construed, this was most often deemed a diplomatic concern, one in which the answer was mediated by the give-and-take of diplomatic exchange and rhetorical positions. There was no right answer and no wrong answer; no faithful interpretation and no corrupt one. In order to avoid, though, this moral relativism in treaty interpretation, the Greeks developed superb technical sophistication in the drafting of treaty obligations, believing (erroneously, I think) that the more complex and detailed the agreement, the more impervious it would be to sophistic interpretation, or, worse, outright trickery. But, still, the sentiment seemed right. And, ironically enough, despite the legendary factiousness of classical Greek international life, treaty compliance was more the rule rather than the exception.

Compare this result with what I have just called a "legal" approach to treaty interpretation. At first blush, this seems more appealing. After all, a treaty is a *legal* text, is it not? States entering into an international agreement must wish that their relations be governed by what we take as the attributes of legal culture: regularity, certainty, and respect for mutual rights and obligations. The Greeks certainly had an appreciation for this aspect of international life, as well. But they could not hold a candle to the Romans in this respect.

Why? Because the Romans developed not one, not two, but *three* fully-articulated elements in a legal approach to treaty compliance. The first was a prime directive of treaty construction and enforcement: the maxim that agreements were to be respected in good faith (*bona fides*). And while the origins of this first principle of Roman law have been hotly-disputed,[217] it remains at least received wisdom that the principle of good faith in treaty interpretation meant something to the Romans. The Romans prided themselves in their observance of good faith. When they spoke of that of their enemies (*punica fides* or *graeca fides*), it was no compliment.

But good legal intentions, even if supported by snappy maxims, could not support a structure of effective Roman treaty compliance. That required social institutions. And, during the time where it most mattered in Roman history — in that early period of Roman expansion into central and southern Italy and into the Western Mediterranean — the Roman College of Fetials operated as a guarantor and enforcer of Roman good faith with her treaty partners. Whether the fetials were more priests than lawyers, or whether fetial ceremonial was borrowed (rather than corrupted) from private law contractual formulas, does not matter. What does signify is that the Roman Republic's freedom of action in observing its treaty obligations was internally constrained by the operation of this social institution. The college of fetials, unlike the Senate or the magisterial offices of the Republic, were largely unpersuaded by rhetoric. The parochial, religious and mystical origins of the fetial institution were hostile to newfangled Greek ideas of rhetorical persuasion.

First principles and legal institutions could not alone have placed Roman treaty compliance on a purely legal footing. What remained was the articulation of concrete *rules* for treaty interpretation, precepts that were independent and autonomous from the merits of the legal text being examined. And that, of course, is my story here. The Romans had such canons, of course. But, as shall be seen in the next chapter, there was waged a vicious intellectual battle between Roman rhetoricians and Roman jurists to capture the soul of these rules. The result of that battle was to determine the fate of the idea that legal texts could be subject to neutral principles of construction.

---

[217]   See Hyland, supra note 207, for a full treatment of the origins of this notion in Roman private law.

The Roman intellectual history of oratorical insight and legal science also dictated the modern reception of these ideas. And, despite the great influence that Greek classicism had on later intellectual developments in Europe, ancient Greek legal principles, institutions, and traditions have had virtually no currency in modern legal culture, aside from antiquarian interest. Let us face it. The Romans bequeathed us law. The Greeks gave us the more dubious legacy of rhetoric.

IV Roman Legal Science

i. Now I must say a few words about the state of the legal profession in Rome, contemporaneous with Cicero and Quintilian, while also abstracting what we today know about the practice of law in late-Republic and early-Empire Rome.[218] Long before the time of Christ, in the archaic period of Roman jurisprudence and the law of the Twelve Tables (450 B.C.),[219] the authority to interpret the law was largely vested in the sacerdotal colleges of priests (*sacerdotes publici*). Lay jurists did periodically give advice on private law matters under the civil law (*ius civile*). After a time, a branch of secular law grew to be coequal with the sacred law administered by the pontiffs and priests.[220] It seems that private law disputes in early Rome were not lawyered in any way we would recognize today and that litigants were expected to represent themselves.[221] Professor Fritz Schulz has characterized legal interpretation in this archaic period as largely formalistic,

---

[218] A full exposition of the legal profession during this period is, obviously, beyond the scope of this study.

For the best, most recent treatment of the subject, *see* Bruce Frier's 1985 volume, *The Rise of the Roman Jurists*, supra note 44. Professor Frier is a classicist, and his work was the subject of some criticism by Roman law scholars. *See, e.g.*, Peter Birks, 7 OXFORD J. LEG. STUD. 444 (1987); Charles J. Reid, Jr., 47 THE JURIST 589 (1987); Alan Watson, 85 MICH. L. REV. 1071 (1987). For works by Roman law scholars, *see* Nicholas, Introduction, supra note 115; Fritz Schulz, HISTORY OF ROMAN LEGAL SCIENCE (1946). Professor Schulz's book was likewise controversial. *See* Nicholas, Introduction, at 272.

[219] *See* Nicholas, Introduction, supra note 115, at 15-16.

[220] *See* Schiller, supra note 238, at 735-36; Schulz, supra note 218, at 6-12. *See also* Richard E. Mitchell, *Roman history, Roman law, and Roman priests: the common ground*, 1984 U. ILL. L. REV. 541.

[221] *See* Kennedy, Rome, supra note 6, at 8-9. *See also* John Crook, LAW AND LIFE OF ROME (1967).

with jurists adhering strongly to the text of the law in developing new causes of action (*legis actio*).[222]

What has come to be called the Hellenistic or Greek-influenced period of Roman jurisprudence, from the end of the Second Punic War (200 B.C.) to the founding of the Principate in 27 B.C.,[223] marked the transformation of Roman law into a sophisticated and supple system. As was considered in the last chapter, this period heralded momentous political and legal change in Rome. This time saw the fulfillment of Rome's transmarine expansion and the conquest of all competing powers. It also saw the rapid transformation of Roman institutions. Roman citizenship was vastly extended. Social mobility also accelerated. At the same time, political power became more and more concentrated in the hands of competing factions, and, ultimately, with the accession of Octavian Augustus to the Principate in 27 B.C., into the hands of a single leader and law-maker who still retained vestiges of Roman republican constitutionalism.[224]

---

[222] *See* id. at 29. Schulz suggested, *see* id. at 30, however (and this has been considered controversial), that the provisions of the Twelve Tables and the *lex Aquilia* — the well-springs of Roman private law — were alternatively given strict and liberal constructions in the fourth and third centuries B.C.

For more on the *lex Aquilia*, *see* Neil H. Andrews, *'Occidere' and the* Lex Aquilia, 46 CAMBRIDGE L. J. 315 (1987); Nicholas, Introduction, supra note 115, at 17, 218. The Lex Aequila has been dated to the third century B.C. and concerned remedies for *iniuriae*, what we would call delicts, torts, or civil wrongs. *See* id. *See also* Stein, supra note 18, at 11.

[223] *See* Schulz, supra note 218, at 38-39. For more on the penetration of Greek influences on Roman law, *see* 1 Bernhard Gustaf Adolf Kubler, ATTI. DI. CONG. INTERN. DI DIRITTO ROMANO 79-98 (1934); von Lubtow, *Cicero und die Methode der Römischen Jurisprudenz*, in 1 FESTSCHRIFT FÜR LEOPOLD WENGER 224 (1944); Villey, *Logique d'Aristotle et droit romain*, 29 REVUE HISTORIQUE DE DROIT FRANÇAIS ET ÉTRANGER 309 (1951); Wieacker, *Über das Verhältris der römischen Fachsjurisprudenz zur griechisch-hellenistichen Theorie*, 20 IVRA 448 (1969).

[224] This historical treatment is abstracted from Nicholas, Introduction, supra note 115, at 3-12. By 300 A.D. all relics of republicanism were destroyed and the period of the Dominate began with the Emperor being the lord and master (*dominus*) of the Roman world. *See also* Tony Honoré, EMPERORS AND LAWYERS (1981); Baade, supra note 106, at 50-53; Richard A. Bauman, *The* "leges iudicorum publicorum" *and their Interpretation in the*

This period of social change coincided with the emergence of non-pontifical jurisconsults (*iurisconsulti*) who were constituting themselves as a distinct career. "Career" may, in fact, be too definitive a description, because the jurisconsults of Cicero's day were men of means who devoted themselves to public lives by (among other things) participating in the legal system as officers of the state, as judges of private disputes, as advisors on legal matters, and as law teachers.[225] Being a jurist was not, at least until well after Cicero's time, considered a very promising way to achieve social status apart from noble birth or vast wealth. Most well-born men saw law as a means only for achieving the great, annually-elected magistracies: one of the eight urban praetors (charged with public peace and the administration of justice), or, the greatest office of all, one of the two consuls of the republic.[226]

ii.   Greek influences on the development of Roman law were notable, but probably not overwhelming.[227] The most important of these — and the one that occupies the center of attention in this study — is the introduction of rhetoric as a distinct liberal art, and the appearance of the judicial orator in a well-defined profession. The relationship between jurist and orator was subtle and fraught with rivalry at both practical and professional levels of contact. There were, for example, commonalities of education. A young man showing

---

Republic, Principate and Later Empire, 13 AUFSTIEG UND NIEDERGANG DER RÖMISCHEN WELT 103, 153-231 (H. Temporini & W. Haase eds. 1980).

[225] *See* Nicholas, Introduction, supra note 115, at 28-30; Schulz, supra note 218, at 40-43, 49-59. *See also* Peter Birks, *New Light on the Roman legal system: the appointment of judges*, 47 CAMBRIDGE L. J. 36 (1988).

[226] *See* especially, Frier, supra note 44, at 44-57, 92-94, 139-71. Professor Frier has shown that in the period from 201 B.C. to 95 B.C., some fifteen jurisconsults achieved the consulship including the brothers, Q. Mucius Q.f. Scaevola (101 B.C.) and Q. Mucius P.f. Scaevola (95 B.C.). Between 95 B.C. and 39 B.C. only Ser. Sulpicius Rufus achieved that station in the year 51. *See* id. at 142-43, 148, 154-55, 253-54. *See also* Tacitus, DIALOGUES 307 (William Peterson transl. Loeb Classical Library ed. 1914) (passage xxviii) (whether a man engaged in military matters or in law or in oratory, he "might make that its sole aim and its all-absorbing interest.").

[227] *See* Hyland, supra note 207, at 411-13; Wieacker, supra note 76, at 152-53. *See also* supra notes 12 and 110 and accompanying text.

predisposition to the law would be trained in rhetoric, but not to the extent that a young orator would be.[228] Instead, a jurist in the making would have either been apprenticed to a senior *iurisconsultus* or would have (sometime later in the first century A.D.) affiliated with an actual law school for theoretical instruction (what was known as *paideia* (παιδεία) or systematic training).[229] Orators and jurists also shared common rules concerning remuneration of services, preferring to receive social status and patronage instead of cash fees.[230]

But to see the points of tension between the two groups one has to consider the typical way that a civil court case was instituted in late-Republic and early-Principate Rome. If a citizen were desirous of instituting a civil action against (say) a neighbor in adjudicating a disputed piece of land, he would seek the advice of a jurist who would then make an appearance before one of the urban praetors in Rome or a provincial praetor elsewhere in the republic or empire.[231] That praetor charged with administering the civil law (*ius civile*) was obliged, at the outset of his annual term of office, to proclaim an edict which enunciated all of the civil causes of action he was prepared to act upon, and give remedy for, during his incumbency.[232] The job of the jurist was, in appearing

---

[228] *See* Bonner, supra note 9, at 48-50; Schulz, supra note 218, at 54.

[229] *See* Bonner, supra note 9, at 45; Nicholas, Introduction, supra note 115, at 32-33; Schulz, supra note 218, at 55-58.

Two general schools of law were known — the Sabinian and Proculian. The speculation that the difference between the two groups was based on attitudes toward interpretation of legal texts has been rejected. *See* H.F. Jolowicz, HISTORICAL INTRODUCTION TO THE STUDY OF ROMAN LAW 388-91 (2d ed. 1939). *See also* Peter Stein, *Two Schools of Jurists in the Early Roman Principate*, 31 CAMBRIDGE L.J. 8 (1972).

[230] *See* Kennedy, Rome, supra note 6, at 12-14. *See also* Nicholas, Introduction, supra note 115, at 28-30. *But see* Baade, supra note 106, at 48 (suggesting that orators took fees, while jurists accepted only honoraria).

[231] A foreigner wishing to sue another alien or a Roman citizen would appear before the peregrine praetor, charged with administering the *ius gentium* or law observed by all peoples. *See* Frier, supra note 44, at 47, 52.

[232] The law that the praetor made through his edict was called the *ius honorarium*. *See* Frier, supra note 44, at 44-57; A. Arthur Schiller, ROMAN LAW: MECHANISMS OF

before the praetor, to formulate his client's cause of action in such a way as to make it acceptable under the edict. The potential defendant would obviously appear (with his or her jurist) to block the issuance of a formula or to insure that a suitable (and successful) defense or exception was included within its terms.[233] If the arguments were successful, the praetor issued a formulary[234] which established the proofs to be decided on the facts before a judge (*iudex*), or, more exceptionably, before a jury of citizens (known variously as *recuperatores* in civil cases or *quaestiores* in criminal prosecutions).[235] Appearing before a

---

DEVELOPMENT 402-41 (1978); Alan Watson, LAW MAKING IN THE LATER ROMAN REPUBLIC 64-82 (1982); Leopold Wenger, INSTITUTES OF THE ROMAN LAW OF CIVIL PROCEDURE (English transl. 1940); Franz Wieacker, VOM RÖMISCHEN RECHT 112-20 (2d ed. 1961). *See also* O. Carrelli, LA GENESI DEL PROCEDIMENTO FORMULARE (1946); A.H.J. Greenidge, THE LEGAL PROCEDURE OF CICERO'S TIME (1901 rep. 1971); Hyland, supra note 207, at 411-12.

[233] *See* Greenidge, supra note 232, at 132-263. *See also* Herbert Hausmaninger, *Publius Iuventius Celsus - The Profile of a Classical Roman Jurist*, in PRESCRIPTIVE FORMALITY AND NORMATIVE RATIONALITY IN MODERN LEGAL SYSTEMS: *FESTSCHRIFT* FOR ROBERT S. SUMMERS 245, 245-46 (1994).

[234] Such might read: "X be the judge. Whereas Y has deposited a silver table with Z, concerning which matter this suit is brought, whatever on account of this matter Z ought in good faith give or do to Y, for this do you, judge, condemn Z to Y, unless Z restore the table. If it does not so appear, acquit Z." *See* id. at 150-61. *See also* Otto Lenel, DAS EDICTUM PEPRPETUUM (3d ed. 1927). The praetor's formula was divided into standard parts: a demonstration (describing the matter concerning which suit is brought), an intention (the plaintiff's claim), an adjudication (an instruction to the judge to decide an issue), a condemnation (giving the *iudex* the power to condemn the defendant), and an exception (providing a defense to the defendant which also may be proved). *See* 1 Charles Phineas Sherman & Thomas Raymond Robinson, ROMAN READINGS IN ROMAN LAW 229-33 (1933); Leopold Wegner, INSTITUTES OF THE ROMAN LAW OF CIVIL PROCEDURE 140-63 (Otis Harrison Fisk transl. 1955).

[235] *See* id. at 37-49, 263-77; Frier, supra note 44, at 197-212 (on the court of the *recuperatores*). *See also* J.P. Dawson, HISTORY OF LAY JUDGES 15-30 (1960); Max Kaser, DAS RÖMISCHE ZIVILPROZESSRECHT 37-44, 138-42, 222-24, 273-74 (1966). For more on criminal tribunals, *see* Erich S. Gruen, ROMAN POLITICS AND THE CRIMINAL COURTS, 149-78 B.C. (1968); James L. Strachan-Davidson, PROBLEMS OF THE ROMAN CRIMINAL LAW (1912).

praetor was thus the primary role for the *iurisconsultus* in the civil justice system.

But after the civil case was set before a judge or commission, it was handed over to the orators for trial. (Likewise, if it were a criminal prosecution, orators would represent both the accused and accuser at the trial.)[236] It was the orators who examined the witnesses at these proceedings and who made the long speeches that came to be associated with both Greek and Roman judicial rhetoric.[237] Once a matter reached trial, the role of the jurist was limited to providing written legal opinions (*responsa*) or providing occasional advice to the litigants.[238] The judge or commissioners — who were all likely to be novices in the law — may also have engaged the services of jurists to serve as their *consilium* (advisors) during the trial,[239] an ancient version of today's institution of judicial lawclerks.

iii. The epitome of the oratorical professional of the Roman republic was, of course, Marcus Tullius Cicero. He was a brilliantly skilled court advocate and avid office-seeker who held both the praetorship and consulship.[240] Likewise, the embodiment of the jurisconsult was Q. Mucius Scaevola, who flourished in the period between 125 and 82 B.C, and has been credited with establishing Roman jurisprudence as a distinct science and professional

---

[236] *See* Kennedy, Rome, supra note 6, at 8-14.

[237] *See* id. at 15-16.

[238] *See* Frier, supra note 44, at 139-83. For more on the role of *responsa* in shaping Roman law, *see* H.F. Jolowicz & Barry Nicholas, HISTORICAL INTRODUCTION TO THE STUDY OF ROMAN LAW 96-97 (3d ed. 1972); Nicholas, Introduction, supra note 115, at 31-32; A. Arthur Schiller, *Roman* Interpretatio *and Anglo-American Interpretation and Construction*, 27 VA. L. REV. 733, 734-37 (1941).

[239] *See* Frier, supra note 44, at 205, 209, 213, 222.

[240] For recent biographical sketches, *see* Christian Habicht, CICERO THE POLITICIAN (1990); W.K. Lacey, CICERO AND THE END OF THE ROMAN REPUBLIC (1978); Thomas N. Mitchell, CICERO, THE SENIOR STATESMAN (1991); Thomas N. Mitchell, CICERO, THE ASCENDING YEARS (1979); Torsten Petersson, CICERO: A BIOGRAPHY (1962); Elizabeth Rawson, CICERO: A PORTRAIT (1975); D.R. Shackleton Bailey, CICERO (1971).

calling.[241] It was a much-needed innovation. The jurists (and the *ius civile* they advised on) was, as already indicated, being severely challenged in the period around 150 B.C. The dynamic development of the praetor's formulary procedure and its *ius honorarium*[242] — in effect, annual revisions of the civil law — put stress on the older, highly formalistic *legis actio* system.[243] The appearance of formally trained orators further challenged the professional identity of jurists. Scaevola's response was nothing less than revolutionary.[244]

α. Scaevola first rationalized and organized the then-extant materials of the law. He sought to reconcile legal sources based on the archaic Twelve Tables and ancient statutes with the dynamic causes of action pronounced by successive praetors.[245] Scaevola also developed an analytic jurisprudence which emphasized the importance of legal definitions (*definitio*, or ὅρος in Greek) and of categories (*genera*) of legal characterizations.[246]

---

[241] *See* Frier, supra note 44, at 155-71; Schulz, supra note 218, at 64; Stein, supra note 18, at 26.

[242] *See* supra note 232 and text. *See also* Schiller, supra note 238, at 740-41.

[243] *See* Frier, supra note 44, at 157; Watson, Law Making, supra note 232, at 31-62.

[244] This view is attributable to the jurists whose extracts appear in the Digest of Justinian, *see* supra note 80. Dig. 1.2.2.39 as much as says that three men — M. Manilius, M. Junius Brutus, and P. Mucius Scaevola — "laid the foundations of the *ius civile*." *See* 1 id. at 8 (1.2.2.39; Pomponius). For a gloss on this text, *see* Frier, supra note 44, at 155-56. It is Professor Frier who calls Scaevola's contribution to Roman private law "revolutionary." *See* id. at 156, 184-96. *See also* Stein, supra note 18, at 26.

[245] *See* Frier, supra note 44, at 158-60. Scaevola's treatise, *Ius Civile* has been partially reconstructed and analyzed in Watson, Law Making, supra note 232, at 137-58.

[246] *See* Frier, supra note 44, at 160-62; Schiller, Mechanisms, supra note 232, at 291-97, 570; Stein, supra note 18, at 36, 39. *See also* R. Martini, LE DEFINIZIONI DEI GIURISTI ROMANI 90-99 (1966); Dietrich Behrens, *Begriff und Definition in den Quellen*, 74 ZEITSCHIFT DER SAVIGNY-STIFTUNG FUR RECHTSGESCHICHTE ROMANISTISCHE ABTEILUNG [SAVIGNY'S ZEITSCHRIFT] 352 (1957).

Cicero highly-regarded Scaevola's use of definitional reasoning.[247] Fragments from the post-classical *Digest* of Justinian,[248] show that, as one recent scholar has written, "such definitions ... are highly normative, in that they become a basis for applying or not applying pertinent law to specific cases."[249] Likewise, Scaevola's "classificatory activity" through the creation of *genera* "served as a foundation for larger legal concepts."[250]

What Scaevola achieved by *definitio* and *genera* was the same intellectual rigor and organization for law, as that advanced by Cicero and (later by) Quintilian for the study of rhetoric. It was, at one and the same time, a more modest and more extraordinary achievement. The Roman rhetoricians, as I have already related, made their mark by transforming Greek ideas into a workable taxonomy for any area of human intellect actuated through speech or persuasion. The orator, after all, had to be prepared to speak on any topic, with an understanding of any technical subject matter, and in defense of any cause. The Roman jurist, on the other hand, needed *genera* to organize only legal principles, but he was obliged to give definition and content to those postulates. Definition mattered more to the jurist than to the orator.[251] This is no surprise for any area of human intellect that seeks the status of science. And, make no

---

[247] *See* Cicero, de Inventione, supra note 21, at 403 (*Topica*, passage vi. 29).

[248] *See* supra note 80. *See also* infra note 267 and accompanying text.

[249] Frier, supra note 44, at 161.

[250] Id. at 161.

[251] Nevertheless, some jurists were opposed even to the process of definition. This was best reflected in the extract from Javolenus in 4 Justinian's Digest, supra note 80, at 969 (50.17.202; Javolenus, *Letters* 11) ("Every definition in civil law is dangerous; for it is rare for the possibility not to exist of its being overthrown."). *See also* B. Schmindlin, DIE RÖMISCHEN RECHTSREGELN (1970); Dieter Nörr, *Spruchregel und Generalisierung*, 89 SAVIGNY'S ZEITSCHRIFT 18 (1972).

mistake, Roman jurisprudence saw itself as legal science,[252] while Roman rhetoric perceived itself as art.

β. The primary challenge for jurisconsults in the second and first centuries B.C. was, as Professor Bruce Frier has written, to "link this new legal science to the hurly-burly of the courts, while at the same time preserving its autonomy as a discipline."[253] Scaevola imagined legal principles being held constant against a backdrop of ever-changing combinations of facts. Scaevola is thus credited with developing the teaching technique of hypothetical cases, which Frier describes as having been "sundered from any particular social background, simplified to remove all extraneous circumstances, and then presented for discussion. [But] the hypothetical case is still recognizably a legal case."[254]

These hypothetical cases (called *quaestiones* or *disputationes*)[255] had a strong affinity for the declaimer's *controversiae*.[256] They were — when used by the jurist or by the orator — an outstanding teaching tool.[257] The hypothetical

---

[252] *See* Harold J. Berman, LAW AND REVOLUTION: FORMATION OF THE WESTERN LEGAL TRADITION 151-64 (1983).

[253] Frier, supra note 44, at 163.

[254] Id. at 164.

[255] *See* Schulz, supra note 218, at 223-24.

[256] *See* supra § I.ii.

[257] *See* Frier, supra note 44, at 167 n.116; Schulz, supra note 218, at 91. This is implied in Cicero, de Inventione, supra note 21, at 415 (*Topica*, passage x. 45).

Interestingly, when the Roman Catholic Church's canon law was systematized by Gratian in his *Concordance of Discordant Canons*, written in Bologna in 1140, he structured his work around a series of hypothetical cases, which he also called *causae*. *See* 1 Johann F. von Schulte, DIE GESCHICHTE DER QUELLEN UND LITERATUR DES CANONISCHEN RECHTS 46-75 (1875) (rep. Akademische Druck - U. Verlagandstadt 1956). *See also* R.R. Bolgar, THE CLASSICAL HERITAGE AND ITS BENEFICIARIES 272 (1954). There is also a strong connection between classical and canonical *causae* and *exempla* used as evidentiary material for legal rules. *See* J. Inst. 1.2.6 ("ad exemplum trahere").

character of the exercise is what gave it such power over the imagination. But the jurists' use of the *disputationes* was meant (as we might expect) to elucidate legal principle, a theoretical solution to a problem where the facts were incidental. Conversely, the declamation exercise was meant to train the orator to make the best use of factual circumstances. Legal principle was secondary. In short, a jurist arguing a *disputatio* never let an inconvenient fact get in the way of a legal argument, while the rhetorician never let a legal principle embarrass his spirited oratory.

But the jurists' play with *disputationes* had another aspect. This was found in its relation with the jurisconsult's regular activity of issuing opinions (*responsa*) to clients. These, of course, were very factual in character.[258] Indeed, Cicero said that the giving of *responsa* discouraged systematic learning of the law since they were so dependant in character on the facts and the parties requesting them.[259] Yet, it was the intellectual combination of the hypothetical *disputatio* and the work-a-day *responsa* which some modern writers have attributed to the distinctive casuistic character of Roman law and legal science. Again, as Professor Frier has said:

> [T]he hypothetical cases in juristic writings serve a large number of purposes; they range from entirely plausible and everyday situations to which rules can be straightforwardly applied, to farfetched "limiting" cases" through which highly theoretical propositions can be elucidated. The one common characteristic they share is that their purpose is always to clarify the law, and for this reason a legal principle or rule (usually a new one) is always involved in their solution; the case thus implies a capacity to generalize beyond the case.[260]

Professor Fritz Schulz, probably the leading historian of Roman jurisprudence, said of the *disputationes* that they were

---

[258] *See* Schiller, supra note 238, at 736-38; Schulz, supra note 218, at 112-17; Stein, supra note 18, at 27.

[259] *See* Cicero, de Oratore, supra note 5, at 301 (passage ii.33.142).

[260] Frier, supra note 44, at 167. *See also* Berman, supra note 252, at 138 (who discusses the Roman jurists antipathy to rules (*reglae*)).

casuistic in a peculiar way. They do not — as in a modern commentary — illustrate abstract principles by means of true or fictitious cases; rather does the work consist of a series of cases in which the legal rule occurs, but is not abstracted from them in a formula. The authors make no theoretical deduction from the series of cases; they confine themselves to the 'merely paratactic association of the analogy'.[261]

γ. The consensus among today's legal historians is that Scaevola's casuistic methodology kept Roman law from getting hardened by systematic theory.[262] It was, of course, the rhetoricians who sought precisely that goal of a grand systematization for law. Cicero's writings were replete with instances in which he argued against the jurist's casuistry and in favor of a methodical restatement for the *ius civile*.[263] So it was that at this final level of theoretical abstraction the rivalry between jurists and orators was played out. The rhetoricians sought nothing less than to deny the jurists of their monopoly of legal expertise[264] by superimposing a system of law on top of the case-by-case

---

[261] Fritz Schulz, PRINCIPLES OF ROMAN LAW 51-52 (2d ed. 1956) (*citing* Max Weber, WIRTSCHAFT UND GESELLSCHAFT 396 (4th ed. 1956)). Professor Harold J. Berman has criticized Weber's conclusion about Roman juridical casuistry. *See* Berman, supra note 252, at 139. *See also* Stein, supra note 18, at 74-89.

For more on the jurist's casuistry, *see* John P. Dawson, THE ORACLES OF THE LAW 114-15 (1968) ("The primary task of the jurists as they conceived it was to provide solutions for cases that had arisen or might arise, testing and revising their central ideas by observing their effects on particular cases.").

[262] *See* Frier, supra note 44, at 169; Manfred Fuhrmann, DAS SYSTEMATISCHE LEHRBUCH 186-88 (1960); Stein, supra note 18, at 48. *See also* 1 Paul Jörs, RÖMISCHE RECHTSWISSENSCHAFT ZUR ZEIT DER REPUBLIK 295-97 (1888).

[263] *See, e.g.*, 1 Cicero, de Oratore, supra note 5, at 133 (passage i.42.190), 301 (passage ii.33.142); Cicero, Brutus, supra note 8, 263, at 131-35 (passage xli. 152 - xliii. 155). Cicero's ambition may have gone so far as to drafting a systematic treatment of the civil law, entitled *De iure civili in artem redigendo*, a manuscript which has been lost to history. *See* Berman, supra note 252, at 139; Schulz, supra note 218, at 69; Stein, supra note 18, at 102; Viehweg, supra note 18, at 39, 53; Hyland, supra note 207, at 413-14.

[264] A handful of jurists sought a grand systematization of the civil law and were often co-opted by the rhetoricians. One of these may have been Ser. Sulpicius Rufus (a/k/a "Servius") whose two-volume treatise on Praetor's Edict was widely admired in oratorical

accretion of legal rules. But the *iurisconsulti* saw this challenge for what it was: a denial that law was, as Professor Frier has said,[265] an "autonomous" institution in Roman society, one which the jurists (and not the rhetoricians) were the guardians. Scaevola was the first of these defenders. But, for all of these virtues, he was not well-regarded as an advocate.[266]

Despite all of this, contemporary legal scholars have, I believe, overly dramatized the conflict between orators and jurists in ancient Rome, perpetuating a rivalry that was admittedly tangible but also ignoring the very real contributions that rhetoric made to law.

---

circles. *See* Cicero, Brutus, supra note 8, 263, at 131-35 (passages xli. 152 - xliii. 155). *See also* Frier, supra note 44, at 170; 1 Digest, supra note 80, at 9 (1.2.2.44; Pomponius) (indicating that Servius dedicated his book to the orator Brutus). Servius is said to have written 180 books. See 1 Digest, supra note 80, at 9 (1.2.2.43; Pomponius). For more on Servius' career and influence, *see* Stein, supra note 18, at 42-45.

[265] *See* Frier, supra note 44, at 185-96. *See also* 1 Digest, supra note 80, at 12 (1.3.16; Paul, *Jus Singulare*) (criticizing "law brought in by authority of a decision maker against the general tenor of legal reason on account of a specific policy goal.").

[266] *See* Cicero, Brutus, supra note 8, 263, at 127 (passage xxxix. 145), wherein Cicero described the jurist "with all of his acuteness and readiness in technical law . . was completely overwhelmed by the wealth of arguments and precedents adduced by his opponent [Crassus]. . . . Scaevola was [nonetheless] the best orator in the ranks of jurists." Id. For more on Cicero's assessment of Scaevola's speaking skills, *see* Schulz, supra note 218, at 54, 335-36 (notes J & K).

V *IUS INTERPRETANDI* AND *CONSTITUTIO LEGITIMA*

I believe the best place to see this curious professional synergy was in the relationship between the jurists' *ius interpretandi* and the rhetorician's *constitutio legitima*. What I quickly discovered was that for the Roman jurists the process of developing rules of interpretation for legal texts was very uncomfortable. It was something they had to do, because the jurisconsult's work centered around giving *responsa* to concrete legal problems, many of which concerned the construction of an ambiguous will or the acceptability of a cause of action under a praetor's edict or a prosecution under a disputed exception to a criminal statute. On the other hand, developing rules of interpretation for legal texts had nothing to do with casuistry. Acceptance of a case-by-case approach to reading a disputed will or an ambiguous statute was possible, but led to its own problems of legal indeterminacy and confusion, precisely what the jurists so desperately sought to avoid. The very intellectual exercise of legal interpretation required, therefore, that the jurisconsults consider the views of the rhetoricians. It was the one subject that the lawyers and orators of late-Republic and early-Principate Rome were obliged to converse with each other on a footing of intellectual equality.

      i. As we might expect, Scaevola was the first to opine canons of construction for legal texts. As transmitted through Justinian's *Digest*, these rules were rudimentary and largely confined to problems of construction in private law writings such as wills and contracts. Using the process of definition, which he pioneered,[267] he was able to make sense of verbose and badly-drafted

---

[267] *See* supra note 248 and accompanying text.

testaments and conveyances.[268] Scaevola also proposed expansive interpretations to resolve ambiguous texts, whether an agreement to let a widow use a house[269] or the praetorian edict prohibiting threats or uses of force.[270] Scaevola has been credited with liberalizing the construction of the laws (*leges*) of the Twelve Tables and the *Lex Aequilia* which had grown formalistic by lawyers attempting to "hedge every clause [of a contract or formulary] with safeguards," in what was known as *leges rogatae*.[271]

Scaevola's fellow jurist, Ser. Sulpicius Rufus (who was known as "Servius")[272] was (if anything) even more emphatic that in cases of disputed wills the presumed intention of the testator be followed.[273] The disagreement among

---

[268] *See* 2 Digest, supra note 80, at 523 (18.1.66.2; Pompoinus, *Quintus Mucius* 31), 840 (28.5.35.3; Ulpian, *Disputationes* 4). *See also* 4 id. 961 (50.17.73.3; Quintus Mucius Scaevola, *Definitiones*) ("Those things that are written in a will in such a way that they cannot be understood are as if they were not written."). For a gloss on these provisions, *see* 1 Franz Horak, RATIONES DECIDENDI 123-26 (1969); Watson, Succession, supra note 115, at 143-44; Alan Watson, THE LAW OF OBLIGATIONS IN THE LATE ROMAN REPUBLIC 95 (1965).

[269] 1 Digest, supra note 80, at 243 (7.8.4.1; Ulpian, *Sabinus* 17) (extending widow's use of the house to include a husband (if she remarried) and her father-in-law). *See also* H.J. Wieling, TESTAMENTSAUSLEGUNG IM RÖMISCHEN RECHT 37-38, 46-47, 130-31 (1972); Alan Watson, THE LAW OF PROPERTY IN THE LATER ROMAN REPUBLIC 219-20 (1968).

[270] *See* 4 Digest, supra note 80, at 604 (43.24.5.8; Ulpian, *Edict* 70) (where Scaevola noted that the words of the edict "what has been done by force or stealth" includes "what has been done by you, or one of yours, or by your order."). *See also* Schulz, supra note 218, at 77; Watson, Law Making, supra note 232, at 126-28 (on the interpretation of praetorian interdicts); Watson, Property, supra note 269, at 222-23. *See* 4 Digest at 602 (43.24.1.5; Ulpian, *Edict* 71) (quoting a definition by Scaevola).

[271] Schulz, supra note 218, at 77. *See also* Jolowicz, supra note 7, at 185-87; Stein, supra note 18, at 10-11; supra note 222 and accompanying text.

[272] For more on which *see* Stein, supra note 18, at 45; and supra note 264.

[273] *See* 3 Digest, supra note 80, at 140 (33.10.7.2; Celsus, *Digest* 19) (abstracting Servius).

the jurists was how, exactly, that intent should be proved. In the case of the testator who regarded clothing as a kind of furniture, later jurists sharply disagreed with whether the testator's eccentric uses of language could be admissible in court,[274] although most agreed that if ambiguity in one clause of a will could be resolved by examination of another provision, then it should be.[275]

ii. Scaevola's influence on the law of legal interpretation was probably best reflected, however, in a *cause célèbre* in which he served not as an advisor, but as an actual advocate for one of the litigants. This was the *causa Curiana* which arose around the year 93 or 91 B.C., information about which has largely come down to us through the writings of Roman rhetoricians.[276] The facts were fairly straightforward. A testator, Coponius, expecting the birth of a son, instituted him as an heir, and, in the event that the expected son died before reaching puberty, provided that Curius would be substituted as his heir.[277] The testator died and no posthumous son was born. The dispute was between Curius

---

[274] *See* Watson, Law Making, supra note 232, at 124 (*comparing* 3 Digest, supra note 80, at 141 (33.10.10 (Javolenus, *Lebeo* 10) (rejecting eccentric language) *with* id. at 154 (34.2.32.1; Paul, *Vitellius* 2) (accepting it)). *See also* Schiller, supra note 73, at 761 (citing Carlo Alberto Maschi, STUDI SULL' INTERPRETAZIONE DEI LEGATI. VERBA E VOLUNTAS 53, 71-75 (1938)).

[275] *See* 3 Digest, supra note 80, at 99 (32.100.1; Javolenus, *Labeo* 2); 2 id. at 847-48 (28.5.79(78); Papinian, *Replies* 6).

[276] *See, e.g.*, 1 Cicero, de Oratore, supra note 5, at 125 (passage i.39.180), 175 (passage i.57.242); 299 (ii.32.140); Brutus, supra note 8, 263, at 127 (xxxix. 144); De Inventione, supra note 21, at 291 (passage ii.42.122); 3 Quintilian, supra note 6, at 141 (passage vii.6.9-10). For additional sources, *see* Schiller, supra note 238, at 752 n.85 (who mentions a similar case, abstracted in Cicero, DE OFFICIIS 337-39 (Walter Miller transl. Loeb Classical Library ed. 1913) (passage iii.16.67)).

[277] Cicero reported the actual terms of Coponius' will. They were: "If one or more offspring be born to me, let him be my heir . . . If my offspring dies before reaching the age of majority, let M.' Curius be my heir." Cicero, de Inventione, supra note 21, at 291 (passage i.42.122). For a slightly different rendering, *see* Cicero, de Oratore, supra note 5, at 299-301 (passage ii.32.141). *See also* J.W. Tellegen, Oratores, Iurisprudentes *and the* "Causa Curiana", 30 RIDA (3d ser.) 293 (1983).

(claiming the inheritance under the will and the law of pupillary substitution)[278] and the agnates as Coponius' heirs on intestacy (on the theory that the will was invalid).

Scaevola represented the heirs on intestacy, arguing that the literal terms of the will had not been satisfied and that if the testator had intended for Curius to collect even if no son had been born, he would have so stipulated. Appearing for Curius, the orator Lucius Licinius Crassus submitted that the manifest intention of the testator was to institute Curius as an heir under both contingencies. It was, from what Cicero said,[279] an oratorical *tour de force* with Scaevola (the best orator among the jurists) matched-up against Crassus (the best lawyer among the rhetoricians). It also came to be represented as a sort of show-down between the competing principles of text (*scriptum*) and intent (*sententia*) in the construction of legal texts, with each side championed by the profession one would expect: the jurist defending the literal words of the will and the rhetorician advancing the intent of the testator.[280]

---

[278] For more on which, *see* Watson, Succession, supra note 115; Wieacker, supra note 76, at 153-55.

[279] *See* Cicero, Brutus, supra note 8, 263, at 127 (xxxix. 144-46). *See also* Viehweg, supra note 18, at 39 40.

[280] For the best reconstruction of the arguments used by both sides, *see* Wieacker, supra note 76, at 157-61.
It was important to remember, however, that Scaevola appeared as an advocate in the case, and not as a more neutral and objective jurisconsult. *See* id. at 130 (citing Giuseppe Gandolfi, STUDI SULL'INTERPRETAZIONE DEGLI ATTI NEGOZIALI IN DIRITTO ROMANO 293 (1966)). His writings are, as just noted, strongly suggestive that he believed the intent of a will-maker should be given every possible effect. *See* 3 Digest, supra note 80, at 155 (34.2.33; Pomponius, *Quintus Mucius* 4) (discussing situation where Senator was in the habit of wearing women's clothing and so a bequest of clothing may well be interpreted to include lady's dinner dress). This *disputatio* was identical to one suggested by id. at 140 (33.10.7.2; Celsus, *Digest* 19) (bequests of furniture including togas); *see* supra note 80 and accompanying text.
See also 2 id. at 840 (28.5.35.3; Ulpian, *Disp.* 4) (groom not to be included in legacy of land); Watson, supra note 232, at 130-31.

iii. Much has been made of this case, and particularly of its outcome with the centumviral court finding in favor of Curius and the testator's intent.[281] Indeed, it spawned what may even be characterized as a violent debate among contemporary scholars of Roman law and rhetoric, a disputation which I now (with very great reluctance) will enter. The crux of the battle is this: were Roman jurists persuaded by the rhetorical *stasis* of *constitutiones legitimae* to modify their views about the interpretation of legal texts and was the *causa Curiana* a pivotal moment in that transformation?

It will probably come as no surprise that disciplinary allegiances are quite strong: modern scholars have lined-up on the sides of their ancient colleagues. Philologists, classicists, and writers on ancient rhetoric have either advanced the idea that there may have been a strong influence of rhetoric on law or have sought some sort of intellectual middle ground. Legal historians have adopted a take-no-prisoners attitude, viciously attacking any such notion of a rhetorical sway on the Roman law of interpretation. I would go so far to say that legal academics have been positively caustic on this point. It is worth summarizing this intellectual history here and for me to reach some conclusions of my own.

α. The historiography begins with the writings of German academics at the end of the nineteenth century and the beginning of the

---

[281] *See* Frier, supra note 44, at 136; Trimpi, supra note 2, at 280-84; Watson, Law Making, supra note 232, at 130 (criticizing Wieacker, supra note 76).

Professor Wieacker carefully examines the jurisprudential outcome in *causa Curiana* and suggests that it may not have been a complete victory for intentionalism in testamentary interpretation. *See* Wieacker, supra note 76, at 154-57. He wrote:

> The crucial point of the discussion was therefore not the confrontation of *verba* and *voluntas*, *rigor* and *aequitas* as Stroux would have us believe, led astray by Cicero's and Quintilian's rhetorical interpretation of the *causa Curiana*. It was in reality a matter of linguistic usage and word-meaning as they had been formed by the juristic tradition of the *ius civile*.

Id. at 161.

A similar — if more genteel — debate has formed around Professor Frier's pathbreaking (and thus controversial) analysis of Cicero's speech in *Pro Caecina*. *See* Frier, supra note 44, at 171-83. For criticisms, see works indicated at note 218.

twentieth. Moriz Voigt, writing in the 1870s,[282] was the first to speculate about the relationship between the grammatical principle of rigor, the rhetorician's use of *stasis*, and the jurists' *ius interpretandi*. He believed that the idea of *aequitas* was introduced by Hellenized-inspired lawyers into the *scriptum et sententiam* debate: "The doctrine of *interpretatio* was expressed and developed by the rhetors in the theoretical systems, and was taken over and applied by the jurists for the interpretation of legal transactions as well as statutes."[283]

Voigt's thesis was, however, taken one critical step forward in a 1926 work by Professor Johannes Stroux.[284] Voigt, a classicist, had been reluctant to argue that Roman law had developed a cogent and comprehensive theory of interpretation for legal texts.[285] Stroux was a philologist and he dared tread where angels feared to go. He began his argument by reasserting Voigt's point[286] that the Greek notion of *aequitas*— a principle that allowed an orator to seek rhetorical invention outside the strict letter of a document[287] — was key to

---

[282] *See* supra note 60.

[283] 2 Voigt, supra note 60, at 100 (as translated in Schiller, supra note 238, at 754 n.93).

[284] Johannes Stroux, SUMMUM IUS SUMMA INIURIA. EIN KAPITEL AUS DER GESCHICHTE DER INTREPETATIO IURIS (1926). This was reprinted in Johannes Stroux, RÖMISCHE RECHTSWISSENSCHAFT UND RHETORIK 7-80 (1949). For more on those scholars who wrote between Voigt and Stroux, *see* Ernst Levy, 47 SAVIGNY'S ZEITSCHRIFT 672 (1928) (reviewing Stroux's book).

[285] 3 Voigt, supra note 60, at 356-57. *See also* Schiller, supra note 238, at 754 n.93 (who makes this same point).

[286] *See* supra note 60 and accompanying text.

[287] *See generally* Schiller, supra note 238, at 756-57 (tracing the notion of equity back to Aristotle's comments that equity "is the correction of the law where the latter is defective by reason of its universality" or as "justice that goes beyond the written law"). *See* Aristotle, NICOMACHEAN ETHICS, supra note 33, at 317 (passage v.10.6); Aristotle, Rhetoric, supra note 24, at 145 (passage i.13.13).
    See also Bonner, supra note 9, at 47; 1 Cohen, supra note 64, at 38-39; Rhetorica ad Herennium, supra note 11, at 90-91 n.b & 94-95 n.d (editor's notes) (paraphrasing

understanding the status system's treatment of *constitutiones legales*. In short, Stroux maintained that the entire, elaborate construct of *quaestiones* concerning the interpretation of legal documents boiled down to the spirit or intent side of the *scriptum et sententia* equation.[288]

Stroux's entire thesis was thus premised on a slim reed of his understanding of the underlying purpose and object of the status system. But, undeterred, he went on from there to argue (in the most forceful terms imaginable) that the rhetorical construct of *aequitas* penetrated Roman jurisprudence and changed it forever.[289] Literal (grammatical) interpretation gave way to more liberal, but also more analytically defensible, construction based on logical principles.[290] Stroux maintained that Roman law after the *causa Curiana* adhered to strong principles of interpretation of legal texts which primarily looked to the intent of the drafter. And, most audacious of all, Stroux suggested that the later compilers of Justinian's *Digest* purposefully obscured this complete theory of legal interpretation in order to insulate imperial edicts from the dangers of statutory construction.[291]

β. Some Italian scholars, motivated by a desire to show the continuity of law from the late-Republican era to its compilation by the Byzantine emperor Justinian, did eagerly embrace Stroux's theory as part of that

---

Stroux's argument that the concept of equity came from Greek philosophy to Greek rhetoric to Roman rhetoric to Roman law); Viehweg, supra note 18, at 49.

[288] *See* supra notes 55-56 and accompanying text. *See also* 1 Cohen, supra note 64, at 45-47.

[289] *See* Stroux, supra note 284, at 40-41. *See also* Bonner, supra note 9, at 47; W.W. Buckland, EQUITY IN ROMAN LAW (1911); Berbard E. Jacob, *Ancient Rhetoric, Modern Legal Thought, and Politics: A Review Essay*, 89 NW. U. L. REV. 1622, 1652-53 (1995) (reviewing Viehweg, supra note 18).

[290] *See* Stroux, supra note 284, at 40-41. *See also* Viehweg, supra note 18, at 47-48.

[291] *See* Stroux, supra note 284, at 45-46. *See also* Erich-Hans Kaden, *Die Lehre von Vertragsschluss im klassichen römischen Recht und die Rechtsregel:* Non videntur qui errant consentire, in 1 FESTSCHRIFT PAUL KOSCHAKER 334 (1939); H.F. Jolowicz, ROMAN FOUNDATIONS OF MODERN LAW 9-10 (1957 rep. 1978); Jolowicz, supra note 7, at 183.

proof.[292] Stroux certainly had a point regarding the frankly bizarre treatment that issues of legal interpretation were given in the *Digest*. If one were to read the *Digest* fragments one would be reluctantly forced to agree with Stroux or conclude (instead) that the Roman *ius interpretandi* had disintegrated in the classical period of Roman jurisprudence (during the Principate from Augustus to Diocletian),[293] and was utterly corrupted by the time of Justinian's *Digest*. The *Digest* was, after all, intended to be the epitome of post-Classical legal rationalization, a sort of "end of history" for Roman jurisprudence.[294] Nevertheless, the only systematic treatment of legal interpretation issues in the *Digest* is found in a cluster of disparate extracts in the first and last books of the work.[295]

The *Digest* does, however, contain enough material to be suggestive of Stroux's thesis. In Book One, section 3 on "Statutes, *Senatus Consulta*, and

---

[292] *See, e.g.*, Professor Salvatore Riccobono's introduction to the Italian translation of Stroux's book, which appeared in 12 ANNALI DEL SEMIN. GIURIDICO D. R. UNIV. DI PALERMO 647-91 (1929). For a description of this peculiar debate among Italian legal historians, *see* Schiller, Mechanisms, supra note 232, at 570-71; Arthur Schiller, *Sources and Influences of the Roman Law, III-IV Centuries A.D.*, 21 GEO. L. J. 147 (1933).

For those Italian scholars that emphasized Stroux's conception of *aequitas*, *see* Lauro Chiazzese, INTRODUZIONE ALLO STUDIO DEL DIRITTO ROMANO PRIVATO 128-30 (1931); 2 Salvatore Riccobono, CORSO DI DIRITTO ROMANO 318-86 (1933-34).

See also Jolowicz, supra note 7, at 183-84; Wieacker, supra note 76, at 155-56 n.17.

[293] *But see* Schulz, supra note 218, at 132-34, 295 (for a partial refutation of this supposition); Fritz Schulz, GESCHICHTE DER RÖMISCHEN RECHTSWISSENSCHAFT 155-57 (1961).

[294] *See* 1 Digest, supra note 80, at xlvi - liv (on the composition and holistic nature of the Digest). *Compare with* THE CODE OF JUSTINIAN, reprinted in [12] 6 THE CIVIL LAW (S.P. Scott ed. 1932 rep. 1973), which was a collection of imperial rescripts and letters issued by late Roman and Byzantine emperors and which reflected then-current "legislation." *See* id. at 85-89 (Code J. 1.14). *See also* 1 Cohen, supra note 64, at 45 & n.89; T. Honore, TRIBONIAN (1978).

[295] *See* Berman, supra note 252, at 138; Jolowicz, Foundations, supra note 291, at 8-9; Jolowicz, supra note 7, at 184-85.

Long-Established Custom"[296] there were some very broad principles for statutory construction, extracted from such classical writers as Celsus, Julian, Ulpian and Paul. For example,

> [No S]tatute can be written in such a way that all cases which might at any time [occur] are covered.... And, therefore, as to matters on which decisions of first impression have been made, more exact provision must be made either by [juristic] interpretation or by a legislative act.... [B]ut wherever the[] sense of [the law] is clear, the president of the tribunal ought to proceed by analogical reasoning and declare the law accordingly.[297]

This was the same language that Cicero used in discussing the rhetorical problem of *syllogismus* or analogous laws.[298] Likewise, Celsus noted that "Knowing the laws is not a matter of sticking to their words, but a matter of grasping their force and tendency,"[299] which was a paraphrase (again) from Cicero's *de Inventione*.[300]

But, despite Stroux's observation, the *Digest* does contain some strong admonitions for textualism. The most famous of these appears in an isolated fragment in the book on legacies: "Where there is no ambiguity in the words,

---

[296]   1 Digest, supra note 80, at 11.

[297]   Id. at 12 (1.3.10-12; Julian, *Digest* 59, 90, 15).

[298]   *See* supra notes 117-18 and accompanying text. *See generally* supra § II.iv.

[299]   1 Digest, supra note 80, at 12 (1.3.17; Celsus, *Digest* 26). For more on Celsus' use of equity, *see* Hausmaninger, Celsus, supra note 233, at 252-53, 254. For a searching review of Celsus' contributions to the jurisprudence of statutory interpretation, *see also* Herbert Hausmaninger, *Zur Gesetzesinterpretation des Celsus*, in 5 STUDI IN ONORE DI GIUSEPPE GROSSO 245 (1972). Celsus flourished in the period AD 100 - 130, well after the Republican period explored here.

To the same effect is 4 Digest, supra note 80, at 934 (50.16.6.1; Ulpian, *ad Edictum* 3 ("The expression 'according to the laws' is to be taken to mean both according to the spirit of the laws as well as according to the words.").

[300]   *See* supra note 105 and accompanying text.

the question of intent ought not to be admitted."[301] Likewise, Celsus enunciated a rule that it was only proper to break from the text in order to "avoid[] an absurdity,"[302] the same suggestion made by Quintilian.[303] To the same effect was the pronouncement that "in matters that are obscure [adopt] the least difficult view."[304] The *Digest* is thus mixed with its endorsement of intent over text in most forms of legal interpretation. So, to the extent that Stroux's theory was endorsed by the Italians because of its vindication of *aequitas* as a new, supple approach to the harsh formalisms of Roman law, such reliance seemed misplaced.

The Roman *ius interpretandi* did, it seems, make a crucial distinction between rules of statutory construction and those for private law instruments. And, indeed, the distinction may have originated in Greek times, and was manifested (as we have seen) in questions of treaty interpretation.[305] For such writings as wills and contracts, the jurists were free to use principles of logical and grammatical construction in order to reach some gloss on the text, even if that was demonstrably contrary to the intent of the writer.[306] This tendency was clearly evinced in the *causa Curiana* and other testacy disputes during the

---

[301] 3 Digest, supra note 80, at 76 (32.25.1; Paul, *Neratius* 1) ("Cum in uerbis nulla ambiguitas est, non debet admitti uoluntatis queastio."). Consider also: "One ought only to depart from the sense of the words when it is clear that the testator meant something else." Id. at 92 (32.69.pr; Marcelllus, *Replies*). *See also* 1 id. 13 (1.3.21 & 23; Neratius, *Parchments* 6 & Paul, *Plautius* 4); Jolowicz, Foundations, supra note 291, at 9, 12 (glossing these texts).

[302] 1 id. 13 (1.3.19; Celsus, *Digest* 33).

[303] *See* supra note 99 and accompanying text.

[304] 4 Digest, supra note 80, at 957 (50.17.9; Ulpian, *Sabinus* 15). For a gloss on this extract, *see* 1 Cohen, supra note 64, at 45-46.

[305] *See* supra § III.i.γ.

[306] *See* Helmut Coing, *Zur Methodik der republikanischen Jurisprudenz: Zur Enstehung der gramatisch-logischen Auslegung*, in 1 STUDI IN ONORE DI VINCENZO ARANGIO-RUIZ 365, 378-87 (1952). For discussion of the interpretation of contracts in the classical period of Roman jurisprudence, *see* Hausmaninger, Celsus, supra note 233, at 258-59.

classical period.[307] "Statutory interpretation, on the other hand, looked to the *vis et potestas* of the lex, not its *verba*, and did so by a set of canons assuring a central place to jurists in the interpretive process."[308]

The *Digest* did, indeed, offer canons of construction (chiefly for statutes, but also for wills) which strongly resonated with the rhetorical writings on *status legitimus*. Aside from helpful rules concerning number and gender in legal writings,[309] there are substantive canons such as:

> Whenever there is any doubt over liberty in an interpretation, a reply must be given in favor of liberty.[310]
>
> It is [impermissible] that measures introduced favorably to men's interests should be extended by us through a sterner mode of interpretation on the side of severity and against those very interests.[311]
>
> When a law pardons something as to the past, it impliedly forbids it for the future.[312]

---

[307] *See* supra note 280 with text (for Digest extracts with similar admonitions). *See also* Hausmaninger, Celsus, supra note 233, at 256; V. Scarano Ussani, VALORI E STORIA NELLA CULTURA GIURIDICA FRA NERVA E ADRIANO: STUDI SU NERAZIO E CELSO 136, 172, 199 (1979).

[308] Baade, supra note 106, at 48.

[309] *See* 4 Digest, supra note 80, at 947 (50.16.158; Celsus, *Digest* 25), 949 (50.16.195.pr; Ulpian, *Edict* 46); 963 (50.17.110; Paul, *Edict* 6) ("the greater includes the lesser"). *See also* Stein, supra note 18, at 123.

[310] 4 id. at 958 (50.17.20; Pomponius, *Sabinus* 7).

[311] 1 id. at 13 (1.3.25; Modestinus, *Replies* 8); 4 id. at 960 (50.17.56; Gaius, *Legacies* 3) ("semper in dubiis benigniora praeferenda sunt"). *See also* Jolowicz, Foundations, supra note 291, at 13-14, who comments on similar constructions of "mildness" (*benignitas*) favoring lenity in criminal proceedings, debtors over creditors, and institutions of heirs rather than disherisons. See also Baade, supra note 106, at 48-49 & n.25. *See also* A. Berger, *In dubiis benigniora*, 9 SEMINAR 36 (1951); Herbert Hausmaninger, *"Benevolent" and "Humane" Opinions of Classical Roman Jurists*, 61 B. U. L. REV. 1139 (1981).

[312] 1 id. at 13 (1.3.22; Ulpian, *Edict* 35).

Where a formulation in an action or defense is ambiguous, the most appropriate rule is rather to accept the interpretation which validates the instrument than that which nullifies it.[313]

It is not lawyer-like practice to give judgment or to state an opinion on the basis of one particular part of a statute without regard to the whole.[314]

Each of these canons had a direct analogue among the rhetorical writings that I have discussed in this study.

γ.   Nevertheless, Professor Stroux bypassed this modest observation in his haste to make a far more expansive point concerning the rhetorical construct of *aequitas* and its alleged impact on the course of Roman jurisprudence. There was just one problem, of course: Stroux was misguided in both his premises and conclusions. *Aequitas* and the *scriptum et sententia* debate was not the alpha-and-omega of classical rhetorical theory of legal status. Nor were classical Roman jurists captured by this methodology. Like too many theorists, Stroux pushed his otherwise significant conclusions one step too far, a misstep that the legal historians seized upon to savage his research.

But, as can be expected, legal scholars went themselves too far in their criticism. Both Professors Albertario and Himmelschein contended that any trend in the *ius interpretandi* in giving effect to the intent (*voluntas*) of the legal drafter was actually post-classical in origin.[315] The juristic extracts to that effect

---

[313] 3 id. at 173 (34.5.12; Julian, *Digest* 50).

[314] Id. at 13 (1.3.24; Celsus, *Digest* 8). For additional Digest provisions bearing on this point, *see* 1 Cohen, supra note 64, at 45-47.

[315] *See* Emilio Albertario, STUDI IN ONORE DI PIETRO BONFANTE 629-54 (1930); Emilio Albertario, INTRODUZIONE STORICA ALLO STUDIO DEL DIRITTO ROMANO GIUSTINIANEO 110 n.93 (1935); Emilio Albertario, 5 STUDI DI DIRITTO ROMANO 91 (1937); Albrecht Dihle, THE THEORY OF WILL IN CLASSICAL ANTIQUITY 135-38 (1982); J. Himmelschein, *Studien zu der antiken Hermeneutica iuris* in SYMBOLAE FRIBERGENSES IN HONOREM OTTONIS LENEL 373, 393-95, 422-24 (1931); Artur Steinwenter, *Rhetorik und römischer Zivilprozess*, 67 SAVIGNY'S ZEITSCHRIFT 69 (1947). *See also* Bonner, supra note 9, at 47-48; 1 Cohen, supra note 64, at 47 n.105.

appearing in the *Digest*,[316] they suggested, were interpolated there by Justinian's compilers.   Classical rhetoric could not have influenced a move against textualism in legal interpretation, they argue, precisely because there was no such change in Roman legal practice.

Yet this line of attack on Stroux and his followers seems to be unsupportable. First, even if the *causa Curiana* is minimized in its doctrinal importance (as at least Professors Albertario and Wieacker have maintained),[317] late-Republican and classical-period writers were clearly drafting *responsa* and *disputationes* involving substantial deference to the intent of legal drafters. It would appear incredible that these had been manufactured in Justinian's time, just as Stroux's suggestion (that Justinian's digesters had purposefully suppressed a *stasis*-inspired *ius interpretandi*) was equally implausible.

In any event, all of the legal historians who commented on Stroux's thesis were clear in their belief that Roman law had no use for classical rhetoric. Some were relatively mild in this reproof, saying only that the status system was "impractical"[318] and unlikely to be of help in concrete cases where Roman juristic casuistry was already preeminently favored.[319]   Other legal historians reached the conclusion that it was coincidental that juristic writings employed the language of the *constitutio legitima*.[320] Although there was a syntactic similarity between the rhetor's *scriptum et sententia* and the jurists dilemma of *verba et voluntas* in matters having to do with legal intent,[321] writers such as Arthur

---

[316] *See* supra notes 301 - 304 and accompanying text.

[317] *See* Wieacker, supra note 76, at 161-64.

[318] This view is found in Levy, supra note 284.

[319] *See* Paul Jörs & Wolfgang Kunkel, RÖMISCHES PRIVATRECHT 22 (1935).

[320] *See* Himmelschein, supra note 315, at 392-93; F. Serrao, CLASSI, PARTITI, E LEGGE 142-48 (1974); Bernhard Vonglis, LA LETTRE ET L'ESPRIT DE LA LOI DANS LA JURISPRUDENCE CLASSIQUE ET LA RHETORIQUE (1968).

[321] *See* Fritz Pringsheim, *Animus in Roman Law*, 49 L. Q. REV. 46 (1933).

Schiller contended that this was either accidental or the product of post-classical interpolations.[322] Indeed, he said that the

> last century of the Republic, the age from which the great number of these *definitiones* derive, was ... the period of flourishing linguistic studies, and ... there is a close relation between the older Roman word interpretation and the newer grammatical interpretation, it seems more likely that the rhetors borrowed from the jurists than vice versa.[323]

Other legal writers were more unforgiving in their assessment of ancient rhetoric. Professor H.F. Jolowicz, otherwise quite balanced in his opinions on Roman legal history, said that

> Roman jurists occasionally gave utterance to statements referring to the construction of statutes and other documents, some of which were suggested by the commonplaces of the rhetoricians, but there was no developed science of construction and rhetoric could not supply one, for its aims were different from those of the lawyers.... It is, indeed, surprising how little there was for lawyers to take from rhetoric, considering that rhetoric was intended to deal with argument in Court.[324]

It was, however, Professor Fritz Schulz, acclaimed as the leading intellectual historian of Roman law, who directed the greatest invective against classical rhetoric. He threw this knock-out punch in his 1946 classic, *Roman Legal Science*, and it has stung our professional discourse to this day:

---

[322] *See* Schiller, supra note 238, at 759-62. *See also* Uwe Wessel, Rhetorische Statuslehre und Gesetzesauslegung der Römischen Juristen 31-41 (1967). For a comment on Wessel's work, see Herbert Hausmaninger, 85 Savigny's Zeitschrift 469, 477 (1968) (for reviews of Wessel's and Vonglis', supra note 320, books). *See also* Schiller, Mechanisms, supra note 232, at 576-77 (for subsequent historiography on this subject).

[323] Id. at 762. *But see*, Hausmaninger, Celsus, supra note 233, at 255 ("It has been noted that the principles of interpretation formulated by Celsus bear the mark of Roman rhetoric. This is not to be taken as a sign of intellectual dependence, but rather as one of courage and originality.").

[324] Jolowicz, supra note 7, at 184-85. To a similar effect is A. Bürge, Die Juristenkomik in Ciceros Rede Pro Murena 46-48 (1974).

The question of law, namely which of two interpretations, the literal or the equitable, ought to prevail, was simply outside the province of rhetoric.... Rhetoric is a theory of advocacy, not of law .... The result was that the Roman jurists found nothing worth learning in rhetoric....

Jurisconsults were ... not at ease in the unscrupulous atmosphere of Hellenistic forensic rhetoric .... [T]hey were not mere partisans, ready to forward a client's cause by any and every available means, including falsehood, calumny, and emotional appeals, but [were, instead,] guardians and promoters of the law. To this tradition they were resolved to be true, and fortunate it was for Roman legal science that they stood fast and refused to suffer the noisome weed of rhetoric, which choked so much else that was fine and precious, to invade their profession.[325]

iv. The war that has been fought by academic lawyers against classical rhetoricians has really been about a set of misunderstandings. The mistakes have been mutual, perhaps, but they are by no means insuperable. Comprehending the tangled historiography I have narrated here is about identifying the sources of miscommunication between Roman orators and Roman jurists, mistakes that we are (it appears) condemned to relive even two millennia after. These errors must be resolved before a clear appreciation can be had of how rhetorical constructs of legal interpretation have influenced our discussions today.

α. The first error is the ostensible claim that classical rhetoric made that *aequitas* was a competing source and even higher form of law. Roman jurists took this as being a very real challenge to their professional authority and legitimacy, an ultimate attack on what Professor Frier called their "autonomy."[326] But I think that a careful reading of the rhetorical texts by Cicero, Quintilian, and others, does not indicate that such a claim was really

---

[325] Schulz, supra note 218, at 76-77, 54-55 (citations omitted). To the same effect is W. Kunkel, RÖMISCHE RECHTSGESCHICHTE 101, 103 (5th rev. ed. 1968) (who associates rhetoric with a "fog of commonplaces and empty phrases" and as "poison"). *But cf.* Ludvicio V. Cifferi, *The Spectre of Contradiction in Cicero's orations, a Study Based on His Conception of* iurisprudentia *and Some Other Speeches*, 39 R.I.D.A. 84, 120-22 (1992).

Of course, this view was shared in antiquity, *see* 6 Philo 289 (F.H. Colson transl. Loeb Classical Library ed. 1935) (*Moses*, passage i. 24).

[326] *See* Frier, supra note 44, at 184-96.

made.   The jurists were, in short, over-reacting to their professional competitors.

It is true, though, that some rhetorical treatises did purport to provide the orator guidance on the sources of law and legal rules. The author of the *ad Herennium* said simply that when dealing with the question whether an act was lawful or not (*quale sit*) it was important to remember the "constituent departments" of the Law, to wit: "Nature, Statute, Custom, Previous Judgements, Equity, and Agreement."[327]   The *ad Herennium*'s subsequent discussion of these sources of law is quite superficial and circumspect,[328] and no attempt is made (aside from the very act of listing these sources) to imply that one is superior to the other. As for equity, all that is said is that "[t]he Law rests on Equity when it seems to agree with truth and the general welfare," followed by the somewhat enigmatic comment that "according to circumstances and a person's status virtually a new kind of Law may well be established."[329] Quintilian does not even venture an opinion on this issue.[330] Cicero, in his *de*

---

[327] Rhetorica ad Herennium, supra note 11, at 91 (passage ii.13.19). *See also* Kroll, 90 PHILOLOGUS 211 (1935) (for Stoic background of the *ad Herennium*'s theory of law).

[328] Legal historians can, and have, disagreed about whether some of these sources were really regarded as rules of decision. Especially subject to this attack have been not only equity (given as *aequo et bono* in the *ad Herennium* text) but also custom (*consuetudo*). The subject of whether and how custom was recognized as a source of law in ancient Rome is beyond the scope of this study. For some background, *see* 1 E.C. Clark, HISTORY OF THE ROMAN PRIVATE LAW 342-76 (1914 rep. 1965); Arthur A. Schiller, *Custom in Classical Roman Law*, 24 VA. L. REV. 268 (1938).

[329] Rhetorica ad Herennium, supra note 11, at 95 (passage ii.13.20). It is important that the phrase used by the author of the *ad Herennium* is not *aequitas*, but *ex aequo et bono*, literally what is "right and good." For the difference, *see* Fritz Pringsheim, Bonum et Aequum, 52 SAVIGNY'S ZEITSCHRIFT 78 (1932). *See also* 1 Cohen, supra note 64, at 44.

[330] *But see* 3 Quintilian, supra note 6, at 133-35 (passage vii. 5) (for a very short passage on "points of law").

Inventione, touches on the same ground as the *ad Herennium* saying only that "[e]quity is what is just and fair to all."[331]

But it bears repeating that all of these statements appearing in the Roman rhetorical handbooks had to do with a matter fundamentally different from the status concerned with the interpretation of legal texts, the *constitutiones legales*. All of these extracts appear in the parts of rhetorical treatments having to do with issues of quality (*constitutio generalis*). As already mentioned,[332] the "assumptive branch of the equitable issue" did not have much to do with *constitutiones legales*; it was a sort of adjunct to be used by the orator when speaking in favor of the intent of a law. The same was true when Cicero made his comment in his political testament, *De Officiis*, that "[i]njustice often arises by a certain chicanery, indeed, by an over-subtle even fraudulent interpretation of the law. From which arose that now old saw, 'the more law, the less justice' (*summum ius summa iniuria*)."[333] This was not intended, as the context clearly reveals,[334] to be an indictment of the jurist's *ius interpretandi*. It is not even clear that it was meant to be an attack on the profession of *iurisprudentia*. Cicero was certainly not coy about such matters; when he did wish to criticize the lawyers he did so with precision and relish. Nevertheless, the jurists who were Cicero's contemporaries saw his remark of *summum ius summa iniuria* as the ultimate insult. Is it any wonder that Roman legal historians had the same reaction to Johannes Stroux's work which bore the same legend?[335]

---

[331]   Cicero, de Inventione, 21, at 233 (passage ii.22.68). To the same effect is the text from *de Partitione Oratore*, supra note 67.

[332]   *See* supra § II.iii.γ.

[333]   Cicero, de Officiis, supra note 276, at 35 (passage i.10.33).

[334]   *See* id. at 31-35 (passage i. 10) (on the nature of promises and changed circumstances). For more on stoic influences on Cicero's philosophy of law, *see* H.A.K. Hunt, THE HUMANISM OF CICERO (1954); Elizabeth Rawson, INTELLECTUAL LIFE IN THE LATE ROMAN REPUBLIC (1985); D.H. Van Zyl, CICERO'S LEGAL PHILOSOPHY (1986); Neal Wood, CICERO'S SOCIAL AND POLITICAL THOUGHT (1988).

[335]   *See* supra note 284.

There may well have been an abstract debate between rhetoricians and jurists over the relative merit of *aequitas* in characterizing legal conduct. Seneca certainly implies such in one of his *controversiae*,[336] and, indeed, many of them were structured around a conflict of the text of the law as against its spirit.[337] This debate may have permeated to the level of a professional challenge to the jurists, with the orators seeking to use the philosophy of *aequitas* to deny Roman lawyers their monopoly of technical legal knowledge. But there is no indication that classical rhetoricians countenanced the philosophical "death" of law by its absorption under *aequitas*.

β. But, even if that is what the rhetors desired, it is not clear that the notion of equity was the single, organizing principle of the orator's approach to the interpretation of legal texts. While Quintilian may have speculated that each of the *quaestiones legales* was really a reflection of the *scriptum et sententia* dialectic,[338] he certainly did not press his point and it (very likely) was not widely shared by earlier rhetorical writers. His observation has, however, been repeated in the modern literature and taken as truth. This, I believe, was Stroux's fundamental mistake.

Although the Roman rhetoricians were somewhat clumsy with their categories of *quaestiones*, there was no doubt that they understood that there were a number of different kinds of problems in legal interpretation. Some of these (like definition and ambiguity) were simply not of much interest to the orators, and, consequently, they dismissed their treatment as being (almost) unworthy of their talents and skills. But they did see — and very clearly so — that a question having to do with the intent underlying a statute was very different in character from a problem of conflicting laws or an issue arising when there was no legal text directly on point.

All of this is not to dispute that the concept of intent (*sententia*) was important for the orator in resolving questions other than the letter and spirit of

---

[336] *See* 1 Seneca, supra note 34, at 43 (passage i.1.13).

[337] *See* 1 id. at xviii (editor's introduction).

[338] *See* text with supra note 61.

a single law.[339] But to grasp this as the only effective axiom of the *status legalis* would be to ignore the very real tension between rules and principles in the rhetor's world. Once again, the orator's intellect was schematic: his tasks were (in order) to classify a problem, identify the issues, frame the points of argument, apply the particular facts of the case, and then seek to achieve the client's objectives. After Scaevola's revolution, the Roman jurist thought much the same way, but with one crucial difference: definition mattered appreciably more than categories. The casuistic reasoning employed by Roman jurists also meant that the process of applying law to facts was one that was achieved less by categorization than by successive patterns of results.

γ. This was really lost on the Roman rhetoricians who craved regularity and system above all else. But, despite that, they realized that the process of construing legal texts was fraught with some uncertainty. The orator knew that the process of identifying an interpretive problem (letter/spirit, conflict, or syllogism) led to some rule-based inquiries. Was there a real conflict between two statutes? Was the intent of the drafter conditional or relative? Did the legislator intend that a lacuna in the law be filled? It was these questions — at least in the schematic way they were asked — which were most like the substantive canons of construction which did find their way into the juristic writings, and thence into Justinian's *Digest*.

What I mean to suggest here is a middle ground in the doctrinal debate that has transpired between classicists and legal historians over the Roman *ius interpretandi*. I believe there were substantial cross-influences between juristic science and judicial oratory in late-Republic Rome. These influences were felt at the level of common education and experience among these two professional groups. There was, to a more limited degree, a common language employed in identifying problems of interest to both lawyers and rhetoricians. Neither side, however, let the other's ideas penetrate so far as to upset their respective professional outlook on knowledge and its organization. The rhetoricians remained taxonomists; the jurists retained their casuistry.

But, at the level of the principles and rules for interpreting legal texts, there was a substantial synergy. The jurists had to modify (to some degree) their textual approaches in order to accommodate the orator's arguments in favor

---

[339] *See* text at § II.iv.

of intent.   The rhetoricians were, likewise, obliged to recognize that categorization and definition alone could not give firm guidance in cases involving substantial issues of construction.   This synthesis of rhetoric and jurisprudence made for a particular outlook on legal interpretation, one which recognized an uneasy combination of principles and rules, categories and canons.   And, despite all the bickering between lawyers and orators (and, today, between philologists and legal historians), there existed a shared expectation and methodology for constructions of legal texts.

Intermezzo

VI TRANSMISSION OF THE CLASSICAL TRADITION OF LEGAL INTERPRETATION

i. I suppose the supreme irony is that as the classical tradition for legal interpretation was received in medieval and modern times, the distinction between juristic and rhetorical postures utterly vanished. It bears remembering that, as time went on, Roman legal sources (except for the post-classical *Digest*, Institutes, and Code of Justinian) became less and less accessible, while the rhetorical writings of Cicero and Quintilian continued to be in wide circulation.

Even so, probably the most influential work of classical rhetoric was one which was largely derivative of these earlier writings. This was Hermogenes text *On Staseis*,[340] composed around 170 A.D., which, as the rhetorical historian, George A. Kennedy, has written, became "the fundamental rhetorical textbook from the Fifth to the Fifteenth Century."[341] Hermogenes work, for

---

[340] HERMOGENIS OPERA 28 (Hugo Rabe ed. 1913) (Rhetores Gracei volume VI) [hereinafter "Rabe"].

[341] Kennedy, Christian, supra note 2, at 74. For more on Hermogenes' influence, *see* T.W. Baldwin, WILLIAM SHAKSPERE'S SMALL LATINE & LESSE GREEKE (1944); Ian MacLean, INTERPRETATION AND MEANING IN THE RENAISSANCE: THE CASE OF LAW 75-82 (1992); William K. Wimsatt, Jr. & Cleanth Brooks, LITERARY CRITICISM 143 (1957).

For more on rhetoric in the middle ages and Renaissance, *see* E.R. Curtius, EUROPEAN LITERATURE AND THE LATIN MIDDLE AGES 76 (W.R. Trask transl. 1953); Frost, Introduction, supra note 18, at 620-24; Wilbur S. Howell, *Renaissance Rhetoric and Modern Rhetoric: A Study in Change* in THE RHETORICAL IDIOM: ESSAYS IN RHETORIC, ORATORY,

which over a hundred different manuscripts were produced during the middle ages,[342] was given preference even over Cicero's *de Inventione*, the *ad Herennium*, or Quintilian's *Institutio Oratoria* because of the "dialectical qualities of his work: the formal validity, systematic method, and the clarity of his treatment."[343]

There was something else distinctive about Hermogenes' approach to status. He broke from the co-equal categories of inquiries (fact, definition, and quality)[344] and developed what a modern logician would call a decision-tree, in which one inquiry led to another in a systematic, progressive way until one was left with the proper characterization of the issue to be addressed. What Hermogenes did, in effect, was to superimpose an additional level of order on the already highly-refined status system developed by the Romans. In short, the Greeks recaptured *stasis* and added an approach "typically Stoic in its consideration of the different categories in which a single entity might be studied from the successively subordinate standpoints of its being, definition, quality, and relation to other persons or things."[345]

Nevertheless, Hermogenes did not substantially alter the received tradition for the rhetorical treatment of legal interpretation. He maintained four *quaestiones legales*: letter and intent, contrary law, ambiguous law, and

---

LANGUAGE AND DRAMA 53 (Donald C. Bryant ed. 1966); J.J. Murphy, THREE MEDIEVAL RHETORICAL ARTS (1971).

[342] *See* Rabe, supra note 340, at xiii-xx (editor's introduction).

[343] Kennedy, Christian, supra note 2, at 74.

[344] *See* supra notes 5-8 and accompanying text.

[345] Nadeau, supra note 10, at 67. For more on Stoicism and these revised *stasis* categories, *see* Benson Mates, STOIC LOGIC (1953) (University of California Publications in Philosophy no. 26); Viehweg, supra note 18, at 49-50; Margaret E. Reesor, *The Stoic Categories*, 78 AJP 63 (1957). *See also* Harry Coplan, *The Decay of Eloquence at Rome in the First Empire*, in STUDIES IN SPEECH AND DRAMA IN HONOR OF ALEXANDER M. DRUMMOND 292-325 (H.A. Wichelns ed. 1944).

inference from law.[346] He did put a sharper point on the *quaestio* of letter and intent, calling it, instead, ῥητὸς καὶ διάνοια, which is translated to "letter and spirit." This, in turn, may have reflected scriptural language, the most famous is Paul's epigram, "for the letter killeth, but the spirit giveth life."[347] As Boaz Cohen, the great comparative scholar of Jewish and Roman law has said, "in Paul's time ῥητὸς καὶ διάνοια was the usual Greek form of the antithesis between letter and spirit."[348]

ii. The classical tradition of legal interpretation thus merged into a single stream of thought, although carried by a number of distinct intellectual traditions. There were the juristic writings of Justinian's *Digest*, containing an abbreviated glimpse of the casuistic reasoning of Roman lawyers on matters of textual construction. Next, there was a tradition of New Testament scholarship which examined the moral implications of right and justice. Finally, there was the continuation of the strongly logical and schematic approaches of oratory and rhetoric. Taken together — as they would have been by any well-educated person of the late Renaissance and early-modern period in Europe — they

---

[346] *See* Rabe, supra note 340, at 83-91 (passages 56-62).

[347] 2 *Corinthians* 3:6. *Cf.* Euripides' comment, rendered at supra note 12. For more on Patristic hermeneutics, including the views of Augustine, *see* Eden, supra note 2, at 41-63.

The spirit-letter distinction is a common trope in modern, American legal usage. *See, e.g., Gulf, Colorado, & Sante Fe Ry. v. Ellis*, 165 U.S. 150, 160 (1897) (Brewer, J.) ("it is always safe to read the letter of the Constitution in the spirit of the Declaration of Independence."); *McCulloch v. Maryland*, 17 U.S. (4 Wheat.) 316, 421 (Marshall, C.J.) ("all means which are appropriate, which are plainly adapted to that end, which are not prohibited, but consist with the letter and spirit of the Constitution, are constitutional.").

[348] 1 Cohen, supra note 64, at 41. For more on the Jewish law of interpretation, *see* id. at 47-57; David Daube, *Rabbinic Methods of Interpretation and Hellenistic Rhetoric*, 22 HEBREW UNION COLLEGE ANNUAL 239 (1949); id., *Alexandrian Methods of Interpretation and the Rabbis*, in ESSAYS IN GRECO-ROMAN AND TALMUDIC LITERATURE 165 (Henry A. Fischel ed. 1977); id., *Texts and Interpretation in Roman and Jewish Law*, in id. at 240; Aaron M. Schreiber, JEWISH LAW AND DECISION-MAKING: A STUDY THROUGH TIME (1979). For more on the Christian heritage of legal interpretation, *see* Jack Bartlett Rogers & Donald K. McKim, THE AUTHORITY AND INTERPRETATION OF THE BIBLE (1979); Geoffrey P. Miller, *Pragmatics and the Maxims of Interpretation*, 1990 WISC. L. REV. 1179, 1184-1189.

formed an overall sense of the way that the interpretation of legal texts had to be approached.

The exercise of legal interpretation in the middle ages was devoted to three branches of the law: the *ius commune* of the received Roman law, the canon law of the Church, and the *statuta* of local and municipal ordinances.[349] Although a detailed examination of the process of legal interpretation in each of these three, distinct legal systems is beyond the scope of this book,[350] it is worth making one point about the manner in which the classical tradition of interpretation was transmitted through the middle ages. The fine distinctions developed in the classical period were lost. The divergent approaches to private law writings and statutory texts, seemingly practiced by the Roman *iurisprudentes*,[351] were largely wiped away in the canon law.[352] Likewise, distinctions between the reason (*ratio*), spirit or will (*voluntas*), and intent (*intentio*) of a legal writing were collapsed into a single inquiry.[353]

---

[349] *See generally*, Baade, supra note 106, at 53-54. For more on the origins of the phrase "jus commune," *see* 1 Sir Frederick Pollock & Frederic William Maitland, THE HISTORY OF ENGLISH LAW BEFORE THE TIME OF EDWARD I 176-80 (1898).

[350] Professor Hans Baade's recent article, supra note 106, is a superb discussion of these developments. For other treatments, *see* Philippe Godding, *L'interprétation de la "Loi" dans le Droit Savant Médiéval et dans le Droit des Pays-Bas Méridionaux*, in L'INTERPRÉTATION EN DROIT, APPROCHE PLURISDISCIPLINAIRE 446, 460-62 (Michel van der Kerchove ed. 1978); Stephan Kuttner, *Urban II and the Doctrine of Interpretation: A Turning Point?*, in Stephan Kuttner, THE HISTORY AND DOCTRINES OF CANON LAW IN THE MIDDLE AGES NO. IV, at 62-63, 78-81 (1980); T.F.T. Plucknett, STATUTES AND THEIR INTERPRETATION DURING THE FIRST HALF OF THE THIRTEENTH CENTURY (1922).

[351] *See* supra notes 306 - 308 and accompanying text.

[352] *See* Baade, supra note 106, at 59 (glossing the reported decision of an ecclesiastical appeal from Padua in 1561 and the writings of Francisco de Suarez); Frost, Introduction, supra note 18, at 620-22.

[353] *See* Baade, supra note 106, at 54. For the first use of *intentio* by a civil law scholar to denote the actual intent of a law-maker in statutory interpretation, *see* the sources cited in id. at 54 n.67. This unification of *ratio*, *voluntas*, and *intentio* was fully described in the work of Constantinus Rogerius, TRACTATUS DE IURIS INTERPETATIONE (1463), cited in id.

Professor Harold J. Berman has also noted that the medieval scholastics had transformed the crudely-transmitted *regulae* of classical Roman law,[354] into universal maxims of legal science.[355]   In short, the scholastics encountered ancient rules which were (at most) intended to help the process of casuistry and, through Aristotelian methods, transformed them into universal principles.[356] Sometimes the results of this transformation were salutary, as in the parable of the Barber of Bologna who, while shaving a judge negligently cut him, thus "letting blood in the palace." This was a capital offense according to the *statuta* of the city.[357] The barber was acquitted by a theory of beneficial interpretation of a statute, borrowing from the Roman law maxim of lenity in criminal statutes[358] and an approach emphasizing, as the canonists put it, the object and purpose of the law (*cessante ratione [causae] legis cessat ipsa lex*).[359]

iii. So it was that by the late 1500s and early 1600s, with the birth of modern jurisprudence, any contrasts that had existed between the Roman *ius interpretandi* and the rhetorician's *status legalis* had been forgotten.[360]   The

---

at 55-56.

[354] Found in book 50, title 17 of 4 Justinian's *Digest*, supra note 80, at 956-69.

[355] *See* Berman, supra note 252, at 139-43. *See also* Jacob, supra note 289, at 1653-56; Stein, supra note 18, at 127.

[356] *See also* Gerhard Otte, DIALEKTIK UND JURISPRUDENZ 214-15 (1971). A similar process was replicated in Gratian's use of hypothetical cases (*causae*) as the organizing principle of his work. *See* supra note 257. *See also* Ian MacLean, supra note 341, at 104-14, 128-31, 142-47.

[357] For a narration of this case, *see* Samuel E. Thorne, Statuti *in the Post-Glossators*, in ESSAYS IN ENGLISH LEGAL HISTORY 3, 7 (1985).

[358] *See* supra note 311 and accompanying text.

[359] *See* C. 26 X *de iureiurando* 2, 24 (1206). *See also* Kuttner, supra note 350.

[360] *See* Viehweg, supra note 18, at 51-64 (for a history of rhetoric and the *mos italicus* — the intellectual milieu of the canon law and the revival of civil law in Bologna and other

"mathematically-minded seventeenth century," as Professor Theodor Viehweg has pointed out, had a strong "aversion to prudence (*prudentia*)."[361] This antipathy was directed against the medieval Glossators and post-Glossators of the *Digest* who had emphasized a jurisprudence of maxims.[362] These were pretty crude constructs, though, with little of the finesse that was shown either under Roman juristic casuistry or by the rhetorical status system.[363]

After time, though, medieval scholasticism did begin to yield to a "systematic legal science."[364] Moreover, as Professor Berman has noted, this sixteenth century legal science was strongly humanist.[365] As a consequence,

---

European universities).

[361] Viehweg, supra note 18, at 54. *See also* his discussion of Leibniz's theories, id. at 65-68. For a consideration of scientific revolutions and the impact on legal science in the fifteenth and sixteenth centuries, *see* Berman, supra note 252, at 151-64. *See also* Jacob, supra note 289, at 1655-56 (for more on the relation between Leibniz's symbolic logic and maxims of interpretation). For additional sources of a "mathematical jurisprudence," *see* Erhard Weigel, PHILOSOPHIA MATHEMATICA (Jena 1693); Hyland, supra note 207, at 422.

[362] *See* Schiller, supra note 238, at 766. *See also* Berman, supra note 252, at 149-51; Ward E. Lattin, *Legal Maxims and their Use in Statutory Interpretations*, 26 GEO. L. J. 1, 1-4 (1937); Paul Vinogradoff, ROMAN LAW IN MEDIEVAL EUROPE (1929).

[363] *See* Viehweg, supra note 18, at 50-55. For the treatment of Roman law-derived maxims in English law in the period before 1550, *see* Stein, supra note 18, at 155, 160-62.

[364] Viehweg, supra note 18, at 54. A path-breaking study of this phenomenon is Harold J. Berman's LAW AND REVOLUTION: FORMATION OF THE WESTERN LEGAL TRADITION (1983). See especially id. at 120-64. *See also* Harold J. Berman & Charles J. Reid, *The Transformation of English Legal Science: From Hale to Blackstone*, 45 EMORY L. J. 438, 457-509 (1996).

[365] *See* Hans Erich Trojen, HUMANISTISCHE JURISPRUDENZ (1993); Harold J. Berman & Charles J. Reid, Jr., *Roman Law in Europe and the Jus Commune: A Historical Overview with Emphasis on the Legal Science of the Sixteenth Century*, 20 SYR. J. INT'L L. & COM. 1, 11-16 (1994); Charles M. Gray, *Reason, Authority and Imagination: The Jurisprudence of Sir Edward Coke*, in CULTURE AND POLITICS FROM PURITANISM TO THE ENLIGHTENMENT 25 (Perez Zagarin ed. 1980); John U. Lewis, *Sir Edward Coke: His Theory of Artificial Reason as a Context for Modern Basic Legal Theory*, 84 L.Q. REV. 330 (1968); Desmond

proponents of this jurisprudence associated themselves with the classical rhetoricians and their lessons.[366]   That is why most early-modern writers, including those that perceived of themselves as legal historians, simply assumed that the rhetorical manuals fairly summarized the jurist's approaches to problems of legal interpretation.   It is no wonder that some of the most significant jurists of this period — including Sir Christopher Hatton[367] and Sir Edward Coke[368] —

Manderson, Statuta *v. Acts: interpretation, music and Early English legislation*, 7 YALE J. L. & HUMAN. 317 (1995); J. Stanley McQuade, *Medieval "Ratio" and Modern Formal Studies: A Reconsideration of Coke's Dictum that Law is the Reflection of Reason*, 38 AJJ 359 (1993).

[366]   *See* Stein, supra note 18, at 162-65 (for more on humanists' treatment of legal maxims). *See also* J. Franklin, JEAN BODIN AND THE SIXTEENTH-CENTURY REVOLUTION IN THE METHODOLOGY OF LAW AND HISTORY (1963); Frost, Introduction, supra note 18, at 624-30.

[367]   *See* Sir Christopher Hatton, TREATISE CONCERNING STATUTES, OR ACTS OF PARLIAMENT: AND THE EXPOSITION THEREOF 26 (1670) (written c. 1570) (*citing* Cicero's *de Legibus*).   Hatton lived from 1540 to 1591, and wa Lord Chancellor in 1587.   For more on this figure, *see* Ian MacLean, supra note 341, at 182-83.

[368]   *See* 1 Sir Edward Coke, SYSTEMATIC ARRANGEMENT OF LORD COKE'S FIRST INSTITUTE OF THE LAWS OF ENGLAND § 1.24b (J.H. Thomas ed., Philadelphia, Alexander Towar 2d American ed. 1836).   *See also* Heydon's Case, 3 Coke Rep. 7a, 76 Eng. Rep. 637, 642 (K.B. 1584) (establishing a rule of favorable construction of statutes in order to "suppress[] mischief" and "advancing the remedy").   *See* Ian Maclean, supra note 341, at 183-85; Baade, supra note 106, at 63-68; William S. Blatt, *The History of Statutory Interpretation: A Study in Form and Substance*, 6 CARDOZO L. REV. 799, 800 (1985) (examining the doctrine of the "equity of a statute"); Jacob, supra note 289, at 1662 & n.140; L.H. LaRue, *Statutory Interpretation: Lord Coke Revisited*, 48 U. PITT. L. REV. 733 (1987); Stein, supra note 18, at 161-62.

See also Richard Helgerson, FORMS OF NATIONHOOD: THE ELIZABETHAN WRITING OF ENGLAND (1992) (for more on Roman republican analogues to Elizabethan English political culture); Jolowicz, Foundation, supra note 291, at 15. *See also* Wilbur S. Howell, RHETORIC AND LOGIC IN ENGLAND, 1500-1700 (1956); Berman & Reid, Emory, supra note 364, at 493-95; Peter Goodrich, LANGUAGES OF THE LAW 15-110 (1990); Allen D. Boyer, *The Last Ciceronian: Sir Edward Coke and Classical Rhetoric* (forthcoming); John W. Cairns, *Rhetoric, language, and Roman law: legal education and improvement in Eighteenth-Century Scotland*, 9 LAW & HIST. REV. 31 (1991); R.J. Schoeck, *Rhetoric and the Law in Sixteenth-Century England*, 50 STUDIES IN PHILOLOGY 110, 115-27 (1953).

were strongly influenced by Cicero and Quintilian in their writings on how to interpret legal texts.[369]   A contemporaneous reference to classical rhetorical sources appears in a comment in Plowden's Reports of Common Pleas in 1574. Glossing the case of *Eyston v. Studd*,[370] Plowden endorses a liberal rule of statutory construction, looking to the "Equity" of the law. This proposition was supported by an indirect citation to Cicero,[371] for the *controversia* of the foreigner who climbs the walls of the city to defend it against attackers.[372] Plowden, however, attributes the example to a Renaissance commentary on Aristotle.[373]

So it should also come as no surprise that in the civil law tradition in Europe — with its strong desire to trace its intellectual roots back to Roman law[374] — the notion of *stasis* remains somewhat influential to this day.[375] And,

---

For a modern application of the "suppressing the mischief" rule in equitable interpretation, *see Potter v. United States*, 269 F. Supp. 545, 549 (N.D. W.Va. 1967) (describing it (incorrectly) as an "ancient canon of interpretation of remedial statutes").

[369]   *See* Ian MacLean, supra note 341, at 175-77; Schiller, supra note 238, at 758-59 (discussing the Elizabethan concept of "equity of a statute"). For more on this see *Wimbish v. Tailbois*, 1 Plowden 38, 53, 57, 75 Eng. Rep. 63, 85-93 (K.B. 1551); Y.B. 21 Hen. VII, Hil. 28 (1506) (Rede, J.) ("No equity can be taken of statutes in abridgement of the common law."). *See also* John Austin, LECTURES ON JURSIPRUDENCE 1028-29 (4th ed. 1879); 1 William Blackstone, COMMENTARIES ON THE LAWS OF ENGLAND *62; 2 Sir Fortunatus Dwarris, GENERAL TREATISE ON STATUTES 720-34 (1831); Baade, supra note 106, at 78-80; Samuel E. Thorne, *The Equity of a Statute and Heydon's Case*, 31 ILL. L. REV. 202 (1936).

[370]   2 Plowden 459a, 467, 75 Eng. Rep. 688, 689 (C.P. 1574).

[371]   de Inventione, supra note 21, at 291-93 (passage ii.42.123) .

[372]   *See* supra note 97 with text.

[373]   2 Plowden at 466a, 75 Eng. Rep. at 698. *See also* Baade, supra note 106, at 81.

[374]   *See* John Henry Merryman, THE CIVIL LAW TRADITION 6-13 (2d ed. 1985); Troje, supra note 365. For examples of current scholarship on this point *see* James Q. Whitman, THE LEGACY OF ROMAN LAW IN THE GERMAN ROMANTIC ERA (1990); Olympiad S. Ioffe, *Soviet Law and Roman law*, 62 B.U. L. REV. 701 (1982); Peter J. Riga, *The influence of*

as a general rule, civil law jurisdictions have shown a great tolerance for breaking from textual rules of construction for most legal writings.[376]

iv. The revival of interest in classicism in Renaissance and early-Modern European intellectual circles soon had an impact on the conduct of diplomacy and the development of international law. The study of classical political history and statecraft deepened. At the same time, and just as canons for statutes were being resurrected, there was a movement towards the systematization of rules in the interpretation of agreements between countries.

It remained for one, towering intellectual figure of the day to synthesize the first modern "system" of international law, a structure in which rules of treaty construction figured prominently. That man was Grotius. And, from

---

Roman law on state theory in the eleventh and twelfth centuries, 35 AJJ 171 (1990); Reinhard Zimmerman, *Roman-dutch jurisprudence and its contribution to European private law*, 66 TUL. L. REV. 1685 (1992).

For similar scholarship on the introduction of Roman law in England, Scotland, and the United States, *see* W. Hamilton Bryson, *The Use of Roman law in Virginia courts*, 28 AJLH 135 (1984); John W. Cairns, *The Teaching of Roman Law in England around 1200*, 38 AJLH 96 (1994); Lewis C. Cassidy, *The Teaching and Study of Roman Law in the United States*, 19 GEO. L. J. 297 (1930-31); Robin Evans-Jones, *Unjust enrichment, contract and the third reception of Roman law in Scotland*, 109 L. Q. REV. 663 (1993); M.H. Hoeflich, *Roman law in American legal culture*, 66 TUL. L. REV. 1723 (1992); id., *Roman and Civil Law in American Legal Education and Research Prior to 1930: A Preliminary Survey*, 1984 U. ILL. L. REV. 719; Edward D. Re, *The Roman contribution to the common law*, 39 LOY. L. REV. 295 (1993); Peter Stein, *The Attraction of the Civil Law in Post-Revolutionary America*, 52 VA. L. REV. 403 (1966); Douglas G. Smith, *Citizenship and the Fourteenth Amendment*, 34 SAN DIEGO L. REV. 681, 738-40 (1997); Bernard Keith Vetter, *Louisiana: the United States' unique connection to Roman law*, 39 LOY. L. REV. 281 (1993).

[375] *See* Braet, supra note 20, at 90-92; Hohmann, supra note 14, at 183-90; Viehweg, supra note 18, at 83-98. For a discussion of the parallels between status theory and modern German and Austrian conceptualizations of the criminal act, *see* F. Horak, *Die rhetorische Statuslehre und der moderne Aufbau des Verbrechensberifts*, in FESTGABE FÜR ARNOLD HERDLITCZKA 121 (F. Horak & W. Waldstein eds. 1972).

[376] *See, e.g.*, the influential work of 1 François Gény, MÉTHODE D'INTERPRETATION ET SOURCES EN DROIT PRIVÉ POSITIF 304-14 (2d ed. 1919); 2 id. at 117-30. *See also* Jolowicz, Foundations, supra note 291, at 12-13.

where else could he have divined his canons for treaty interpretation than from classical rhetoric, law, and diplomacy?

VII   Grotius and His Followers on Treaty Construction

i. Hugo de Groot, also known by his Latin eponym, Grotius, has been called the "father of the law of nations."[377] Although it hardly matters today whether he deserves such credit, his treatise, *De Jure Belli ac Pacis* (On the Rights of War and Peace), first published in 1625,[378] justifiably remains a classic. His

---

[377] *See, e.g.*, Maurice Bourquin, *Grotius est-il le père du droit des gens*? in GRANDES FIGURES ET GRANDES OEUVRES JURIDIQUES (Geneva 1948) (collecting sources suggesting that Grotius was the progenitor of modern international law). *But see* Benedict Kingsbury & Adam Roberts, *Introduction: Grotian Thought in International Relations*, in HUGO GROTIUS AND INTERNATIONAL RELATIONS 1, 3 (Hedley Bull, Benedict Kingsbury & Adam Roberts ed. 1990) (suggesting that "scholars have (for the most part) long-ceased to debate the *question mal posée* whether or not Grotius was 'the father of the law of nations'....") ["Kingsbury & Roberts, Introduction"].

[378] The standard English text of this work is the Francis W. Kelsey translation, Classics of International Law ed. 1925 (number 3, volume 2 of the series). This edition was drawn from the second, vastly revised version by Grotius in 1646, near the conclusion of the Thirty Years' War. See Edward Gordon, Book Review, 89 AJIL 461, 463 (1995) (reviewing A NORMATIVE APPROACH TO WAR: PEACE, WAR AND JUSTICE IN HUGO GROTIUS (Onuma Yasuaki ed. 1993)) (noting that Grotius made nearly a thousand corrections to the first edition).

    The majority of references in this essay to *De Jure Belli ac Pacis* will be to the Kelsey translation [hereinafter "1646"]. In a few instances I have chosen to cite the 1901 translation by A.C. Campbell, published as part of the Universal Classics Library. This was a reprint of the first, 1625 edition of the book [hereinafter "1625"]. References will be made to pages in either the Campbell ["1625"] translation or Kelsey translation ["1646"], as well as to standard indications of the relevant passage (including book, chapter, section, sub-section).

book has been considered the first systematic treatment of international law. Adam Smith, in lectures delivered in 1762 on the subject of moral philosophy and the law of nations, said that "Grotius seems to have been the first who attempted to give the world anything like a regular system of natural jurisprudence, and *De Jure Belli ac Pacis* with all of its imperfections, is perhaps at this day the most complete work on the subject."[379] Later writers have suggested that the key influence of Grotius' treatise was as a "systematic reassembling of practice and authorities on the traditional but fundamental subject of the *jus belli* [laws of war], organized for the first time around a body of principles rooted in the law of nature."[380] One way to see how Grotius "reassembl[ed] [the] practice and authorities on the traditional" subject of international law is to examine his discussion (and those of his contemporaries) on the classical tradition in rhetoric and treaty interpretation.

The extent and depth of Grotius' citations to classical sources in the *The Rights of War and Peace* was staggering. My reading of the text indicates that Grotius made specific references to at least 120 different classical writers. These writers span virtually all of the classical canon, and include not only the prominent Greek and Roman historians and jurists, but also quite a number of philosophers and poets. Grotius' selection of source material, at least in its classical focus, was certainly eclectic and diffuse.

The reason for this was that Grotius sought to use classical materials not so much to provide authority for fine legal points, but, instead, to offer evidence of the practice and customs of ancient States. For the principles of natural justice, which he believed guided State conduct in international affairs, Grotius did have recourse chiefly to using scriptural interpretation. But for his account of State practice, Grotius did not need to rely solely on Roman jurisconsults,

---

Henceforth, *De Jure Belli ac Pacis* will be abbreviated "DJBaP" in the citations.

[379] Adam Smith, LECTURES ON JUSTICE, POLICE, REVENUE AND ARMS 1 (E. Canaan ed. 1896).

[380] Kingsbury & Roberts, supra note 377, at 3-4. *See also* Benedict Kingsbury, *Grotius, Law and Moral Scepticism: Theory and Practice in the Thought of Hedley Bull*, in CLASSICAL THEORIES OF INTERNATIONAL RELATIONS 42 (Ian Clark & Iver B. Neumann eds. 1996).

who were relatively thinly represented in his text. Indeed, Grotius seemed to have a definitive bias against using, as authority, the texts of leading legal schools, including the more contemporaneous civil and canon lawyers.[381]   In short, Grotius was not so much writing a legal treatise as he was drafting a compendium of the rules of international law as reflected in actual State conduct.

Further analysis of Grotius' citations to ancient authorities indicate substantial emphasis being placed on historical or narrative texts. Chief among these were the works of Diodorus Siculus, Demosthenes, Livy, Plutarch, Polybius, Tacitus, Thucydides, and Xenophon. These were certainly regarded as being the leading classical historians. Relatively underrepresented in Grotius' book are citations to Herodotus, Josephus, and Sallust. Of these, Grotius' three scant references to Herodotus (in his 1625 edition) probably represent the biggest surprise in his handling of classical historical texts.

The next largest group of citations are those to the leading classical texts on oratory, statecraft and political conduct. In this category I would include Cicero, Pliny, Quintilian, and Seneca. Indeed, Cicero is the classical author whom Grotius cites most often. Cicero makes over eighty appearances in the 1625 edition.   In the next group of citations I would include mentions of philosophical works, most notably those by Aristotle and Plato. Next are epic, poetic, or dramatic sources, including those by Euripides, Homer, and Virgil. In the last group are references to the Roman jurisconsults, Paulus and Ulpian.

---

[381]   *But see* Grotius' DE JURE PRAEDAE COMMENTARIUS (Commentaries On the Law of Prize), originally drafted in 1604-06, but only published upon its discovery in 1868. The best modern translation is that of Williams-Zeydel, in the Classics of International Law edition in 1950. In DE JURE PRAEDAE, the number of citations to the canonist writers is quite extensive. *See* Peter Haggenmacher, *Grotius and Gentili: A Reassessment of Thomas E. Holland's Inaugural Lecture*, in Kingsbury & Roberts, supra note 377, at 133, 146.

This is in sharp contrast to the 1625 edition of DE JURE BELLI AC PACIS where there is not a single reference to the canonists. The absence of these citations may have reflected Grotius' belief that both the civil and canon laws had little relevance to the modern reincarnation of the Roman *jus gentium ac publicum*, what Grotius renamed *jus belli ac pacis*. See Haggenmacher, supra, at 152. Dutch authorities imposed strict censorship requirements in the early 17th century for any publication referring to Popish or canon law sources. These restrictions were, apparently, lifted by the time the 1646 edition of the book appeared.

That still leaves over a hundred other classical writers, for each of which Grotius made a few, isolated references.

ii. *De Jure Belli ac Pacis* thus exhibited the mind of an extraordinary scholar. Grotius was, after all, more than an international law publicist. A child prodigy, entered at the University of Leiden at age 11, presented to the court of King Henry IV of France and acclaimed "the miracle of Holland," Grotius found time in his long life to write nearly sixty books in Latin, ranging in subjects from theology, biblical criticism, history, philology, and poetry.[382] He may well have been the best-read man of his generation in Europe, the equal in many respects of his countryman, Erasmus.[383]

Grotius was, by disposition, a Romanist. Cicero was, indeed, his favorite classical author, and certain Ciceronian turns of phrase permeated Grotius' thinking. Consider, for example, the very title of Grotius' project: *De Jure Belli ac Pacis*. This was a borrowing from what Cicero denominated as the Roman law of nations (or at least that part of Roman law dealing with private law relations with foreigners), the *jus gentium*.[384] Although some modern writers[385] have indicated that Grotius proceeded from a historical mistake — the *jus gentium* was analytically distinct from a law of nations (*jus inter gentes*) — it hardly matters in the context of Grotius' understanding of ancient sources.

Grotius conceived of international law as being a set of rules which governed the conduct of peoples in distinct communities. For example, in the

---

[382] *See* Hedley Bull, *The Importance of Grotius in the Study of International Relations* in Kingsbury & Roberts, supra note 377, at 65, 67.

[383] Erasmus himself was much influenced by classical rhetorical approaches to interpretation. *See* Eden, supra note 2, at 64-78; Kathy Eden, *Equity and the Origins of Renaissance Historicism: The Case of Erasmus*, 5 YALE J. OF L. & HUMAN. 137 (1993). For Cicero's influence on Malancthon, *see* Eden, supra note 2, at 79-89.

[384] *See* Haggenmacher, supra note 381, at 152. See also Ludwik Ehrlich, *L'Interprétation des Traités*, 24 RCADI 1, 12-13, 16 (1928 - IV) (discussing Cicero's influence on Gentili and Grotius).

[385] *See* Kingsbury & Roberts, supra note 377, at 28-29.

part of his book on the conduct of hostilities,[386] Grotius opined on whether there was a generally-accepted, universal rule to not enslave enemies captured in war. He concluded that in wars amongst Christians this was so. Likewise, Muslim countries followed the same practice *inter se*. But the absence of the rule in inter-faith conflicts indicated that such a rule lacked the status of *jus gentium*.

Grotius' preoccupation with universal rules derived from right reason (the *sine qua non* of natural law) suggests that he was strongly influenced by Cicero's notion of *humani generis societas*, a "society of mankind rather than of states."[387] This phrase appears in a number of places in Cicero's works, particularly in *De officiis*[388] and *De finibus bonorum et malorum*.[389] Cicero may have inherited this phrase, in turn, from Stoic philosophers,[390] a debt that Grotius

---

[386] *See* DJBaP (1646), supra note 378, at 696 (passage iii.7.9.2). *See also* Theodor Meron, HENRY'S WARS AND SHAKESPEARE'S LAWS 93-94 (1993) (who discusses other publicists contemporary with Grotius who concurred in this opinion).

[387] *See* Jules Basdevant, *Hugo Grotius*, in LES FONDATEURS DU DROIT INTERNATIONAL. LEURS OEUVRES — EURS DOCTRINES 125, 254 (A. Pillet ed. 1904). *See also* Max Hamburger, THE AWAKENEING OF WESTERN LEGAL THOUGHT 125-27 (Bernard Miall transl. 1942); Jean Moreau-Reibel, *Le Droit de Société Interhumaine et le 'Jus Gentium': Essai sur les origines et le developpement des notions jusqu'à Grotius*, 77 RCADI 485, 489-99 (1950 - II).

[388] *See* 21 Cicero, DE OFFICIIS 47, 289 (Walter Miller transl. 1913) (Loeb Classical Library rep. 1968) (passages i.14.42 & iii.5.21).

[389] *See* 17 Cicero, DE FINIBUS BONORUM ET MALORUM 281-83 (H. Rackham transl. 1914) (Loeb Classical Library rep. 1983) (passage iii.19.62).

[390] *See* Haggenmacher, supra note 381, 172. See also Ernst Cassirer, THE MYTH OF THE STATE 165-66, 172 (1946); Miquel, 87 SAVIGNY'S ZEITSCHRIFT 85 (1970) (both noting Grotius' debt to neo-Stoicists). Grotius' views of the state and international relations may have also been strongly influenced by Aristotle. *See* Tanaka Tadashi, *Prolegomena* in Onuma, supra note 378, at 21-22.

himself noted.[391] The thrust of many of these references was to establish rules of law which were universal or near-universal in character.

This pattern of reliance is repeated throughout *De Jure Belli ac Pacis.* A proposition of international law is made. Historical "evidence" is then offered in the form of scripture or of historians writing in Greek or Latin. Finally, a legal authority is cited (and often quoted) to support the proposition. More often than not, that legal authority was Cicero, although on some occasions the views of jurists like Ulpian were substituted. This pattern was by no means invariable. Grotius could use Cicero as just another citation, without any particular emphasis.[392]   In some instances, Cicero provided the *only* support for the argument being advanced by Grotius.[393]

Grotius' reliance on Cicero was emblematic of his substantial ambivalence about the reliability of ancient sources in the enunciation of rules of "modern" international law. In order to accord with his theories of natural law, the rules governing State relations had to be *both* universal *and* based on right reason. How did a scholar writing in the early seventeenth century prove both elements in the creation of a customary international law? Antiquity provided the raw narrative of international history. Greek and Latin texts, especially of the breadth that Grotius consulted, provided him historical data for nearly five centuries of authentic State relations. To have ignored such a wealth of historical fact would have been foolish. If the ancient historical record was clear in the depiction of certain rules of State relations, the element of universality was certainly satisfied.

---

[391] DJBaP (1646), supra note 378, at 51 (passage i.2.1.1). Grotius often directly quoted Cicero in his book, even though his transliterations were not always accurate. *See* Haggenmacher, supra note 381, at 150-51 (suggesting that Grotius may have borrowed directly from the quotation supplied by Alberico Gentili (1552-1608)).

[392] For examples *see* id. (1646) at 560-63 (passage ii.23.7 & 8) (on doubtful causes in just war theory).

[393] *See* id. at 811 (passage iii.20.16) (debts owed to individuals at the beginning of war are not discharged as a result of the war).

iii. Nowhere is Grotius' debt to classical scholarship more evident than in his treatment of the subject, as he styled it, of "interpretation."[394] Grotius begins his discussion of the proper construction of treaties by considering the problem of intent in the making of any agreement. What gives any contract its enforceable character is the notion that one who makes a promise should intend to keep it. But, as Grotius quotes Cicero as writing, "In good faith what you meant, not what you said, is to be considered."[395]

The study of the interpretation of agreements is governed, Grotius then suggested, by "natural reason," which "demands that one to whom the promise has been made should have the right to compel the promisor to do what the correct interpretation suggests."[396] Grotius' assumption was that it is, in all cases, possible to discern the correct interpretation of any legal writing, "[f]or otherwise the matter would have no outcome, a condition which in morals is held to be impossible."[397] In short, Grotius was making a plea for objective rules of treaty interpretation, making it possible to resolve disputes as to the proper construction of agreements. He was also eschewing a doctrinal void, and avoiding a *non liquet* in interpreting a text.

Grotius, following Aristotle, believed that the act of making faith through a promise was one governed by natural reason and by notions of "judgement," "good sense," and "the perception of what is fair."[398] Likewise,

---

[394] DJBaP (1646), supra note 378, at 409 (passage ii.16.1). *See also* György Haraszti, SOME FUNDAMENTAL PROBLEMS OF THE LAW OF TREATIES 33 (1973); Ehrlich, supra note 384, at 16.

[395] DJBaP (1646), supra note 378, at 409 (passage ii.16.1.1) (quoting, Cicero, DE OFFICIIS, supra note 276, at 45 (passage i.13.40) ("In the matter of a promise one must always consider the meaning and not the mere words.")).

[396] Id.

[397] Id.

[398] *See* id. at 425 (passage ii.16.26.1) (quoting, 18 Aristotle, MAGNA MORALIA 575-77 (G. Cyril Armstrong transl. 1935) (Loeb Classical Library rep. 1977) (passage ii. 2). *See also* Ehrlich, supra note 384, at 17.

in citing one of the Elder Seneca's *controversiae*, Grotius made the point that "In the law ... there is no exception. But there are many things which, though not considered exceptions, are understood, and the written form of the law is restricted, the interpretation broad. Some things, however, are so manifest that they have no need of provision."[399] Grotius also made clear that the principles he was divining from the classical rhetorical theory of *stasis* and its application to statutes were applicable, "within proper limits," to "wills ... and compacts."[400]

This was not the first time that the subject of interpretation of legal texts (and especially agreements between countries) was linked to natural reason or to natural law principles. Nor would it be the last. Alberico Gentili, writing in his 1612 edition of his volume, *De Iure Belli Libri Tres* (The Laws of War in Three Volumes) paraphrases Aristotle's admonition to interpret legal texts in "equity and the opinion of a good man,"[401] while also refuting Bartolus' earlier contention that treaties were not to be construed in accordance with a "universal law" of "good faith."[402] "For all contracts," Gentili wrote,

> with sovereigns and communities are in good faith, according to my firm conviction.... It is in harmony with the simplicity of international law, to which agreements on truces, treaties, and peace belong. I am [also] surprised Baldus

---

[399] Id. at 425 n.1 (quoting 2 Seneca, CONTROVERSIAE, supra note 34, at 291 (passage ix.4.9) (although cited by Grotius as passage iv. 27)).

[400] Id. at 425. *See also* V.D. Degan, L'INTERPRETATION DES ACCORDS EN DROIT INTERNATIONAL 28-33 (1963).

[401] Alberico Gentili, DE IURE BELLI LIBRI TRES 191 (1612 ed.) (John C. Rolfe transl.) (Classics of International Law 1964 rep.) (passage ii. 13). *See also* Ehrlich, supra note 384, at 12-15. For Gentili's influence on the eighteenth century Spanish writer, Ignacio Ortega y Cotes, *see* Degan, supra note 400, at 34-37; Ehrlich, supra note 384, at 22-23.

[402] Id. (glossing the passage from Bartolus, *On the Digest*, xxxix.4.15). *See also* Haraszti, supra note 394, at 31; Marcelle Jokl, D'INTERPRETATION DES TRAITES NORMATIFS D'APRÈS LA DOCTRINE ET LA JURISPRUDENCE INTERNATIONALES 95 (1936).

writes, that the contracting of a treaty is a matter of strict law, and that nothing enters into it which has not been expressly mentioned.[403]

This was a point made nicely by Christian Wolff in his *Jus Gentium Methodo Scientifica Pertractatum* (The Law of Nations Treated According to a Scientific Method), a treatise which appeared in 1764 (over 150 years after Gentili), and which marked a high-point of natural reason discourse in international law:

> [I]t cannot happen otherwise than that controversies should arise between parties to a treaty concerning that which has been promised in the treaty, or excepted from it, to be terminated in no other way than by admitting the interpretation made in accordance with rules, which each party to the treaty is bound to admit as true.... [F]or this reason it cannot be said that interpretation of treaties is useless, and that controversies are not to be terminated except by force of arms. In the law of nations the question is, what is right and what ought nations and their rulers to do, but not what is necessary to do if they are unwilling to submit to the truth....[404]

What is surprising is the extent to which many of the great, early-Modern scholars of international law,[405] perceived the impelling need to create exogenous rules for international relations, norms which were separate from the whim and will of State behavior, but which were also consistent with the general trends of State conduct. To this end, these writers devoted substantial attention to rules of treaty interpretation, for precisely the reason that international

---

[403] Id. (critiquing the passage from Baldus, *On the Digest*, i.3.32). Gentili's interpretation of Baldus may have been unwarranted. Richard Zouche, who lived from 1590 - 1661, wrote in IURIS ET IUDICII FECIALIS (Exposition of the Fetial Law and Procedure, or of Law Between Nations) (J.L. Brierly transl. The Classics of International Law series rep. 1964), that Baldus believed that treaties were to be interpreted in good faith and not according to strict legal rules. Id. at 104 (passage 30 [34]).

[404] Christian Wolff, JUS GENTIUM METHODO SCIENTIFICA PERTRACTATUM 194 (1764) (Joseph H. Drake transl. Classics of International Law series) (§ 375). *See also* Degan, supra note 400, at 37-39; Ehrlich, supra note 384, at 24-25.

[405] *But see* David Kennedy, *Primitive Legal Scholarship*, 27 HARV. INT' L. J. 1 (1986) (who critiques Grotius and Gentili, at least, as "primitive" international law scholars, to be distinguished from those of the "classical" period, including Vattel and Wolff). *See also* Ehrlich, supra note 384, at 21-24 (who also makes this point).

agreements were perceived as being the primary vehicle for the development and attachment of international obligations. In any event, it was Grotius' work that was positively crucial in developing rules of treaty interpretation that every civilized nation was "bound to admit as true."[406] Every writer that sought a synthesis for rules of treaty interpretation — precepts which combined natural law principles of equity and fairness, as well as concrete legal principles — acknowledged his debt to Grotius. Samuel Pufendorf, the great English jurist of the late seventeenth century, discussed "the whole subject ... following almost κατὰ πόδα [in the very footsteps] of Grotius,... who has handled the presentation of this subject most precisely."[407]

iv. The precision of Grotius' handling of the interpretation of treaty texts was directly attributable to his understanding of, and his willingness to modify, the *stasis* system of classical rhetoric. Grotius' exegesis "On Interpretation" is a direct response to his readings of Cicero, Quintilian, and the *Rhetorica ad Herennium*. Just as Hermogenes added a logical overlay to the unruly categorical inquiries of fact, definition, and quality,[408] Grotius specifically focused on a rational taxonomy for the five *quaestiones legales* or *constitutio legitima* which described every kind of problem involving interpretation of a legal text. Grotius' insight was to recast questions surrounding the construction of agreements — and especially those with a public law flavor — into a single inquiry, and, from that single scrutiny, to fashion a legal taxonomy that could provide greater guidance to the interpreter of a treaty.

α. Grotius said that "modern" treaty interpretation might do well to observe the "ancient treaty formula given by Livy: 'Without wicked

---

[406] Wolff, supra note 404, at 194.

[407] Samuel Pufendorf, DE JURE NATURAE ET GENTIUM LIBRI OCTO 793 (2d ed. 1688) (C.H. Oldfather & W.A. Oldfather transl. Classics of International Law series rep. 1964) (passage v.12.1).

[408] *See* supra notes 340 - 348 and accompanying text. *See also* Haraszti, supra note 394, at 32.

deceit, and as these words here to-day have been most rightly understood'."[409] This short quotation to the Roman fetial's treaty-making oath is telling, and has already been the subject of analysis here.[410] It not only establishes a classical provenance for his discussion,[411] it also undergirds his observation that: "The measure of correct interpretation is the inference of intent from the most probable indications.   These indications are of two kinds, words and implications; and these are considered either separately or together."[412] In these two sentences are three unprecedented thoughts.

A. The first, as has already been hinted at, is that rules of interpretation are expected to lead to a "correct" result. The application of principles of interpretation was not intended by Grotius as an oratorical pursuit for persuasion. Rather, it was an exercise in legal reasoning. It was thus possible to have a measure of success or failure in the process, and, more importantly, to immunize objective, exogenous rules of interpretation from the whims of one State party wishing to make a sophistic or self-serving construction of a disputed treaty provision. Interpretation of legal texts (even those which

---

[409] DJBaP (1646), supra note 378, at 409 (passage 11.16.1.2) (quoting Livy, supra note 135, at 85 (passage i.24.7)). *See also* supra notes 202 - 205 and accompanying text.

[410] See supra § III.iii.β.

[411] Discussed in DJBaP (1646), supra note 378, at 415-17 (passage ii.16.13), are the great *cause célèbres* of ancient treaty interpretation. Among these are the problems of after-acquired allies, as arose in the Peace Treaty ending the First Punic War, *see* 2 Polybius, supra note 157, at 60-65 (passages iii.25.3 & iii.26.6), and the conflict in obligations that Athens encountered in its relations with Corcyra and Corinth. *See* 1 Thucydides, supra note 142, at 70-81 (passages i. 35 & 45). *See also* supra § III.ii & iii.

For other early-Modern publicists commenting on these events, *see* Cornelius van Bynkershoek, QUAESTIONUM JURIS PUBLICI LIBRI DUO 62-63 (1737) (Tenney Frank transl. 1930 Classics of International Law series rep. 1962) (passage i.9.71-73) (supporting Grotius); Johann Wolfgang Textor, SYNOPSIS JURIS GENTIUM (Synopsis of the Law of Nations) 259-61 (1680) (John Pawley Bate transl. Classics of International Law series rep. 1964) (for a sharp criticism of Grotius' reading of Livy and Polybius); Zouche, supra note 403, at 103. *See also* Haraszti, supra note 394, at 33.

[412] Id. at 409 (passage ii.16.1.2).

implicated State sovereignty and will as much as treaties) was thus part and parcel of an autonomous science of law.

B. The second point, though, is that intent *did* matter in any agreement. And as soon as that notion was embraced, the interpreter must also have realized that the use of exclusively textual means of construction could lead to "incorrect" results. Likewise, recourse to literal approaches of interpretation — in which the words of the instrument are exalted to the detriment of the agreement's object and purpose — were disclaimed by Grotius as being inconsistent with a "natural reason" that encompasses fairness and justness.

By using the idiom of "intent," Grotius was impliedly making reference to the *constitutio legitima* of "letter and exceptions thereto" (*scriptum et sententia*).[413] This invocation of one of the *quaestiones legales* would be made express in Grotius' following pages, but its purpose in his opening passages was to resurrect an old synthesis of the subject: all questions of legal interpretation are really aspects of the discrepancy between the letter and intent of legal texts. Of course, Quintilian made exactly the same point,[414] but still persisted in cleaving to the traditional division of the *quaestiones* into five categories: definition, ambiguity, conflicts in laws, analogous laws, and letter and exceptions. And although Grotius discussed each of these *constitutio* in his chapter on interpretation, they were clearly subordinated to his primary thesis that the chief dynamic in legal interpretation is to balance the words of the instrument with their implications. In this respect, Grotius self-consciously revisited the debate between Roman jurists and rhetoricians as to the proper balance to be struck between the text and intent of any legal writing.[415]

---

[413] *See generally* supra § II.iii. Interestingly, Pufendorf, in glossing Grotius' text refers to the "rhetorician['s] term [of] περὶ ῥητοῦ καὶ διάνοιας, 'the letter and design of the writing'." Pufendorf, supra note 407, at 800 (passage v.12.6).

[414] *See* 3 Quintilian, supra note 6, at 163 (passage vii.10.2).

[415] *See* DJBaP (1646), supra note 378, at 422 (passage ii.16.20.3 & 4) (discussing the *causa Curiana* and Cicero's speech in *Pro Caecina*). *See also* Pufendorf, supra note 407, at 812 (passage v.12.17) (discussing these cases). For discussion of the significance of these two cases in the history of Roman jurisprudence, *see* supra §§ V.ii & iii.

Γ. The idea of balance, of synthesis, is the final idea redolent in Grotius' summary, and one largely absent from the classical sources: words and implications can be "considered ... *together.*"[416] Text and context, words and intent, were not merely a dialectic established as a rhetorician's plaything. And even though the orators sensitively used the categories of *scriptu et sententia*, they were still utterly beholden to them. Not Grotius. He could, instead, combine taxonomic rules with the broader implications of interpreting certain kinds of treaty provisions in certain ways. Grotius was providing an approach which was actually keyed to the content of various types of treaty clauses and even the divergent power grades of the States making the agreements. This, as shall be seen, produced new and powerful canons of interpretation for treaties.

Elsewhere in his work Grotius opined that "the contracts of kings and peoples ought [not] to be interpreted according to Roman law, [because] it is [not] apparent that among certain peoples the body of civil law has been received as the law of nations in respect to the matters which concern the law of nations." Id. at 429 (passage ii.16.31). *But cf.* Textor, supra note 411, at 264-65 (passage xxiv. 29 & 30) (who argues that while Grotius is correct, "there is a balance of probability on the side of that King or people who can claim the support of the Roman law, a system which, by the consent of nearly all mankind, is uniquely just.").

[416] DJBaP (1646), supra note 378, at 409 (passage ii.16.1.2) (emphasis added).

NATURAL REASON (1.1)
"correct interpretation" =
inference of intent from the most probable indications (1.2)
basis of word and intent

WORDS

A. *"Grammatical" Canons*
  1. Plain Meanings of Words
      bases of definition
      and ambiguity
  2. Technical Meanings
  3. Related Passages

B. *"Substantive" Canons*
  1. Resort to Textual Conjectures
      a. subject-matter (5)
      b. effects (6)
      c. connected elements (7)
      d. motives (8)

  2. Broad v. Narrow Meanings (10 &
      20.1)
      a. favorable clauses
      b. odious clauses
      c. mixed or median clauses

  3. Avoiding.... (12.2 & 22)
      a. absurdity
      b. injustice
      c. ineffectiveness

IMPLICATIONS
basis of analogy

A. *Reasons for Broadening Terms* (20)

B. *Reasons for Restricting Terms*

  1. Cessation of Reason or Defect of Subject
      Matter (23-25)

  2. Obligations too Burdensome (27)

  3. Intent Incompatible with
      [Natural] Law (26)

  4. Document Self-Contradictory (28 & 29)
      basis of conflicts of law
      "Conflict" Canons

Numbers in parentheses refer to §§ of Book ii, ch. 16 of DJBaP

Figure 2 - Grotius' Schematic on Treaty Interpretation

β. The first great division in Grotius' schematic of treaty interpretation was the handling of the words of the agreement. "If there is no implication which suggests a different conclusion, words are to be understood in their natural sense," he wrote, "not according to the grammatical sense which comes from derivation, but according to current usage."[417] This basic tenet of interpretation was designed to prevent sophistic interpretations of treaties, and Grotius delighted in citing to classical sources where States sought foolishly to liberate themselves from the terms of oaths by giving to words preternatural meanings.[418] Such incidents undoubtedly included Rome's disagreements with Carthage and the Aetolians regarding their respective, improper treaty interpretations (as previously considered in chapter III).

But Grotius also believed that technical terms should be given technical meanings, and in so doing, mentioned the first of the *quaestiones legales*: the problem of definition.[419] Grotius does not dwell long on the problem of defining technical terms, just as the classical rhetoricians realized the futility of crafting canons of interpretation for difficult words.[420] Rather, Grotius recognized that words or sentences could be "interpreted in different ways, that is, admit of several meanings."[421] This is the *constitutio* of "ambiguity."[422]

---

[417] Id. at 409 (passage ii.16.2) (citing 2 Procopius, THE VANDALIC WAR 103 (H.B. Dewing transl. 1916) (Loeb Classical Library rep. 1979) (passage iii.11.4) ("Length of time is not wont to preserve words in the sense originally given them. Things themselves, in fact, are changed as men wish, and men care not at all for the names first assigned to things."). *See also* Ehrlich, supra note 384, at 18.

[418] Id. at 410 (passage ii.16.2) (citing 1 Polybius, supra note 157, at 251-55 (passage ii. 6)). *See also* id. at 421 (passage ii.16.20.2).

[419] *See* id. (passage ii.16.3).

[420] *See* supra § II.ii.

[421] DJBaP (1646), supra note 378, at 411 (passage ii.16.4.1).

[422] *See* id. Grotius mistakenly calls this the "*topic* of ambiguity." Id. (emphasis added). *See* supra § II.ii. Pufendorf would later gloss Grotius' text on ambiguity in treaty interpretation. *See* Pufendorf, supra note 407, at 797 (passage v.12.5) (citing Cicero,

What Grotius concludes here is that within this first category of treaty interpretation — methods which begin with the text of the agreement — recourse can quickly be made to "conjectures" about the text.[423] Of this process, Grotius said, "[t]he Greek rhetoricians call the topic 'concerning the word and the meaning'; and the Latins call it 'of the written word and the meaning of the word'. The elements from which are derived conjectures as to meaning are especially the subject-matter, the effect, and the connexion."[424] Grotius thus superimposed upon the *constitutio legitima* of "*scriptum et sententia*" a new typology of *topoi* and a fresh set of substantive canons.

A. Grotius' checklist of types of conjectures derived from treaty texts was intended to be more helpful in the actual exercise of "correctly" interpreting an agreement than the classical *stasis*. Conjectures based on the subject-matter of the writing were significant, for as Grotius quoted Tertullian: "Speech ought to be explained according to the nature of the matter spoken of."[425] "As regards to effect," Grotius wrote, "especially important is the case when a word taken in its more common meaning produces an effect contrary to reason."[426] Additionally, some conjectures could be generated from textual elements that are connected, "either in origin or in place."[427] Thus two provisions in the same writing, or in different agreements concluded at different times could be used to divine meaning. Or, as Grotius glossed St. Augustine, "They choose out certain portions of the Scriptures in order to deceive the

---

Quintilian and the *Rhetorica ad Herennium*).

[423]   Id. at 411 (passage ii.16.4.2).

[424]   Id.

[425]   Id. at 411 (passage ii.16.5) (quoting Tertullian, *On Modesty*, passage viii). *See also* Ehrlich, supra note 384, at 54-56.

[426]   Id. at 412 (passage ii.16.6).

[427]   Id. (passage ii.16.7).

ignorant, without connecting these with the context which precedes and follows, from which the will and intent of the author can be understood."[428]

When Samuel Pufendorf later had occasion to revisit questions of interpretation in his book *On the Law of Nature and Nations*, he expanded the examples offered by Grotius in support of his three categories of conjectures based on subject-matter, effects, and connected elements.[429] Pufendorf noted that on those occasions "when words, if taken in their plain and simple meaning, will produce an absurd or even no effect, [then] some exception must be made from their more generally accepted sense, that they may not lead to nothingness or absurdity."[430] Likewise, he suggested that

> [a] great light is cast upon the interpretation of obscure phrasings and words if they are compared with others which have some affinity with them; with those passages, for instance, where the same writer discusses a similar subject, or with their antecedents and consequences.[431]

Taken together, Grotius' and Pufendorf's use of textual conjectures form the essence of basic, grammatical canons: (1) the plain meanings of words should be used unless they lead to absurd results; (2) technical words should be given their technical meanings; and (3) a correct interpretation of doubtful words and phrases might be made in relation to the use of the terms or expressions in the same, or related, documents.

B.   If that was all that Grotius proposed, his schematic would have only offered a modest advance in sophistication from that of the classical rhetoricians. Grotius' insight, as already suggested, was to refine the

---

[428]   Id. (quoting Augustine, *Against Adimantus*, passage xiv. 2).

[429]   *See* Pufendorf, supra note 407, at 800-04 (passages v.12.7-9). *See also* Ehrlich, supra note 384, at 21-22.

[430]   Id. at 802 (passage v.12.8) (*citing* 1 Digest, supra note 80, at 13 (1.3.19; Celsus, *Digest* 33 ("When there is an ambiguity in a statute, that sense is to be preferred which avoids an absurdity, especially when by this method the intendment of the act is also secured.")).

[431]   Id. at 803 (passage v.12.9).

topoi of his status system of treaty interpretation one step further by also defining substantive canons of interpretation, covering the likely application of commonly-negotiated clauses in international agreements.   There was an important connection to be made between the grammatical and substantive canons, an affinity that Grotius framed in the following terms: "the fact should be recognized that many words have several meanings, the one narrower, the one broader."[432]

Johann Wolfgang Textor, writing his *Synopsis Juris Gentium* in 1680, construed Grotius' construct as an approach toward

> the presumptive interpretation of treaties, apart from the force of the language used. These presumptions are founded on the reasons for making the treaty, and interpretation by means of them is either restrictive or extensive. A restrictive use of a presumption is the general rule; a presumption is employed extensively only where there is a cogent ground for thinking that the parties contemplated the reason referred to above for making the treaty.[433]

Textor thus perceived in Grotius' text a link between substantive and grammatical canons, as well as a connection between certain subject-matters in treaties and the proper (that is, broad or narrow) construction to be given to ambivalent words and phrases.

Grotius himself provided the critical tie between these two sets of concerns: "it should be noted that of promises which are made[,] some are favourable, some odious, some mixed, and some median."[434]   A favorable promise is one "made on a basis of equality and [to] promote the common advantage."[435]   Likewise, "[o]dious promises are those which impose burden on

---

[432]   DJBaP (1646), supra note 378, at 314 (passage ii.16.9).

[433]   Textor, supra note 411, at 263-64 (passage xxiv. 25). *See also* Ehrlich, supra note 384, at 22.

[434]   DJBaP (1646), supra note 378, at 413 (passage ii.16.10). *See also* Ehrlich, supra note 384, at 23-24 (discussing Barbeyrac's critique of this tripartite distinction in LE DROIT DE LA GUERRE ET DE LA PAIX 500-01 (1724)).

[435]   Id.

one party only; or on one party more than the other."[436]   Mixed and median agreements contain provisions which are both favorable and odious, or "will be considered now favourable and now odious, as the amount of good or of change predominates."[437]   I believe Grotius derived this distinction from Greek and Roman treaty forms, many of which emphasized either parity or subordinated relationships.   Greek *epimachia* or *symmachia* were an example of this duality, as were the Roman *foedera* and *amicitia*.[438]

The culmination of Grotius' schematic for the "distinctions of meanings and promises stated" were the enunciation of "rules ... formulated in regard to interpretations."[439] These rules took the form of a checklist of attributes and a direction for broad or narrow constructions of disputed terms:

> In agreements that are not odious the words should be taken with their full meaning according to current usage; and if there are several meanings, that which is broadest should be chosen....
>
> In more favourable agreements, if the speaker knows the law or avails himself of the advice of lawyers, the words should be taken rather broadly, so as to include even a technical meaning, or meaning imposed by law. But we should not have recourse to meanings that are plainly unsuitable unless otherwise some absurdity or the uselessness of the agreement would result. On the other hand[,] words are to be taken even more strictly than the proper meaning demands if such an interpretation shall be necessary to avoid injustice or absurdity. And even if there be no such necessity, but there is manifest fairness or advantage in this restriction, we ought to confine ourselves to the narrowest limits of the proper meaning unless circumstances persuade to the contrary.[440]

---

[436] Id.

[437] Id.

[438] *See* supra §§ III.i & III.iii.

[439] Id. at 414 (passage ii.16.12).

[440] Id. (passages ii.16.12.1-2) (citation omitted). *See also* Pufendorf, supra note 407, at 806-10 (passage v.12.13).

From this lengthy (and somewhat discursive) passage, the essential attributes of Grotius' substantive canons can be gleaned. The first rule of interpretation is to follow the plain meanings of words. But throughout Grotius' discussion,[441] there is the repetition of the idea that a textualist approach cannot lead to "injust" or "absurd" results, nor even (in less extreme circumstances) compromise the "usefulness" or "advantage" of the agreement. The next theme probed by Grotius was the relative strengths of the States (or parties) making the treaty.   Underlying his exquisitely-wrought distinctions of "odious" and "favorable" agreements was the idea that agreements should be construed in favor of the weaker, or even less legally-sophisticated, party.[442]

γ. It is no surprise, therefore, that when Grotius next addressed "conjectures outside of the meaning of the words in which the promise is contained,"[443] the theme of broad and narrow interpretations persisted. But here there is a twist:

> [n]ow the interpretation which broadens the meanings proceeds with greater difficulty; that which narrows the meaning proceeds more easily.... The difficulty here is much greater than in the case of which we were speaking above, where the *words* admit of a rather broad interpretation, though one less accepted; for here we are in search of a conjecture outside of the words of the promise. Such a conjecture ought to be very certain in order to create the obligation....[444]

So while a textual implication could be made that would widen an obligation under a treaty, such was disfavored when the words conveyed no such burden. Non-textual means of construction were, therefore, fraught with more peril for the interpreter, as one might expect from any exercise in *syllogismus*, the

---

[441]   *See also* DJBaP (1646), supra note 378, at 423 (passage ii.16.22).

[442]   *Accord* Textor, supra note 411, at 262 (passage xxiv. 19) ("As regards odious provisions, a restrictive interpretation must doubtless be adopted....").

[443]   DJBaP (1646), supra note 378, at 421 (passage ii.16.20.1).

[444]   Id. (emphasis added).

constitutio legitima of arguing "beyond the letter of the law."[445]   This was especially so with attempts to impose additional responsibilities on a party, the worst possible form of an "odious" agreement for Grotius.

As for implications which *narrowed* the textual terms of a treaty, Grotius also argued caution. Yet, this circumspection was not entirely shared by later writers, including Pufendorf, who opined: "But when there is a restriction of the interpretation of words in which an undertaking is expressed, it is due either to an original defect in the will of the speaker, or to the repugnancy of some unexpected case to what he had in mind."[446] But here, at least, Grotius identified a number of possible factual conditions that could lead the interpreter to such a conclusion. The first set of these involved situations where the only reason for agreement had ceased or that the actual subject-matter of the treaty was defective or no longer relevant.[447]

In a similar vein,

> [a] second implication will become manifest if, while the literal interpretation may not in itself involve something unlawful, the obligation, in the view of one who judges the matter fairly, shall appear to be burdensome and unbearable, whether the condition of human nature is considered in the abstract, or the person and matter under consideration are brought into comparison with the result of the act itself.[448]

Grotius is clearly referring to the idea of a *clausula rebus sic stantibus*, an implied provision of an agreement which stipulates that the pact becomes voidable if there is an unforeseeable change in circumstances.[449]   Yet, in

---

[445]   *See* supra § II.iv. *Compare* DJBaP (1646), supra note 378, at 421 (passage ii.16.20.2), *with* Pufendorf, supra note 407, at 811 (passage v.16.17).

[446]   Pufendorf, supra note 407, at 815 (passage v.12.19).

[447]   *See* DJBaP (1646), supra note 378, at 424 (passage ii.16.23-25). *See also* Pufendorf, supra note 407, at 816 (passages v.12.19.2-3).

[448]   Id. at 426 (passage ii.16.27.1).

[449]   For the historical background on this doctrine, *see* Vamvoukos, supra note 161.

response to the question "whether promises contain in themselves the tacit condition, 'if matters remain in their present state'," Grotius concluded that they did not, "unless it is perfectly clear that the present state of affairs was included in that sole reason" for the agreement.[450] Grotius was thus uncomfortable, as were classical authorities,[451] with an implication which gives such power to the promisor to liberate himself (or itself) from an otherwise binding obligation: "a certain harm to the promisor is insufficient to prevent the promise from being binding, but the harm should be such as to require that it be considered an exception in view of the nature of the act."[452]

The third set of conditions giving rise to non-textual conjectures occur where "the literal meaning would in any case involve something unlawful, that is, at variance with the precepts of nature, or of divine law."[453] "Of necessity," Grotius concluded, "an exception must be made in such cases, since they are not capable of imposing a legal obligation."[454] And here in his text, Grotius refers specifically to the rhetorical *constitutio legitima* of word and intent,[455] and quotes Quintilian from his *Declamations* as saying that "certain things although not included in any expression of the law are nevertheless by nature excepted."[456]

---

[450]   DJBaP (1646), supra note 378, at 424 (passage ii.16.25.2).

[451]   *See* DJBaP (1646), supra note 378, at 426-27 (passage ii.16.27.3) (quoting 3 Seneca, MORAL ESSAYS 277-79 (John W. Basore transl. 1935) (Loeb Classical Library rep. 1989) (*De Beneficiis*, passage iv.35.2), as saying: "Then I shall break faith, then I shall hear the reproach of inconstancy, if, when all things are the same as they were when I promised, I do not fulfill my promise. Whatever is in any way changed gives me the opportunity to reconsider, and releases my pledge.").

[452]   Id. at 426 (passage ii.16.27.2).

[453]   Id. at 425 (passage ii.16.26.2).

[454]   Id.

[455]   *See* id. at 424-25 (passage ii.16.26.1).

[456]   Quintilian, *Declamations* (passage 315).

The thrust of this section on implicit restrictions of terms in treaties is that there are natural law restraints on State power. Grotius was careful to consider this an aspect of the problem of *verba et voluntas*, and not as an outright conflict in laws. Invocation of this *quaestiones legalis* was reserved for his treatment of the predicament when two parts of the treaty document are in conflict.[457] Here, Grotius reorganized Cicero's discussion of the subject in *De Inventione* and in the *Rhetorica ad Herennium*.[458] Grotius offered these standard "conflict" canons: (1) "that which permits should yield to that which orders," (2) "that which is to be done at a definite time should have preference to that which can be done at any time," (3) "among agreements which are equal in respect to the qualities mentioned, that should be given preference which is most specific and approaches most nearly to the subject at hand; for special provisions are ordinarily more effective than those that are general," (4) "prohibitions which add[] a penalty should be given preference over that which lacks a penalty," (5) "that provision should prevail which has either the more honourable or the more expedient reasons," and (6) "that which was last said should prevail."[459]

Samuel Pufendorf, writing in *On the Law of Nature and Nations*, took especial care in glossing these canons used in resolving textual dissonance. He was particularly interested in rules (3) and (4). And while he endorsed the general rule that specific provisions should prevail over more general ones, Pufendorf disagreed with Grotius' corollary on penalties:

> But what Grotius adds on prohibitions, to the effect that those which have a penalty attached are preferred to such as do not, and those which inflict a graver penalty to those which carry a lighter, is after all not so clear. For a prohibition which is strengthened by no penalty, express or arbitrary, appears to have no force at all.... Therefore, I do not see how this rule can stand, unless it be in the sense that, when a case arises where one of two prohibitions

---

[457] *Compare* DJBaP (1646), supra note 378, at 427 (passage ii.16.28), *with* Pufendorf, supra note 407, at 817-18, 820 (passages v.12.21 & 23).

[458] *See* supra § II.v. Pufendorf, glossing Grotius on this point, freely mixes citations to all the classical rhetorical sources. *See, e.g.,* Pufendorf, supra note 407, at 820 (passage v.12.23.1).

[459] DJBaP, supra note 378, at 427-28 (passage ii.16.29.1).

must be broken, the one the violation of which involves less loss is understood to be permitted.[460]

Additionally, Pufendorf took the opportunity to expand Grotius' natural law principles in treaty construction by offering some additional precepts. Among these is one explicitly couched in natural law terms:

> In the case of laws which emanate from subordinate powers, the law of an inferior power yields to that of a superior, when both cannot be met at the same time. Therefore, it is better to obey God than men (*Acts*, iv. 19); and the commands of kings outweigh those of heads of households.[461]

Other conflicts principles which Pufendorf offered were that "the law of benefaction, when all else is equal, yields to the law of gratitude"[462] and "the closer to bond by which a person is drawn to use, the more do services owed him outweigh those due others, all else being equal."[463]

v. Finally, Grotius and contemporary publicists were, like Greek treaty-makers, preoccupied with preventing sophistic interpretations of treaties made in bad faith by States seeking to liberate themselves from unwanted obligations. This was a consistent theme in the writings of Grotius[464] and contemporary publicists.[465] Alberico Gentili wrote explicitly that "agreements are made in good faith," and that included in them is "not only what is expressed in their actual language, but other things as well which equity and the opinion of a good man are accustomed to understand in addition and to introduce into contracts in

---

[460] Pufendorf, supra note 407, at 822 (passage v.12.23.4).

[461] Id. at 823 (passage v.12.23.9). *See also* Haraszti, supra note 394, at 35.

[462] Id. (passage v.12.23.8).

[463] Id. at 823-24 (passage v.12.23.11) (*quoting* Cicero, De Inventione, supra note 21, at 145-47 (passage ii.49.145-47)).

[464] *See* DJBaP (1646), supra note 378, at 410 (ii.16.2), 421 (passage ii.16.20.2).

[465] *See* Pufendorf, supra note 407, at 801-02 (passage v.12.7), 812-15 (passage v.12.18).

good faith. "[466] Indeed, Gentili went further than this expression of a doctrine of good faith (*pacta sunt servanda*) in treaty-making; he made clear that he would reject all legal rules of interpretation (what he called "subtle discussions on fine points of law"[467]) that would lead to unjust results.

As I have tried to suggest here, however, Grotius rejected this course by fashioning a construct for treaty interpretation which combined rhetorical devices and legal principles, balanced text and intent, and synthesized rules of construction under a first principle of "natural reason." This was completely consistent with Grotius' world view and his intellectual approach to his subject. While the material that Grotius used for *De Jure Belli ac Pacis* was classical or classicist, his scholarship was thoroughly and unmistakably modern.[468] Superbly read, Grotius had the depth of knowledge to collect vast amounts of material and to organize it in rational, and novel, ways. Throughout *De Jure Belli ac Pacis* there is a dramatic tension in the ways that Grotius used classical sources. His dominant approach was deductive. By that I mean that Grotius used evidence of State practice in antiquity to propound rules of international law. His alternative second method was inductive. On these occasions, Grotius devised a categorical approach to characterizing State behavior, and then would fit the classical sources into his preconceived hypothesis.

Grotius eschewed formalism in the construction of international legal doctrines, and, yet, he was also an unrepentant taxonomist. He (along with Samuel Pufendorf)[469] purported to scientifically approach the historical record

---

[466] Gentili, supra note 401, at 191 (passage ii. 13).

[467] Id. at 361 (passage iii. 14).

[468] *But see* some recent writers, most notably David Kennedy, *see* supra note 405, at 5-7, who counts Grotius among "primitive" international legal scholars who devoted "little energy [to] interpretation — even less into methodological elaboration or argument." Id. at 6. Other writers have made much the same point. *See, e.g.*, Elemér Balogh, *The Traditional Element in Grotius' Conception of International Law*, 7 N.Y.U. L. Q. 261 (1929); Basdevant, supra note 387, at 125; Louis Le Fur, *La Théorie du Droit Natural Depuis le XVIIe Siècle et la Doctrine Moderne*, 18 R.C.A.D.I. 263, 310-19 (1927).

[469] *See* Hyland, supra note 207, at 422 (discussing the influence of Erhard Weigel of Jena, philosopher, mathematician, and astronomer on Pufendorf).

of State practice, although he was prepared to modify (and even distort) that evidence in order to fashion rules of enduring significance to modern nations. Grotius thus embodied the modern ambivalence of legal scholarship. He sought to balance the legitimacy of law as descriptive science with its power as social theory. Grotius' dilemma is ours today as international law scholars: divining rules which are descriptive of how States really behave and, yet, are also binding on States irrespective of their will.

Toward the end of this "neo-classical" period of international law theory, however, substantial disillusionment arose with respect to a jurisprudence which combined natural law principles with scientific rationalism and a sense of human progress. Grotius' and Pufendorf's work, coming near the end or just after the Thirty Years War, contained some strong elements of skepticism about State behavior. Pufendorf reacted strongly to the work of Thomas Hobbes and, in *On the Law of Nature and of Nations*, attempted to refute the proposition that international relations was merely a state of nature.[470]

The antidote to Hobbesian disenchantment was the embrace of a strong social contract theory of State relations, one premised on the principle of States making their own positive law through treaties which were to be observed in good faith. Although some scholars disagree whether Grotius or Pufendorf can be properly credited with enunciating the principle of *pacta sunt servanda* in international law,[471] it is manifest that it was a necessary corollary for intelligible rules of treaty interpretation. After all, there would be no point in having autonomous rules for construing disputed treaty texts unless it was widely believed that the obligations contained in treaties were to be performed in good faith.

---

[470] *See* Pufendorf, supra note 407, at 165-78 (passages ii.2.5, 9 & 12). *See also* Hans Welzel, DIE NATURRESCHTSLEHRE SAMUEL PUFENDORFS 31-51 (1958); Hyland, supra note 207, at 423. *See also* Kingsbury, supra note 380.

[471] *See* Hyland, supra note 207, at 425 (arguing that "Grotius was so indebted to the classical jurists that he continued to conceive of the issue, as they did, in terms of identifying the circumstances that render a promise binding. The fact that Grotius did not himself formulate the *pacta* maxim suggests that more fragile view of the social contract, such as Pufendorf's, is the true foundation of the maxim.").

Ironically, though, the embrace of the idea of *pacta sunt servanda* forced the removal of public international law theory to a more positivist basis, much less dependent on "natural reason." And, as a collateral consequence of this, scholarly reliance on classical thought and political experience — the repository of that reason — came to be decreased. In works following Grotius and Pufendorf, citations to classical materials markedly abated. So, by the time of Bynkershoek's *Quaestionum Juris Publici Libri Duo* in 1737 and Emmerich de Vattel's *Le Droit des Gens* in 1758, such references were notably absent, as were direct attributions to classical rhetoricians (and their theories of *stasis*) in the fashioning of rules for treaty interpretation.[472]

Nevertheless, the influence of Grotius' unique construct on treaty interpretation persisted, although on the strength of his own prestige as a publicist rather than because of the putative authority of classical experience. Most of the rules Grotius propounded in the construction of treaty texts were adopted by Emmerich de Vattel, although mostly without attribution and certainly without any sense of the underlying classical authority for the interpretive canons.[473]

Although Vattel seconded Grotius' view that rules of interpretation are "founded on reason, and authorized by the law of nature,"[474] Vattel's interpretive jurisprudence is best remembered for his "golden rule": Il n'est pas permis d'interpreter qui n'est pas besoin interpretation (It is not permissible to interpret

---

[472] *But see* Bynkershoek, supra note 411, at 63-64 (passage i. 9) (discussing sophistic treaty interpretations but directly citing only Grotius); Emmerich de Vattel, LE DROIT DES GENS, OU PRINCIPES DE LA LOI NATURELLE, APPLIQUÉS À LA CONDUITE ET AUX AFFAIRES DES NATIONS ET DES SOUVERAINS (The Law of Nations, or Principles of Natural Law as Applied to the Conduct and Affairs of States and Sovereignties) 191 (1758) (Charles G. Fenwick transl. Classics of International Law series) (passage ch. xv, § 233) (citing classical materials, but through Grotius).

[473] Exceptions can be found in isolated references to a handful of classical sources. *See, e.g.*, Vattel, supra note 472, at 255 (passage bk. II, ch. xvii, § 285) (Dig. 1.3(de legibus).24), 258 (passage ii.xvii.290) (Cicero, *pro Caecina*); 259 (ii.17.292) (Seneca); 264 (ii.xvii.301) (Quintilian).

[474] Vattel, supra note 472, at 244 (ii.xvii.262).

what has no need of interpretation).[475] This ringing call for textualism is then countermanded by a bewildering pastiche of maxims,[476] without any structure or schematic of analysis. Indeed, the sense of utter interpretive confusion is made complete in Vattel's closing words of his disquisition on the topic:

> All the rules contained in this chapter ought to be combined together, and the interpretation made in such manner as to accord with them all, so far as they are applicable to the case. When these rules appear to clash, they reciprocally counterbalance and limit each other, according to their strength and importance, and according as they more particularly belong to the case in question.[477]

Despite all of this, Vattel's treatise exercised inordinate influence on the subsequent consideration of treaty interpretation problems by international law publicists.[478] It also swayed early Republican thought in the United States.[479]

---

[475] *See* id. at 461 (bk. II, ch. XII, §§ 156-57). *See also* Sir Fortunato Dwarris, GENERAL TREATISE ON STATUTES 126-32 (Am. ed. Platt Potter ed. 1871) (collecting Vattel's interpretive maxims). For discussion of Vattel's "non"-canon, *see Kingdom of Saudi Arabia v. Arabian American Oil Co.*, 27 I.L.R. 117, 173-74 (1958) (Sauser-Hall, Badawi/Hassan & Habachy, arbs.).

[476] For a collection of Vattel's interpretive maxims, *see* Dwarris, supra note 475, at 126-31. *See also* Degan, supra note 400, at 39-41; Ehrlich, supra note 384, at 25-28; Haraszti, supra note 394, at 35-37; Ivan Sergeevitch Pereterski, TOLKOVANIE MEJDOUNARUDNYH DOGOVOROV [Interpretation of International Treaties] 143-44 (1959); Charles Fairman, *The Interpretation of Treaties*, 20 TRANSACTIONS OF THE GROTIUS SOC'Y 123, 129-30 (1935). *But see*, Francis Stephen Ruddy, INTERNATIONAL LAW IN THE ENLIGHTENMENT: THE BACKGROUND OF EMMERICH DE VATTEL'S LE DROIT DES GENS 204-10 (1975) (who claims that Vattel's "presentation bore the marked systematization of Wolff.").

[477] Vattel, supra note 472, at 274 (ii.xvii.322).

[478] *See* Ruddy, supra note 476, at 281-310.

[479] This was acknowledged by James Kent in his 1 COMMENTARIES ON AMERICAN LAW 18 (1826). In 1775, Benjamin Franklin acknowledged receipt of three copies of Vattel's new edition, in French, and remarked that the book "has been continually in the hands of the members of our Congress now sitting. . . ." 2 F. Wharton, UNITED STATES

In precisely the same fashion, classical influences on the Anglo-American law for interpreting legal texts persisted, even as references to, and acknowledgments of, that classical tradition waned from the late eighteenth century.

REVOLUTIONARY DIPLOMATIC CORRESPONDENCE 64 (1889). Vattel's work was cited by Thomas Jefferson, Alexander Hamilton, and John Marshall. *See* 3 WRITINGS OF THOMAS JEFFERSON 237 (H.A. Washington ed. 1883); 9 id. 134-35; 16 id. 185-86; 4 THE WORKS OF ALEXANDER HAMILTON 315, 355, 380, 410, 435, 436, 451, 458 (Henry Cabot Lodge ed. 1904); 5 id. at 29, 36, 41, 44, 272, 383, 430-36, 438, 442, 477; 6 id. 87, 110, 117, 131, 224; 7 THE PAPERS OF JOHN MARSHALL 312 (Charles F. Hobson ed. 1993). *See also,* Benjamin M. Ziegler, THE INTERNATIONAL LAW OF JOHN MARSHALL (1939).

VIII THE ANGLO-AMERICAN RECEPTION

i. In the Anglo-American legal tradition,[480] humanist legal science ran a different course than on the continent,[481] with somewhat surprising results for the law of interpretation. The process of "genuine interpretation" — the phrase that John Austin used to distinguish the construction of legal texts from the wider phenomenon of the organic growth of the common law[482] — was seen more as a positivistic process of developing and applying canons of construction.[483] And, somewhat peculiarly, Anglo-American practice has been to construct different

---

[480] For more on how this tradition was influenced by continental jurisprudence, *see* the sources cited in Berman & Reid, supra note 365, at 30 n.55.

[481] *See* Harold J. Berman, *The Origins of Historical Jurisprudence: Coke, Selden, Hale*, 103 YALE L. J. 1651, 1652-73 (1994); Barbara Shapiro, *Law and Science in Seventeenth-Century England*, 21 STAN. L. REV. 727 (1969).

[482] John Austin, LECTURES ON JURISPRUDENCE 578-80, 629-31, 991-93 (5th ed. 1911). *See also* Edwin Charles Clark, PRACTICAL JURISPRUDENCE 235-42 (1883); Robert J. Farley, *Interpretation Re-interpreted*, 11 TULANE L. REV. 266 (1937); Frederick J. deSloovère, *The Equity and Reason of a Statute*, 21 CORN. L. Q. 604 (1936); Roscoe Pound, *Spurious Interpretation*, 7 COLUM. L. REV. 379 (1907).

[483] *See* Schiller, supra note 238, at 764 (who suggests that the strong move toward canons of construction was a reaction to Elizabethan casuistry, for more on which *see* supra note 369 and accompanying text). *See also* Theodore Sedgwick & John Norton Pomeroy, TREATISE ON THE RULES OF INTERPRETATION AND APPLICATION OF STATUTORY AND CONSTITUTIONAL LAW 190-328 (2d ed. 1874).

rules of interpretation for each kind of legal text,[484] so that the canons of statutory construction would be very different than those for, say, contracts or treaties.

The legal science of interpretation for English and American jurists in the eighteenth and nineteenth centuries meant a wholesale rejection of equitable interpretation[485] and a rigorous adoption of substantive rules of construction.[486] They also manifested themselves, at least for statutory construction, with the passage of legislative enactments which purported to give "authentic" interpretations of words and phrases found in the laws.[487] In English practice,

---

[484] *See* Schiller, supra note 238, at 747 (citing Richard R. Powell, *Construction of Written Instruments*, 14 IND. L. J. 199, 204 (1939)).

[485] *See* supra note 369 and accompanying text. *See also* Baade, supra note 106, at 78-81.

[486] William Blackstone, in his *Commentaries* listed ten principal, substantive canons of construction, including such matters as restrictive constructions for penal statutes and broad interpretations for remedial statutes. *See* 2 Matthew Hale, A HISTORY OF THE PLEAS OF THE CROWN 335 (rep. 1980); 1 William Blackstone, COMMENTARIES *87-92 (discussing *Heydon's* case, in which an English court construed a 1547 statute, 1 Edw. VI, c. 12, denying benefit of clergy for the stealing of "horses" to be inapplicable to a defendant who stole just one horse). *See also* Geoffrey P. Miller, *Pragmatics and Maxims of Interpretation*, 1990 Wis. L. Rev. 1179, 1189-90; John Choon Yoo, Comment, *Marshall's Plan: The Early Supreme Court and Statutory interpretation*, 101 YALE L.J. 1607, 1609-10, 1626-30 (1992).

The reaction against equitable interpretation was particularly strong in post-Revolution America. *See* Gordon S. Wood, CREATION OF THE AMERICAN REPUBLIC, 1776-1787, at 10, 302-04 (1969); Yoo, supra, at 1610-11.

[487] *See, e.g.*, Act of July 30, 1947, ch. 388, 61 Stat. 633 (1947), *codified at* 1 U.S.C.A. §§ 1-6; The Interpretation Act, 1889, 52-53 Vict. ch. 63. *See also* Jolowicz, Foundations, supra note 291, at 11. For a modern, American version of authentic interpretation, *see* Model Statutory Construction Act, 14 U.L.A. 513 (1993). *See also* state codifications of such canons. Minn. Stat. ch. 645; Pennsylvania Statutory Construction Act, 1 Pa. Consol. Stat. §§ 1921-28.

a textual "plain meaning" rule[488] was only broken when the literal interpretation made caused an "absurd" result[489] or when it deviated from the manifest purpose of the law in addressing some problem or "mischief" left from the common law.[490]

These canons were far more rigid than the taxonomic rules invented by the rhetors or the intuitive rules of the classical Roman jurists. But they also sometimes reflected the principle of "beneficial" interpretation,[491] in which canons of interpretation were established to benefit different classes of people in disputes over rights. Lastly, the sense of the English opinions was that legal interpretation was fundamentally a juridical exercise, and this view went so far that the actual, stated intent of legislators in making the law was ignored.[492]

---

[488] *See* Sussex Peerage Case, 11 Cl. & F. 85, 143, 8 Eng. Rep. 1034 (H.L. 1844) ("If the words of the statute are in themselves precise and unambiguous, there no more can be necessary than to expound those words in their natural and ordinary sense.") (Tindal, C.J.); *Vacher & Sons, Ltd. v. London Soc'y of Compositers*, [1913] App. Cas. 107, 121-22 (H.L.) (Atkinson, L.J.) ("If the language of a statute be plain, admitting of only one meaning, the Legislature must be taken to have meant and intended what it has plainly expressed, *[even if] it should lead to absurd or mischievous results.*") (emphasis added); *Hill v. East & West India Dock Co.*, 9 App. Cas. 448, 464-65 (H.L. 1884) (Bramwell, L.J.) (to the same effect).

[489] This was known as the "golden rule" of statutory construction in *Grey v. Pearson*, 6 H.L.C. 61, 106, 10 Eng. Rep. 1216, 1234 (H.L. 1857) (Wensleydale, L.J.); *Becke v. Smith*, 2 M. & W. 191, 195, 150 Eng. Rep. 724, 726-27 (Exch. 1836) (Wensleydale, L.J.). *See also* Baade, supra note 106, at 90-91; Elmer A. Driedger, *Statutes: The Mischieveous Literal Golden Rule*, 59 CAN. B. J. 780 (1981); Ian MacLean, supra note 341, at 128.

[490] *See* 1 William Blackstone, COMMENTARIES *87-88 (discussing rule in Heydon's Case, 3 Coke Rep. 7a, 7b-8a, 76 Eng. Rep. 637, 638-39 (K.B. 1584)). *See also* LaRue, supra note 368, at 742-49.

[491] *See* P.B. Maxwell, INTERPRETATION OF STATUTES 68-70 (10th ed. 1953). *See also* Jolowicz, Foundations, supra note 291, at 14-15.

[492] *See Sheffield v. Ratcliffe*, Hob. 334, 336, 80 Eng. Rep. 475, 486 (K.B. 1616); *Millar v. Taylor*, 4 Burr. 2303, 98 Eng. Rep. 201 (K.B. 1769). *See also* 1 William Blackstone, *Commentaries* *70-71.

For more on the controversy about the use of legislative intent in the seventeenth

ii. Each of these types of canons had classical analogues,[493] as well as a strong basis in natural law and reasoning. This was deliberately acknowledged by the leading English thinker on problems of legal interpretation in the eighteenth century: Thomas Rutherforth. His writings really did condition subsequent jurisprudential attacks on canons of interpretation, censures made by such positivist writers as John Austin (in England) and historical jurists as Friedrich Carl von Savigny (on the Continent).

α. Thomas Rutherforth's *Institutes of Natural Law* appeared for the first time in print in 1756, although it was possibly drafted earlier.[494] Rutherforth was a professor in the University of Cambridge, an ecclesiastic fully schooled in the civil law tradition in England.[495]   His volume was self-consciously modeled on Grotius' *De Jure Belli a Pacis*.[496] And just as Grotius had an extended treatment on treaty interpretation, so, too, did Rutherforth.[497] But unlike Pufendorf's and Vattel's writing on the subject, which really was derivative of Grotius' writing, Rutherforth made a fresh start.

---

and eighteenth centuries in England, *compare* Baade, supra note 106, at 77-78; Hans W. Baade, *"Original Intent" in Historical Perspective: Some Critical Glosses*, 69 TEX. L. REV. 1001, 1006-13 (1991); and id., *"Original Intention": Raoul Berger's Fake Antique*, 70 N.C. L. REV. 1523 (1992); *with* Raoul Berger, *Original Intent: A Response to Hans Baade*, 70 TEX. L. REV. 1535, 1536 (1991).

[493] For beneficial rules of construction, *see* supra notes 217-18 and accompanying text. For technical ("authentic") rules of interpretation (such as that concerning number and gender), *see* supra note 309 with text. See also Frost, Introduction, supra note 18, at 628-30.

[494] The edition used here is T. Rutherforth, INSTITUTES OF NATURAL LAW (2d Am. ed. 1832).

[495] *See* Degan, supra note 400, at 42.

[496] *See* id. at frontispiece ("Being the Substance of a Course of Lectures on Grotius De Jure Belli et [sic] Pacis").

[497] *See* Rutherforth, supra note 494, at 404-35 (bk. II, ch. vii).

Rutherforth's analysis began with a first principle of interpretation: "to ascertain our claims, as they arise from promises ... and our obligations, as they arise from instituted laws, is to collect the meaning and intention of the promiser ... or lawmaker, from some outward sign or marks."[498] This was an intelligible paraphrase of Grotius.[499] But Rutherforth went on with a decidedly different taxonomy flowing from that first principle. He reasoned that all interpretation was either "literal, rational [or] mixed."[500]   Literal interpretation was "collect[ing] the intention of the ... writer from his words only."[501] This was textualism. "Rational" interpretation arises when the "words do not express ... intention perfectly, but either exceed it or fall short of it, so that we are to collect it from probable or rational conjectures...."[502] This is intentionalism. Finally, mixed interpretation is needed when "words, although they do express ... intention, when they are rightly understood, are in themselves of doubtful meaning, and we are forced to the like conjectures to find out what sense" the words are used.[503] As Rutherforth made clear, mixed interpretation looked to the underlying purpose or teleology of the legal writing.[504]

This schematic of text-intent-teleology has come to be one of the primary modes of modern discourse about legal interpretation. And, like Grotius, Rutherforth relied on classical sources for the reasoning he provided. Indeed,

---

[498]   Id. at 404 (ii.vii.1).

[499]   *See* supra note 412 with text.

[500]   *See* Rutherforth, supra note 494, at 407 (passage ii.vii.3).

[501]   Id.

[502]   Id.

[503]   Id. at 408.

[504]   *See* id. at 412-19 (passages ii.vii.6-9). *See also* Degan, supra note 400, at 44-45.

perhaps more so than Grotius, Rutherforth hinged his argument on classical *rhetorical* sources.[505]

β.   In short, Rutherforth was trying to provide a sensible justification for rules of interpretation based on natural reason.   His was a defense of classical canons of interpretation from attacks that would develop on no less than three fronts.   One was the kind of unreflective work of such publicists as Vattel, who tried to strip away natural law and classical references in his writing.   Rutherforth tried to restore system and integrity to rules which Vattel had popularized, and, at the same time, bowdlerized.

The second front of attack was far more formidable, though.   It was reflected in the intensely positivistic writings of John Austin.   The problem of legal interpretation was only briefly mentioned in Austin's *Lectures on Jurisprudence*, and that remark was confined to his critique of a form of equity that "by which the defective but clear provisions of a statute are extended to a case which those provisions have omitted."[506]   This, Austin sneered, is "judicial legislation disguised with the name of interpretation,"[507] a sentiment which has echoed to this day.[508]

If all Austin had been reacting to was the then-discredited Elizabethan notion of equitable interpretation,[509] his remarks would have passed largely unnoticed.   But in his *Lectures*, Austin reserved some of his invective for

---

[505]   *See, e.g.*, id. at 413 (citing the *controversiae* of the testator and gift of plate), 414 (Labeo and Antiochus and cutting the ships in two), 421 (the causa Curiana), 423 (Senecan *controversiae* on salvage), 427 (Cicero and the law of the Rhodians), 431 (*controversiae* of a woman killing a tyrant).

[506]   2 Austin, supra note 482, at 274 (1863).

[507]   Id.

[508]   *See* infra § IX.

[509]   *See* supra note 369 and accompanying text.

Grotius, to whom he attributed this "species of pretended interpretation."[510] The connection between *aequitas* and interpretation *ex ratione legis* was derived, Austin conceded, from antiquity. This troubled Austin. He was happy to chide Grotius, but less willing to enter a disputation with Cicero and the classical jurists.[511]

In two notes published after his death,[512] it was manifest that Austin was, in effect, revisiting the great debate between Roman jurists and rhetoricians: whether the letter or the spirit of the law should be observed.[513] Austin was even willing to propose a thoroughly modern compromise: "the reason of a statute and the actual intention of the lawgiver oftener coincide or tally."[514] In short, the divide between text and intent could be bridged: "the literal meaning of the words, the reason of a statute with the actual intention of the lawgiver are commonly styled by the moderns 'the spirit of the laws' by the Roman jurists, and the moderns who adopt their language...."[515] The danger, Austin warned, was to give too much power of interpretation to judges who, by using such classical rhetorical tricks as analogy and syllogism,[516] could subvert the true meaning of the legislation.

---

[510]   2 Austin, supra note 482, at 276 (1863).

[511]   *See* id. at 377.

[512]   *See* 3 Austin, supra note 482, at 231 (1863) ("Note on Interpretation (Proper and Improper)"), 249 ("Excursus on Analogy (Analogical Reasoning and Syllogism)").

[513]   *See* supra § V.

[514]   3 Austin, supra note 482, at 236 (1863). *Cf.* Blackstone, supra note 486, at *59 ("The fairest and most rational method to interpret the will of the legislator, is by exploring his intentions at the time when the law was made, by signs the most natural and probable. And the signs are either the words, the context, the subject matter, the effects and consequences, or the spirit and reason of the law.").

[515]   Id.

[516]   *See* id. at 249, 254 (quoting Quintilian).

γ. Austin also had his own worries, for developing on the Continent was a newfangled historical jurisprudence, expounded by the German writer, Savigny, that posed a real threat to his positivist theories of legal interpretation. In Savigny's *System des heutigen römischen Rechts* (System of the Modern Roman Law), first published in 1840, there was an extended treatment of problems of legal interpretation.[517] Savigny began with the proposition that "Interpretation is an art, and education for it is furnished by the admirable models of ancient and modern times of which we possess a great wealth.... [and] this art ... admits of being imparted or acquired by means of rules."[518] And, it should be noted, Savigny's exposition of the art of interpretation was achieved by a close reading of the Justinianic canon of documents, particularly the *Digest*.

So far, Savigny's thinking would hardly be seen at variance with that of Grotius, Pufendorf or Rutherforth. But the subversive part of the Savigny's philosophy of legal interpretation lay just below the surface. For Savigny made a strong connection between interpretation of a statute (or any legal text) and customary law. He believed that customary practices could, and should, inform the interpretation of legal texts.[519] When he came to develop his schematic of interpretation, Savigny discerned four "elements": *grammatical* ("expl[aining] ... the phraseology of the law-giver"); *logical* (upon which "depends ... the logical relation [that the] several parts of the [text] stand to one another"); *historical* (examining the "jural relation presented [in the text] as determined by the rules of law, at the time... in question); and *systematic* (concerned with the "innate connection in which all the institutions and rules of law are bound up

---

[517] Reference will be made here to SYSTEM OF THE MODERN ROMAN LAW (William Holloway transl., 1867) (rep. 1978). The material on interpretation appears in the first volume ("Law-Sources"), fourth chapter ("Interpretation of Written Laws"). *See also* Karl Heinrich Friauf, *Techniques for the Interpretation of Constitutions in German Law*, in PROCEEDINGS OF THE FIFTH INTERNATIONAL SYMPOSIUM ON COMPARATIVE LAW 9, 11-13 (1968).

[518] Id. at 170 (passage i.4.32).

[519] See id. at 168 (passage i.4.32).

into a great unity").[520] But, unlike Vattel's interpretive maxims, Savigny's elements were "not... four species of interpretation, among which one may select according to taste and pleasure but they are different modes of activity which must work in unity, if the interpretation is to be reached."[521]

Savigny went on in his analysis with a pathology of various interpretive problems, his own gloss on the classical rhetoricians' *constitutio legitima*. Laws could be found defective, Savigny wrote, either because of indefinite expression ("which guides to no complete thought") or erroneous expression (where "the thought... is different from the actual thought of the law").[522] There were three cures for such defects. The first was to compare the indefinite or erroneous expression with another passage of the same law, or a provision from another statute.[523] The second was to look to the "ground of the law," which was Savigny's shorthand for the use of *aequitas* in interpretation.[524] The applicability of this solution was "rather dependent," Savigny wrote,

> upon the degree of certainty with which we know [the ground of the statute] and upon the degree of its relationship to the contents [of the law]. If one of these considerations is unfavorable, it may still be almost always applied to the removal of the first sort of defects (indefiniteness), less frequently however to that of the second (the erroneous expression).[525]

---

[520] See id. at 172 (passage i.4.33). For the intellectual origins of this division, *see* id. at 258-60 (passage i.4.50) (discussing work of Christopher H. Eckhard, HERMENEUTICA JURIS (1802)). For the enduring influence of Savigny's schematic, *see* Haraszti, supra note 394, at 80 & n.4.

[521] Id. at 173 (passage i.4.33).

[522] Id. at 179 (passage i.4.35).

[523] *See* id. at 180.

[524] *See* id. For more on *aequitas*, *see also* id. at 184 (passage i.4.37), 192 (passage i.4.37).

[525] Id. at 181 (passage i.4.35).

The third answer was to embrace "the intrinsic value of the result" of the interpretation. But this, according to Savigny, was "the most questionable of all remedies because... the interpreter [thereby]... oversteps the limits of his occupation and intrude[s] upon that of the legislator."[526]

This last-quoted caution was of little comfort to Austin and other interpretive positivists or textualists. Savigny's theory of "ground of the law" or *aequitas* provided substantial liberty to the interpreter to depart from the imperfect commands of the legislator. This was made clear in Savigny's treatment of conflicts between separate statutes. When laws are read together, Savigny suggested, and yet still incompletely covered legal situations, the interpreter was invited to fill the gaps. Savigny relied heavily on the Roman rhetorical concept of *syllogismus* or analogy for resolving such situations.[527] Likewise, in cases of contradictory laws, the interpreter was permitted to engage in either (1) systematic reasoning, in which the texts are reconciled, or (2) historical harmonization, in which it is determined which law really was favored by the legislator.[528]

γ Savigny's jurisprudence was free-form interpretation, giving substantial discretion to judges. It is no wonder that John Austin reacted so violently to it. Yet, interestingly enough, both Austin and Savigny shared an antipathy towards what they perceived were arid, mechanical maxims of interpretation. Whether such canons were sensitively explained (as in Grotius, Pufendorf, and Rutherforth) or ridiculously simplified and distorted (in Vattel), such rules were unlikely to satisfy either positivistic textualists like Austin or writers like Savigny concerned with the "innate connection in which all the institutions and rules of law are bound up into a great unity." So, by the middle of the nineteenth century, the classically-derived canons of interpretation for legal texts were under intellectual siege from both outside and within.

iii. On the other side of the Atlantic, the classical canons fared better. The political theory behind the canons of construction were recognized as having

---

[526] Id.

[527] *See* id. at 235 & n.(a) (passage i.4.46) (citing Quintilian).

[528] *See* id. at 221-24 (passage i.4.44).

strong classical roots, and the influence of Roman republican ideas (as largely transmitted through Cicero's writings) on the founders of the American Republic being undoubted and well-documented.[529]

The Framers were much concerned with the process of law-making and the problems of statutory interpretation. James Madison, in *Federalist No. 37*, noted that "[a]ll new laws, though penned with the greatest technical skill and passed on the fullest and most mature deliberation, are considered as more or less obscure and equivocal, until their meaning be liquidated and ascertained by a series of particular discussions and adjudications."[530]   This comment acknowledged the understanding of the Founding Generation that laws are inherently obscure, and it is up to judges to give them content and application. The question was how this was fairly to be achieved.

Alexander Hamilton, writing in favor of the use of canons of construction in *The Federalist* said that they were based on the "nature and the reason" of the interpretive process.[531]   "The rules of legal interpretation," he wrote, "are rules of *common sense*, adopted by the courts in the construction of the laws. The true test ... of a just application of them is its conformity to the source from which they are derived."[532]   The canons would be applied to control "unjust and partial laws" by "mitigating the severity and confining the operation

---

[529]   *See* Robert A. Ferguson, LAW AND LETTERS IN AMERICAN CULTURE 72-84 (1984); Richard M. Gummere, THE AMERICAN COLONIAL MIND AND THE CLASSICAL TRADITION (1963); Carl J. Richard, THE FOUNDERS AND THE CLASSICS (1994); John C. Rolfe, CICERO AND HIS INFLUENCE (1963); Mortimer N.S. Sellers, AMERICAN REPUBLICANISM: ROMAN IDEOLOGY IN THE UNITED STATES CONSTITUTION (1994); Wood, supra note 334, at 1-9, 67. For further reflections on Cicero's influence, *see* the essays in CICERO (T.A. Dorsey ed. 1965); Frost, Introduction, supra note 18, at 630-33; Clinton W. Keyes, *Original Elements in Cicero's Ideal Constitution*, 42 AJP 309 (1921).

[530]   FEDERALIST NO. 37, at 229 (James Madison) (Clinton Rossiter ed. 1961).

[531]   THE FEDERALIST No. 78, at 468 (Alexander Hamilton) (Clinton Rossiter ed. 1961).

[532]   THE FEDERALIST No. 83, at 496 (Alexander Hamilton) (original emphasis). For an explication of reason and common sense in statutory interpretation, *see* Paul W. Kahn, *Reason and Will in the Origins of American Constitutionalism*, 98 YALE L.J. 449 (1989).

of such laws."[533] It was to this extent — and this extent only — that the courts were to be given the power to interpret statutory enactments.[534]

Hamilton was not just espousing a theory of judicial review; he was restating Cicero's notion that individualized justice required that judges "not only to read [the] law, which any child could do, but to comprehend it with the mind and interpret [the lawmaker's] intentions."[535]   Likewise, Hamilton was responding to Montaigne's influential point, criticizing those "who thought by a multiplicity of laws to bridle the authority of judges, cutting up their meat for them. [Such men do] not realize that there is as much freedom and latitude in

---

[533] THE FEDERALIST No. 78, at 470. Hamilton mentioned elsewhere the specific canon of narrow construction for penal statutes. Id. No. 81, at 483 (Alexander Hamilton). *See also United States v. Wiltberger*, 18 U.S. (5 Wheat.) 76, 95 (1820). *See also* Ross E. Davies, *A Public Trust Exception to the Rule of Lenity*, 63 U. CHI. L. REV. 1175 (1996).

Hamilton was not alone among the Framing generation in espousing these views. *See* 2 THE WORKS OF JAMES WILSON 478, 486 (Robert G. McCloskey ed. 1967) (supporting equitable interpretation of statutes). *See also* Robert J. Pushaw, Jr., *Justiciability and Separation of Powers: A Neo-Federalist Approach*, 81 CORNELL L. REV. 393, 425 & n.151 (1996).

[534] *See* David F. Epstein, THE POLITICAL THEORY OF *THE FEDERALIST* 185-92 (1984).

This sense of judicial review — as manifested through equitable interpretations of statutes — was a constant subject of debate in nineteenth century American jurisprudence. *See Simonton v. Barrell*, 21 Wend. 362 (N.Y. 1839) (supporting a broad use of equitable readings).   Taken to its logical extreme, it would mean that judges could rewrite the clear terms of statutes in order to achieve equitable results.   That was why the doctrine was so heavily criticized in the United States.   See supra note 486 and accompanying text.   The backlash was reflected in such cases as *Brown v. Somerville*, 8 Md. 444, 456 (1855) ("The words of an Act may be disregarded where that is necessary to arrive at the interpretation of the law-makers but not where the Act admits of only one interpretation."). *See also* G.A. Endlich, A COMMENTARY ON THE INTERPRETATION OF STATUTES (1888); Henry Campbell Black, A HANDBOOK ON THE CONSTRUCTION AND INTERPRETATION OF THE LAWS (1896); Joel Prentiss Bishop, COMMENTARIES ON THE WRITTEN LAWS AND THEIR INTERPRETATION (1882); deSloovère, supra note 482, at 597-98.

[535] Cicero, de Inventione, supra note 21, at 307 (passage ii.47.139). *See also* supra note 106 and accompanying text.

the interpretation of the laws as in their creation."[536] In giving judges a limited power of interpretation, as long as it was exercised consistent with established canons of construction, Hamilton hoped to answer fears of an unelected, anti-democratic, and un-restrained judiciary. And, in order to grant legitimacy to these canons, Hamilton had to provide a standard by which to measure their validity: "the true test of the just application of them is ... conformity to the sources from which they were derived...." The source perceived by Hamilton was right reason as tested by classical experience.

James Madison, another great figure from the Framing Generation, also had occasion to comment on methods of interpretation for legal texts. Writing during the First Congress in 1791, Madison was drawn into a contentious debate involving constitutional interpretation and the federal government's power, under the Constitution, to charter a national bank. Likening constitutional interpretation more to contractual construction (as between coequal parties), rather than like statutory interpretation, Madison developed some "rules" as "preliminaries to right interpretation."[537] Madison generally observed that when the "meaning" of a provision was "doubtful, it is fairly triable by its consequences."[538] "In controverted cases," Madison went on, "the meaning of the parties to the instrument, if to be collected by reasonable evidence, is a proper guide."   And included in that "reasonable evidence" are the "contemporary and concurrent expositions ... of the parties."[539]

Whether or not Madison's statement was a license for originalism in American constitutional interpretation — although hotly debated in the modern

---

[536] Montaigne, *Of Experience* (1588), in THE COMPLETE ESSAYS OF MONTAIGNE 815 (David M. Frame transl. 1943 rep. 1971).

[537] *See* M. St. Clair Clarke & D.A. Hall, LEGISLATIVE AND DOCUMENTARY HISTORY OF THE BANK OF THE UNITED STATES 39-45 (Washington 1832) (rep. 1967) [hereinafter "1791 House debate"].

[538] Id.

[539] Id. at 40-41.

literature[540] — is quite beside the point here. So is the question of whether the Framers saw the Constitution as, in essence, a treaty concluded between sovereign and consenting state parties. What is significant is the understanding of the Framers of the role of canons of construction, this time in the context of the Constitution. Elbridge Gerry, speaking in the same debate, rejected Madison's *ad hoc* use of interpretive canons as "being made for the occasion," and preferred, instead, the "sanctioned" authority of Blackstone's rule of statutory construction: looking to the "intention" of the legislator, "by the signs most natural and probable ... the words, the context, the subject matter, the effect and consequences, or the spirit and reason of the law."[541] All of this indicates the firm reception of canons of interpretation into American legal consciousness just after the Revolution. Whether the vector of transmission was directly through classical sources (Cicero being the favored author), or through such intermediary sources as Vattel, Rutherforth or Blackstone, the result was the same.

Despite this understanding of the Framing Generation, a backlash against these rule-based doctrines of interpretation was inevitable. A consensus in Anglo-American jurisprudence began to develop that the object of genuine interpretation was to construe legal texts according to the true sense and intention of the drafters.[542] But, that being said, the juristic debate broke down

---

[540] *See, e.g.,* Jack N. Rakove, ORIGINAL MEANINGS: POLITICS AND IDEAS AND THE MAKING OF THE CONSTITUTION 351-54 (1996); Benjamin B. Klubes, *The First Federal Congress and the First National Bank: A Case Study in Constitutional Interpretation,* 10 J. OF THE EARLY REPUBLIC 19 (1990); J. Jefferson Powell, *The Original Understanding of Original Intent,* 98 HARV. L. REV. 885 (1984).

[541] 1791 House Debates, supra note 537, at 75-81 (quoting Blackstone, see supra note 514).

[542] *See, e.g.,* 2 Austin, supra note 482, at 989-90; John Chipman Gray, NATURE AND THE SOURCES OF LAW 172-73 (2d ed. 1927); Francis Lieber, LEGAL AND POLITICAL HERMENEUTICS 11 (3d ed. 1880); 1 Joseph Story, COMMENTARIES ON THE CONSTITUTION 305 (5th ed. 1891).

This approach can be traced to William Blackstone, who noted in his Commentaries that judges should seek the will of the legislator when confronted with vague statutory language. *See* 1 William Blackstone, COMMENTARIES *59.

See also M.H. Hoeflich, *John Austin and Joseph Story: two nineteenth century*

in the late nineteenth century into the paradigmatic battle between *scriptum* and *voluntas*.[543] One camp (including Professors Wigram and Wigmore and Justice Holmes)[544] continued to argue for constrictive rules to determine the meaning of words, while another school argued for the jettisoning of text altogether in favor of examining the intention of the writer.[545] Meanwhile, canons of construction — of the sort favored by the Roman rhetors and by some of the juristic writings in the *Digest* — came under a vicious attack, with Professor John Landis (writing in 1930) deploring the blind adherence to "barbaric rules of interpretation"[546] and Professor Karl Llewellyn attacking them as formalistic and merely rhetorical in flavor.[547]

---

perspectives on the utility of the civil law for the common lawyer, 29 AJLH 36 (1985).

[543] One writer as much as made the connection with antiquity, *see* Sidney L. Phipson, *Extrinsic Evidence in Aid of Interpretation*, 20 L.Q. REV. 245, 248 (1904).

[544] Sir James Wigram, EXTRINSIC EVIDENCE IN AID OF THE INTERPRETATION OF WILLS 9-10 (5th ed. 1914); 5 John Henry Wigmore, EVIDENCE § 2459 (2d ed. 1923); Oliver Wendell Holmes, Jr., *The Theory of Legal Interpretation*, 12 HARV. L. REV. 417 (1899).
   This group traced their intellectual roots back to the jurisprudence of Chief Justice John Marshall. *See* such cases as *United States v. Fisher*, 6 U.S. (2 Cranch 358, 387-95 (1805). *See also* Yoo, supra note 486, at 1616-26.

[545] *See, e.g.,* James Bradley Thayer, PRELIMINARY TREATISE ON EVIDENCE 404-05 (1898). Interestingly enough, the parable of the Barber of Bologna reappeared often in U.S. Supreme Court decisions at the turn-of-the century, holding for a liberal interpretation of a statute. *See Rector of Holy Trinity Church v. United States*, 143 U.S. 457, 461 (1892); *Hawaii v. Mankichi*, 119 U.S. 197, 212 (1903). *See also* James Landis, *Statutes and the Sources of Law*, in HARVARD LEGAL ESSAYS 213, 234 (Roscoe Pound ed. 1934).

[546] James M. Landis, *A Note on "Statutory Interpretation,"* 43 HARV. L. REV. 863, 890 (1930).

[547] *See* Karl N. Llewellyn, *Remarks on the Theory of Appellate Decision and the Rules or Canons About How Statutes are to be Construed*, 3 VAND. L. REV. 395, 401 (1950) ("There are two opposing canons on almost every point. . . ."). For glosses on Llewellyn's criticism, *see* R. Dickerson, THE INTERPRETATION AND APPLICATION OF STATUTES 227 (1975); Jonathan R. Macey & Geoffrey P. Miller, *The Canons of Statutory Construction and Judicial Preferences*, 45 VAND. L. REV. 647, 649-56 (1992) (critiquing Llewellyn and suggesting that canons can promote judicial efficiency); R. Perry Sentell, Jr., *The Canons*

iv. We have, it seems, a cyclical intellectual history of reactions to the problem of legal interpretation. Beginning with antiquity, juristic casuistry competed with rhetorical system. "[T]he Latin rhetors and the post-classical lawyers favored hermeneutics, the study of the 'principles' of interpretation, whereas the classical jurists were satisfied with exegesis, the practical application of this art."[548] Later, the civil and canon lawyers of the middle ages embraced the axiomatic jurisprudence that they (falsely) perceived was the heritage of classical Rome. The reaction was a humanist legal revolution which brought a renewed emphasis on equitable construction of statutes. But legal positivism of the eighteenth and nineteenth centuries marked a turn back toward concrete rules of interpretation. These canons were, in turn, attacked by legal realists as unsatisfying and primitive.

It seems, therefore, that the passage of time had cheated the Roman lawyers of the hard-won victory they had gained to protect their profession against the inroads of judicial oratory. Some writers have despaired that there has been an important lesson lost here. Arthur Schiller wrote that:

> The moral is not far to seek. Classical Roman jurists developed a legal system that ranks among the greatest the world has known. They had little use for hermeneutics; they preferred to attack each case involving interpretation on its own merits; they made use of all the techniques that came to hand (as well as their common sense), not to arrive at the intention of the writer, the meaning of the words, the reason for the law, or any one single factor, but to solve that particular question in accordance with the needs of the social and political life of their day. Roman law declined when hermeneutics triumphed....[549]

Time, it seems, has failed to reconcile rhetoric and law, or to harmonize casuistry with hermeneutics. Yet, it certainly has obscured the origins of these conflicts.

---

of Construction in Georgia: "Anachronisms" in Action, 25 GA. L. REV. 365, 366-70 (1991); David Shapiro, *Continuity and Change in Statutory Interpretation*, 67 N.Y.U. L. REV. 921, 925 (1992). For an attack on Llewellyn on another front, *see* [Justice] Antonin Scalia, A MATTER OF INTERPRETATION: FEDERAL COURTS AND THE LAW 26-27 (1997)

[548] Schiller, supra note 238, at 767.

[549] Id. at 768.

Modernity

IX CANONS OF STATUTORY INTERPRETATION TODAY

That concludes the first story I wished to address in this book. It had a quite ambivalent ending, what with my reconciliation of the differences that had drawn legal historians and classicists apart over the issue of legal interpretation. This same discord, of course, had succeeded in sundering law and rhetoric altogether as disciplines with a common interest. Yet, the way in which the classical tradition of legal interpretation was transmitted to us today has had a profound impact on the very current debate about the proper means of construing statutes. It comes to this: we are now reliving the same professional debate that occurred two millennia ago. The worst of it is that academic lawyers (at least) are blissfully unaware of the intellectual history that they are repeating. The next part of my book — the second tale I wanted to narrate — is about how the tension between classical law and rhetoric has been received in our modern discourse on the proper construction of legal texts. Before returning to the main thrust of this volume, the use of canons in treaty interpretation, I need to say a few words here about statutory construction.

This, too, is a history of ideas, although it does not feature philologists and Roman law historians. It stars, instead, legal academics and U.S. Supreme Court justices. This is the story of how classical canons of construction, as primarily conceived by rhetoricians, came to influence our current, and very heated, debate about the interpretation of statutes and the limits of legitimacy for judges. These questions have sparked an extraordinary dialogue, but one in which, somewhat surprisingly, classicists and rhetoricians have been mute. I would like to give voice here to these insights.

i. First, I need to summarize the current state of academic scholarship on statutory construction. I begin where I left off above, with the legal realists' attack on canons of construction. After nearly sixty years in which virtually no self-respecting legal academic bothered to write about the subject, we now have a renaissance in the theoretical debate over the ways and means of statutory construction. It is surely one of the most notable developments in modern legal discourse.[550] It has also become quite a polemic. The resurgence in interest of statutory interpretation (and its methods) revolves around two distinct, but entwined, strands of thoughtful concern.

α. The first is understanding the problem of meaning in any text, but especially legal texts carrying important (but sometimes indeterminate) social norms and values.[551] In this respect, the modern debate in legal academic circles about statutory interpretation has been profoundly influenced by language theory. Indeed, it is doubtful whether the entire process of intellectual introspection in the legal academy would have been initiated had it not been for the injection of three strands of ideology into the conversation.

---

[550] *See* William S. Blatt, *A History of Statutory Interpretation: A Study in Form and Substance*, 6 CARDOZO L. REV. 799 (1985); William N. Eskridge, Jr. & Philip P. Frickey, *Statutory Interpretation as Practical Reasoning*, 42 STAN. L. REV. 321, 321 (1990) [hereinafter "Eskridge & Frickey"]; Philip S. Frickey, *From the Big Sleep to the Big Heat: The Revival of Theory in Statutory Interpretation*, 77 MINN. L. REV. 241 (1992) [hereinafter "Frickey, *Minnesota*"]; Henry M. Hart, Jr. & Albert M. Sacks, THE LEGAL PROCESS 1169 (William N. Eskridge & Philip P. Frickey eds., 1994) (noting that "American courts have no intelligible, generally accepted, and consistently applied theory of statutory interpretation."); Earl M. Maltz, *Rhetoric and Reality in the Theory of Statutory Interpretation: Underenforcement, Overenforcement, and the Problem of Legislative Supremacy*, 71 B.U. L. REV. 767, 767 (1991) [hereinafter "Maltz"]; William L. Reynolds, *A Practical Guide to Statutory Interpretation Today*, 94 W. VA. L. REV. 927 (1992) [hereinafter "Reynolds"]; David L. Shapiro, *Continuity and Change in Statutory Interpretation*, 67 NYU L. REV. 921, 921-22 (1992); Nicholas S. Zeppos, *The Use of Authority in Statutory Interpretation: An Empirical Analysis*, 70 TEX. L. REV. 1073 (1992) [hereinafter "Zeppos, *Texas*"].

[551] *See, e.g.*, Eskridge & Frickey, supra note 550, at 323-24; Maltz, supra note 550, at 773-76; Cass R. Sunstein, *Interpreting Statutes in the Regulatory State*, 103 HARV. L. REV. 405, 414 n.29, 441-43 (1989) [hereinafter "Sunstein"].

I would call these three streams rhetorical,[552] hermeneutic,[553] and

---

[552] Modern rhetorical theory, for example, emphasizes a theory of argumentation based on strong logical principles. *See, e.g.,* Linda Levine & Kurt M. Saunders, *Thinking Like a Rhetor*, 43 J. LEGAL ED. 108 (1993); Kurt M. Saunders, *Law as Rhetoric, Rhetoric as Argument*, 44 J. LEGAL ED. 566 (1994). Although appeals in the construction of a legal text need not be logical to satisfy the rhetor, other kinds of argumentation are subject to criticism as being intellectually dishonest or illegitimate. *See, e.g.,* Richard H. Underwood, *Logic and the Common Law Trial*, 18 AM. J. TRIAL ADVOC. 151 (1994). In this sense, current rhetorical principle approximates classical rhetoric's taxonomic concern for giving guidance to the advocate in deciding which kinds of interpretive arguments are likely to succeed and which are not. *See* supra § II.vi.β.

For more on questions of legitimacy in the relation between rhetoric and law, *see* Anthony T. Kronman, *Rhetoric*, 67 U. CINN. L. REV. 677 (1999); Eileen A. Scallen, *Classical Rhetoric, Practical Reasoning, and the Law of Evidence*, 44 AM. U. L. REV. 1717 (1995); Gerald Wetlaufer, *Rhetoric and its Denial in Legal Discourse*, 76 VA. L. REV. 1545 (1990).

[553] Allied with rhetorical outlooks is a new stream of legal hermeneutics. *See generally* Andrei Marmor, INTERPRETATION AND LEGAL THEORY (1992); Costas Douzinas & Ronnie Warrington, POSTMODERN JURISPRUDENCE: THE LAW OF TEXT IN THE TEXTS OF LAW (1991); INTERPRETING LAW AND LITERATURE: A HERMENEUTIC READER (Sanford Levinson & Steven Mailloux eds. 1988); LAW, INTERPRETATION AND REALITY (Patrick Nerhot ed. 1990); LEGAL HERMENEUTICS: HISTORY, THEORY AND PRACTICE (Gregory Leyth ed. 1992); Delf Buchwald, *Statutory Interpretation in the Focus of Legal Justification: An Essay in Coherentist Hermeneutics*, 25 U. TOL. L. REV. 735 (1994); Goodrich, supra note 18; David Couzens Hoy, *Interpreting the Law: Hermeneutical and Post-Structuralist Perspectives*, 58 S. CAL. L. REV. 135 (1985); Karen M. Gebbia-Pinetti, *Statutory Interpretation, Democratic Legitimacy and Legal-System Values*, 21 SETON HALL LEGISL. J. 233, 296-97 n.174 (for a full bibliography on American legal hermeneutics); Scott Brewer, Comment, *Figuring the Law: Holism and Tropological Inference in Legal interpretation*, 97 YALE L.J. 823 (1988). What distinguishes these fresh approaches to the the study of legal interpretation is a wholesale rejection of even generic rules or canons of construction.

For the historical origins of hermeneutic literature in American jurisprudence, one would have to go back to Francis Lieber's 1839 volume, LEGAL AND POLITICAL HERMENEUTICS, *see* supra note 542.

linguistic[554] theory.   Although a consideration of the extraordinary rich and abstract body of these separate philosophies is well-beyond the scope of this work, the important point that must be kept in mind is that they each suggest that legal texts are particularly subject to the problem of indeterminacy of meaning. They each advance a system of interpretation for legal texts. And, finally, each is strongly opposed to a rules-based methodology of interpretation.

β. The second concern in modern statutory interpretation is the fundamental constitutional dilemma of judicial power — the relationship between an unelected federal judiciary reviewing and interpreting the enactments of a democratically-elected Congress.[555] The new theorists of statutory construction take widely divergent positions on these two concerns. Depending on the postures selected as to the determinacy of texts and the propriety of judicial independence, different paradigms of interpretive method have been selected by scholars and jurists.

Some writers, for example, see the debate as an abstract battle between those that embrace "foundational" sources of statutory interpretation and those

---

[554]   By linguistic theory, I am referring here to a wide body of deconstructionist literature that has strongly suggested that texts can have no independent meaning apart from the whim of the interpreter. For a survey of this philosophical school, *see* Peter C. Schanck, *Understanding Postmodern Thought and its Implications for Statutory Interpretation*, 65 SO. CAL. L. REV. 2505 (1992); Peter C. Schanck, *The Only Game in Town: An Introduction to Interpretive Theory, Statutory Construction, and Legislative Histories*, 38 KAN. L. REV. 815 (1990).

A different strand of linguistic theory is called pragmatics. *See* Paul Grice, STUDIES IN THE WAY OF WORDS (1989); Sanford Levinson, PRAGMATICS (1983); Miller, supra note 348, at 1191-1224. This school has had a strong influence in recent legal reasoning, *see* Steven J. Burton, *Law as Practical Reason*, 62 SO. CAL. L. REV. 747 (1989).

[555]   *See, e.g.*, Eskridge & Frickey, supra note 550, at 325-28; Maltz, supra note 550, at 788-91; William D. Popkin, *An "Internal" Critique of Justice Scalia's Theory of Statutory Interpretation*, 76 MINN. L. REV. 1133, 1161-70 (1992) [hereinafter "Popkin"]; Jane S. Schacter, *Metademocracy: The Changing Structure of Legitimacy in Statutory Interpretation*, 108 HARV. L. REV. 593 (1995); W. David Slawson, *Legislative History and the Need to Bring Statutory Interpretation under the Rule of Law*, 44 STAN. L. REV. 383, 400-05 (1992); Nicholas S. Zeppos, *Legislative History and the Interpretation of Statutes: Toward a Fact-Finding Model of Statutory Interpretation*, 76 VA. L. REV. 1295, 1311-19 (1990) [hereinafter "Zeppos, *Virginia*"].

using "dynamic" or "practical reasoning" approaches.[556] Other scholars see the problem as being more one of the actual selection of sources for construction.[557] They give names to such schools as "textualism," "intentionalism" (with its twin "originalism"), and "purposivism". Yet other thinkers have brought to bear social science critiques on actual exercises in statutory interpretation, revealing disquieting trends in counter-majoritarian and interest-group politics.[558] Lastly, quite a few writers see the entire debate in doctrinal terms, using every new

---

[556] The leading writer on this point is Professor William N. Eskridge, Jr. He can be credited with largely resurrecting the study of statutory interpretation after it fell into disrepute with the rejection of canons of interpretation during the New Deal. *See* Symposium Introduction, 45 VAND. L. REV. 529, 529-30 (1992). Among his leading works, *see* William N. Eskridge, Jr. & Philip P. Frickey, CASES AND MATERIALS ON LEGISLATION: STATUTES AND THE CREATION OF PUBLIC POLICY (1988); William N. Eskridge, Jr., *Gadamer/Statutory Interpretation*, 90 COLUM. L. REV. 609 (1990); William N. Eskridge, Jr., *The New Textualism*, 37 UCLA L. REV. 621 (1990).

Professor Eskridge has taken a leading role in arguing for "dynamic" methods of statutory construction, unfettered by connection to "foundational" sources and their schools. *See* William N. Eskridge, Jr., *Dynamic Statutory Interpretation*, 135 U. PA. L. REV. 1479 (1987); Eskridge & Frickey, supra note 550. *See also* T. Alexander Aleinikoff, *Updating Statutory Interpretation*, 87 MICH. L. REV. 20 (1988).

For more on practical reason and pragmatism in legal interpretation, *see* Scallen, supra note 552, at 1747-51.

[557] *See, e.g.*, Earl M. Maltz, *Statutory Interpretation and Legislative Power: The Case for a Modified Intentionalist Approach*, 63 TUL. L. REV. 1 (1988); Popkin, supra note 555; Scallen, supra note 552, at 1741-59; Sunstein, supra note 551, at 415-34; Zeppos, *Texas*, supra note 550, at 1076-88; Zeppos, *Virginia*, supra note 555, at 1299-1335.

[558] In this group I include the public choice theorists and their critics. For a sampling of the literature, *see* Daniel A. Farber, *Legislative Deals and Statutory Bequests*, 75 MINN. L. REV. 667 (1991); Daniel A. Farber, *Statutory Interpretation and Legislative Supremacy*, 78 GEO. L. J. 281 (1989); Reynolds, supra note 550, at 933-34; Edward L. Rubin, *Beyond Public Choice: Comprehensive Rationality in the Writing and Reading of Statutes*, 66 N.Y.U. L. REV. 1 (1991); Sunstein, supra note 551, at 446-51; Zeppos, *Texas*, supra note 550, at 1081-84; Zeppos, *Virginia*, supra note 555, at 1304-08. *See also* Gebbia-Pinetti, supra note 553 (for a detailed analysis of questions of "legal-system values" and statutory interpretation).

Supreme Court decision as a yardstick for measuring the value of new rules of interpretation and of decision.[559]

ii. The last aspect of the great debate in statutory interpretation is the role of independent and objective values in construction. These have been called "new" canons by some scholars, and they have come to be an important, normative voice in the interpretive discussion.[560] Even more significantly, these new canons are gaining adherents amongst judges, including the justices of the Supreme Court.[561] This should really come as no surprise. Because the scholastic dialectic between textualists, intentionalists, and purposivists is ultimately so unsatisfying, it seems to make more sense to look to principles of interpretation which touch on the underlying substance of the legal text being

---

[559] *See, e.g.*, Maltz, supra note 550, at 773-76; Popkin, supra note 555; Daniel B. Rodriguez, *The Presumption of Reviewability: A Study in Canonical Construction and its Consequences*, 45 VAND. L. REV. 743 (1992); Slawson, supra note 555, 1073, at 388-95; Jeffrey W. Stempel, *The Rehnquist Court, Statutory Interpretation, Inertial Burdens, and a Misleading Version of Democracy*, 22 U. TOL. L. REV. 583 (1991).

[560] The leading advocate of these "new" canons is Professor Cass Sunstein. *See* Reynolds, supra note 550, at 937-38. His seminal article was Cass R. Sunstein, *Interpreting Statutes in the Regulatory State* (*cited at* supra note 551). For some criticisms of Sunstein's work, *see* Eben Moglen & Richard J. Pierce, Jr., *Sunstein's New Canons: Choosing the Fictions of Statutory Interpretation*, 57 U. CHI. L. REV. 1203 (1990); Richard A. Posner, *Statutory Interpretation — In the Classroom and in the Courtroom*, 50 U. CHI. L. REV. 800, 805-14 (1983); Peter L. Strauss, *Sunstein, Statutes, and the Common Law Reconciling Markets, the Communal Impulse, and the Mammoth State*, 89 MICH. L. REV. 907 (1991). *But see* Robert J. Martineau, *Craft and Technique, Not Canons and Grand Theories: A Neo-Realist View of Statutory Construction*, 62 GEO. WASH. L. REV. 1 (1993).

For other examples of new canonists in statutory interpretation, *see* William N. Eskridge, Jr. & Philip P. Frickey, *Quasi-Constitutional Law: Clear Statement Rules as Constitutional Lawmaking*, 45 VAND. L. REV. 593 (1992); Rodriguez, supra note 559.

[561] A number of significant recent cases have turned on the Court's enunciation of a substantive presumption of legislative intent. For a few, *see NLRB v. Catholic Bishop of Chicago*, 440 U.S. 490 (1979) (statutes construed to avoid constitutional difficulties); *Chiarella v. United States*, 445 U.S. 222 (1980) (rule of lenity with criminal statutes); *Dames & Moore v. Regan*, 453 U.S. 654 (1981) (presumption against derogation of Presidential power); *EEOC v. Arabian American Oil Co.*, 111 S.Ct. 1227 (1991) (rule against extraterritorial effect of statutes).

gleaned. In statutory practice, these principles are becoming more and more merged with well-regarded presumptions as to Congressional intent in law-making.

But what I have found startling is that most of the prevailing discussion of canons of construction for statutes track the classical discourse between Roman rhetoricians and jurists. Indeed, I would say that the revival of definitive rules of statutory interpretation *is* the modern expression of the classical construct of canons. The parallels between the ancient and modern discourse appear in the actual structure of the "new" canons of statutory construction. As considered by a number of legal academics,[562] the canons have been organized into categories that are strikingly reminiscent of the rhetoricians' *status legalis*. In most recent commentary, the canons of statutory construction are divided generally into those which deal with (1) textual ambiguity, (2) the use of extrinsic sources of interpretation, and (3) the furtherance of actual policy goals.[563]

α.   Textual ambiguity comes within the ambit of the rhetorician's status of *ambiguitas* and *definitio*. A classical orator would immediately recognize the use of linguistic conventions and the search for the proper threshold of ambiguity in legal texts to be subjects properly committed to these *quaestiones*. And, indeed, much of the current debate about textualism in legal interpretation boils down to a simple, but mischievous, question: how much ambiguity, how much uncertainty, are we prepared to tolerate in a statute? The rhetorical manuals of Cicero and Quintilian advised the judicial orator that he better be able to endure a great deal of doubt in finding the "true" meaning

---

[562] *See* William N. Eskridge & Phillip P. Frickey, *Law as Equilibrium*, 108 HARV. L. REV. 26, 97-108 (1994); Shapiro, supra note 550, at 927-41; Sunstein, supra note 551, at 506-08.

[563] This is the construct offered by Eskridge & Frickey, Harvard, supra note 562, at 97-108. Professor Shapiro's schematic is a little bit different, identifying linguistic canons, substantive ("presumpt[ive]" or "tie-break[ing]") canons, and clear statement rules. *See* Shapiro, supra note 550, at 927-41. At slightly greater variance is Cass Sunstein's "typology" which recognizes linguistic and extrinsic source canons, but subdivides policy-oriented canons into those which (a) promote institutional goals, (b) promote substantive goals, (c) counteract statutory failure. *See* Sunstein, supra note 551, at 506-08.

of words.[564] Remember Quintilian's remarks: "there is not a single word which has not a diversity of meanings"[565] and "it is quite unimportant how ambiguity arises or how it is remedied.... It is a perfectly futile rule which directs us to endeavour ... to turn the word in question to suit our own purpose."[566]

We, however, today have a real problem embracing Quintilian's simple truth and we have profound difficulties accepting linguistic uncertainty. In a more innocent age of jurisprudence, one more confident that words had definite meaning, this would not be an issue.[567] But all seem to agree that a "plain meaning" rule in statutory interpretation passed away in the New Deal era,[568] a casualty of the rise of the regulatory state.[569] But commentators remain divided about whether a plain meaning doctrine has been, in fact, resurrected by the Rehnquist Court.[570] Despite a growing tendency to resort to dictionaries to drain words of their very last drop of connotation,[571] the Supreme Court has not

---

[564] *See supra* § II.ii.

[565] 3 Quintilian, supra note 6, at 153 (passage vii.9.1).

[566] id. at 161 (passage vii.9.14).

[567] *See* Maltz, supra note 550, at 769-70 (discussing first rejection of the plain meaning rule in *Church of the Holy Trinity v. United States*, 143 U.S. 457, 458-59 (1892)). *See also Nix v. Hedden*, 149 U.S. 304, 305-07 (1893) (holding that, while a tomato is botanically a fruit, in "the common language of the people" it is a vegetable, for purposes of import excise).

[568] *See United States v. American Trucking Ass'n*, 310 U.S. 534, 543-44 (1940).

[569] *See* Shapiro, supra note 550, at 931-34; Sunstein, supra note 551, at 408-09.

[570] *See* T. Alexander Aleinikoff & Theodore M. Shaw, *The Costs of Incoherence: A Comment on Plain Meaning*, West Virginia University Hospitals, Inc. v. Casey, *and Due Process of Statutory Interpretation*, 45 VAND. L. REV. 687, 698-706 (1992); Eskridge & Frickey, supra note 550, at 340-45; Popkin, supra note 555.

[571] *See* Eskridge & Frickey, Harvard, supra note 562, at 98 & nn.8-10; David O. Stewart, *By the Book*, A.B.A. J. 46 (July 1993) (discussing use of dictionaries by the

bothered to tell its public why a dictionary is the tool of choice for an interpreter, as opposed, to say, a thesaurus or book of quotations. Have words and phrases really become more vague as of late? Or, are we just less confident of meaning?

If we had a sensible threshold of ambiguity, like the Roman rhetoricians had, courts could avoid the morass of indeterminacy. Although the Supreme Court sometimes gets hung-up on over- and under-inclusiveness problems with statutes,[572] leading to findings of ambiguity,[573] it has remained fairly true to the notion that the plain meaning of a statute should prevail unless it would lead to an "odd"[574] or an "absurd"[575] result. And the threshold of "absurdity" was precisely the benchmark set both by Roman orators and jurists.[576] Even so, the Court has sometimes demanded that Congress craft a law completely free of ambiguity,[577] or else it will proceed to look to extra-textual sources, this does not

---

Court); Note, *Looking It Up: Dictionaries and Statutory Interpretation*, 107 HARV. L. REV. 1437 (1994).

[572] This is simply another version of Quintilian's concern with statutes that refer to a whole or a part of a subject-matter. *See* supra note 121 and accompanying text.

[573] *See* Maltz, supra note 550; Sunstein, supra note 551, at 418-21. *See also* Robert S. Summers, *Statutory Interpretation in the United States*, in INTERPRETING STATUTES: A COMPARATIVE STUDY 407, 412-19 (D. Neil MacCormick & Robert S. Summers eds. 1991).

[574] *Public Citizen v. United States Department of Justice*, 491 U.S. 440, 454 (1989) (*quoting Green v. Bock Laundry Mach. Co.*, 490 U.S. 504, 509 (1989)).

[575] *INS v. Cardozo-Fonseca*, 480 U.S. 421, 452 (1987) (Scalia, J., concurring); *Church of the Holy Trinity v. United States*, 143 U.S. 457, 459 (1892). Some cases have (properly) suggested that the "mischievous result" threshold is, itself, an ancient canon. *See Adams v. Proctor & Gamble Mfg. Co.*, 697 F.2d 582, 586 (4th Cir. 1983).

[576] *See* supra notes 99 & 302 and accompanying text.

[577] *See Chevron v. Natural Resources Defense Council, Inc.*, 467 U.S. 837, 842-43 (1984); *INS v. Cardoza-Fonseca*, 480 U.S. 421, 445 n.29 (1987). In such a case where a statute is ambiguous, courts should defer to the administrative agency (if any) charged with carrying-out the law's mandate. Moreover, only the text of a statute may be employed in

appear to be the rule. In most other respects, though, the linguistic canons of construction that the Supreme Court has developed would be totally familiar to the Roman jurist. Rules about punctuation in statutes, disjunctive language, the use of gender and number, and other grammatical concerns are virtually settled,[578] although the maxims of *inclusio unius* (inclusion of one thing implies the exclusion of another) and *ejusdem generis* (words of the same kind) continue to cause trouble.[579] Indeed, these two canons have been explicitly recognized by courts — alongside the *noscitur a sociis* rule (words should be known by the company they keep) — as being "ancient" rules of legal interpretation.[580]

---

determining whether, under *Chevron*'s first-prong, the law is ambiguous. Legislative history may not be set-up to cloud the plain meaning of a law. *See, e.g., National Railroad Passenger Corp. v. Boston & Maine Corp.*, 112 S.Ct. 1394, 1401 (1992); *City of Chicago v. Environmental Defense Fund*, 114 S.Ct. 1588, 1594 (1994).

The criticisms of this form of deference are legion. *See, e.g.,* Colin Diver, *Statutory Interpretation in the Administrative States*, 133 U. PA. L. REV. 549 (1985); Cynthia Farina, *Statutory Interpretation and the Balance of Power in the Administrative State*, 89 COLUM. L. REV. 452 (1989); Thomas Merrill, *Textualism and the* Chevron *Doctrine*, 72 WASH. U. L.Q. 351 (1994); Sidney Shapiro & Robert Glicksman, *Congress, The Supreme Court, and the Quiet Revolution in Administrative Law*, 1988 Duke L.J. 819; Cass Sunstein, *Law and Administration after* Chevron, 90 COLUM. L. REV. 2071 (1990).

[578]   *See* supra note 309 and accompanying text. For more on rules regarding punctuation, *see* Ray Marcin, *Punctuation and Interpretation of Statutes*, 9 CONN. L. REV. 227 (1977).

[579]   *See* Eskridge & Frickey, Harvard, supra note 562, at 97-98; Shapiro, supra note 550, at 927-31. The "expressio unius" rule has been the subject of harsh judicial attack. *See Sullivan v. Hudson*, 490 U.S. 877 (1989) (refusing to apply the canon, over a vigorous dissent); *National Petroleum Refiners Ass'n v. FTC*, 482 F.2d 672, 676 (D.C. Cir. 1973) (the maxim "stands on the faulty premise that all possible alternative or supplemental provisions were necessarily considered and rejected by the [legislature]."); In re American Reserve Corp., 840 F.2d 487, 492 (7th Cir. 1988). *See also Heathman v. Giles*, 374 P.2d 839 (Utah 1962) (for one recent application of the *ejusdem generis* canon).

[580]   *See National Railroad Passenger Corp. v. National Association of Railroad Passengers*, 414 U.S. 453, 458 (expressio unius est exclusio alterius is "an ancient maxim"); *Sweet Home Chapter Communities for a Greater Oregon v. Babbitt*, 1 F.3d 1, 12 (D.C. Cir. 1993) (Sentelle, J., dissenting), modified on reh'g, 17 F.3d 1463 (D.C. Cir. 1994), rev'd, 115 S.Ct. 2407 (1995) (noscitur a sociis). For more on noscitur a sociis, *see* Sentell, supra

β. The positively incendiary arguments we have today about the propriety of using legislative history to divine the meaning of statutes would, likewise, be prosaic for the Roman rhetor. Many commentators have maintained that the prevailing school of legislative construction today seeks to ascertain the original intent of the law-makers in fashioning the relevant act.[581] This methodology of interpretation certainly has its detractors,[582] and one should also not ignore the internal schism between those that distinguish between an "original" intent and a more dynamic or evolutive design of the statute.

In any event, the search for legislative intent probably reached its highwater mark in Justice Thurgood Marshall's remark that when legislative history is ambiguous, the Court must only then "look primarily to statutes themselves to find the legislative intent."[583] For Justice Scalia — the Court's leading textualist — this is pure anathema: the text *is* the alpha-and-omega of interpretation.[584] Justice Scalia's opposition to the use of legislative history has

---

note 547, at 374-433; David A. Schlesinger, Comment, *Chevron Unlatined: The Inapplicability of the Canon* Noscitur a Sociis *Under Prong One of the Chevron Framework*, 5 N.Y.U. ENV'TL L. J. 638 (1996).

Also recognized for their "ancient" vintage are the rules of *contra proferentem*, *Pan American World Airways, Inc. v. Aetna Casualty & Surety Co.*, 505 F.2d 989, 1003 (2d Cir. 1974); and the rule against implied repealer, *Longmire v. Sea Drilling Corp.*, 610 F.2d 1342, 1351 (5th Cir. 1980).

[581] *See* Eskridge & Frickey, supra note 550, at 325; Frickey, *Minnesota*, supra note 550, at 256; Zeppos, *Texas*, supra note 550, at 1077. *See also* Summers, supra note 573, at 422-30.

[582] *See* Eskridge & Frickey, supra note 550, at 325-32.

[583] *Citizens to Preserve Overton Park v. Volpe*, 401 U.S. 402, 413 n.29 (1971). This peculiar inversion of the textual canon has been vigorously criticized in the literature. *See, e.g.,* William T. Mayton, *Law Among the Pleonasms: The Futility and Aconstitutionality of Legislative History in Statutory Interpretation*, 41 EMORY L. J. 113 (1992). *See also* Scalia, A Matter of Interpretation, supra note 547, at 31 (who savages this inversion of textualism, although without attributing it to Justice Marshall).

[584] *See* Popkin, supra note 555; Nicholas S. Zeppos, *Justice Scalia's Textualism: The "New" New Legal Process*, 12 CARDOZO L. REV. 1597 (1991). For an interesting counterpoint, *see* [Justice] John Paul Stevens, *The Shakespeare Canon of Statutory Construction*,

two thrusts. The first is to question the reliability of statements drafted and made in the legislative process as probative of legislative intent.[585] The second is to doubt the entire enterprise of divining the legislator's intent.[586] This is the "New Textualism." The devotees of the New Textualism — including its chief acolyte, Justice Antonin Scalia — have been ambivalent about canons of construction. Justice Scalia has gone so far as to observe that "[m]any of the canons were originally in Latin, and I suppose that alone is enough to render them contemptible."[587] Indeed, Scalia says simply that, for textualists, the new substantive canons are "a lot of trouble."[588]

But I would submit that the new textualism has, in fact, embraced the old canons.[589] The truth is that, of course, there are many degrees of textualism, something that classical jurists and orators knew quite well. It is one thing, as Cicero supposed, that *no* statute should admit of *any exception*. It is quite another thing to say that a particular exemption should not be allowed under a

---

140 U. PA. L. REV. 1373, 1374-76, 1381-82 (1992).

[585] *See Hirschey v. FERC*, 777 F.2d 1, 7-8 (D.C. Cir. 1985); *Begier v. IRS*, 496 U.S. 53, 67-71 (1990) (Scalia, J., concurring); *Wisconsin Public Intervenor v. Mortier*, 501 U.S. 597, 617-23 (1991) (Scalia, J., concurring in the judgment); *Thunder Basin Coal Co. v. Reich*, 114 S.Ct. 771, 782 (1994) (Scalia, J., concurring in part and in the judgment).
   Nor is Justice Scalia alone on the Supreme Court in expressing such concerns. *See* [Judge] Stephen Breyer, *The Uses of Legislative History in Interpreting Statutes*, 65 S. CAL. L. REV. 845 (1992). For additional (non judicial) scholarship, *see* George Costello, *Average Voting Members and other "Benign Fictions": The Relative Reliability of Committee Reports, Floor Debates, and other Sources of Legislative History,* 1990 DUKE L.J. 39.

[586] For those who share this concern, *see* Frederick Schauer, *Statutory Construction and the Coordinating Function of Plain Meaning*, 1990 SUP. CT. REV. 231; Kenneth Starr, *Observations About the Use of Legislative History*, 1987 DUKE L.J. 371.

[587] Scalia, A Matter of Interpretation, supra note 547, at 25.

[588] Id. at 28.

[589] *See* William N. Eskridge, Jr., *Textualism, The Unknown Ideal*, 96 MICH. L. REV. 1509, 1545 (1998) (reviewing Antonin Scalia, A MATTER OF INTERPRETATION (1997)).

certain statutory scheme.[590] There are few takers today for extreme literalism, even while there are rather more adherents of "soft" textualism.

Today's "new" canons are, as a consequence, very much like their classical counterparts when it comes to the propriety of using extrinsic evidence of legislative intent. Just as the Roman orators had *topoi* under the status of *scriptum et sententia* to appreciate circumstances when recourse to such sources was appropriate (or at least plausible), so too today. For example, Cicero's and Quintilian's distinction between absolute and conditional intent[591] has its parallels in two common pathologies of current statutory construction.

The first is where the statute was clear enough except when it came to resolving the legal controversy raised in the case.[592] This is situational obscurity. The extent to which it should be resolved by looking at legislative history has been the source of much consternation and bitterness within the Supreme Court. Threshold rules of ambiguity and plain meaning have been offered as one guide.[593] So, too, have institutional approaches which give deference to the interpretations of the Executive branch and its agencies.[594] But the arguments made in support of textualism and intentionalism in statutory construction today are really those made two millennia ago. The nub of the dispute is, as it was, the proper role of the judge in interpreting the law. The Romans knew the import of separation of powers arguments and knew how to persuade a judge either to do his duty and apply the law as literally stated or to do his duty and dispense individualized justice.[595]

---

[590] *See* supra notes 82-87 and accompanying text.

[591] *See* supra § II.iii.α.

[592] *See* Summers, supra note 573, at 430-43.

[593] *See* Eskridge & Frickey, Harvard, supra note 562, at 100-01; Stevens, supra note 584, at 1383-87; Sunstein, supra note 551, at 418-24.

[594] *See* Eskridge & Frickey, Harvard, supra note 562, at 99; Sunstein, supra note 551, at 444-46. *See also* supra note 577 and accompanying text.

[595] *See* supra §§ II.iii.β & γ.

The second pathology of interpretation is the issue of structural readings of statutory provisions which (apparently) conflict with each other. This is, of course, its own *constitutio* in the classical status system: *contrariae leges*. Judges today would do well to remember Quintilian's observation that "[I]t is clear ... that one law cannot contradict another in principle (since if there were two different principles, one law would cancel the other), and that [such] laws ... are brought into collision purely by the accidents of chance."[596] Indeed, quite a few "new" canons of construction are nothing more than an attempt to determine whether there is, in fact, a true conflict between provisions of the same law,[597] or between two different statutes,[598] or between a new law and the existing common law.[599]

Legislative intent has been broadly implicated both in conflict circumstances and situational obscurities. The new canons of construction have been presented as sophisticated rules both anticipating and directing congressional law-making.[600] After all, Congress, is expected to act with full knowledge of these rules of interpretation. The canons operate as default rules which Congress is free to deviate from, but if it does so tacitly, it acts at its own peril. These new precepts of statutory interpretation are the fulfillment of Alexander Hamilton's "rules of *common sense* ... in the construction of the laws."[601]

γ. The Roman rhetor would have understood "common sense" in two ways. The first was in the expression of the will of the people. The

---

[596] 3 Quintilian, supra note 6, at 143 (passage vii.7.2). *See also* supra § II.v.

[597] *See* Eskridge & Frickey, Harvard, supra note 562, at 98-99.

[598] *See* id. at 99-100.

[599] *See* Shapiro, supra note 550, at 936-38.

[600] *See* Eskridge & Frickey, Harvard, supra note 562, at 65-71.

[601] THE FEDERALIST No. 83, at 496 (Alexander Hamilton) (original emphasis).

second was in a notion of right reason and logic.[602] Combined in these two ways, the Roman orator would have called common sense, *aequitas*, if only to distinguish it from the literal terms of the *lex*. *Aequitas* may or may not have been at the center of the classical rhetorician's approach to statutory construction. It hardly matters today. For even though modern statutory interpretation is bereft of explicit references to equity (in sharp contrast with early-modern Anglo-American jurisprudence),[603] equitable principles are really what undergird the substantive, policy-oriented rules of construction which are the paradigmatic "new" canon.

Let me consider, first, those substantive canons applicable to particular classes of statutes. One such rule would be that of lenity in construing criminal statutes favorably to the defendant. This is manifestly of classical origin,[604] and modern courts have so recognized its ancient pedigree.[605] This is obviously the precise context in which Alexander Hamilton wrote in *The Federalist* of the need for judges to dispense individualized justice in order to "mitigat[e] the severity and confining the operation of [unjust] laws."[606] And although the rule of lenity is sometimes given uneven treatment of late,[607] it is still widely respected.

---

[602] *See generally* Amy H. Kastely, *Cicero's* De Legibus: *Law and Talking Justly Toward a Just Community*, 3 YALE J. L. & HUMAN. 1 (1991).

[603] *See* supra note 368 and accompanying text.

[604] *See* supra note 310 and accompanying text.

[605] *See United States v. Wilson*, 916 F.2d 1115, 117 (6th Cir. 1990); *United States v. Rippon*, 537 F. Supp. 789, 792 (C.D. Ill. 1982) (both citing 3 J. Sutherland, STATUTES AND STATUTORY CONSTRUCTION § 59.03, at 8 (4th ed. 1973)).

[606] THE FEDERALIST No. 78, at 470. *See* supra note 533 with text.

[607] *Compare United States v. Yermian*, 468 U.S. 63 (1984); and *United States v. Margiotta*, 688 F.2d 108 (2d Cir. 1982), cert. denied, 461 U.S. 913 (1983) (a notorious case in which the canon was ignored) *with Chiarella v. United States*, 445 U.S. 222, 232-33 (1980) (upholding it); and *Williams v. United States*, 458 U.S. 279 (1982).

Likewise, Hamilton wrote of judges being vigilant against "partial" laws.[608]   In this sense, he would have approved of canons that protect "majoritarian" values against encroachment by "special-interest" statutes. An example of this would be a canon against construing acts in derogation of sovereignty.[609] Likewise, interpreting public grants in favor of the government (as opposed to the private beneficiary) would curb "partial" enactments.[610]

A second group of substantive canons operate across different categories of statutes. These establish public policy presumptions which judges embrace.[611] Some of these may address questions of legitimacy in a political order — such as the rule that laws should be interpreted in order to avoid constitutional difficulty or impairment.[612] Likewise, courts have developed presumptions and rules of statutory construction giving voice to ingrained preferences to Indian tribes,[613] the application of international law,[614] the disinclination to apply U.S.

---

[608]   Id.

[609]   *See* 2 Sutherland, supra note 605, §§ 62.01.

[610]   *See* id. § 63.04.

[611]   *See* Scalia, A Matter of Interpretation, supra note 547, at 27-29.

[612]   For doubts on this point, *see* [Judge] Henry Friendly, *Mr. Justice Frankfurter and the Reading of Statutes*, in BENCHMARKS 211-12 (1967); and [Judge] Richard Posner, THE FEDERAL COURTS: CRISIS AND REFORM 285 (1985).

[613]   *See, e.g., Montana v. Blackfeet Tribe*, 471 U.S. 759, 766-68 (1985). *See also* Jill de la Hunt, *The Canons of Indian Treaty and Statutory Construction: A Proposal for Codification*, 17 U. MICH. J. L. REF. 681 (1984); Peter S. Heinecke, Comment, Chevron *and the Canon Favoring Indians*, 60 U. CHI. L. REV. 1015 (1993).

[614]   *See, e.g., Murray v. The CHARMING BETSY*, 6 U.S. (2 Cranch) 64, 118 (1804). For more on this canon, *see* Curtis A. Bradley, *The* Charming Betsy *Canon and Separation of Powers: Rethinking the Interpretive Role of International Law*, 86 GEO.L. J. 479 (1997).

law overseas,[615] the defense of the President's inherent powers,[616] and the protection of the authority of the courts themselves.[617]

Now, these presumptions were intended to act merely as "tie-breakers": when in doubt, apply the presumption. But no less an authority than Justice Scalia has recently suggested that they have transcended this role, and become metaphorical "thumbs on the scales," or "dice-loading rules."[618] But, by the same token, Scalia notes that any confusion in these presumptions' application "are a fair price to pay for preservation" of important constitutional principles.[619] Lately, courts have attempted to harden these presumptions into self-expressed canons of interpretation. The process that has been chosen is to express these preferences as requiring a "clear statement" by Congress before a law will be interpreted contrary to the preference. So, for example, some courts have held that if Congress wishes to breach a treaty obligation or legislate extraterritorially or intrude on states' rights, it must quite literally insert into the statute bold-faced language expressing such a peculiar (or, at least, suspect) intent.[620]

---

[615] *See, e.g., Foley Bros. v. Filardo*, 336 U.S. 281 (1949). For more on this canon, *see* William S. Dodge, *Understanding the Presumption Against Extraterritoriality*, 16 BERKELEY J. INT'L L. 85 (1998).

[616] *See, e.g., Haig v. Agee*, 453 U.S. 280 (1981).

[617] *See, e.g., United States v. Nordic Village, Inc.*, 503 U.S. 30, 33-34 (1992) (federal sovereign immunity); *Hecht Co. v. Bowles*, 321 U.S. 330 (1944) (presumption against acts withdrawing courts' equitable jurisdiction); *South Carolina v. Regan*, 465 U.S. 367 (1984) (same for remedial rights); *Abbott Laboratories v. Gardner*, 387 U.S. 136 (1967) (presumption in favor of judicial review). *See also* Scalia, A Matter of Interpretation, supra note 547, at 29; William N. Eskridge, Jr. & Philip P. Frickey, *Quasi-Constitutional Law: Clear Statement Rules as Constitutional Law-Making*, 45 VAND. L. REV. 593 (1992).

[618] Scalia, A Matter of Interpretation, supra note 547, at 28-29.

[619] Id. at 28.

[620] *See, e.g., Gregory v. Ashcroft*, 501 U.S. 452 (1991) (federalism); *Atascadero State Hosp. v. Scanlon*, 473 U.S. 234 (1985) (same); *EEOC v. Arabian American Oil Co.*, 499 U.S. 244 (1991) (extraterritoriality); *Palestine Liberation Organization v. United States*, 695 F. Supp. 1456 (S.D.N.Y. 1988) (treaty violation).

iii.   What should be obvious after this long disquisition is that substantive canons are not new at all. We would just like to think they are. Their origins lie, I believe, in Quintilian's notion of looking "beyond the letter"[621] of the law, the quintessential activity of legal analogy or *syllogismus*. "Beyond the letter," one invariably finds the object and purpose of the law. In the teleology of the statute one can embrace substantive legal values. Substantive canons provide sources for those values. No one is fooled, however, that these sources — or the values they lead to — are neutral in any policy function. These rules are simply the linguistic embodiment of policy preferences made by judges. When the preferences change, the canon is discarded, modified, or supplanted by a new rule.

The classical rhetoricians knew well of substantive canons. The entire *constitutio* of *ratiocinatio* is really based on the notion that "no one can include every case in one statute but that he makes the most suitable law who takes care that some things may be understood from certain others."[622] Likewise, the entire "assumptive branch of the equitable issue"[623] was merely a catalogue of social values that were to be applied whenever the judge had to go "beyond the letter." The rule of lenity, applied to this day,[624] is a direct descendant from the equitable principle propounded by the orators, adopted by the Roman lawyers,[625] and revived by the medieval Glossators and the early-Modern humanist publicists.

Roman jurists and orators understood the full dimensions of what we perceive to be the central questions of the statutory interpretation debate. They recognized the tension between rules and principles in construing any legal text.

---

[621] 3 Quintilian, supra note 6, at 149 (passage vii.8.1). *See also* supra notes 103-05 and accompanying text.

[622] Cicero, de Inventione, supra note 21, at 321 (passage ii.50.152).

[623] *See* supra notes 89-92 and accompanying text.

[624] *See* Eskridge & Frickey, Harvard, supra note 562, at 104; Shapiro, supra note 550, at 935-36. *See* supra notes 604 - 607 and accompanying text.

[625] *See* supra notes 217-18 and accompanying text.

They appreciated the structure of argument that was necessitated by the adoption of certain interpretive canons. They sensed that intelligent statutory construction depended on a supple understanding of the role of the judge in respecting the will of a law-maker, while, at the same time, embracing the capacity of the judge as a dispenser of equity. Lastly, both Roman jurists and rhetoricians agreed that they respectively added something to the process of statutory construction. They managed to strike the essential compromise that is required in any interpretive exercise: balancing the demands of fidelity to the sovereign, of certainty in applying the law, and of beneficence in granting justice.

X THE DEVELOPMENT OF MODERN RULES OF TREATY INTERPRETATION

i. But was this evolution in understanding of statutory construction matched by a similar epiphany for treaty interpretation? I believe it was. To pick up the thread of the story on the evolution of treaty interpretation, I must return to the work of nineteenth century publicists. The leading figure was probably Sir Robert Phillimore, Queen's Advocate in the High Court of Admiralty and the leading civil law scholar of his age in England.[626] Phillimore's volume, *Commentaries Upon International Law*, went through three editions before his death in 1885, and became a standard reference work afterwards.[627] His treatment of the subject of treaty interpretation was to have broad influence, insofar as it combined the best elements of classical writers (such as Grotius, Pufendorf and Rutherforth) with more recent jurisprudential insights of such scholars as Savigny. Indeed, Phillimore can be credited with introducing Savigny's interpretive jurisprudence to English-reading audiences,[628] and also to

---

[626] *See* Degan, supra note 400, at 45; Ehrlich, supra note 384, at 30-32.

[627] The volume used in my survey is 2 Robert Phillimore, COMMENTARIES UPON INTERNATIONAL LAW (Philadelphia 1855).

[628] For those that have documented Phillimore's debt to Savigny, *see* Degan, supra note 400, at 46; Ehrlich, supra note 384, at 46-47. Phillimore's citations to Savigny in his chapter on Interpretation of Treaties are many. *See* Phillimore, supra note 627, at 70 n.(a), 71 n.(h), 77 n.(n), 78 nn.(q) & (s), 79 n.(z), 80 n.(c).

180

practically applying it in one, particular context: to international treaties, which he acknowledged had aspects of both contract and statute.[629]

Phillimore's treatment had two other virtues, not previously embraced by earlier writers: it was succinct and powerfully written. To Phillimore's enduring fame is the canard: "interpretation is the life of the dead letter."[630] But it is worth reading the entire passage in which that famous remark is embedded:

> The interpretation is the life of the dead letter; but what is meant by the term "interpretation"? The meaning which any party may choose to affix? or a meaning governed by settled rules, and fixed principles, originally deduced from right reason and rational equity, and subsequently formed into laws? Clearly the latter.[631]

Phillimore's remark clearly bridges the gap between natural law thinkers (like Grotius, Pufendorf and Rutherforth) and positivists (like Vattel and Austin). With a tip of his hat to the positivists, Phillimore conceded that rules of interpretation were "governed by settled rules" — made by the practice of the States that were engaged in the ongoing process of treaty interpretation. Moreover, Phillimore seemed to imply, these inchoate rules could, themselves, be the subject of formal law-making through codification. From natural law, Phillimore still insisted that the rules of interpretation for treaties were "originally deduced" from "right reason and rational equity." Implicit in this was a warning that the application of canons of construction should not deviate too much from first principles of justice.

This balance between natural and positive law formulations was observed in the rest of Phillimore's treatment. For example,

> The general heads under which ... we may range the principles and rules of Interpretation, are the following:-

---

[629] *See* id. at 78 (passage ii.8.77) ("the Treaty or International Covenant, it must be remembered, partakes of the character both of a law and a contract.").

[630] Phillimore, supra note 627, at 71 (passage ii.8.66).

[631] Id.

α. *Authentic* Interpretation, that is, the exposition supplied by the Lawgiver himself.

β. *Usual* Interpretation, that which is founded upon usage and upon precedent.

γ. *Doctrinal* Interpretation; that which is founded upon a scientific exposition of the terms of the instrument....[632]

In Phillimore's view, only doctrinal interpretation is "properly so called," and, as a consequence, he devoted only two paragraphs to authentic and usual interpretation.

---

[632]   Id. at 72 (passage ii.8.67).

I.   AUTHENTIC INTERPRETATION (**68**)

II.   USUAL INTERPRETATION (**69**)

III. DOCTRINAL INTERPRETATION (**70**)
  A. *Grammatical Rules*
        1. Plain Meaning
        2. Whole Instrument
        3. Technical Words

  B. *Logical Rules* (**72**)
        1. General Principles of Construction (**73**)
                a. Reconcile Whole Text
                b. Ground of Reason of Text (*Ratio Legis*)
                c. Earlier Treaties
                d. Justice and Equity
                e. Effectiveness
                f. Common Usage in Affected Countries
                g. Customarily Implied Clauses

        2. Problems of Uncertainty (**74**)
                a. Incompleteness (**75**)
                b. Ambiguity (**76**)
                        i. Single Expressions (**77**)
                        ii. General Construction (**78**)
                c. *Contra Proferentum* Rule (**80**)

        3. Problems of Impropriety (**81-83**)
                a. Extensive Interpretation (**84-86**)
                b. Restrictive Interpretation (**87-89**)
                c. Favorable v. Odious Obligations (**95**)

  C. Conflict between Clauses in Different Treaties (**97**)

(Numbers indicate section in book 2, ch. 3 of Phillimore's COMMENTARIES)

Figure 3 - Phillimore's Schematic on Treaty Construction

For his discussion of doctrinal interpretation, Phillimore divided canons of construction into two categories: grammatical and logical.[633] Grammatical interpretation Phillimore likened to "literal interpretation."[634] "The principal rule," he wrote, is "to follow the ordinary and usual acceptation, the plain and obvious meaning of the language employed."[635] Added to this rule — "a cardinal maxim of interpretation [embraced] equally by civilians, and by writers of International Law"[636] — were two corollaries: (1) that the language of the whole instrument is to be consulted, and (2) "[w]ords of art, or technical words are to be construed according to their technical meaning."[637]

Phillimore's logical rules of treaty interpretation were directly influenced by classical rhetorical forms as reshuffled in Savigny's model, which divided all interpretive pathologies into two categories: problems of uncertainty and of impropriety.[638] Certain principles of interpretation were, however, susceptible of use in resolving either quandary. These included reconciling a disputed passage with the balance of the writing; looking to the "ground of reason" (*ratio legis*) of the provision; effectuating the underlying purpose of the agreement; and applying customary (although implied) clauses of treaties.[639]

---

[633] *See* id. at 72-73 (passages ii.8.67 & 70). By so doing, he self-consciously adopted two of Savigny's four categories of interpretive method. *See* Savigny, supra note 517, at 172 (passage i.4.33). Savigny's third category of "historical" interpretation was probably subsumed under Phillimore's "usual" interpretation (dictated by custom). Savigny's fourth category of "systematic" interpretation was an amalgam of his three other forms. *See* id.

[634] Id. at 73 (passage ii.8.70).

[635] Id.

[636] Id.

[637] Id. at 75 (passage ii.8.70).

[638] *See* Savigny, supra note 517, at 179 (passage i.4.35).

[639] See Phillimore, supra note 627, at 75-77 (passage ii.8.73).

If these principles did not satisfy, then Phillimore pointed out that it was important to distinguish two sorts of textual uncertainties: incompleteness and ambiguity. Of these two, ambiguity was the more serious problem, and could arise in reference to single expressions (*singulorum verborum*) and general constructions (*compositione orationis*).[640] This part of Phillimore's schematic is heavily-influenced by the works of Roman orators and jurists, and classical citations (and more modern glosses) are sprinkled throughout. He, in any event, concludes the discussion of ambiguity by citing the *contra proferentum* rule: "the contracting party, who might and ought to have expressed himself clearly and fully, must take the consequences of his carelessness, and cannot, *as a general rule*, introduce subsequent restrictions or extensions of his meaning."[641]

As for defects in language which lead to inappropriate outcomes, Phillimore borrowed heavily from the *scriptum-voluntas* debate of antiquity and Grotius' insights on extensive and restrictive interpretations. There are cases, Phillimore posited,"in which the expression does convey a meaning, and, abstractly considered, an unambiguous meaning, but one which, when the circumstances are considered, evidently does not convey *the* meaning intended by the authors.... In such cases is the word or the intent to prevail?"[642] And Phillimore repeated Celsus' admonition that "[k]nowing the laws is not a matter of sticking to their words, but a matter of grasping their force and tendency."[643] This study of extensive and restrictive constructions, Phillimore (borrowing from Savigny) declared to be both logical and historical, "necessitating a recurrence to the record of the facts which preceded or accompanied the formation of the Treaty."[644] But, Phillimore cautioned,

---

[640] *See* id. at 77-78 (passage ii.8.76).

[641] *See* id. at 79 (passage ii.8.80) (original emphasis) (citing Dig. 45.1.38.18 & 2.14.39, as well as Savigny).

[642] *See* id. at 80 (passage ii.8.81) (original emphasis).

[643] Id. (passage ii.8.81) (quoting 1 Digest, supra note 80, at 12 (1.3.17; Celsus, *Digest* 26)). For more on Celsus, *see* supra note 299.

[644] Id. (passage ii. 8.82). *See also* supra note 520.

In the application, equally of *restrictive* as of the *extensive* modes of *interpretation*, the most scrupulous caution is to be observed, lest the true bounds of the doctrine which we are considering be overpassed, and inference or analogy be substituted for interpretation, in which case it is clear, that the expression is not rectified by being brought into unison with the idea, but that a *new idea* is substituted by the interpreter in the place of that which was present to the mind of the framers of the Treaty.[645]

Phillimore's subsequent discussion of broad and narrow interpretations of improperly-drafted treaty clauses attempted a synthesis of publicists (Grotius, Pufendorf and Vattel) with classical writers (particularly Quintilian, Seneca and various Digest extracts).[646] Phillimore tended to side with Vattel's very cautious use of these interpretive techniques,[647] and Phillimore was emphatic in rejecting the distinction (fashioned by Grotius) between favorable and odious obligations, calling it "disputable" and "[]not found [in] any safe rules of interpretation."[648] But Phillimore did fully endorse Cicero's and Grotius' rules for dealing with situations in which two treaties are in conflict.[649]

Robert Phillimore's writing was the last attempt made at synthesizing a general theory for interpreting treaties. By the latter part of the nineteenth century, the emphasis in treaty construction shifted to the elaboration of very specific rules of interpretation for treaty provisions, often with little sense or appreciation of how the rules were to be connected or related to each other. Despite this change, classical rhetorical and juristic writings continued to exert a marked, if more subliminal, influence on the three major vehicles for the elaboration of treaty interpretation rules: publicists' writings, international

---

[645] Id. (passage ii.8.83) (original emphasis) (citing to Savigny and a Pandect source).

[646] See id. at 81 (passages ii.8.84-85).

[647] *See* id. at 84-88 (passages ii.8.84-92). Phillimore's consideration culminated in a case study of a well-known diplomatic contretemps of the time, the Russo-Dutch Loan, in which British Parliamentary attempts to repudiate a treaty with Russia (premised on grounds of "extensive" interpretation) were rebuffed. *See* id.

[648] Id. at 89-90 (passage ii.8.95).

[649] See id. at 90-92 (passage ii.9).

arbitral or judicial decisions, and codification attempts. I will look at each of these sources in turn.

ii. The important thing to emphasize about publicists' writings is the extraordinary historical continuity of their work. International law scholars continue to rely on early-modern writers (like Grotius, Pufendorf and Vattel) to this very day, and this seems particularly so in the development of doctrines on treaty interpretation. Modern publicists are careful to acknowledge their intellectual debt to these earlier writers,[650] but the intellectual history used by modern publicists to explain the origin of systematic canons of treaty construction is quite incomplete, and thus deeply flawed.

The leading explanation, first made by Charles Fairman, is that Vattel represented the epitome of treaty construction rules, which "have entered generally into the treatises of international law, and were elaborated by Phillimore, who was, of course, an accomplished civilian."[651] Not only are Grotius and Pufendorf curiously absent from this history, but Fairman also suggests that Vattel influenced Pothier's famous 1761 civil law treatise, *On The Law of Obligations*, and thus the resurrection of Digest rules in the leading civil codes of the nineteenth century.[652] Fairman's point was that, under civil law precepts, the question of what a contract means is a question of *fact*, not *law*, and, therefore, rules of construction are not binding in any legal sense.[653]

---

[650] *See, e.g.,* Degan, supra note 400, at 49-54; William Edward Hall, INTERNATIONAL LAW 284-85 & n.2 (1880); Haraszti, supra note 394, at 85, 92, 95, 109, 193; Lord Arnold McNair, THE LAW OF TREATIES 371-72 (1961); Henry Wheaton, ELEMENTS OF INTERNATIONAL LAW 389 (5th ed. Coleman Phillipson ed. 1916).

[651] Charles Fairman, *The Interpretation of Treaties*, 20 TRANSACTIONS OF THE GROTIUS SOC'Y 123, 129 (1935).

[652] See id. at 129-30 (citing C. Civ. art. 1156 (Fr.); C.c. art. 1131 (It.)).

[653] See id. at 130-31 (citing Cass. req., Feb. 16, 1892, S. 1893, 1, 409 (Fr.) (*Tain c. Cimetière*); Cass. civ., Roma, Apr. 28, 1880, Giur. It. 1880, I, 866 (It.) (*Benigni c. Gregori*)). *See also* James Brierly, THE LAW OF NATIONS 325 (6th ed. Sir Humphrey Waldock ed. 1963) ("There are no technical rules in international law for the interpretation of treaties. . . ."); Charles G. Fenwick, INTERNATIONAL LAW 331 (1924) (ascribing only "inchoate legal value" to rules of treaty construction); Amos S. Hershey, THE ESSENTIALS

This conclusion was repeated by Hersh Lauterpacht,[654] but with a very different thrust: he wished to divorce treaty interpretation from private-law contract rules, and in this effort he largely succeeded.[655] But in so doing, Lauterpacht was obliged to characterize the classical canons of treaty interpretation as quintessentially contractual in character, and this (as I have previously noted) was just not true. Grotius, Pufendorf, Vattel and Phillimore were constructing rules applicable to international agreements, and they self-consciously acknowledged that treaties had both the character of contract and legislation. Indeed, it was this dynamic tension that was the source of much of their methodological difficulties.

The primary vice, however, of Fairman's "private-law" account of the intellectual origins of treaty canons was that it ignored the classical rhetorical roots of the rules. These have, however, been appreciated by other writers.[656]

OF INTERNATIONAL PUBLIC LAW AND ORGANIZATION 445 (rev. ed. 1927) (canons "form no part of International Law proper").

[654] *See* Hersh Lauterpacht, INTERNATIONAL LAW: COLLECTED PAPERS 361 (1970); Hersh Lauterpacht, PRIVATE LAW SOURCES AND ANALOGIES OF INTERNATIONAL LAW 178-79 (1927). *See also* Serge Sur, L'INTERPRÉTATION EN DROIT INTERNATIONAL PUBLIC 251 (1974); Research in International Law, Harvard Law School, Draft Convention on the Law of Treaties, art. 19, 29 AJIL SUPP. 937, 939 (1935) ["Harvard Draft"].

[655] See, e.g., Maarten Bos, *Theory and Practice of Treaty Interpretation (pt. 1)*, 27 NETH. INT'L L. REV. 3, 15-16 (1980) (citing *Reservations to the Convention on the Prevention and Punishment of the Crime of Genocide*, 1951 I.C.J. 3, 23-24 (Opinion of May 28) (noting that in treaties like the Genocide Convention "one cannot speak of individual advantages or disadvantages to States, or of the maintenance of a perfect contractual balance between rights and duties," as would be afforded by private-law rules of contractual interpretation)).

[656] I must point out that virtually no current writer has identified the tap roots of modern treaty interpretation in classical rhetorical forms. The one exception is Ilmar Tammelo, TREATY INTERPRETATION AND PRACTICAL REASON: TOWARD A GENERAL THEORY OF LEGAL INTERPRETATION (1967). Tammelo's challenging book, as it acknowledges, is really about the application of practical reasoning, not interpretive theory. *See* id. at 48-50. Ironically, Tammelo's rhetorical history focuses exclusively on Aristotelian forms and ignores the more pragmatic approach taken by Roman rhetors like Cicero and Quintilian. *See* id. at 35-41.

One strand of thinking has emphasized, like Vattel, Savigny and Phillimore, that interpretation is about following logical rules, founded on "right reason." Dionisio Anzilotti, the leading Italian publicist of the inter-War generation, wrote that treaty interpretation is a "logical operation subject only to the laws of logic, the very general criteria inherent in the special character of a particular legal order being taken for granted."[657]

But this emphasis on logic was, of course, quite problematic, because as D.P. O'Connell wrote, "Logic itself is a deceptive notion, for the mind will utilize different techniques of logic at different times, and the choice between them is not itself, often enough, dictated by logic."[658] Or, put another way, it was impossible "to prescribe any system of rules of interpretation for cases of ambiguity in written language that will readily avail to guide the mind in the decision of doubt."[659] In short, the interpretation of treaties was impervious to a logic-based system of rules or canons.

So, if "logic" could not satisfy modern thinkers, that left one other alternative: rules of treaty construction could effectuate equity and "good faith." This, of course, was the central premise of Grotius and Pufendorf, and the natural law principles inherent in that position have been embraced by a number of writers today, including Ludwik Ehrlich,[660] Charles De Visscher,[661] and Rudolf Bernhardt.[662] The problem with this approach is its standardless quality: how can an equitable interpretation be discerned? The critics of this revived

---

[657] 1 Dionisio Anzilotti, LEHRBUCH DES VÖLKERRECHTS 82 (1929).

[658] 1 D.P. O'Connell, INTERNATIONAL LAW 272 (1965). *See also* Ioan Voïcu, DE L'INTERPRÉTATION AUTHENTIQUE DES TRAITÉS INTERNATIONAUX 44-45 (1968).

[659] Hannis Taylor, TREATISE ON INTERNATIONAL PUBLIC LAW 394 (1901).

[660] *See* Ehrlich, supra note 384, at 16, 70.

[661] *See* Charles de Visscher, PROBLÈMES D'INTERPRETATION JUDICIARE EN DROIT INTERNATIONAL PUBLIC (1963).

[662] *See* Rudolf Bernhardt, DIE AUSLEGUNG VÖLKERRECHTLICHER VERTRÄGE 28 (1963).

school of naturalists have doubted whether treaty canons could possibly be neutral and objective.

Indeed, the critics made the point that treaty canons based on equity are too malleable and too prone to abuse: "for many of the so-called rules of interpretation that one party may invoke before a tribunal the adverse party can often, by the exercise of a little ingenuity, find another rule to serve as an equally attractive antidote."[663] Even J.H.W. Verzijl, who as an arbitrator in the *Georges Pinson* case,[664] attempted to formulate such rules, later gave up the enterprize in disgust, noting that such rules, "on concrete application ... often abrogate each other and frequently appear worthless."[665]

Finally, the entire structure of treaty canons was savaged as rigid and mechanical. Modern publicists were intensely critical of what they perceived as the formalism of the "systematic" approaches they took.[666] The formalism of a "system" or "general theory" of interpretation thus gave way to a "new" functionalism for treaty construction.[667] T.J. Lawrence considered the entire intellectual exercise of devising rules of treaty interpretation as "a vast amount of misplaced energy."[668] Consider this attack, made by Tsune-Chi Yü in his 1927 monograph, worth quoting at length:

> [P]ublicists ever since the days of Grotius and Vattel have resorted to metaphysical formulae and arbitrary distinctions as their polestar in interpreting international agreements. They have made painful efforts to lay down artificial yet precise specifications of method, and to induce nations to observe their imaginary canons. In order to put their conjectures into a system, oftentimes

---

[663] McNair, supra note 650, at 365. *See also* de Visscher, supra note 661, at 70-71.

[664] 1927-28 Ann. Dig. no. 292; 5 R.I.A.A. 422 (Fr.-Mex. Claims Comm'n 1927).

[665] Quoted in 26 BRIT. Y.B. INT'L L. 48, 52 (1949).

[666] *See* Degan, supra note 400, at 54 (noting that Vattel's "system" of treaty interpretation broke down before the First World War).

[667] *See* Degan, supra note 400, at 52.

[668] T.J. Lawrence, PRINCIPLES OF INTERNATIONAL LAW 302 (7th ed. 1923).

a nomenclature of classes, modes and species of interpretation has been frequently elaborated whereby various cases, actual or hypothetical, have been described for the sake of elucidating their definitions and for the purpose of exhibiting the application of particular canons which they have deliberately framed.... [T]hey have presented their artificial maxims with assiduous nicety .... [T]ext writers have accumulated a mass of fanciful rules which, on account of their sweeping, mechanical nature, have caused the task of interpretation to become dangerous.[669]

Yü thus assailed the very structure of interpretive canons. It is not just that the rules have proliferated into a congested, contradictory mass. Nor is it only that the rules are unsupported either by neutral logic or dispassionate equity. It is their very emphasis on "method," on "system," and on taxonomy ("classes, modes and species of interpretation") that is problematic.

iii. But, even in this hostile intellectual environment, canons of treaty construction continued to be employed in arbitral and judicial decisions, and persisted as an important influence in codification efforts. Judges and arbitrators took little heed of the academic grumblings, and continued to apply (and elaborate) rules of treaty construction in their decisions handed-down in the late nineteenth[670] and early twentieth centuries.[671] This, of course, obliged the

---

[669] Tsune-Chi Yü, THE INTERPRETATION OF TREATIES 27 (1927) (1968 rep.). The Harvard Draft, supra note 654, at 945, quite correctly points out that Yü's work was heavily influenced by Charles Cheney Hyde's writing, especially *Concerning the Interpretation of Treaties*, 3 AJIL 46 (1909).

[670] There were but a handful of these decisions, *see, e.g.*, *San Juan* Arbitration (Gr.Brit. v. U.S.) (1872) (German Emperor, arb.), reprinted in 3 A. Lapradelle & N. Politis, RECUEIL DE ARBITRAGES INTERNATIONAUX 20 (1872-75) (see also Wheaton, supra note 209, at 389-90 (for a reprint of the British submissions in that case)); *Van Bokkelen* Case (U.S. v. Haiti) (1888) (A. Porter More, arb.), 2 John Bassett Moore, HISTORY AND DIGEST OF THE INTERNATIONAL ARBITRATIONS TO WHICH THE UNITED STATES HAS BEEN A PARTY 1848 (1898) (quoting extensively from Vattel); *Aspinwall* Case (U.S. v. Ven.) (1890) (J.V. Findlay, arb.), reprinted in 4 id. at 3621 (quoting Grotius).

[671] *See, e.g.*, *Aroa Mine (Ltd.)* Case (Gr.Brit v. Ven.) (1903) (Ralston, arb.), reprinted in Jackson H. Ralston, VENEZUELAN ARBITRATIONS OF 1903, at 844, 852-54 (1904); *Sambiaggio Case*, id. at 689; *Kummerow Case*, id. at 557; *North Atlantic Fisheries* Case (Gr.Brit. v. U.S.), Hague Court Reports (Scott) 141, 186 (Perm. Ct. Arb. 1910).

publicists to comment upon, and respond to, these decisions and so reconsider the robust character of these canons that they had declared intellectually dead.[672] In this exercise, publicists were forced also to acknowledge their own irrelevance to the actual process of treaty interpretation and international dispute settlement. No matter how much the scholars railed against "mechanical" rules of construction, their use persisted.

The creation of the Permanent Court of International Justice in 1920 offered, for the first time in international history, an authoritative institution for interpreting treaties. Every decision of the World Court touching on that issue was carefully parsed and analyzed.[673] It soon became clear that the Court would countenance some use of interpretive canons, "but with such qualifications as to leave itself completely free to apply them or not accordingly as the circumstances and evidence in a particular case may require."[674]

International decisions were quick to adopt, in almost the very words of Robert Phillimore, "as a cardinal principle of interpretation[,] that words must be interpreted in the sense which they would normally have in their context, unless such interpretation would lead to something unreasonable or absurd."[675] Indeed, the Court showed a reluctance to deviate from the "natural,"[676]

---

[672]   *See* Degan, supra note 400, at 51 (listing these scholars).

[673]   *See, e.g.,* G.G. Fitzmaurice, *The Law and Procedure of the ICJ: Treaty Interpretation and Certain Other Treaty Points*, 28 BRIT. Y.B. INT'L L. 1 (1951); 5 Green Haywood Hackworth, DIGEST OF INTERNATIONAL LAW 222-69 (1943); 1 Edvard Hambro, LA JURISPRUDENCE DE LA COUR INTERNATIONALE, 1922-1951 (1961); Manley O. Hudson, THE PERMANENT COURT OF INTERNATIONAL JUSTICE 640-61 (1943); Charles Rousseau, PRINCIPLES GÉNÉRAUX DU DROIT INTERNATIONAL PUBLIC 631-764 (1944); Fairman, supra note 651, at 131-39; Charles Cheney Hyde, *Interpretation of Treaties by the Permanent Court of International Justice*, 24 AJIL 1 (1930).

[674]   Harvard Draft, supra note 654, at 943.

[675]   *Polish Postal Service in Danzig*, 1925 P.C.I.J. (ser. B) No. 11, at 39 (Opinion of May 16) (paraphrasing Phillimore, supra note 627, at 73 (passage ii.8.70)).

[676]   *Interpretation of the 1919 Convention on Women Working in the Night*, 1932 P.C.I.J. (ser. A/B) No. 50, at 373, 378 (Opinion of Nov. 15); *Conditions of Admission,*

"literal,"[677] "ordinary,"[678] "normal,"[679] "logical,"[680] "reasonable,"[681] "clear,"[682] or "sufficiently clear"[683] meaning of a provision.[684] The Court has also sought to look at the entire text of an instrument, and not to interpret one provision in isolation.[685] But, as Judge Dionisio Anzilotti noted in his dissenting opinion in *1919 Convention on Women Working in the Night*, ascertaining whether a text reaches a benchmark of "naturalness," "logic," or "reasonableness" is a subjective task:

> But I do not see how it is possible to say that an article of a convention is clear until the subject matter and aim of the convention have been ascertained, for the article only assumes its true import in this convention and in relation thereto. Only when it is known what the Contracting Parties intended to do,

---

1948 I.C.J. 57, 63 (Opinion of May 28).

[677] *Chorzow Factory* (Jurisdiction) (Ger. v. Pol.), 1927 P.C.I.J. (ser. A/B) No. 21, at 37 (Judgment of 26 July).

[678] *Polish Postal Service in Danzig*, 1925 P.C.I.J. (ser. A/B) No. 11, at 37.

[679] Id. at 39.

[680] *Chorzow Factory* (Jurisdiction), 1927 P.C.I.J. (ser. A/B) No. 21, at 37.

[681] *Polish Postal Service in Danzig*, 1925 P.C.I.J. (ser. B) No. 11, at 39.

[682] *Women Working in the Night*, 1932 P.C.I.J. (ser. A/B) No. 50, at 373.

[683] *Interpretation of Article 3, paragraph 2 of the Treaty of Lausanne* (Mosul Frontier Case), 1925 P.C.I.J. (ser. A/B) No. 17, at 22 (Opinion of Nov. 21).

[684] *See also* Haraszti, supra note 394, at 83-104; Harvard Draft, supra note 654, at 942; Hudson, supra note 673, at 645-46.

[685] *See, e.g., Competence of the International Labor Organization*, 1922 P.C.I.J. (ser. A/B) Nos. 2-3, at 23 (Opinion of Aug. 12); *Marine Safety Committee of the Intergovernmental Marine Consultative Organization*, 1960 I.C.J. 150, 158, 166 (Opinion of June 8). For the use of textual preambles in interpretation, *see* Haraszti, supra note 394, at 106-07.

and the aim they had in view, is it possible to say either that the natural meaning of the terms used in a particular article corresponds with the real intention of the Parties, or that the natural meaning of the term used falls short of, or goes further than such intention.[686]

So interpretation was further defined by the World Court as understanding "the text as it stands, taking into consideration all the materials at the Court's disposal."[687] The goal was to determine the drafters' intent.[688] But this led to a problem: when was it appropriate to look at sources extraneous to the treaty text in order to divine the drafters' intent, and precisely which sources were legitimate to examine? This spurred contention in many different directions.

There was, for example,[689] a heated debate about the use of *travaux préparatoires* — the drafts, debates, and negotiations leading-up to the signing of an agreement. Some scholars had held the view that such proceedings were

---

[686] *Women Working in the Night*, 1932 P.C.I.J. (ser. A/B) No. 50, at 383 (Anzilotti, J., dissenting).

[687] *Treatment of Polish Nationals in Danzig*, 1932 P.C.I.J. (ser. A/B) No. 44, at 40 (Opinion of Feb. 4).

[688] For more on intentionalism in treaty interpretation, *see* Degan, supra note 400, at 117-34; 1 Paul Guggenheim, TRAITÉ DE DROIT INTERNATIONAL PUBLIC 133 (1953); Haraszti, supra note 394, at 104-09; Hudson, supra note 673, at 643-45; Paul Reuter, DROIT INTERNATIONAL PUBLIC 70 (1958).

[689] Other issues included whether the subsequent conduct of the parties in applying a treaty was dispositive, for more on which, *see* the sources discussed in Degan, supra note 400, at 130-32; Ehrlich, supra note 384, at 36; Harvard Draft, supra note 654, at 966-70; Hudson, supra note 673, at 658; Paul Pic, *De l'Interprétation des Traités Internationaux*, 17 R.G.D.I.P. 1, 7-8 (1910).

The leading cases include, *Competence of the International Labor Organization*, 1922 P.C.I.J. (Ser. A/B) No. 2, at 39 ("If there was any ambiguity, the Court might, for the purpose of arriving at the true meaning, consider action which has been taken under the Treaty."); *Jurisdiction of the Danzig Courts*, 1928 P.C.I.J. (Ser. A/B) No. 28, at 18 (Opinion of March 3) ("The intention of the Parties ... [may be determined by] taking into consideration the manner in which the Agreement has been applied....").

"merged" with the treaty and were thus fair game in its interpretation.[690] At the other extreme were those publicists who utterly rejected the use of *travaux*.[691] Middle views were apparent, too, such as Quincy Wright's principle that for bilateral treaties (having the flavor of contract), *travaux* was a reliable indicator of intent, while for multilateral treaties (or those having the indicia of international legislation), it was not.[692] International arbitral institutions[693] and the World Court, as expected, rejected the extreme positions, and accepted that

---

[690] *See, e.g.*, Hershey, supra note 653, at 448; Alexander P. Fachiri, *Interpretation of Treaties*, 23 AJIL 745 (1929).

[691] *See, e.g.*, Samuel B. Crandall, TREATIES, THEIR MAKING AND ENFORCEMENT 377 (2d ed. 1916); Ehrlich, supra note 384, at 118; Charles Cheney Hyde, *Judge Anzilotti on the Interpretation of Treaties*, 27 AJIL 502 (1933); Hersh Lauterpacht, *Some Observations on Preparatory Work in the Interpretation of Treaties*, 48 HARV. L. REV. 549 (1935).

[692] Quincy Wright, *The Interpretation of Multilateral Treaties*, 23 AJIL 94 (1929). *Cf.* Andrew McNair, *The Functions and Differing Legal Character of Treaties*, 11 BRIT. Y.B. INT'L L. 107 (1930) (declaring that Wright's distinction is "intrinsically reasonable" but may be difficult to discern in practice).

[693] *See, e.g., Chilean-Peruvian Accounts* Case, 2 J.B. Moore, supra note 670, at 2095 (*travaux* has "only a corroboratory value"); *Island of Timor* Case (Neth v. Port.), Hague Court Reports (Scott) 354, 369, 375 (1914) (*travaux* "throws positive light on the real and mutual intention of the parties"); *Ascherberg Hopwood & Crew, Ltd. v. Quaritch*, 5 Trib. Arb. Mixtes 332, 335-36 (U.K.-Ger. 1925) (rejecting use of *travaux* when "the Treaty has a clear meaning") (for more on this case, see Bin Cheng, THE INTERPRETATION OF TREATIES BY JUDICIAL TRIBUNALS 49-51 (1953) (critical of its holding)).

travaux — in some limited circumstances[694] — was an appropriate, supplemental means to aid the interpreter in divining the intent of the drafters.[695]

To complete the theoretical trinity of treaty interpretation,[696] courts and arbitrations had also to develop a teleological approach.[697] They quickly obliged. One strand of decisions[698] simply emphasized the objective purpose of

---

[694] *See Competence of the International Labor Organization*, 1922 P.C.I.J. (ser. A/B) Nos. 2-3, at 41 (rejecting use of *travaux*, because terms of the ILO Convention "clearly excluded" disputed interpretation); *Lotus* Case (Fr. v. Turk.), 1927 P.C.I.J. (ser. A/B) No. 22, at 16, 17 (Judgment of Sept. 7) ("there is no occasion to have regard to the preparatory work if the text of the convention is sufficiently clear in itself" and nothing in the *travaux* was "calculated to overrule the construction indicated by the actual terms" of the treaty); *European Commission of the Danube*, 1927 P.C.I.J. (ser. A/B) No. 25, at 28, 31 (Opinion of Dec. 8) ("preparatory work should not be used for the purposes of changing the plain meaning of a text.").

[695] *See, e.g., Treatment of Polish Nationals in Danzig*, 1932 P.C.I.J. (ser. A/B) No. 44, at 33 ("This text not being absolutely clear, it may be useful, in order to ascertain its precise meaning, to recall here somewhat in detail the various drafts which existed prior to the adoption of the text now in force."); *Lighthouses* Case (Fr. v. Gr.), 1934 P.C.I.J. (ser. A/B) No. 62, at 13, 15-16 (Judgment of March 17) ("Where the context does not suffice to show the precise sense in which the Parties to the dispute have employed these words in their Special Agreement, the Court, in accordance with its practice, has to consult the documents preparatory to the Special Agreement, in order to satisfy itself as to the true intentions of the Parties."); *Reservations to the Genocide Convention*, 1951 I.C.J. 3, 22 (Opinion of May 28).

[696] *See, e.g.*, Degan, supra note 400, at 75; Fitzmaurice, supra note 673, at 1-8; id., 33 BRIT. Y.B. INT'L L. 203, 204-09; Sir Ian Sinclair, THE VIENNA CONVENTION ON THE LAW OF TREATIES 115 (2d ed. 1984); Max Sørensen, LES SOURCES DU DROIT INTERNATIONAL 230-33 (1946).

[697] *See, e.g.*, Degan, supra note 400, at 137-46; Fitzmaurice, supra note 673, at 1-8; id., 33 BRIT. Y.B. INT'L L. 203, 204-09;

[698] *See, e.g., Competence of the International Labor Organization*, 1922 P.C.I.J. (ser. A/B) No. 2, at 21-28; *Reparations for Injuries*, 1949 I.C.J. 174, 179-80, 182-83 (Opinion of Apr. 11); *Effects of Judgments of the U.N. Administrative Tribunal*, 1954 I.C.J. 47, 57-58 (Opinion of July 13).

an international agreement, quite apart from its bare text or the original intent of its framers.[699] The other stream of cases[700] had a more ambitious form of teleology in mind. Originally propounded by Grotius, Vattel and Phillimore (under the maxim *ut res magis valeat quam pereat*),[701] it was advocated by some modern publicists:[702] to maximize the effectiveness of treaty régimes. This variant of teleology has, however, been subject to a withering attack by writers. As Lord McNair wrote, "Many treaties fail — and rightly fail — in their object by the reason of the words used, and tribunals are properly reluctant to step in and modify or supplement the language of the treaty."[703] In that vein, the International Court of Justice held in *Interpretation of Peace Treaties* that "[T]he rule of effectiveness[] cannot justify the Court in attributing to the provisions ... [of] the Peace Treaties a meaning which ... would be contrary to their letter and spirit."[704]

---

[699] *See also* Hudson, supra note 673, at 650-51 (noting that the PCIJ looked to the "nature," "scope," "object," "spirit," "tenor," "function," "rôle," "aim," "purpose," "system," "scheme," "general plan" and "principles underlying" treaties) (citing various cases), 656-57 (discussing PCIJ cases where mention was made of political and social background of a treaty).

[700] *See Cayuga Indian* Claims (U.K. v. U.S.), 20 AJIL 574, 587 (1926); *Acquisition of Polish Nationality*, 1923 P.C.I.J. (ser. A/B) No. 7, at 16-17 (Opinion of Sept. 15) ("an interpretation which would deprive the ... Treaty of a great part of its value is inadmissible."); *Exchange of Greek and Turkish Populations*, 1925 P.C.I.J. (ser. B) No. 10, at 25 (Opinion of Feb. 21); *Corfu Channel Case* (U.K. v. Alb.), 1949 I.C.J. 4, 25 (Judgment of Apr. 9) ("It would indeed be incompatible with the generally accepted rules of interpretation to admit that a provision ... should be devoid of purport or effect.").

[701] *See* Degan, supra note 400, at 102; Haraszti, supra note 394, at 168 n.42.

[702] *See, e.g.,* de Visscher, supra note 661, at 84-92, 121-27 (with some reservations); Degan, supra note 400, at 102 (citing a number of writers); Ehrlich, supra note 384, at 81; Haraszti, supra note 394, at 167-70.

[703] McNair, supra note 650, at 383.

[704] *Interpretation of Peace Treaties with Bulgaria, Hungary and Roumania* (Second Phase), 1950 I.C.J. 221, 229 (Opinion of July 18); *cf.* id. at 231 (Read, J., dissenting).

Rules of interpretation were thus vitally significant in fashioning the modern trichotomy of text-intent-purpose. But where they exercised their greatest influence was in the interstices of this three-way schematic. First, the maxims were used in a grammatical sense as a handy approach to what were regarded as situationally obscure provisions. Examples of such rules are *expressio unius est exclusio alterius*[705] and *ejusdem generis.*[706]

Second, canons of construction were applied by tribunals in offering default positions on interpretive matters. One such rule was *contra proferentum*, in which an ambiguous text was construed against the drafter.[707] Despite the different handling of this rule in common law and civil law systems,[708] and the fact that few treaties were acknowledged to be the product of only one nation's

---

[705] *See, e.g., S.S. Wimbledon* Case (Fr./It./Jap./U.K. v. Ger.), 1923 P.C.I.J. (ser. A) No. 1, at 23 (Judgment of Aug. 17); *Lusitania* Case, 7 Rep. Int'l Arb Awards 91, 111 (U.S.-Ger. Mixed Comm'n 1924) (calling this principle a rule "both [of] law and logic"); *Conditions of Admission of Members to the United Nations*, 1948 I.C.J. 57, 62 (Opinion of May 28). *See also* Haraszti, supra note 394, at 110-11 (although calling this the *a contrario* principle); Hersh Lauterpacht, 44 ANNUAIRE DE L'INSTITUT DE DROIT INTERNATIONAL 219 (1952 - I) (suggesting that the rule has not been applied consistently); McNair, supra note 650, at 399-402 (saying that the maxim "would find a place in the logic of the nursery.").

[706] *See Competence of the International Labor Organization*, 1922 P.C.I.J. (ser. A/B) Nos. 2-3, at 59; *Serbian Loans* Case, 1929 P.C.I.J. (ser. A) Nos. 20 & 21, at 30. *See also* Hudson, supra note 673, at 661; McNair, supra note 650, at 393-96.

[707] *See* de Visscher, supra note 661, at 110-12; Haraszti, supra note 394, at 188-92.

[708] *See* Lauterpacht, 26 BRIT. Y.B. INT'L L. at 57 ("the same principle of interpretation which in English and American law has led to the acceptance of the rule that the contract is to be construed against the giver of the promise was responsible in, the Roman law system for the appropriate principle of restrictive interpretation in favour of the debtor). For a typical Civil Law formulation, *see* C. Civ. art. 1162 ("Dans le dout, la convention s'interprète contre celui qui a stipulé, et en faveur de celui qui a contracté obligation.") (Fr.).

drafting,[709] the canon was sometimes invoked by tribunals confronted with ambiguous bilateral agreements.[710]

This maxim was, moreover, closely related to a more problematic cluster of (contradictory) substantive principles: restrictive interpretations to protect state sovereignty[711] and liberal constructions to fully effectuate the object and purpose of international undertakings.[712] Consider these equivocal statements of the World Court: "in case of doubt a limitation of sovereignty must be construed restrictively,"[713] but while this principle is "sound of itself," it

---

[709] *See* id. at 64. *See also Pensions of the Officials of the Saar Territory* Case (Ger. v. Governing Comm'n of the Saar), 3 R.I.A.A. 1555, 1564 (1934) ("The rule that in case of doubt the text of a treaty is to be interpreted against the party which drafted it can only be applied when … one of the parties handed a prepared text to the other party for signature.").

[710] *See, e.g., Lusitania* Case (U.S. v. Ger.), reprinted in 18 AJIL 361, 373 & nn. 26 & 27 (1924) (citing Vattel); *Goldenberg & Sons* Case, 1927-1928 Ann. Dig. 544 (Rom.-Ger. 1927); *Brazillian Loans* Case (Fr. v. Brz.), 1929 P.C.I.J. (ser. A/B) No. 34, at 114 (Judgment of July 12) (where the *contra proferentum* rule was called a "reglè bien connue d'interprétation," but in the context of construing a loan instrument, not a treaty *per se*); *Islamic Republic of Iran and United States of America* (Case A-18) (Dual Nationality), 5 Iran-U.S. Claims Trib. Rep. 251, 260 (1984 - I).

[711] *See* Hudson, supra note 673, at 660-61. A number of sources have (quite rightly) traced this canon back to Grotius' distinction between "odious" and favorable" treaty obligations. *See* Haraszti, supra note 394, at 163 n. 29; Harvard Draft, supra note 654, at 942.

[712] *See* supra notes 700 - 704 and accompanying text.

[713] *Free Zones* Case (Switz v. Fr.), 1932 P.C.I.J. (ser. A/B) No. 46, at 167 (Judgment of June 7). To the same effect are the *Lotus* Case, 1927 P.C.I.J. (ser. A) No. 10 at 18 ("Restrictions upon the independence of States cannot therefor be presumed."); *Mosul Boundary* Case, 1925 P.C.I.J. (ser. B) No. 12, at 25 ("[I]f the wording of a treaty provision is not clear, in choosing between several admissible interpretations, the one which involves the minimum of obligations for the Parties should be adopted. This principle must be admitted to be sound.").

"must be employed only with the greatest caution."[714]   Indeed, the Court has made very clear that these principles are only valid in a limited sense: "[T]he rules as to strict or liberal construction of treaty stipulations can be applied only when ordinary methods of interpretation have failed."[715]

iv. α. The pervasive use of classical canons of interpretation by modern international tribunals compelled codification efforts to do the same. But the very process of codifying principles of treaty interpretation was often seen as rationalizing discordant maxims, and imposing a new system, a new order, on these unruly rules. At the outset, some attempts at codification were merely re-ordering of classical maxims, as handed-down by Grotius and Vattel, into "new" categories (as suggested by Savigny and Phillimore).[716] But by the 1930s, this started to change, and there was a strong movement to discard all the old maxims and impose a new, functionalist approach to treaty interpretation.[717] Of course, this trend coincided with the larger inclination to eschew formalism in all forms of legal interpretation, as we have already seen in the Legal Realists' attack on American statutory construction theory.[718]

---

[714] *Territorial Jurisdiction of the River Oder Commission* (Ger. v. Pol.), 1929 P.C.I.J. (ser. A/B) No. 36, at 26 (Judgment of Sept. 10).

[715] *Polish Postal Service in Danzig*, 1925 P.C.I.J. (ser. B) No. 11, at 39. *See also Wimbledon* Case, 1923 P.C.I.J. (ser. A) No. 1, at 24-25 (the Court was "obliged to stop at the point where the so-called interpretation would be contrary to the plain terms of the article and would destroy what has been clearly granted.").

[716] *See* Pasquale Fiore, INTERNATIONAL LAW CODIFIED 341-46 (Edwin M. Borchard transl. 1918) (§§ 797-821).

[717] An early example is the Declaration on Treaty Interpretation of the Seventh International Conference of American States (Dec. 24, 1933), *reprinted in* Harvard Draft, supra note 654, at 1225-26, which attempts a concise formulation of rules and also notes the relevance of "rules governing the interpretation of domestic law," but only "so far as those rules are common to the legal system of the parties to the controversy." Id. art. 1. *See also* Haraszti, supra note 394, at 216.

[718] *See* supra notes 546 - 547 and accompanying text.

It is no surprise, therefore, that the Harvard Draft Convention on the Law of Treaties, published (with commentary) in 1935, launched a fusillade against the canons, "even in the face of so much doctrine and apparent jurisprudence."[719]   The Draft concluded that "[i]t seems evident that the prescription in advance of hard and fast rules of interpretation — even ... if they amount only rebuttable presumptions — contains an element of danger which is to be avoided."[720]   Indeed, the Harvard Draft inveighed against rules altogether, calling treaty interpretation "a task which calls for investigation, weighing of evidence, judgment, foresight, and a nice appreciation of a number of factors varying from case to case."[721]   After all this damning, the Harvard Draft did have some faint praise for interpretive rules: "[t]his is not to say that all the so-called canons of interpretation are of absolutely no utility."[722]

Nonetheless, the Harvard Draft's key provision on treaty interpretation, article 19(a), was a non-rule: an instruction that all evidence was probative of a treaty's meaning, without any hierarchy of sources:

> A treaty is to be interpreted in the light of the general purpose which it is intended to serve.   The historical background of the treaty, *travaux préparatoires*, the circumstances of the parties at the time the treaty was entered into, the change in these circumstances sought to be effected, the subsequent conduct of the parties in applying the provisions of the treaty, and the conditions prevailing at the time the interpretation is made, are to be considered in connection with the general purpose which the treaty is intended to serve.[723]

---

[719]   Harvard Draft, supra note 654, at 944.

[720]   Id. at 946.

[721]   Id. *See also* Degan, supra note 400, at 64-65.

[722]   Id. at 946-47.

[723]   Id. at 937.

Indeed, there seems to be only one source that is not mentioned on this laundry list: the actual *text* of the treaty. It is no surprise that the Harvard Draft provision on treaty interpretation was regarded as worthless.[724]

β. It was inevitable that the intellectual pendulum would swing back to rule-based treaty construction which insisted on a relative ordering of interpretive techniques. Such a move began with the work of the International Law Institute in the 1950s, and, despite Hersh Lauterpacht's attempts to maintain the pure "functionalist" approach epitomized by the Harvard Draft,[725] the textualists won the day.[726]

It remained for the 1969 Vienna Convention to complete this process. The language of articles 31 and 32 of the Vienna Convention on the Law of Treaties[727] as adopted is virtually identical to that prepared by the International Law Commission (ILC) when it completed its deliberations on the Law of Treaties in 1966.[728] However the ILC's language itself reflected a revision of the language originally proposed by the Special Rapporteur, Sir Humphrey Waldock.

In the process of identifying clear and binding rules of interpretation, the Special Rapporteur ran head-on into the status of the myriad interpretive canons.

---

[724]   *See* Degan, supra note 400, at 64-65.

[725]   *See* 43 ANNUAIRE DE L'INSTITUT DE DROIT INTERNATIONAL 423, 433 (1950 - I).

[726]   *See* 46 ANNUAIRE DE L'INSTITUT DE DROIT INTERNATIONAL 358 (1956). *See also* Degan, supra note 400, at 65-66.

[727]   Vienna Convention on the Law of Treaties, U.N. Doc. A/CONF. 39/27 (1969), 1155 U.N.T.S. 331, 63 AJIL 875 (1969), done at Vienna on May 23, 1969; entered into force on January 27, 1980 [hereinafter Vienna Convention].

[728]   The provisions on treaty interpretation were adopted as articles 69 and 70 of the ILC's Draft Articles at the ILC's 884th meeting, on July 5, 1966. *Summary Records of the 884th Meeting*, [1966] 1 Y.B. Int'l L. Comm'n 270, U.N. Doc. A/CN.4/SER.A/1966. The provisions adopted there differ from the final treaty text only by six words, the inclusion in the final text of the phrase "or the application of its provisions" to the end of paragraph 3(a) of article 69, which became article 31.

In coming to terms with these canons, Waldock (quoting from the Harvard Draft) first acknowledged the difficulty of imposing any rules on the interpretive process:

> The process of interpretation, rightly conceived, cannot be regarded as a mere mechanical one of drawing inevitable meanings from the words in a text, or of searching for and discovering some preexisting specific intention of the parties with respect to every situation arising under a treaty.... In most instances interpretation involves *giving* a meaning to a text – not just any meaning which appeals to the interpreter, to be sure, but a meaning which, in the light of the text under consideration and of all the concomitant circumstances of the particular case at hand, appears in his considered judgment to be one which is logical, reasonable, and most likely to accord with and to effectuate the larger general purposes which the parties desired the treaty to serve. This is obviously a task which calls for investigation, weighing of evidence, judgment, foresight, and a nice appreciation of a number of factors varying from case to case. *No canons of interpretation can be of absolute and universal utility in performing such a task, and it seems desirable that any idea that they can be should be dispelled.*[729]

Indeed the Special Rapporteur acknowledged that some scholars rejected the utility of canons of interpretation as anything other than "mere *prima facie* guides to the intention of the parties in a particular case."[730] However, Waldock chose to side with those writers who, "although they may have reservations as to the obligatory character of certain of the so-called canons of interpretation, have shown less hesitation in recognizing the existence of some general rules for the interpretation of treaties."[731]

He approached this difficult task first by asserting the relevance of interpretive canons to international jurisprudence:

---

[729] Third Report on the Law of Treaties, by Sir Humphrey Waldock, Special Rapporteur, U.N. Doc. A/CN.4/167 and Add. 1-3, at 53 [hereinafter Waldock III] (quoting Harvard Draft, supra note 654, at 946) (emphasis added to final sentence).

[730] Id. (quoting McNair, supra note 650, at 366).

[731] Id. (counting among this group the previous Special Rapporteur, Sir Gerald Fitzmaurice).

> The great majority of cases submitted to international adjudication involve the interpretation of treaties, and the jurisprudence of international tribunals is rich in references to principles and maxims of interpretation. In fact, statements can be found in the decisions of international tribunals to support the use of almost every principle or maxim of which use is made in national systems of law in the interpretation of statutes and contracts; for example, those frequently referred to in their Latin forms, *ut res magis valeat quam pereat, contra proferentum, eiusdem generis, expressio unius est exclusio alterius, generalia specialibus non derogant.* Treaty interpretation is, of course, equally part of the everyday work of Foreign Ministries and, if it is less easy to give chapter and verse than in the case of arbitral jurisprudence, it may safely be said that appeal to these principles and maxims of interpretation is no less frequent in State practice.[732]

Neither Waldock nor other members of the ILC referred to the precise source of these canons, suggesting that evidence of their use in the practice of states and judges was sufficient. And their discussions reveal a tacit assumption or assertion that their existence, content, and possibly their sources, were common knowledge.

But establishing (or positing) the prevalence of interpretive canons only begged the question of their authoritativeness:

> In short, it would be possible to find sufficient evidence of recourse to these principles and maxims in international practice to justify their inclusion in a codification of the law of treaties, if the question were simply one of their relevance on the international plane. But ... the question posed by many jurists is rather as to the non-obligatory character of many of these principles and maxims; and it is a question which arises in national systems of law no less than in international law. *They are, for the most part, principles of logic and good sense valuable only as guides to assist in appreciating the meaning which the parties may have intended to attach to the expressions which they employed in a document.* Their suitability for use in any given case hinges on a variety of considerations which have first to be appreciated by the interpreter of the document: the particular arrangement of the words and sentences, their relation to each other and to other parts of the document, the general nature and subject-matter of the document, the circumstances in which it was drawn up, etc. Even when a possible occasion for their application may appear to exist, their application is not automatic but depends on the conviction of the

---

[732] Id. at 54 (citations omitted).

interpreter that it is appropriate in the particular circumstances of the case. *In other words, recourse to many of these principles is discretionary rather than obligatory, and the interpretation of documents is to some extent an art, not an exact science.*[733]

One wonders what Waldock was about with his mysterious qualification "for the most part," and his general pronouncements about the discretionary character of "many of the principles." His meaning becomes clear when one sees his attempt to distinguish "methods of interpretation," which his draft articles record as binding principles, from mere canons of interpretation. He acknowledged:

> The position in regard to the methods of interpretation is somewhat analogous. The jurisprudence of international tribunals furnishes examples of all the different approaches to interpretation – textual, subjective and teleological. But it also shows that, if the textual method of interpretation predominates, none of these approaches is exclusively the correct one, and that their use in any particular case is to some extent a matter of choice and appreciation.[734]

However, he hastened to interpret the patterns of practice as generously for his project as possible: "This [absence of uniformity] does not necessarily mean that there is no obligatory rule in regard to methods of interpretation; but it does mean that there is a certain discretionary element also on this point."[735] Given these constraints, he saw his task as an attempt "to isolate and to codify the comparatively few rules which appear to constitute the strictly legal basis of the interpretation of treaties."[736] He justified undertaking this admittedly problematic task first because of the potential that codifying clear rules may reduce the arbitrariness of treaty interpretation, second because he felt the Commission could strengthen the trend of increased reliance on the texts of treaties, and third because some indication of how treaties are to be interpreted

---

[733] Id. (emphasis added).

[734] Id.

[735] Id.

[736] Id.

was necessary to give meaning to other parts of the draft convention that include phrases like "unless a contrary intention appears from the treaty."[737]

To formulate the specifics of his draft articles, Waldock drew primarily on the 1956 Resolution of the Institut de Droit International and on Gerald Fitzmaurice's formulation of the "major principles" of interpretation in a 1957 article in the *British Yearbook of International Law*.[738] These principles elevated the text of the treaty over other sources of interpretation, but they also contemplated consultation of the *travaux préparatoires*, reference to practice under the treaty and a teleological approach.

As a starting point the draft:

> takes as the basic rule of treaty interpretation the primacy of the text as evidence of the intentions of the parties. It accepts the view that the text must be presumed to be the authentic expression of the intentions of the parties; and that, in consequence, the starting point and purpose of interpretation is to elucidate the meaning of the text, not to investigate *ab initio* the intentions of the parties.[739]

---

[737] Id.

[738] 33 Brit. Y.B. Int'l L. 203 (1957).

[739] Waldock III, supra note 729, at 56. In elaborating the textual approach Waldock identifies four separate principles of text-driven interpretation, drawn principally from his main sources, but justifiable also on logical grounds: interpretation in good faith; utilizing the natural and ordinary meaning of the terms; such meaning to be interpreted by reference to the context in which the terms occur; and "interpretation by reference to the linguistic usage current at the time of the conclusion of the treaty." Id.
Waldock's Draft Article 70.–General rules, provided that

> 1. The terms of a treaty shall be interpreted in good faith in accordance with the natural and ordinary meaning to be given to each term–
> (a) in its context in the treaty and in the context of the treaty as a whole; and
> (b) in the context of the rules of international law in force at the time of the conclusion of the treaty.
>
> 2. If the natural and ordinary meaning of a term leads to an interpretation which

Article 71 of Waldock's Draft spelled-out[740] what materials may be consulted as the "context of the treaty as a whole" and the Special Rapporteur was at pains to clarify that:

> for purposes of interpreting the treaty, the specified categories of documents should not be regarded as mere evidence to which recourse may be had for the purpose of resolving the ambiguity or obscurity but as part of the context for

---

is manifestly absurd or unreasonable in the context of the treaty as a whole, or if the meaning of a term is not clear owing to its ambiguity or obscurity, the term shall be interpreted by reference to–
  (*a*) its context and the objects and purposes of the treaty; and
  (*b*) the other means of interpretation mentioned in article 71, paragraph 2.

3. Notwithstanding paragraph 1, a meaning other than its natural and ordinary meaning may be given to a term if it is established conclusively that the parties employed the term in the treaty with that special meaning.

[740] The text of draft article 71 was:
1. In the application of article 70 the context of the treaty as a whole shall be understood as comprising in addition to the treaty (including its preamble)–
  (*a*) any agreement arrived at between the parties as a condition of the conclusion of the treaty or as a basis for its interpretation;
  (*b*) any instrument or document annexed to the treaty;
  (*c*) any other instrument related to, and drawn up in connexion with the conclusion of, the treaty.

2. Reference may be made to other evidence or indications of the intentions of the parties and, in particular, to the preparatory work of the treaty, the circumstances surrounding its conclusion and the subsequent practice of parties in relation to the treaty, for the purpose of–
  (*a*) confirming the meaning of a term resulting from the application of paragraph 1 of article 70;
  (*b*) determining the meaning of a term in the application of paragraph 2 of that article;
  (*c*) establishing the special meaning of a term in the application of paragraph 3 of that article.

the purpose of arriving at the natural and ordinary meaning of the terms of the treaty.[741]

Article 72 was an attempt to accommodate the principle of "effective" interpretation among the general rules without letting it overwhelm the focus on the parties' intent revealed through the text.[742]   This limitation is ensured by clarifying that effective interpretation "does not call for 'extensive' or 'liberal' interpretation in the sense of an interpretation going beyond what is expressed or necessarily implied in the terms."[743]

γ. The response of the International Law Commission to the Waldock Draft was enthusiastic. Characteristic of this was the reaction of Professor Herbert Briggs, who said that:

> He strongly supported the approach adopted by the Special Rapporteur in articles 70 to 73 and thought it not inconsistent with the wise caution displayed in the Harvard Research Draft. The canons of interpretation were not always rules of international law but, as Judge de Visscher had said, they were working hypotheses, and the Special Rapporteur's decision to distill the essence of such fundamental principles as could properly be treated as rules of international law was sound. Extensive State practice, precedent and doctrine permitted of the precise formulation and systematization of rules of the kind he had set out.
>
> The Special Rapporteur had rightly emphasized the primacy of the text of the treaty as an expression of the intentions of the parties.[744]

---

[741] Waldock III, supra note 729, at 58.

[742] The text of draft article 72 was:
In the application of articles 70 and 71 a term of a treaty shall be so interpreted as to give it the fullest weight and effect consistent–
        (*a*) with its natural and ordinary meaning and that of the other terms of the treaty; and
        (*b*) with the objects and purposes of the treaty.

[743] Waldock III, supra note 729, at 58.

[744] *Summary Records of the 765th Meeting*, [1964] 1 Y.B. Int'l L. Comm'n 275, U.N. Doc. A/CN.4/SER.A/1964 [hereinafter *765th Meeting*] (comments of Prof. Briggs).

Professor Ruda differed from what appears to be majority sentiment in favor of codifying rules of interpretation, asserting that:

> at the present stage of development of international law, there did not as yet exist for States any obligatory rules upon the subject of interpretation; he stressed that he was referring to rules binding upon States. At least, if any rules existed, they were subject to considerable doubt, except for the rule *in claris non fit interpretatio*, which had been first formulated by Vattel and which meant that there could be no question of interpretation where the sense was clear and there was nothing to interpret.
>
> Interpretation occurred at two different levels. First, as between States, the only legally valid interpretation of a treaty was the authentic interpretation by the parties to the treaty. The other level was that of interpretation by arbitration, for which there were fundamental principles; that form of interpretation, however, fell outside the discussion because the Commission was engaged in drafting a convention between States.
>
> Although he did not wish to imply that the Commission could not formulate rules in the matter, he stressed that those rules would not constitute a codification of existing law; they would represent proposals for the progressive development of international law. With a view to progressive development, rules could thus be submitted to States for their guidance in the interpretation of treaties. Such rules would have the advantage, from the theoretical point of view, of being conducive to the certainty of international transactions. From the practical point of view, as had been indicated by other speakers, it would be useful to submit to States draft articles on interpretation, so as to elicit from them specific comments.
>
> On the second problem, the choice of method, he agreed with the approach adopted by the Special Rapporteur, who had taken the text of the treaty as the authentic expression of the intention of the parties.[745]

With respect to the specifics of Waldock's proposed method, despite his insistence that the materials making up the "context of the treaty" were integral to the process of interpretation, several members of the commission were still uncomfortable with the seeming priority given to textual methods of interpretation. Mr. Yasseen clarified that he:

---

[745]   Id. at 277 (comments of Mr. Ruda).

approved the Special Rapporteur's approach to the subject matter of article 70. The text of the treaty should form the basis of any inquiry into the scope and meaning of its provisions; but interpretation could not be confined to the context of the treaty, for a treaty also had to be regarded as an expression of will in the light of the legal order in force at the time of its conclusion.[746]

Likewise Mr. Bartos complained that:

> The draft articles were based on the general concept, so dear to the English .school of legal thought, that interpretation meant interpretation of the text rather than of the spirit of a treaty. Like Mr. Tunkin, he thought it would be better to take as a basis the general principles of international law than to concentrate on the "terms" of the treaty. He did not greatly favour the exegetical method in international law. Where interpretation was concerned, the autonomy of the will of the parties was paramount. What the parties had intended was more important than what they had actually said in the treaty.[747]

The ILC then considered whether or not it could agree to establish "a sort of order of importance among sources of interpretation."[748] This discussion concluded, vaguely that "If the 'context of a treaty' was understood in a fairly liberal sense and defined on the lines suggested by the Chairman, some measure of hierarchical order would be given to the different elements of interpretation without going too far in that direction."[749] And Waldock was asked to redraft articles 70 and 71 in light of the Commission's discussion. Article 72, incorporating the problematic and controversial maxim *ut res magis valeat quam pereat*, was dealt with by deciding that:

> [it] should not form the subject of a separate rule. In so far as it stated a logical rule, it was in any case implicit in the earlier provisions of sections III of the draft and there was perhaps no need to state it explicitly....

---

[746] Id. at 279 (statement of Mr. Yasseen).

[747] Id. (response of Mr. Bartos).

[748] *Summary Records of the 766th Meeting*, [1964] 1 Y.B. Int'l L. Comm'n 285, U.N. Doc. A/CN.4/SER.A/1964 (statement of M. de Luna).

[749] Id. at 288.

Accordingly, [the Chairman] suggested that for the time being article 72 should not appear in the section on the interpretation of treaties.[750]

δ.   In response to the reactions of the governments who submitted comments on the formulation of the draft articles, Waldock undertook a revision of the articles that was reexamined by the International Law Commission in 1966, which, after lengthy debate, referred the issues to a Drafting Committee.

Charged with collating the disparate positions of the delegates and reducing them to text, the Drafting Committee interpreted the various approaches to these issues in the following way. With respect to the hierarchy of interpretive rules, the final draft should reflect two somewhat contradictory conclusions, first, the primacy of the text as a reflection of party intent,[751] and second, the undesirability of establishing any formal hierarchy of rules or methods.   On this point the Special Rapporteur clarified the Commission members' sentiments:

> Neither in [the 1964] text nor in the one now proposed was there any intention of creating an order in which a series of rules should be successively applied; the Commission's idea was rather that of a crucible in which all the elements of interpretation would be mixed: the result of that mixing would be the correct interpretation. It was important that that should be made clear in the commentary....[752]

The Final ILC Draft articles on treaty interpretation read as follows, and were (with only slight stylistic changes) adopted in the 1969 Vienna Convention:[753]

---

[750]   Id. at 291.

[751]   *Summary of the 869th Meeting*, [1966] 1 Y.B. Int'l L. Comm'n, pt. I, 185, U.N. Doc. A/CN.4/SER.A/1966 [hereinafter *869th Meeting*] (exemplifying delegates statements in support of this rule, which was not accepted without controversy).

[752]   *Summary of the 883rd meeting*, [1966] 1 Y.B. Int'l L. Comm'n 267, U.N. Doc. A/CN.4/SER.A/1966 (statement of Sir Waldock, Special Rapporteur).

[753]   This was so despite the United States' attempt to moderate the strong textualist tone of the provisions, a provision that was overwhelmingly defeated. *See* Sinclair, supra note 696, 859, at 115; id., *The Vienna Conference on the Law of Treaties*, 19 INT'L & COMP.L.

ARTICLE 69 [31]

General rule of interpretation

1. A treaty shall be interpreted in good faith in accordance with the ordinary meaning to be given to the terms of the treaty in their context and in the light of its object and purpose.

2. The context for the purpose of the interpretation of a treaty shall comprise, in addition to the text, including its preamble and annexes:

(*a*) any agreement related to the treaty which was made between all the parties in connexion with the conclusion of the treaty;

(*b*) any instrument which was made by one or more parties in connexion with the conclusion of the treaty and accepted by the other parties as an instrument related to the treaty.

3. There shall be taken into account, together with the context:

(*a*) any subsequent agreement between the parties regarding the interpretation of the treaty;

(*b*) any subsequent practice in the application of the treaty which establishes the understanding of the parties regarding its interpretation;

(*c*) any relevant rules of international law applicable in the relations between the parties.

4. A special meaning shall be given to a term if it is established that the parties so intended.

ARTICLE 70 [32]

Supplementary means of interpretation

Recourse may be had to supplementary means of interpretation including the preparatory work of the treaty and the circumstances of its conclusion, in order to confirm the meaning resulting from the application of article 69 [31], or to determine the meaning when the interpretation according to article 69 [31]:

(*a*) leaves the meaning ambiguous or obscure; or

Q. 47, 60 (1970).

(*b*) leads to a result which is manifestly absurd or unreasonable.[754]

The final discussion of the Draft Articles adopted by the International Law Commission suggests that in many ways they deliberately did not resolve the difficult issues of creating a hierarchy of interpretive method. One should not lose sight of the fact, however, that the very process of reaching out into the jurisprudence of international and national tribunals and the doctrinal writings of publicists (which seemed to serve as the main sources for the canons they identified) to collect a small group of canons for codification or proposal as binding rules of international law, was both a controversial and meaningful achievement.[755]

Transforming even a small number of these prudential guidelines and logical approaches to interpretation into rules of law entangled the Commission in the issue of whether, and to what extent, these canons were or could be binding. The approach taken by the Special Rapporteur, and by the Commission under his leadership, does not seem to have resolved many of the deeper philosophical issues hinted at by the ILC's trepidation even to engage in this process, but by making the choice to make the effort, the ILC made some law.

Whether this approach made new law, by elevating some of these canons to the status of law, or was simply a recognition of the binding nature of long-standing practices, was debatable even among the members of the Commission and the governments who participated in drafting the articles.[756] But given the diversity of practices on which the Commission drew, and the general view of these interpretive canons as mere "rules of thumb," it seems most likely that

---

[754] *Summary of the 883rd & 884th Meetings*, [1966] 1 Y.B. Int'l L. Comm'n 267-70, U.N. Doc. A/CN.4/SER.A/1966 (recording votes of ILC).

[755] *See* Bos, supra note 655, at 36-37, 143-46; Sinclair, supra note 2, at 117 ("the Convention rules on interpretation reflect an attempt to assess the relative value and weight of the elements to be taken into account in the process of interpretation rather than to describe the process of interpretation itself.").

[756] *See* Georg Schwarzenberger, *Myths and Realities of Treaty Interpretation* 22 CURRENT LEGAL PROBLEMS 205 (1969) (suggesting that the Vienna Convention creates new law for treaty interpretation).

Articles 31 and 32 go beyond their stated codificatory function to the creation of new binding rules of interpretation.

v. What seems to be clear, is that the ILC's codification effort drew on classical insights of interpretation of legal texts, as received in the treatise literature and the international arbitral jurisprudence. Although the influence of classical sources may not always have been apprehended in this process, they were certainly present. Aside from the analysis of particular maxims of interpretation, there was the general treatment of approaches to construction of treaty texts, and the consideration of the critical question of whether treaty interpretation was even susceptible to the application of rules of construction. The ultimate conclusion reached — as with that for modern statutory interpretation — was a resounding "yes" in principle.

What remains for my consideration in this study is how canons of construction have been actually applied in treaty practice. While I might have continued to deepen my discussion of international treaty interpretation practice, I have decided to offer, instead, a synthesis of developments in treaty and statutory construction by examining the development of canons in a domestic legal order. Although I might have chosen to explore the British, French, German or Japanese jurisprudence of treaty construction, I will stick to what I know best, which is the United States law on this subject. I would like to think that this selection transcends parochialism, although it probably does not. But I did need to select a domestic legal order that had substantial depth of experience — and sophistication — in judicial attempts to interpret treaties, and United States' practice surely fills that bill.

XI A PRIMER ON MODERN AMERICAN TREATY INTERPRETATION

This part of my volume begins by trying to find the method in the madness of treaty interpretation by United States courts. We know that treaties are law of the land.[757] Their provisions have as much force as statutes. Yet, unlike Acts of Congress, treaties begin their life in constitutional obscurity. They are the creation not of the law makers, but of the Executive Branch, receiving only a limited form of legislative concurrence. Born into legal limbo, treaties live a double life: one half as part of the American legal system, the other as an expression of an international undertaking with other nations.

This dual character of treaties — and of the treaty-making power — was recognized by the Framers of the American Constitution. Alexander Hamilton, writing in *The Federalist*, had occasion to comment on this problem, in language that was strongly reminiscent of his comments concerning the use of canons of statutory construction as a form of judicial review.[758] He wrote that the treaty power:

> does not seem strictly to fall within the definition of either [the legislative or executive power]. The essence of the legislative authority is to enact laws; or, in other words, to prescribe rules for the regulation of society; while the execution of the laws and the employment of the common strength, either for this purpose or for the common defense, seem to comprise all the functions of

---

[757] *See* U.S. Const. art. VI, § 2.

[758] *See* supra § VIII.i.

the executive magistrate [the Presidency]. The power of making treaties is plainly, neither the one nor the other.... Its objects are CONTRACTS with foreign nations which have the force of law, but derive it from the obligations of good faith. They are not rules prescribed by the sovereign to the subject, but agreements between sovereign and sovereign. The power in question seems therefore to form a distinct department, and to belong, properly, neither to the legislative nor to the executive.[759]

Important in this passage are two ideas. The first is the recognition of the insight made a century earlier by Grotius and Pufendorf[760] that the defining principle of making and enforcing international agreements is that they contain real "obligations" which are to be observed in "good faith." Hamilton's understanding appeared to be shared by the Framing generation[761] and thus influenced the terms of the Constitutional text. The second point that Hamilton made was, as already suggested, that treaties have a dual character as international agreement and as domestic law, as legislation and as contract. And while Hamilton dismissed the idea that a treaty can create rights and obligations for individuals, a question of greater relevance today than in 1787, he does acknowledge the enigmatic character of treaties.

The strange birth and schizophrenic life of treaties, as succinctly described by Hamilton, has led, however, to their being considered as something fundamentally *other* than public law. Nowhere has this treatment been most tellingly seen than in the efforts of American courts to give meaning and content to treaty provisions. This section summarizes the manner in which international[762] agreements are interpreted in the courts of the United States.[763]

---

[759] THE FEDERALIST No. 75, at 450-51 (Alexander Hamilton) (Clinton Rossiter ed. 1961) (original emphasis).

[760] *See* supra § VII.

[761] *See also* James Madison, writing as Helvedius, who noted that the treaty power should not be considered legislative in character. James Madison, *Letters of Helvedius*, No. 1 (Aug. 24, 1793), in 6 THE WRITINGS OF JAMES MADISON 145 (G. Hunt ed. 1906).

[762] From the beginning of the Republic until 1871, the United States concluded treaties with the Indian nations on the North American continent. *See* Act of March 3, 1871, ch. 120, 16 Stat. 566 (1871) (codified at 25 U.S.C. § 71 (1988)) (ending the practice of calling

The goal here is to discover whether there is a consistent pattern or practice in the judicial interpretation of treaties. To this end, it is necessary first to examine the constitutional allocation of power between the branches of the federal government. This exercise is important in order to ascertain whether judges and courts have unfettered power to construe treaties, and, if they do not, to determine what constrains them. These inhibitions traditionally manifest themselves as judicial deference to those branches which make treaties under U.S. law (the President and the Senate) or which generally manage the country's foreign affairs (the Executive branch alone).

Next, this section will set forth some basic substantive rules of treaty interpretation as enunciated by our courts, particularly those canons articulated by the United States Supreme Court. It should be said, though, that a search for first principles in treaty interpretation is fraught with peril. The reason is that

---

agreements with Indian tribes "treaties"). A substantial jurisprudence has been generated concerning the proper methods of interpreting and applying such treaties. *See, e.g., United States v. Winnans*, 198 U.S. 371, 380-81 (1905); *Choctaw Nation v. United States*, 119 U.S. 1, 28 (1886); *Worcester v. Georgia*, 31 U.S. (6 Pet.) 515, 582 (1832). For the purposes of this article, however, cases concerning treaties with Indian tribes will not be directly considered. For more on the problem of Indian treaties, *see* Lawrence H. Tribe, *Taking Text and Structure Seriously: Reflections on Free-Form Method in Constitutional Interpretation*, 108 HARV. L. REV. 1223, 1263-64 (1995).

[763] Both the federal courts of the United States and the courts of the individual states are free (in principle) to interpret treaties. Treaty interpretation by state courts is infrequent. *But see, Sei Fujii v. California*, 38 Cal.2d 718, 242 P.2d 617 (1952) (in which the California Supreme Court interpreted the U.N. Charter in such a way as to make its non-discrimination provisions non self-executing); *Oregon v. Kolovrat*, 220 Or. 448, 349 P.2d 255 (1960), *rev'd*, 366 U.S. 187 (1961) (construing Friendship, Commerce and Navigation (FCN) Treaty with Yugoslavia). The United States Constitution gives to the federal courts jurisdiction over "all Cases ... arising under this Constitution, the Laws of the United States, and Treaties made, or which shall be made, under their Authority ...." U.S. Const. art. III, § 2.

An interpretation of a treaty made by the U.S. Supreme Court is definitive and binding on state courts, pursuant to the Supremacy clause of the Constitution. U.S. Const. art. VI, ¶ 2. Indeed, any general canons of treaty interpretation enunciated by the U.S. Supreme Court would likewise be binding on all courts in the country. *See Restatement (Third) Foreign Relations Law of the United States* § 326, cmt. d (1987) [hereinafter "Restatement"].

a court's selection of an interpretive method for construing any legal instrument (whether a contract, statute, or treaty) is often driven by the substantive result desired. It is not enough to credit what a court *says* in how it construes a treaty; one must understand what the court then *does* in applying the method of interpretation to reach some legal conclusion.

Finally, this section will look at the influence of generally-agreed, international methods of treaty construction on domestic practice in the United States. Courts here have always been sensitive to the concern that, because treaty interpretation has both municipal and international implications, care must be taken to interpret treaties consistently with the expectations of other countries. In the past, this concern has sometimes manifested itself in the form of great deference to the President's Executive branch interpretation of a treaty. While this deference remains strong, a trend is developing for courts to at least consider the interpretive rules of the 1969 Vienna Convention on the Law of Treaties.[764] As yet, there exists little consistency in applying the Vienna Convention canons. This should not be surprising since it is difficult to discern even a core set of deferential or substantive principles that United States courts faithfully employ in interpreting treaties.

    i. *Allocation of Constitutional Power to Interpret Treaties.* Courts ultimately decide the meaning of treaties in the United States.[765] As Justice

---

[764] Vienna Convention on the Law of Treaties, May 23, 1969, arts. 31 & 32, 1155 U.N.T.S. 331 [hereinafter "Vienna Convention"]. *See* supra §§ X.iv.β & γ.

[765] *See Sullivan v. Kidd*, 254 U.S. 433, 442 (1921); *Jones v. Meehan*, 175 U.S. 1, 32 (1899); *Ware v. Hylton*, 3 U.S. (3 Dall.) 199, 283 (1796). The Executive branch and administrative agencies are sometimes called upon to construe treaties in the first instance, but their interpretations are typically subject to judicial review. *See* Restatement, supra note 2, at § 326; Senate Comm. on Foreign Relations, *The INF Treaty*, S. Exec. Rep. No. 15, 100th Cong., 2d Sess. 107 (1988). *See also* Stefan A. Riesenfeld & Frederick M. Abbott, *The Scope of U.S. Senate Control over the Conclusion and Operation of Treaties*, 67 CHI.-KENT L. REV. 571, 582-84 (1991).

    For the allocation of power to interpret treaties (which have been enacted into statute) in the United Kingdom and most Commonwealth countries, *see* C.H. Schreuer, *The Interpretation of Treaties by Domestic Courts*, 45 BRIT. Y.B. INT'L L. 255, 256-61 (1971) (collecting cases holding that British courts have the power to interpret such agreements). For French practice, *see* id. at 261-63 (indicating that French tribunals show substantially

Black wrote in *Kolovrat v. Oregon*,[766] "courts interpret treaties for themselves."[767] As already noted, an interpretation made by a federal court, particularly the U.S. Supreme Court, is binding on the other branches of the federal government, as well as the states.[768] Indeed, our courts have a *duty* to interpret treaties. They may not abstain from doing so because of delicate foreign relations concerns or fears of embarrassing the President or Congress with an unexpected or unfortunate reading of a treaty.[769] Courts, however, remain under an obligation to merely construe treaties — not to rewrite them. As Justice Story wrote in 1821, "this Court is bound to give effect to the stipulations of a treaty in the manner and the extent which the parties have declared, and not otherwise."[770]

Courts and other interpreting authorities have at their disposal a wide range of materials from which they can develop a construction which is true to the text, intent, and purpose of the international agreement. The use of these materials, and the priority to be accorded to them, will be discussed in greater

---

greater deference to the political branches).

[766] 366 U.S. 187 (1961).

[767] Id. at 194 (Black, J.).

[768] *See, e.g., Japan Whaling Ass'n v. American Cetacean Soc'y*, 478 U.S. 221, 230 (1986); *Nielsen v. Johnson*, 279 U.S. 47, 52 (1929) ("meaning of treaty provisions [should not be] restricted by any necessity of avoiding possible conflict with state" laws); *Jones v. Meehan*, 175 U.S. 1, 32 (1899).

[769] *See* Restatement, supra note 763, at § 1, note 4 and § 326, note 3. For more on a "political question" exception to justiciability of treaty interpretation questions, *see United States v. Decker*, 600 F.2d 733, 737 & n.6 (9th Cir.), *cert. denied*, 444 U.S. 855 (1979).
It was not always true that courts felt free to interpret treaties. *See The Cherokee Nation v. Georgia*, 30 U.S. (5 Pet.) 1, 20 (Marshall, C.J.), 30 (Johnson, J., concurring) (1831). *See also* Thomas M. Franck, POLITICAL QUESTIONS/JUDICIAL ANSWERS: DOES THE RULE OF LAW APPLY TO FOREIGN AFFAIRS? 11-12, 59-60 (1992) (for more on the enunciation of a "rule" of judicial abstinence in treaty interpretation cases — and its later rejection).

[770] *The AMIABLE ISABELLA*, 20 U.S. (6 Wheat.) 1, 71-73 (1821) (Story, J.).

detail below. But it needs to be said here that there are no rules of treaty interpretation which are mandated by the Constitution itself, or are legitimately derived directly from constitutional allocations of authority.[771]

α. *Judicial Deference to Senate Interpretations of Treaties.* Under the Constitution, the Senate has a privileged role in the conclusion of international agreements entered into by the United States. The President has the "Power ... to make treaties."[772] But in order for a treaty to become "the supreme Law of the Land,"[773] it must receive the "Advice and Consent of the Senate ... provided two thirds of the Senators present concur."[774] The Senate may lawfully condition its advice and consent on the adoption of any number of reservations (which purport to change the legal effect of the treaty upon the

---

[771] *See* Kenneth S. Gallant, *American Treaties, International Law: Treaty Interpretation after the Biden Condition*, 21 ARIZ. ST. L. J. 1067, 1091 (1989).

[772] U.S. Const. art. II, § 2, cl. 2.

[773] Id. art. VI, ¶ 2.

[774] Id. art. II, § 2, cl. 2. The President does have the power to alone conclude executive agreements with other countries. *See* Restatement, supra note 763, § 303, cmts. g - j. Sole executive agreements are presumably subject to the same canons of construction as treaties, save that the Senate's understanding is irrelevant.

Beyond the scope of this study is the newly-raging debate as to whether all (or most) international agreements entered into by the United States must be adopted pursuant to the treaty power (by two-thirds of the Senate), or whether a complete alternative exists in adopting an international agreement as an Act of Congress (by a majority vote of the House and Senate). For more on this, *compare* Bruce Ackerman & David Galove, *Is NAFTA Constitutional?*, 108 HARV. L. REV. 799 (1995) (contending that any agreement can be adopted by an Act of Congress); *with* Tribe, supra note 762 (taking the position that the treaty power must be used, at least for those international agreements implicating important derogations of sovereignty).

United States)[775] or declarations and interpretations (which merely attempt to clarify the terms of the agreement prior to ratification).[776]

There is no question that the terms of a permissible reservation are material — and binding — on a court in interpreting a treaty.[777] Nor is there any real doubt that an otherwise valid and *express* senatorial declaration as to the meaning of a treaty provision, transmitted to the President with its advice and consent,[778] is likewise dispositive on courts later construing the agreement.[779] Within the last twenty years, however, great dispute has arisen whether the courts must honor the Senate's *unstated* assumptions about the interpretation of a treaty, constructions formed in view of the Executive branch's representations as to the negotiated meaning of the international agreement. In short, the question is whether it is proper for a court to take into account a treaty's

---

[775] A discussion of U.S. practice as to reservations is beyond the scope of this article. For further details, *see* Restatement, supra note 763, §§ 313 & 314; Vienna Convention, supra note 764, arts. 2(d), 19-21. Sometimes the Senate attaches a condition to a treaty which does not purport to change the international legal effect of the instrument for the United States. This is not considered a reservation. *See, e.g., Power Authority of New York v. Federal Power Comm'n*, 247 F.2d 538 (D.C. Cir.), *vacated as moot*, 355 U.S. 64 (1957).

[776] *See* Restatement, supra note 763, § 313, cmt. g.

[777] *See* id., § 314(1) & cmt. b.

[778] The President is under no obligation to proceed with ratifying a treaty after receiving the Senate's advice and consent. Sometimes the President does not wish to conclude a treaty in view of the Senate's reservations or understandings. *See* Restatement, supra note 2, § 303, note 3.

[779] *See Northwestern Bands of Shoshone Indians v. United States*, 324 U.S. 335, 351-51 (1945); *Haver v. Yaker*, 76 U.S. (9 Wall.) 32, 35 (1869); Restatement, supra note 763, § 314, cmt. d. *But see, New York Indians v. United States*, 170 U.S. 1, 23 (1898), where a stated Senate understanding to an Indian treaty was not used by the Court because the President had expressly rejected the interpretation. Id. at 23.

"legislative history" — the record of Senate-Executive interchanges in the treaty-making process — as a tool of interpretation.[780]

Few courts have discussed the actual propriety of using Senate treaty ratification debates.[781] Nonetheless, there appears to be some resistance to their being employed as an interpretive source. The problem seems to be that, while the Senate is presumed to consent to both the clear and implied terms of a

---

[780] This debate was fueled by the dispute between the Senate and President Reagan concerning the proper interpretation of the Anti-Ballistic Missile (ABM) Treaty made with the Soviet Union, May 26, 1972, U.S.-U.S.S.R., 23 U.S.T. 3435, T.I.A.S. No. 7503, and its relevance to restricting a proposed "Strategic Defense Initiative" (SDI).

In reaction to the President's interpretation of the ABM Treaty, the Senate initiated a move to include in all subsequently ratified treaties a clause, known as a "Biden Condition" (in honor of the Senator who originally formulated it), that the treaty would be interpreted based on the common understanding of the President and Senate at the time of advice and consent. See 134 Cong. Rec. 12,849 (1988). In response, the State Department, led by its Legal Advisor, Abraham Sofaer, enunciated a doctrine that the President was not bound to follow the interpretations made at the time of ratification. *See The ABM Treaty and the Constitution: Joint Hearings Before the Senate Comm. on Foreign Relations and the Senate Comm. on the Judiciary*, 100th Cong., 1st Sess. 130, appendix at 357-58, 372-73 (1987); S. Exec. Rep. No. 15, supra note 4, at 90, appendix at 447.

The literature on this debate is vast. For a sampling, *see*, Gallant, supra note 771; Michael J. Glennon, *Interpreting "Interpretation": the President, the Senate, and when Treaty Interpretation becomes Treaty Making*, 20 U.C. DAVIS L. REV. 913 (1987); Malvina Halberstam, *A Treaty is a Treaty is a Treaty*, 33 VA. J. INT'L L. 51 (1992); David A. Kopolow, *Constitutional Bait and Switch: Executive Reinterpretation of Arms Control Treaties*, 137 U. PA. L. REV. 1353 (1989); W. Michael Reisman, *Necessary and Proper: Executive Competence to Interpret Treaties*, 15 YALE J. INT'L L. 316 (1990); Eugene V. Rostow, *The Reinterpretation Debate and Constitutional Law*, 137 U. PA. L. REV. 1451 (1989); Gary Michael Buechler, Comment, *Constitutional Limits on the President's Power to Interpret Treaties: The Sofaer Doctrine, the Biden Condition, and the Doctrine of Binding Authoritative Conditions*, 78 GEO. L. J. 1983 (1990).

[781] A number of courts, including the U.S. Supreme Court, have cited to treaty ratification history, although uncritically. *See, e.g., Air France v. Saks*, 470 U.S. 392, 397, 403 (1985); *Immigration & Naturalization Service v. Stevic*, 467 U.S. 407, 417-18 (1984); *Trans World Airlines v. Franklin Mint Corp.*, 466 U.S. 243, 250, 257 (1984); *Warren v. United States*, 340 U.S. 523, 527 n.5 (1951); *Cook v. United States*, 288 U.S. 102, 119 n.19 (1932); *In re Korean Airlines Disaster of Sept. 1, 1983*, 932 F.2d 1475, 1489-90 (D.C. Cir. 1991); *Frolova v. U.S.S.R.*, 761 F.2d 370, 376 (7th Cir. 1985).

treaty,[782] there is just no credible way to divine the Senate's "understanding" of a treaty, absent an express declaration.[783] Despite some judicial criticism,[784] federal courts are beginning to rely expressly on the statements made by Executive branch officials in testifying before the Senate as to the meaning of an agreement's provisions. Use of such material seems to be particularly justified when the Executive branch is espousing a position in later litigation contrary to that taken during the advice and consent process.[785]

In contrast to the weight given the Senate's express, contemporaneous understandings of a ratified treaty, *later* senatorial interpretations of international agreements are accorded no deference at all by the courts.[786] Despite earlier occasions in which the Senate was asked by the President to help interpret a treaty,[787] it has been settled since 1901 that "[t]he meaning of a treaty cannot be

---

[782] *See Wilson v. Girard*, 354 U.S. 524, 528-29 (1957).

[783] In diplomatic correspondence the United States has maintained that a treaty partner should not rely on informal Senate interpretations made during the advice and consent process. *See* 5 Green Hackworth, DIGEST OF INTERNATIONAL LAW 262 (1943) (quoting correspondence from then-Secretary of State Charles Evans Hughes to U.S. ambassador in Berlin).

[784] *See Coplin v. United States*, 6 Cl. Ct. 115 (1984), *rev'd on other grounds*, 761 F.2d 688 (Fed. Cir. 1985), *aff'd on other grounds sub nom. O'Connor v. United States*, 479 U.S. 27 (1986), where the U.S. Claims Court declined to adopt an interpretation embedded in a short exchange between an Executive branch witness and a Senator, because the proposed interpretation was not made express and transmitted to the other contracting party for approval. 6 Cl. Ct. at 143-46.

[785] *See, e.g., Rainbow Navigation, Inc. v. Department of the Navy*, 688 F. Supp. 354, 357 & n.17 (D.D.C. 1988), *later proceeding*, 699 F. Supp. 339, 343 (D.D.C. 1988). *See* infra notes 1049 - ? and accompanying text.

[786] *See* Restatement, supra note 763, § 326, note 1. *But see Cameron Septic Tank Co. v. Knoxville*, 227 U.S. 39, 49 (1913) (seemingly relying on interpretive views of subsequent Congress).

[787] *See* Senate Comm. on Foreign Relations, *Treaties and Other International Agreements: The Role of the Senate*, 98th Cong., 2d Sess. 35 (1984) (practice from the

controlled by subsequent explanations of some who may have voted to ratify it."[788] Of course, the Senate (acting with the House of Representatives) may seek to initiate legislation to "overrule" an earlier treaty.[789]

β.   *Judicial Deference to Executive Interpretation.* Very significant questions exist today as to the proper respect U.S. courts should extend to the President's treaty interpretations. These concerns have proven to be far more intractable than the recent competition between the Senate and President in forming a "common understanding" of treaties at the time of ratification.   The truth is that the Senate is rarely prepared to confront the President on a question of treaty interpretation.   On the other hand, the Executive branch of the federal government is continuously called upon to provide authoritative interpretations of treaties. This is so not only in diplomatic practice, but also in litigation in U.S. courts.   The trouble arises when the Executive branch's interpretation of a treaty changes with administrations, or when the Executive adopts a clearly self-serving interpretation in order to advance its interests.   Judicial deference to the Executive branch's treaty interpretations is so ingrained that when Justice Black said that "courts interpret

---

administration of George Washington).

[788] *Fourteen Diamond Rings v. United States*, 183 U.S. 176, 180 (1901) (Fuller, C.J.) (refusing to give effect to a Senate resolution of February 6, 1899, *reprinted in*, Cong. Rec. 55th Cong., 3d Sess. 1847 (1899)). *See also* Justice Brown's concurrence, which further elaborates the issue of subsequent Senate interpretation, without the approval of the President or House of Representatives. 183 U.S. at 182-84 (Brown, J., concurring).

In an even earlier decision, *Foster v. Neilson*, 27 U.S. (2 Pet.) 253 (1829), the Supreme Court noted that "We think then, however individual judges might construe [a] treaty..., it is the province of the Court to conform its decisions to the will of the legislature, if that will has been clearly expressed." Id. at 307.

[789] For more on this, the "last-in-time" rule, *see* Restatement, supra note 763, at § 115(1)(a), cmt. 1, note 1. *See also La Abra Silver Mining Co. v. United States*, 175 U.S. 423, 460 (1899); *Chae Chan Ping v. United States*, 130 U.S. 581, 600 (1889); *Head Money Cases*, 112 U.S. 580, 599 (1884). *See also* Jordan J. Paust, *Rediscovering the Relationship between Congressional Power and International Law: Exceptions to the Last in Time Rule and the Primacy of Custom*, 28 VA. J. INT'L L. 393 (1988).

treaties for themselves,"[790] he also noted in the same breath that "the meaning given [to treaties] by the departments of the government charged with their negotiation and enforcement is given great weight."[791]

Some authorities have argued that substantial deference to the Executive is warranted if the desire is to capture, via interpretation, the intent of the treaty's framers. It is, after all, the President who negotiates, signs, and concludes the international agreement.[792] While this contention has equal force in the debate between the Senate and Executive branch over "common understanding," it has been the courts which have given it the greatest credence.

The origins of this judicial deference can be traced to the early case of *Foster v. Nielson*,[793] but it only found its full expression by the Supreme Court

---

[790] *Kolovrat v. Oregon*, 366 U.S. 187, 194 (1961) (Black, J.).

[791] Id. *See also United States v. Curtiss-Wright Export Corp.*, 299 U.S. 304, 319-20 (1936) (for basis of President's power in foreign relations area).

[792] *See* Abraham D. Sofaer, *The ABM Treaty, Part II: Ratification Process, reprinted in* 133 Cong. Rec. 12,881, at 12,891 (1987), where the "role reversal" between the President and Senate is elaborated. In the treaty-making process, Sofaer suggests, the President is the "legislator," while the Senate has an unqualified veto. *See also United States v. Chadha*, 462 U.S. 919, 955 (1983) (recognizing constitutionality of absolute Senate veto over treaties); Louis Henkin, FOREIGN AFFAIRS AND THE CONSTITUTION 167 (1972) (judiciary may be incapable of understanding the delicate diplomatic concerns leading to the framing of a treaty). *But see* James Madison, writing as Helvedius, who noted that the treaty power should not be considered legislative in character. James Madison, *Letters of Helvedius*, No. 1 (Aug. 24, 1793), in 6 THE WRITINGS OF JAMES MADISON 145 (G. Hunt ed. 1906).

[793] 27 U.S. (2 Pet.) 253, 307 (1829). *See also United States v. The SCHOONER PEGGY*, 5 U.S. (1 Cranch) 103, 110 (1801) (suggesting deference to the Executive branch abrogation of a treaty). *But see Ware v. Hylton*, 3 U.S. (3 Dall.) 199, 283 (1797) (suggesting that courts are not bound by the opinions of the treaty negotiators).
British courts have stated that they do not owe deference to the treaty interpretations of their government. *See Inland Revenue Comm'rs v. Commerzbank AG*, 63 T.C. 218 (1990) (Mummery, J.). For additional comparisons of United States and United Kingdom approaches to treaty interpretation, *see* AMERICAN LAW INSTITUTE, FEDERAL INCOME TAX PROJECT, *Tentative Draft No. 16*, at 30-31 (Apr. 15, 1991) [hereinafter "Tax Treaty Draft

in the first few decades of the twentieth century. While in some of these cases the Court was careful to say that the Executive branch's determination was not "conclusive" as to a proper interpretation,[794] the vast majority of these decisions did ultimately adopt the President's proposed reading.[795] A few of these cases appear to accept an Executive determination as to the meaning of a treaty, as manifested through diplomatic correspondence, even though our treaty partner or partners contested the proposed construction.[796] Similarly, where the other contracting party to a treaty with the United States concurred in an interpretation propounded by the Executive, courts have credited that construction, despite proof that it contradicted an earlier, espoused position by an Executive department or agency.[797]

Project"].

[794] *Factor v. Laubenheimer*, 290 U.S. 276, 294-95 (1933) (Stone, J.) (relying on diplomatic correspondence by the Secretary of State, written shortly after the extradition treaty in question was signed). *But see*, id. at 319-21 (Butler, J., dissenting) (where the use of such diplomatic letters was criticized as not being probative of a legal meaning to the treaty, but, rather, as being only suggestive of a diplomatic resolution of a dispute with Great Britain). *See also Sumitomo Shoji America, Inc v. Avagliano*, 457 U.S. 176, 184-85 (1982) ("Although not conclusive, the meaning attributed to treaty provisions by the Government agencies charged with their negotiation and enforcement is entitled to great weight.") (*citing Factor v. Laubenheimer*); *cf. Trans World Airlines, Inc. v. Franklin Mint Corp.*, 466 U.S. 243, 276 n.5 (1984) (treaty interpretation of agency "not entitled to any special deference").

[795] *See, e.g., United States v. Pink*, 315 U.S. 203, 220-21 (1942); *Nielsen v. Johnson*, 279 U.S. 47, 52-53 (1929); *Terrance v. Thompson*, 263 U.S. 197, 223 (1923); *Charlton v. Kelly*, 229 U.S. 447, 468 (1913); *Ortman v. Stanray Corp.*, 371 F.2d 154, 157 (7th Cir. 1967). *See* infra notes 1174 - 1193 with text. *See also* David J. Bederman, *Deference or Deception: Treaty Rights as Political Questions*, 70 U. COL. L. REV. 1439 (1999)

[796] *See Factor v. Laubenheimer*, 290 U.S. 276, 295, 298 (1933) ("Until a treaty has been denounced, it is the duty of both the government and the courts to sanction the performance of the obligations reciprocal to the rights which the treaty declares and the government assents, even though the other party to it holds a different view of its meaning.") (*citing Charlton v. Kelly*, 229 U.S. 447, 472-73 (1913)). For more on deference to the views of our treaty partners, *see* infra notes 818 - 836, 1124 - 1127 and accompanying text.

[797] *See Sumitomo Shoji America, Inc v. Avagliano*, 457 U.S. 176, 184 n.10 (1982).

There have, however, been instances where a federal court specifically refused to follow the Executive's lead in interpreting an international agreement. Courts have departed from a Presidential construction of a treaty where the interpretation manifestly contradicted previous Executive branch practice,[798] would have led to an unconstitutional result,[799] or was just poorly reasoned.[800] While there appear to be limits to a court's deference to a Presidential determination of the meaning of a treaty provision, little guidance exists for judges in choosing an alternate construction. Procedural rules of treaty construction continue to be manifested in a search for "original understanding" between the Senate and President, or in deference to the Executive branch's subsequent interpretations. They remain a potent, albeit unpredictable, guide to the process of treaty interpretation in United States courts.

ii. *Basic Methods of Treaty Construction.* Courts in the United States have been known to apply different substantive canons of construction to different kinds of treaties. Most of the confusion concerning essential principles in treaty interpretation has to do with whether international agreements are more like contracts than legislation, or whether there are something altogether *sui*

---

[798] *See Clark v. Allen*, 331 U.S. 503, 513 (1947); *Perkins v. Elg*, 307 U.S. 325, 347-48 (1939) (1869 Naturalization Treaty with Sweden); *Haitian Centers Council, Inc. v. McNary*, 969 F.2d 1350, 1364 (2d Cir. 1992), *rev'd sub nom. Sale v. Haitian Centers Council, Inc.*, 113 S.Ct. 2549 (1993) (article 33 of the 1954 U.N. Convention on the Status of Refugees).

[799] *See Reid v. Covert*, 354 U.S. 1, 15-19 (1957) (Black, J.) (Court interpreted treaty waiver of right to jury trial as inapplicable to civilian spouse charged with murdering her husband stationed in Germany); *Liberato v. Royer*, 270 U.S. 535, 538-39 (1926) (Court narrowly interpreted court access provision in treaty with Italy); *Maiorano v. Baltimore & Ohio RR. Co.*, 213 U.S. 268, 274 (1909) (same).

[800] *See United States v. California*, 381 U.S. 139, 161-67 (1965) (construing 1958 U.N. Convention the Territorial Sea and Contiguous Zone); *Johnson v. Browne*, 205 U.S. 309, 320-22 (1907) (interpreting extradition treaty with Britain); *De Lima v. Bidwell*, 182 U.S. 1, 194-96 (1901) (reading of Treaty of Peace with Spain in 1898 as annexing Philippines and Puerto Rico); *United States v. Enger*, 472 F. Supp. 490, 544-45 (D.N.J. 1978) (interpreting 1961 Vienna Convention on Diplomats as raising a justiciable question of diplomatic immunity).

generis.[801] Some treaties clearly have the flavor of legislation;[802] indeed, some rise to the level of organic, "constitutional" texts.[803] For these charters, rules of interpretation approximating those for statutory construction would seem to be most appropriate. Other agreements clearly evidence contractual features. Interpreting courts in this country have thus sought to apply basic contractual usages to these texts.[804] The most essential of these forms is the notion of

---

[801] It does not really matter whether the agreement in question is multilateral or bilateral. Some multilateral treaties have a contractual aspect, while some bilateral conventions are legislative in character. See also *The BLONDE*, [1922] 1 App. Cas. 313, 331 ("The principle of ascertaining the intention of the parties to an agreement by giving due consideration to what they have said is no doubt valid in international matters, but there are many rules both as to the formation, the interpretation and the discharge of contracts, which cannot be transferred indiscriminately from municipal law to the law of nations.").

[802] For those cases which have recognized the legislative character of treaties, *see In re Ross*, 140 U.S. 453, 475 (1891) (construing consular treaty with Japan); *Geofroy v. Riggs*, 133 U.S. 258, 270 (1890) (Treaty of Amity with France); *Whitney v. Robertson*, 124 U.S. 190, 194 (1888); *Edye v. Robertson*, 112 U.S. 580, 599 (1884); *Foster v. Nielson*, 27 U.S. (2 Pet.) 253, 314 (1829) (Marshall, C.J.) ("Our Constitution declares a treaty to be the law of the land. It is, consequently, to be regarded in courts of justice as equivalent to an Act of Legislature...."). *See also* Michael P. Van Alstine, *Dynamic Treaty Interpretation*, 146 U. PA. L. REV. 687, 704-05 (1998).

[803] *See* Restatement, supra note 763, § 325, cmt. d. *See also Reparations for Injuries Suffered in the Service of the United Nations Case*, 1949 I.C.J. 174, 178-79, 196-98 (Hackworth, J., dissenting) (Opinion of 11 April) (construing U.N. Charter as constitutional instrument); *Competence of the General Assembly for the Admission of a State to the United Nations Case*, 1950 I.C.J. 4, 15-19 (Alvarez, J., dissenting) (Opinion of March 3) (same).

[804] *See, e.g., Washington v. Washington Commercial Passenger Fishing Vessel Ass'n*, 443 U.S. 658, 675 (1979) ("A treaty is essentially a contract between or among sovereign nations."); *Santovincenzo v. Egan*, 284 U.S. 30, 40 (1931); *Rocca v. Thompson*, 223 U.S. 317, 331-32 (1912); *United States v. American Sugar Ref. Co.*, 202 U.S. 563, 577 (1906). *See also* Van Alstine, supra note 802, at 691.

perfect equality between the parties[805] and the fact that one State's interpretation is not to be privileged over another's, absent objective evidence of intent.

Finally, there is an argument to be made that treaties are special and that they should not be interpreted in the same fashion as either contracts or statutes. After all, in United States practice, treaties are not concluded by a legislative body.[806] Likewise, a treaty is a contract in only the most generic sense. Many established norms of contract law are simply inapplicable to treaties. The problem, however, is that arguments about the distinctiveness of treaties — and of treaty interpretation — are usually made as a preface to an invitation to adopt the Executive branch's construction of the text. A unique approach to treaty interpretation does not, therefore, have to lead to substantive canons of interpretation. It can as easily send the court back to deference.

Depending upon the paradigm selected, interpreting authorities are likely to choose among three canons of treaty construction. Judicial descriptions of these interpretive methods only roughly approximate the international denominations of the textualist, intentionalist, and teleological schools.[807] What may seem a mere rhetorical difference is, however, very important. United States courts have yet to adopt a consistent vocabulary in characterizing approaches to treaty construction. This explains some judges' resistance to the Vienna Convention, as well as their predilection to unwittingly apply the rules of statutory construction to treaties. So the essential confusion in the American doctrine of treaty interpretation arises, really, from the problem of deciding where to place treaties within the American matrix of public law.

---

[805] Although this does not necessarily mean perfect reciprocity of obligations. *See* *Charlton v. Kelly*, 229 U.S. 447, 476 (1913). For more on the international aspects of this problem, *see* Evangelos Raftopoulos, THE INADEQUACY OF THE CONTRACTUAL ANALOGY IN THE LAW OF TREATIES (1990).

[806] See supra note 792 and accompanying text.

[807] These phrases characterize the international debate regarding treaty interpretation. *See* Restatement, supra note 763, § 325, cmt. g, note 4; *see also* Maria Frankowska, *The Vienna Convention on the Law of Treaties Before United States Courts*, 28 VA. J. INT'L L. 281, 328 (1988).

α. *Canon One*: *Begin interpretation with the treaty's text.* It has often been complained that American courts are too quick to look behind the text of a treaty and thus ignore the plain meaning of the words.[808] This criticism is wholly justified. The unfortunate tendency to deviate from the text has persisted, despite Supreme Court pronouncements that if a treaty's language is clear, no other means of interpretation may be employed.[809] This stricture is easily defeated by a judge's ready acceptance that an article is capable of more than one meaning.[810] Such a finding sends a court quickly away from a textualist

---

[808] *See* Restatement, supra note 763, § 325, note 4. *See also* Haraszti, supra note 394, at 42-43. For the intellectual origins of the textualist first canon of treaty interpretation, *see* Emmerich de Vattel, LE DROIT DES GENS OU PRINCIPES DE LA LOI NATURELLE, at 461 (livre II, ch. XII, §§ 156-57), *reprinted in* 1 Emmerich de Vattel, Classics of International Law Series (1916) (*"Il n'est pas permis d'interpreter ce quis n'a pas besoin d'interpretation"* or "It is not permissible to interpret what has no need of interpretation.") For even an earlier discussion of this first canon of treaty construction, *see* the discussion in part VII of this book.

For earlier invocations of textualism in treaty interpretation by the U.S. Supreme Court, see *The NEREIDE*, 13 U.S. (9 Cranch) 388, 419-20 (1815); *The PIZARRO*, 15 U.S. (2 Wheat.) 227, 245-46 (1817); and *The AMIABELLE ISABELLA*, 19 U.S. (6 Wheat.) 1, 70-74 (1821).

[809] *See, e.g., Maximov v. United States*, 373 U.S. 49, 54 (1963) (construing double taxation treaty with Britain). *But see* those cases like *Air France v. Saks*, 470 U.S. 392 (1985), where the Court says that an interpreter must look first to "the text of the treaty and the context in which the written words are used." Id. at 397. The implication might be that a contextual reading of the words may be broader than a mere review of the text. *See* infra note 1010.

[810] The decision of the U.S. Court of Appeals for the Second Circuit in *Day v. Trans World Airlines, Inc.*, 528 F.2d 31 (2d Cir. 1975), shows how a responsible interpreter only makes the jump from the text most reluctantly. At issue was article 17 of the Warsaw Convention, Oct. 12, 1929, 49 Stat. 3000, T.S. No. 876 (1934), and whether it applied to a passenger's claim for damages sustained by a terrorist bomb in a boarding lounge. Article 17 made a carrier liable for injuries in the "course of any of the operations of embarking or disembarking." Id. The Circuit Court held that the language was ambiguous in application to passengers waiting to board in the terminal. 528 F.2d at 33. The Court proceeded to apply the two other canons of treaty construction, while considering other material sources.

See also, United States v. American Sugar Refining Co., 202 U.S. 563 (1906), which suggests that a treaty ambiguity can be either textual or situational. Id. at 577.

basis for construction. Of course, many clauses in international agreements *are* ambiguous, and it is usually only the problematic provisions which become the subject of dispute.

Textual ambiguity is often created, though, when courts attempt to apply rules of statutory construction which are only really suited to domestic legislation. While reminding a judge to not read the terms of a treaty in isolation sounds good in principle,[811] it is but one step to look at the "context in which the written words are used."[812] Any invocation of context invariably leads away from the text. In the same fashion, giving too much credit to the precise language of a treaty can lead a court to give too much weight to an apparent omission, despite the clear meaning of the text.[813]

The worst problem lies in those cases where judges purport to apply a textualist approach, and yet readily concede that an interpreter should not really be bound by the words in the international agreement. The Supreme Court has as much as said this in the past: the treaty's text does not control if "application of the words of the treaty according to their obvious meaning effects a result inconsistent with the intent or expectations of its signatories."[814] This is manifestly at variance with more international norms of treaty interpretation.[815]

---

[811] As in *Sullivan v. Kidd*, 254 U.S. 433, 439 (1921) and *Geofroy v. Riggs*, 133 U.S. 258, 270 (1890) ("It is a rule, in construing treaties as well as laws, to give a sensible meaning to all their provisions if that be practicable."). For those cases discussing the analogue rule in statutory construction, *see White v. United States*, 305 U.S. 281 (1938); *Missouri K. & Tr. Co. v. Haber*, 169 U.S. 613 (1898). *See also* supra notes 1202 - 1202 and text.

[812] *Air France v. Saks*, 470 U.S. 392, 397 (1985) (O'Connor, J.); *Rocca v. Thompson*, 223 U.S. 317, 331 (treaties "to be read in the light of the conditions and circumstances existing at the time" it was drafted).

[813] *See, e.g., Rocca v. Thompson*, 223 U.S. 317, 331-32 (1912); *United States v. Rausher*, 199 U.S. 407, 420 (1886).

[814] *Maximov v. United States*, 373 U.S. 49, 54 (1963).

[815] *See* Vienna Convention, supra note 764, art. 32 (allowing recourse to subsidiary methods of interpretation only where a textual reading "leaves the meaning [of the text]

But, more than that, it subverts the integrity of the entire exercise of determining an agreement's meaning.[816] Departures from the text should be the exception, not the rule.

β. *Canon Two*: *Treaties should be construed liberally and in good faith*. It is an oft-repeated maxim that treaties ought to be construed liberally and in good faith.[817] This canon is obviously two rules of construction rolled into one, and has strong classical origins — as received by early-Modern publicists such as Grotius and Vattel.   The notion of liberal, expansive interpretation has its domestic well-spring in the 1890 Supreme Court opinion in *Geofroy v. Riggs*,[818] where Justice Field noted that:

---

ambiguous or obscure; . . . or . . . leads to a result which is manifestly absurd or unreasonable."). *See also* infra part XI.iii

[816] An excellent illustration of the confusion this can cause is in *Sumitomo Shoji America, Inc. v. Avagliano*, 457 U.S. 176 (1982), in which the Supreme Court was asked to determine the applicability of the U.S.-Japan FCN Treaty to a Japanese business subsidiary incorporated in the United States. The Court concluded that, under article 22, para. 3, of the Treaty, the subsidiary was not a Japanese corporation covered by the protection of the Treaty. But the Court was not content with stopping at the crystal-clear text, id. at 180-83, and went on to review the current interpretations held by the U.S. and Japanese governments, id. at 183-85, and the underlying purpose of the Treaty. Id. at 185-89. Each source led to the same result. The problem is that if use of these different interpretive tools had produced different meanings, the Court might have been at a loss to choose among them.

See also *Great-West Life Assurance Co. v. United States*, 678 F.2d 180, 183 (Ct. Cl. 1982) (for an instance where a court proceeded to review the negotiating and legislative history of a treaty, the terms of which the litigants had conceded were perfectly clear).

[817] This maxim has been considered previously. *See* supra note 313 and accompanying text.

[818] 133 U.S. 258 (1890) (Field, J.). This case concerned the 1853 Consular Treaty with France, and whether its non-discrimination provisions as to property ownership applied in the District of Columbia, even though article 7 of the Treaty limited application to the "States of the Union." The Court concluded that they did. Id. at 272-73.

For British practice, *see* Schreuer, supra note 765, at 288-90. German practice stood in sharp contrast to Anglo-American liberalism, *see* id. at 29-94 (majority of German courts electing for restrictive or literal interpretation).

[i]t is a general principle of construction with respect to treaties that they be liberally construed, so as to carry out the apparent intention of the parties to secure equality and reciprocity between them. As they are contracts between independent nations, in their construction words are to be taken in their ordinary meaning, as understood in the public law of nations, and not in any artificial or special sense impressed upon them by local law, unless such restricted sense is clearly intended.... [W]here a treaty admits of two constructions, one restrictive of rights that may be claimed under it and the other favorable to them, the latter is to be preferred.[819]

This passage fully captures the "liberal interpretation" prong of this canon. The underlying thrust is to protect treaties from parochial readings that will result in interpretations not consonant with international expectations. The reference to the "public law of nations" seems to be a reminder that terms of art are to be construed in view of international usages[820] and customary international law,[821]

---

[819] Id. at 271-72 (citing, for the proposition contained in the last sentence, *Hauenstein v. Lynham*, 100 U.S. 483, 487 (1879) and *Shanks v. Dupont*, 28 U.S. (3 Pet.) 242, 249 (1830) (Story, J.)). *See also Fothergill v. Monarch Airlines*, 3 W.L.R. 209, 223 (1980) ("The language of an international convention has not been chosen by an English parliamentary draftsmen. It is neither couched in traditional English legislative idiom nor designed to be construed exclusively by English judges.") (Diplock, L.J.); *Bacardi Corp. v. Domenech*, 311 U.S. 150, 163 (1940); *Santovincenzo v. Egan*, 284 U.S. 30, 40 (1931); *Jordan v. Tashiro*, 278 U.S. 123, 127 (1928); *Shanks v. Dupont*, 28 U.S. (3 Pet.) 242, 249-50 (1830). For more on British practice in this regard, *see* Schreuer, supra note 765, at 267-68.

[820] For some cases employing international meanings for words and phrases, *see Volkswagenwerk Aktiengesellschaft v. Schlunk*, 486 U.S. 694, 699-703 (1988) (use of foreign treatises and law dictionaries); *Immigration & Naturalization Service v. Cardozo-Fonseca*, 480 U.S. 421, 431 & n.22 (1987) (United Nations material).

[821] For those cases where the background principles of customary international law were invoked to provide an "international" meaning to the words and phrases of a treaty, *see Wildenhus's Case*, 120 U.S. 1, 14-16 (1886); *The AMISTAD*, 40 U.S. (15 Pet.) 518, 594-95 (1841); *The PIZARRO*, 15 U.S. (2 Wheat.) 227, 246 (1817) ("The language of the law of nations is always to be consulted in the interpretation of treaties."); *Ware v. Hylton*, 3 U.S. (3 Dall.) 199, 223-28, 239 (1796). *But see United States v. Alvarez-Machain*, 112 S. Ct. 2188, 2210-11 (1992) and *Eastern Airlines v. Floyd*, 111 S. Ct. 1489, 1495-96, 1499-1502 (1991) (both suggesting that customary practices must relate directly to the subject matter of the treaty).

not domestic constructions. Likewise, the last sentence of the passage sets forth a general principle that, when in doubt, an interpreter should construe in favor of granting rights under a treaty, rather than restricting them.

The "liberal interpretation" language of *Geofroy v. Riggs* is not, however, an open invitation to determine the intent of the parties. Justice Field seems to imply that such an exercise would be difficult, and maybe even fruitless. Instead, he creates a set of interpretive values that act independently of evidence of intent. The chief of these is that the treaty is presumed to be completely equal and reciprocal in its terms,[822] and that a peculiarly American gloss of the text is by no means to be preferred.

The corollary of liberal interpretation is good faith. The notion of good faith in the interpretation of international agreements was best expressed by Justice Brown in *Tucker v. Alexandroff*,[823] where he said that a treaty

> should be interpreted in a spirit of *uberrima fides*, and in a manner to carry out its manifest purpose.... [They] should be interpreted in that broad and liberal spirit which is calculated for the existence of perpetual amity [between nations], so far as it can be done without the sacrifice of individual rights or those principles of personal liberty which lie at the foundation of our jurisprudence. It is said by Chancellor Kent in his Commentaries (vol. 1, p. 174): "Treaties of every kind are to receive a fair and liberal interpretation according to the

---

[822] See *Jordan v. Tashiro*, 278 U.S. 123, 127 (1928) (treaties to be construed so as "to secure equality and reciprocity between them"). See also supra note 805.

[823] 183 U.S. 424 (1902). The case concerned the proper construction of article 9 of the Treaty of Amity with Russia, 8 Stat. 444 (1832), which gave consuls the right to seek the "imprisonment of deserters from the ships of war or merchant vessels of their country." Alexandroff, a Russian subject, had been detailed to serve on board a vessel being constructed at Philadelphia, but not yet commissioned or launched. He deserted, but claimed that he was outside the scope of article 9 since he was not a member of the "crew" of the ship, as the term was used in that provision. A sharply-divided Court rejected Alexandroff's argument. 183 U.S. at 449. A vigorous dissent was written by Justice Gray, joined by three other justices. Id. Although he agreed with the majority's general approach to treaty interpretation, id. at 466-67, Gray rejected the Court's conclusion.

> intention of the parties, and are to be kept with the most scrupulous good faith...."[824]

Good faith is closely linked with liberal interpretation in this passage, as it should be. One distinction is that a good faith interpretation of a treaty text may not necessarily be the most liberal reading. It is, rather (as illustrated by the context of *Tucker*), the judicial desire to give credence to the meaning ascribed by one of our treaty partners. In this fashion, the courts believe they are serving the interests of United States foreign policy by ensuring that a treaty is given domestic effect consistent with its terms, thus protecting the United States from a charge of treaty breach.[825]

Comparing two other cases will suffice to show that liberal interpretation and good faith need not go hand-in-hand. In *Nielsen v. Johnson*,[826] the Court was able to neatly reconcile the two by concluding that the Amity Treaty with Denmark[827] required that a bequest from an American decedent be passed on to the Danish family without any inheritance tax imposed by state law. The relevant provision of the treaty was silent on the question of waiver of estate taxes, but the Court ruled that as a liberal interpretation was to be preferred,[828] such levies would be presumed to be prohibited.[829]

---

[824] Id. at 437. (citing 1 James Kent, COMMENTARIES ON AMERICAN LAW *174 (O.W. Holmes 12th ed., 1884) (citing Grotius, Pufendorf, Rutherforth and Vattel).

[825] *See United States v. The SCHOONER PEGGY*, 5 U.S. (1 Cranch) 103, 109-10 (1801) (recognizing that if the Court does not effectuate U.S. obligations under a treaty, other party may utilize self-help measures); *See also Chew Heong v. United States*, 112 U.S. 536, 540 (1884). *See* infra notes 1148 - 1150 and accompanying text.

[826] 279 U.S. 40 (1929).

[827] Treaty of Amity, U.S.-Den., Apr. 26, 1826, art. 7, 8 Stat. 340, 342 (1826), as later renewed, 11 Stat. 719, 720 (1857).

[828] 279 U.S. at 52.

[829] Id. at 57-58. In *Day v. Trans World Airlines, Inc.*, 528 F.2d 31 (2d Cir. 1975), the Court of Appeals considered arguments as to the policy goals and purposes of the Warsaw Convention's absolute liability provisions. *See* supra note 810. The Court

But in *Ford v. United States*,[830] handed down just a few years before *Nielsen*, the Court adopted a decidedly strict interpretation of a treaty, made between Britain and the United States,[831] giving the United States the right to search and seize British vessels suspected of illegal importation of alcoholic products into the United States, in violation of Prohibition-era laws. The treaty expressly allowed only the confiscation and condemnation of the vessel engaged in rum-running; it was silent as to whether the crew and passengers of the ship were subject to United States criminal penalties.[832] The Court construed the British government's failure to object as an indication of acquiescence to the interpretation advanced by the United States,[833] and held that the Treaty did allow criminal prosecutions of British subjects.

The *Ford* decision was clear in its repudiation of a liberal interpretation.[834] The Court, nonetheless, believed it was interpreting the treaty in good faith. More than that, it held that any other interpretation would have frustrated the object of the treaty: to suppress smuggling.[835] The canon of good faith and liberal interpretation can thus disintegrate into an unprincipled search for purpose. While rhetorically consistent with "international" values in treaty

---

concluded that a broad reading of article 17 was consistent with the purpose of the Convention in allocating the costs of accidents. 528 F.2d at 34. Liberal interpretation and good faith thus coincided.

[830]   273 U.S. 593 (1927) (Taft, C.J.).

[831]   May 22, 1924, 43 Stat. 1761 (1924).

[832]   Id. art. 2, para. 2.

[833]   *See* 273 U.S. at 613-14.

[834]   *See* id. at 610-13.

[835]   *See* id. at 612-13, 618 ("Considering the friendly purpose of both countries in making this treaty, we do not think any narrow construction should be given which would defeat it.").

interpretation,[836] it can also be used to reach results that would certainly seem surprising — and unwelcome — by the United States' treaty partners.

γ. *Canon Three*: *Treaty interpretation should effectuate the intent of the parties*. This method of interpretation, fully embraced in U.S. treaty practice today, requires judges to divine the intent of a provision and give effect to that intention.   But American courts have not always been so preoccupied with this process.   Prior to the 1930s, in fact, courts in this country would have thought it peculiar to give effect to the proven intentions of States.[837] A treaty provision would have been assigned a meaning based on its clear language, as possibly altered by application of liberal interpretation and good faith.

This unified approach to treaty interpretation was transformed in a 1943 Supreme Court case, *Choctaw Nation of Indians v. United States*.[838]   There the Court wrote that "[t]reaties are construed more liberally than private agreements, and to ascertain their meaning we may look beyond the written words to the

---

[836]   *See* Vienna Convention, supra note 764, art. 31, para. 1 ("A treaty shall be interpreted in good faith in accordance with the ordinary meaning to be given to the terms of the treaty in their context and in light of its object and purpose."). *See also* Harvard Research on International Law, *Draft Convention on Treaties*, art. 19(a), 29 AJIL SUPP. 666, 937 (1935) ("A treaty is to be interpreted in the light of the general purpose which it is intended to serve.").

[837]   *See Valentine v. United States*, 299 U.S. 5 (1936), where it is first suggested that the intent of treaty parties is decisive.   Id. at 10.   The 1930s was also the time that the use of legislative history, generated by Congress in the process of passing Acts, came to be more and more relied upon by the courts for statutory interpretation.   *See* Restatement, supra note 2, § 325, note 1; John W. Johnson, *Retreat from the Common Law? The Grudging Reception of Legislative History by American Appellate Courts in the Early Twentieth Century*, 1978 DET. C. L. REV. 413.

For German practice in this regard, *see* Schreuer, supra note 765, at 275-76.   For British practice, *see* id. at 274-75. *See also Daniel v. Commissioner for Claims on France*, 2 Knapp 23, 49, 12 Eng. Rep. 387, 397 (P.C. 1825) (Gifford, L.J.) ("Treaties, like other compacts, are to be construed according to the intention of the contracting parties. . . .").

[838]   318 U.S. 423 (1943).   For more on Indian treaties *see* supra note 762.   The Court made clear in *Choctaw Nation*, however, that its intentionalist interpretive method applied equally to international agreements.

history of the treaty, the negotiations, and the practical construction adopted by the parties."[839]   Liberal interpretation was invoked as the justification for intentionalism.   The *Choctaw Nations* language also sanctioned the use of extrinsic or external sources for finding the intent of the treaty parties.   Two such sources are clearly contemplated, and have been extensively used by later courts:[840] the negotiating history (or *travaux préparatoires*) of the international agreement and evidence of subsequent practice by the parties under the treaty.

Even in early cases, some forms of negotiating history had been deemed to be of such significance as to have been accorded judicial recognition. Indications as to which treaty language was to have been considered authoritative,[841] or regarding the deliberate omission of a key provision found in other, similar instruments,[842] have always been considered material.   Recently, the use of negotiating history by courts has become much more sophisticated — and problematic.   Litigants (including the government itself) have been more and more successful in bringing courts' attention to a wide variety of treaty negotiation materials.   These include statements and speeches by delegates at international codification conferences[843] and renditions of successive drafts of

---

[839]   Id. at 431-32.

[840]   The interpretive method of *Choctaw Nation* has become so ingrained in treaty jurisprudence that courts nowadays rarely bother to acknowledge authority for the notion that the intent of the parties is controlling.   *But see Air France v. Saks*, 470 U.S. 392, 396-97 (1985) (where rule of *Choctaw Nation* is placed side-by-side with the textual canon of *Maximov v. United States*, 373 U.S. 49, 53-54 (1963) (*see* supra notes 814 - 816 with text)). *See* infra notes 1013 - 1034, 1084 - 1109 and accompanying text.

[841]   *See United States v. Percheman*, 32 U.S. (7 Pet.) 51, 86-87 (1833).

[842]   *See Kolovrat v. Oregon*, 366 U.S. 187, 195-96 (1961); *Santovincenzo v. Egan*, 284 U.S. 30, 37 (1931); *Terrace v. Thompson*, 263 U.S. 197, 223 (1923).   *See also* supra note 813 and accompanying text.

[843]   *See Air France v. Saks*, 470 U.S. 392, 401-03 (1985); *Trans World Airlines, Inc. v. Franklin Mint Corp.*, 466 U.S. 243, 259 & n.33 (O'Connor, J.), 266-70 (Stevens, J., dissenting) (1984); *Sale v. Haitian Centers Council, Inc.*, 113 S.Ct. 2549, 2565-67 (1993); *In re Korean Airlines Disaster of Sept. 1, 1983*, 932 F.2d 1475, 1486-87, 1489 (D.C. Cir. 1991).

provisions.[844] Nonetheless, it has been pointed out by one judge that "the biggest possible pitfall in the use of legislative history [for a treaty is] what do we do when the legislative history is [itself] ambiguous."[845]

In a mad dash to find intent, courts have — when confronted with ambiguity in the *travaux* — moved even farther afield into the subsequent practice of the State parties under the international agreement. Some American courts have called this an inquiry into the "practical construction" placed on the terms of the treaty by the parties.[846] At any rate, it has led courts to consider materials as diverse as treaties containing identical language,[847] municipal case law or statutes shedding light on analogous or related points,[848] diplomatic correspondence between two treaty parties,[849] and subsequent, amendatory

---

[844] *See Air France v. Saks*, 470 U.S. 392, 401-03 (1985); *Nielsen v. Johnson*, 279 U.S. 47, 52-53 (1929); *Terrace v. Thompson*, 263 U.S. 197, 223 (1923). Extensive treatment of conference minutes and drafts was given in *Day v. Trans World Airlines, Inc.*, 528 F.2d 31, 34-35 (2d Cir. 1975). *See* supra notes 810 and 829 with text.

[845] *Haitian Centers Council, Inc. v. McNary*, 969 F.2d 1350, 1365 (2d Cir. 1992) (Pratt, J.), *rev'd sub nom. Sale v. Haitian Centers Council, Inc.*, 113 S.Ct. 2549 (1993). *Cf. Sumitomo Shoji America, Inc. v. Avagliano*, 457 U.S. 176, 185 (1982) (a court's "role is limited to giving effect to the intent of the parties").

[846] *See, e.g., Nielsen v. Johnson*, 279 U.S. 47, 52 (1929) ("When the[] meaning [of treaties] is unclear, recourse may be had . . . to the[] [contracting parties'] own practical construction of it."). *See also Pigeon River Improvement Slide & Boom Co. v. Cox*, 291 U.S. 138, 158 (1934); *Terlinden v. Ames*, 184 U.S. 270, 285 (1902). For a very early use of subsequent practice in construing a treaty, *see The LES QUATRES FRÉRES*, 165 Eng. Rep. 40, Hay & M. 170, 172 (Adm. 1778) (construing 1670 treaty between England and Denmark).

[847] *See Tucker v. Alexandroff*, 183 U.S. 424, 430 (1902).

[848] *See Eastern Airlines, Inc. v. Floyd*, 111 S. Ct. 1489, 1501-02 (1991); *Air France v. Saks*, 470 U.S. 392, 400, 404-05 (1985); *Trans World Airlines v. Franklin Mint Corp.*, 466 U.S. 273, 258 n.31 (1984); *Tucker v. Alexandroff*, 183 U.S. 424, 442-43 (1902).

[849] *See Factor v. Laubenheimer*, 290 U.S. 276, 295-96 (1933) (*see also* supra note 33 with text); *United States v. Reynes*, 50 U.S. (9 How.) 127, 147-48 (1850) (sanctioning use

international agreements.[850] On occasion, American judges have expressed some reluctance about using some of these sources, particularly case law from other jurisdictions and later treaty modifications.[851] Nonetheless, they have now become an accepted tool of treaty interpretation.

iii. *Reconciling Vienna Convention Methods of Treaty Interpretation.* Now, more than ever, there is a conflict between U.S. practice and more "international" approaches to treaty interpretation. The chief division is over American courts' willingness to deviate from the text of a treaty in search of intent, and to also embrace a meaning advanced by the Executive branch which may not accord with international expectations or the canon of liberal interpretation and good faith. This schism in method has been well-documented,[852] and judges in the United States are more frequently realizing that

---

of "the public acts and proclamations of [foreign] governments, and those of their publicly recognized agents, in carrying into effect" treaties); *Cementos Anahuac de Golfo, S.A. v. United States*, 687 F. Supp. 1558, 1565 (Ct. Int'l Trade 1988); see also supra note 794 and accompanying text.

[850] The most-litigated of these have been the later modifications to the Warsaw Convention. *See, e.g., Air France v. Saks*, 470 U.S. 392, 403-04, 407-07 (1985) (1971 Guatemala City Protocol and 1966 Montreal Agreement); *Trans World Airlines v. Franklin Mint Corp.*, 466 U.S. 273, 257-58 (1984) (Montreal Agreement). *See also* supra note 810. Examination of subsequent practice — in the form of the Montreal Agreement — was done in *Day v. Trans World Airlines*, 528 F.2d 31, 36-37 (2d Cir. 1975). *See* supra notes 810, 829 and 844.

[851] *See, e.g., Eastern Airlines, Inc. v. Floyd*, 111 S. Ct. 1489, 1501-02 (1991) (rejecting applicability of Hague, Montreal and Guatemala City Protocols to Warsaw Convention concerning question of allowance for pain and suffering damages); *Onyeanusi v. Pan Am*, 952 F.2d 788, 791-92 (3d Cir. 1992) (rejecting applicability of a French case because of lack of a stated reason for the judgment).

[852] *See* Restatement, supra note 763, § 325, note 4. *See also* Frankowska, supra note 807, at 328; Kenneth J. Vandevelde, *Treaty Interpretation from a Negotiator's Perspective*, 21 VAND. J. TRANSNAT'L L. 281, 287-89 (1988); Tax Treaty Draft Project, supra note 793, at 31-35.
    The United States has yet to ratify the Vienna Convention, but some sources have viewed the Convention's provisions on treaty interpretation to be customary international law. See Restatement, supra note 763, § 325, note 4.

the approach taken by the Vienna Convention on the Law of Treaties may lead to interpretive outcomes very different than those suggested by some of the litigants.

As already discussed in the previous chapter, the Vienna Convention's primary focus is on the text of the international agreement, but as conditioned by its "context and in light of its object and purpose."[853] Resort to extrinsic evidence of the parties' intent, including *travaux*, is meant to be only an exceptional occurrence.[854]   The use of peculiarly national materials for interpretive purposes is manifestly disapproved by the Vienna Convention.[855] This latter category would include Executive branch representations as to the meaning of an provision,[856] or even a contemporaneous record of Presidential-Senate "common understandings" of treaty interpretation at the time of advice

---

[853]   *See* Vienna Convention, supra note 764, art. 31, para. 1.

[854]   *See* id. art. 32, which describes the use of *travaux* as a "supplementary means of interpretation," only to be used where a textual reading "leaves the meaning ambiguous or obscure; or . . . leads to a result which is manifestly absurd or unreasonable." Id. *See* Degan, supra note 400 (for a European view supporting textualism); Shabtai Rosenne, *Interpretation of Treaties in the Restatement and the International Law Commission's Draft Articles: A Comparison*, 5 COLUM. J. INT'L L. 205 (1966) (for a review of earlier distinctions). *Compare* Myres McDougal, Harold Lasswell & James C. Miller, THE INTERPRETATION OF AGREEMENTS AND WORLD PUBLIC ORDER: PRINCIPLES OF CONTENT AND PROCEDURE (1967) (supporting teleological approach to treaty interpretation, emphasizing "object and purpose" of agreement) *with* Sir Gerald Fitzmaurice, Review Article, Vae Victis *or Woe to the Negotiators! Your Treaty or Our "Interpretation" of It?*, 65 AJIL 358 (1971) (fearful that such an approach would lead to anarchy in interpretation).
The Vienna Convention is, however, somewhat more forgiving of the use of materials shedding light on later interpretations by the parties. *See* id. art. 31, para. 3 ("There shall be taken into account, together with the context [of the treaty]: (a) any subsequent agreement between the parties regarding the interpretation of the treaty or the application of its provisions; [and] (b) any subsequent practice in the application of the treaty which establishes the agreement of the parties regarding its interpretation . . . .").

[855]   *See* Restatement, supra note 763, § 325, note 5. The Vienna Convention, supra note 764, art. 32, mentions only "preparatory work (travaux préparatoires) of the treaty and circumstances of its conclusion."

[856]   *See* supra notes 790 - 797 with accompanying text.

and consent.[857]   Notwithstanding its narrower thrust — and the more limited range of materials it allows to the interpreter — the Vienna Convention has a growing following by the U.S. State Department and the federal courts.[858]

Recently, federal courts have become reluctant to deviate from the text of a treaty unless failing to do so "leaves the meaning ambiguous or obscure; or ... leads to a result which is manifestly absurd or unreasonable."[859] This would be a higher threshold of ambiguity than previously tolerated by American judges.[860] Recent decisions make clear that the move from text to intent is not to be taken lightly;[861] in some cases, the step is contemplated, but actually rejected.[862]

---

[857] *See* supra notes 777 - 785 and accompanying text. *See also* Gallant, supra note 771, at 1084-90 (arguing that the Biden Condition, *see* supra note 780, is flatly inconsistent with the Vienna Convention).

[858] *See* Restatement, supra note 763, § 325, cmt. a. *See also Haitian Centers Council, Inc. v. McNary*, 969 F.2d 1350, 1362 (2d Cir. 1992) (Pratt, J.), *rev'd sub nom. Sale v. Haitian Centers Council, Inc.*, 113 S.Ct. 2549 (1993); S. Exec. Doc. L, 92d Cong., 1st Sess. 1 (1971) (State Department official testifying that treaty interpretation rules of the Vienna Convention are authoritative).

[859] Vienna Convention, supra note 764, art. 32. For more on the threshold of ambiguity pegged by the Vienna Convention, *see* T. O. Elias, THE MODERN LAW OF TREATIES 79-80 (1974); Sir Ian Sinclair, THE VIENNA CONVENTION ON THE LAW OF TREATIES 116, 118, 141-42 (2d ed. 1984).

[860] *See* supra notes 810 - 813 and accompanying text. A good example of the countervailing tendency is in *Day v. Trans World Airlines, Inc.*, 528 F.2d 31 (2d Cir. 1975), where the court moved quickly from the text (citing the Vienna Convention) to the *travaux* (without citing the Convention's cautionary language). Id. at 34. For criticism of this decision, *see* Frankowska, supra note 807, at 334. *See also* supra notes 810, 829, 844, and 850.

[861] *See, e.g., Acrillos v. Regan*, 617 F. Supp. 1082, 1086 n.15 (Ct. Int'l Trade 1985); *Coplin v. United States*, 6 Cl. Ct. 115, 125-35 (1984).

[862] *See Haitian Centers Council, Inc. v. McNary*, 969 F.2d 1350, 1362 (2d Cir. 1992), *rev'd sub nom. Sale v. Haitian Centers Council, Inc.*, 113 S.Ct. 2549 (1993).

One difficulty that has arisen, though, is that the Vienna Convention is apparently in agreement with the recently-developed U.S. practice accepting the use of subsequent interpretations of a treaty made by the parties.[863] Unfortunately, in embracing such materials (like later diplomatic correspondence or analogous international agreements), courts have not realized that the Vienna Convention, by its very silence, has eschewed the notion of subsequent modification of treaty terms by later interpretation.[864] It still seems that article 31(3)(b) of the Vienna Convention has been (erroneously) cited in some cases as support in using, for example, the Montreal Agreement as a basis for amending the terms of the Warsaw Convention,[865] as well as in modifying the terms of other treaties.[866]

One last point to mention is that the Vienna Convention does allow the interpreter to look to the "object and purpose" of a treaty,[867] shorthand for a teleological approach. A few courts in this country have accepted the Vienna Convention's invitation on this point to depart from the text and to divine some underlying, purposeful meaning of a provision. But, interestingly enough, in the few cases where judges have cited the Vienna Convention for this methodology,

---

[863] *See* Vienna Convention, supra note 764, art. 31, para. 3. *See also* Sinclair, supra note 696, 859, at 135-38.

[864] The diplomatic conference which adopted the Vienna Convention, in fact, rejected a draft article which would have allowed a "treaty [to] be modified by subsequent practice in the application of the treaty establishing the agreement of the parties to modify its provisions." Commentary to Draft article 47, [1966] 2 Y.B. Int'l L. Comm'n 245. *See also* Frankowska, supra note 807, at 346-47.

[865] *See, e.g., Day v. Trans World Airlines*, 528 F.2d 31, 35-36 (2d Cir. 1975); *Husserl v. Swiss Air Transport*, 351 F. Supp. 702, 707 (S.D.N.Y. 1972).

[866] *See Barr v. United States Dep't of Justice*, 819 F.2d 25, 28 (2d Cir. 1987) (construing Mutual Assistance Treaty with Switzerland).

[867] *See* Vienna Convention, supra note 764, art. 31, para. 1. *See also* Sinclair, supra note 696, 859, at 130-35.

they have ultimately returned to a textual reading of the agreement.[868]   The overall effect of the Vienna Convention on American treaty jurisprudence has been to slightly check the use of extra-textual means of interpretation.

But one thing that is surprising is that no American judge has relied upon the Vienna Convention for the canons of construction embedded in its text. Instead, U.S. courts have preferred to distill these rules of construction from an earlier, domestic jurisprudence.   For United States jurists, rules of treaty construction are truly judge-made law, and they remain largely ignorant of international glosses on the subject.   Indeed, I would go further and say that the sort of canons emphasized in earlier American treaty decisions tended to either structural   concerns   (such   as   judicial   deference   to   Executive   branch interpretations) or generic values (such as achieving a liberal interpretation or effectuating the intent of the parties).   There appears to have been little appreciation of substantive canons of treaty interpretation — default rules which favor particular interpretive results or policy outcomes.

The absence of recognition for substantive canons has recently been addressed in the jurisprudence of the U.S. Supreme Court.   The following chapter looks at the Rehnquist Court's treaty interpretation case-law, and charts its parallels with both classical debates and internationalist approaches to this subject.

---

[868]   *See, e.g., Westar Marine Services v. Heerema Marine Contractors*, 621 F. Supp. 1135, 1139 (N.D. Cal. 1985) (interpreting the 1910 Salvage Treaty). This case might as easily be considered an application of the canon of "good faith and liberal interpretation." *See* supra notes 818 - 836 and accompanying text. *See also Denby v. Seaboard World Airlines*, 575 F. Supp. 1134, 1145 (E.D.N.Y. 1983); Frankowska, supra note 807, at 339-40.

XII TREATY READINGS BY THE REHNQUIST COURT

The United States Supreme Court, since the elevation of William Rehnquist to Chief Justice in 1986, has decided thirteen significant treaty interpretation cases.[869] This averages to little more than one a term, but nonetheless indicates that cases turning on weighty issues of treaty construction have come to be a staple of Supreme Court jurisprudence. These thirteen decisions taken together also reveal much about the current state of methods and applications of treaty interpretation in the United States. For that reason they will form the basis of the following discussion which will focus on the most vexing theoretical problems in the judicial enterprise of gleaning the meaning and content of international agreements.

---

[869] See *O'Connor v. United States*, 479 U.S. 27 (1986) [hereinafter "O'Connor"]; *Immigration & Naturalization Service v. Cardoza-Fonseca*, 480 U.S. 421 (1987) [hereinafter "Cardoza"]; *Société Nationale Industrielle Aérospatiale v. United States District Court for the Southern District of Iowa*, 482 U.S. 522 (1987) [hereinafter "SNIAS"]; *Volkswagenwerk Aktiengesellschaft v. Schlunk*, 486 U.S. 694 (1988) [hereinafter "Volkswagen"]; *United States v. Stuart*, 489 U.S. 353 (1989) [hereinafter "Stuart"]; *Chan v. Korean Air Lines, Ltd.*, 490 U.S. 122 (1989) [hereinafter "Chan"]; *Eastern Airlines, Inc. v. Floyd*, 499 U.S. 530 (1991) [hereinafter "Floyd"]; *United States v. Alvarez-Machain*, 504 U.S. 655 (1992) [hereinafter "Alvarez"]; *Itel Containers Int'l Corp. v. Huddleston*, 507 U.S. 60 (1993) [hereinafter "Itel"]; *Sale v. Haitian Centers Council, Inc.*, 509 U.S. 155 (1993) [hereinafter "Haitian Centers"); *Zicherman v. Korean Air Lines Co., Ltd.*, 516 U.S. 217 (1995) [hereinafter "Zicherman"]; *Breard v. Greene*, 523 U.S. 371 (1998) [hereinafter "Breard"]; *El Al Israel Airlines, Ltd. v. Tseng*, 525 U.S. 155 (1999) [hereinafter "Tseng"].

For a further consideration of the important Rehnquist Court cases, *see* Martin A. Rogoff, *Interpretation of International Agreements by Domestic Courts and the Politics of International Treaty Relations: Reflections on Some Recent Decisions of the United States Supreme Court*, 11 AM. U. J. INT'L L. & POL'Y 559 (1996).

i. *Breaking from the Treaty Text.* One issue has been confronted consistently by the Rehnquist Court in these treaty construction cases. Alluded to briefly already,[870] the problem can be simply stated as what is the proper threshold of ambiguity at which a treaty interpreter should deviate from the terms of the agreement and go in search of extrinsic sources of meaning? After all, the first principle of all construction is to begin interpretation with the text. One consistent pathology of treaty interpretation by U.S. courts has been an avid willingness to depart from the actual terms of a treaty instrument and to seek confirmation of meaning in outside sources, such as legislative history, *travaux préparatoires*, subsequent practice, and representations made by the Executive branch of the government. In short, the threshold of tolerable textual ambiguity in treaties has been set quite low, much lower than the Rehnquist court has allowed in pursuing a textualist approach for statutes.[871] There has been a vigorous debate within the federal judiciary as to whether this is proper as a method of interpretation.[872] This debate has been rehearsed in the Supreme Court over the past eight years.

Ironically enough, the wellspring of the intellectual conflict was the 1986 unanimous decision in *O'Connor v. United States*.[873] The interpretive problem in *O'Connor* seemed straight-forward enough: should Article 15 of one of the Implementing Agreements[874] to the 1977 Panama Canal Treaty[875] be construed so as to allow U.S. citizens working for the Panama Canal Commission to avoid paying taxes either in Panama or in the U.S. on their salaries? This issue had

---

[870] *See* supra notes 808 - 816 and accompanying text.

[871] *See* supra § IX.ii.

[872] *See* supra notes 809, 812 and 816 and accompanying text.

[873] 479 U.S. 27 (1986).

[874] Panama Canal Treaty: Implementation of Article III, U.S.-Pan., Sept. 7, 1977, art. 15, 33 U.S.T. 141, T.I.A.S. No. 10031, 1280 U.N.T.S. 79 [hereinafter "Implementing Agreement"].

[875] Panama Canal Treaty, U.S.-Pan., Sept. 7, 1977, 33 U.S.T. 39, T.I.A.S. No. 10030, 1280 U.N.T.S. 79 (entered into force Oct. 1, 1979).

been extensively litigated in the lower courts, with surprising results. A number of judges had construed Article 15 of the Agreement[876] to insulate U.S. Commission employees from paying U.S. income tax. Many of these courts had believed that Article 15 was badly drafted, and so the government had to live with this peculiar, and unexpectedly generous, concession.[877] This was obviously an application of a form of the *contra proferentum* canon,[878] with the government hung on its own textual petard.

The government waged a broad attack on these results, and ultimately won review in the U.S. Supreme Court. In its opinion, Justice Scalia writing, the Court made an effort to provide a meaning to the disputed language so that it was clear that the exemption to taxes applied only to Panamanian authorities.[879] But this was hard, as already noted, since Article 15, paragraph 2, swept the exemption to "any" taxes.[880] Justice Scalia as much as admitted that the textual support for limiting the exemption was weak. He noted that "[t]here is some purely textual evidence, albeit subtle, of the understanding that Article XV applies only to Panamanian taxes...."[881] This was a case where a quick break from the text was necessary, as Justice Scalia made clear. "More persuasive

---

[876] The taxpayers' relied on the provision that said in pertinent part that "United States citizen employees and dependents shall be exempt from any taxes, fees or other charges on income received as a result of their work for the Commission." Implementing Agreement, supra note 874, art. 15, para. 2.

[877] *See Harris v. United States*, 768 F.2d 1240, 1244 (11th Cir. 1985); *Coplin v. United States*, 6 Cl. Ct. 115,149 (Cl. Ct. 1984), *rev'd*, 761 F.2d 688 (Fed. Cir. 1985), *aff'd sub nom. O'Connor v. United States*, 479 U.S. 27 (1986). *But see* those lower court decisions ruling against the taxpayers, *Rego v. United States*, 591 F. Supp. 123 (W.D. Tenn. 1984); *Watson v. United States*, 592 F. Supp. 701 (W.D. Wash. 1983); *Corliss v. United States*, 567 F. Supp. 162 (W.D. Ark. 1983).

[878] *See* supra note 707 with text.

[879] *O'Connor*, 479 U.S. at 30-31.

[880] *See* supra note 876.

[881] *O'Connor*, 479 U.S. at 31.

than the textual evidence," he wrote, "and in our view overwhelmingly convincing, is the contextual case for limiting Article XV to Panamanian taxes."[882] The Court responded favorably to the government's submission, made by the Solicitor General,[883] that the treaty text *was* ambiguous, and, in any event, the Court should reject "efforts to wrench snippets of [treaty] language out of context."[884]

If anything, the Court seemed intent to show that the taxpayers' reading of the treaty would lead to an absurd, or at least undesirable, result. In effect, Justice Scalia said that accepting Petitioners' interpretation of the plain meaning of the language would lead to a "tax immunity of unprecedented scope."[885] When counsel for the taxpayers' attempted to argue textually that "these broader tax consequences need not follow from their interpretation,"[886] Justice Scalia returned to textualism and concluded that the taxpayers' saving reading was "unnatural"[887] and "flatly inconsistent with the language"[888] of another treaty provision.

O'Connor has had a problematic legacy for the Rehnquist Court — and particularly for its author, Justice Scalia. But it really was a *tour de force*. As will shortly be seen,[889] its use of a wide variety of extrinsic sources in

---

[882]   Id.

[883]   *See* Brief for the United States, *O'Connor* (85-558, 85-559, 85-560) (U.S. Sept. 30, 1986).

[884]   Id. at 15 n.8.

[885]   *O'Connor*, 479 U.S. at 32.

[886]   Id. *See also* Petitioners' Reply Brief, *O'Connor* (85-558, 85-559, 85-560), at 4 (U.S. Mar. 22, 1986).

[887]   *O'Connor*, 479 U.S. at 32.

[888]   Id.

[889]   *See* infra notes 1025 - 1034, 1103 - 1109 and accompanying text.

interpretation had a significant impact on later cases.   But the intellectual premise of the exercise was troublesome.   Justice Scalia apparently felt uncomfortable in making the quick switch to extratextual means of construction. The contrast is particularly striking with Justice Scalia's own concurrence in *United States v. Stuart*,[890] another tax case.   This time the Court was struggling with a nettlesome question of the Internal Revenue Service issuing administrative summons[891] under Articles 19 and 21 of the 1942 U.S.-Canada Double Taxation Convention.[892]   In the decision, Justice Brennan tackled the problem of interpreting the Double Taxation Convention in almost precisely the same manner as Justice Scalia in *O'Connor*. It was not even really a very complicated matter of construction because the treaty's text did not support Respondent's proposition that the Convention imposed restrictions on the ability of the I.R.S. to cooperate with Canadian tax authorities.[893] Nor, Justice Brennan concluded, did other "[n]ontextual sources" for the treaty's meaning help their case.[894]

Justice Scalia, in a concurrence, took issue with the majority's use of such extrinsic sources as the Senate hearings and debates in ratifying the treaty,[895] as well as the subsequent practice of the parties in enforcing the

---

[890]   489 U.S. 353 (1989).

[891]   This technical controversy was whether the American revenue authorities had to be assured that any summons they issued on behalf of Canadian authorities was not in pursuance to a criminal prosecution. *Stuart*, 489 U.S. at 355-56. The Court ruled that nothing in the Treaty required such a precondition for cooperation. *See* id. at 356, 370.

[892]   Convention Respecting Double Taxation, U.S.-Can., Mar. 4, 1942, 56 Stat. 1405, T.S. No. 983.

[893]   The taxpayers had somehow convinced the Court of Appeals, *see* 813 F.2d 243 (9th Cir. 1987), that the very language of articles 19 and 21 of the Double Taxation Convention, supra note 892, was a substantive limitation on I.R.S. discretion. Id. at 246-47, 249-50. As Respondents, they renewed this argument before the Court, but Justice Brennan summarily rejected it. 489 U.S. at 365-66.

[894]   489 U.S. at 366-70.

[895]   *See* id. at 366-68.

Convention.[896]   This aspect of the discordance of views in the *Stuart* decision will be addressed below,[897] but it is significant to note that Scalia expressed his opposition in principle to the use of *any* extrinsic sources when the treaty text is clear.   "Given that the Treaty's language resolves the issue presented," Justice Scalia wrote, "there is no necessity of looking further to discover 'the intent of the Treaty parties'."[898]   In developing this theme, Justice Scalia said that

> no one can be opposed to giving effect to 'the intent of the Treaty parties.' The critical question, however, is whether that is more reliably and predictably achieved by a rule of construction which credits, when it is clear, the contracting sovereigns' carefully framed and solemnly ratified expression of those intentions, or rather one which sets judges in various jurisdictions at large to ignore that clear expression and discern a 'genuine' contrary intent elsewhere. To ask that question is to answer it.[899]

This is as clarion an expression of the textualist canon of treaty interpretation that one is likely to find in a Supreme Court opinion. To be sure, it begs the decisive issue of what makes a text "unclear" and what level of ambiguity an interpreter can tolerate.   Nonetheless, Justice Scalia was intent on extending his jurisprudence of statutory construction to the treaty area.   In his *Stuart* concurrence he conducted a quick review of the origins of the now-accepted search for intent in treaty construction.[900]   Although he did not manage to trace the notion back to its intellectual taproots in the *Choctaw Nation* opinion,[901] he did manage a swipe at the oft-repeated phrase from *Maximov v.*

---

[896]   *See* id. at 369-70.

[897]   *See* infra notes 1057 - 1083 with text.

[898]   Id. at 371 (Scalia, J., concurring) (quoting the majority opinion, id. at 366).

[899]   Id. (Scalia, J., concurring). *See also Snap-on Tools, Inc. v. United States*, 26 Cl. Ct. 1045, 1065-66 (1992) (where Justice Scalia's concurrence in *Stuart* was followed in establishing a methodology to interpret a tax treaty).

[900]   489 U.S. at 371-73 (Scalia, J., concurring).

[901]   318 U.S. 423 (1943). *See* supra notes 838 - 839 with text.

United States[902] that the clear import of treaty language controls unless "application of the words of the treaty according to their obvious meaning effects a result inconsistent with the intent or expectations of the parties."[903] The irony cannot be lost, though, that Justice Scalia himself relied on the *Maximov* intent canon in his *O'Connor* opinion, even though he only cited to it indirectly.[904]

While stirring in its appeal for a return to first principles in treaty construction, the Scalia concurrence in *Stuart* rings a bit hollow. Was not, after all, the language in the Panamanian Agreement every bit as clear — or as ambiguous — as the Canadian Tax Treaty? The only difference had to be the desired result: in *O'Connor* the only possible support for the favored interpretation was found in extrinsic sources, while in *Stuart* the text could stand alone. Quite clearly the threshold of ambiguity was raised sometime between *O'Connor* and *Stuart*.

Or was it? In a number of other cases the Supreme Court has seemed ambivalent in saying exactly what kind of textual or circumstantial vagueness will qualify the terms of an international agreement as "unclear" so as to allow a break from the first canon of treaty interpretation. These cases tended to turn on two sorts of occurrences. The first was when the language used seemed clear enough except when it came to a resolution of the legal controversy raised in the case. This is situational obscurity. The second occurrence is where (usually) mandatory language is missing in an instrument, but is present in a related provision or agreement. What is the interpreter to deduce from this omission? This could be called the "slip of the pen" problem.[905]

---

[902] 373 U.S. 49 (1963).

[903] Id. at 54 (as quoted in *Sumitomo Shoji America, Inc. v. Avagliano*, 457 U.S. 176, 180 (1982)).

[904] *O'Connor*, 479 U.S. at 33 (citing *Sumitomo*, 457 U.S. at 184-85, which in turn cites *Maximov*).

[905] Justice Scalia has been critical of judges that would intend to cure a *lapsus linguae* (slip of the tongue) or "scrivener's error" in a statute. Although he recognizes "extreme cases" where there was an error, a judicial correction is the exception and not the rule. *See* Scalia, A Matter of Interpretation, supra note 547, at 20-21.

A few examples will suffice for these two scenarios. *O'Connor* was arguably a slip of the pen case. After all, the Court concluded that the text of the Panama Canal Treaty could not mean what it said in exempting "all taxes."[906] Likewise, in *Société Nationale Industrielle Aerospatiale ("SNIAS")*[907] the question presented was the proper construction of the Hague Evidence Convention[908] and whether its terms were mandatory on American courts in the conduct of overseas discovery.[909] But nowhere in the text of the Convention was there any mention that the provisions were to be considered as mandatory. Was this obvious? The Supreme Court, Justice Stevens writing, concluded that the text meant what it said — but only by omission.[910] After all, Stevens could point to a related treaty, the Hague Service Convention, which *did* contain the expected language that its terms were to be construed as obligatory.[911] That observation was dicta, of course, but by deduction the interpreter could assume that the Evidence Convention was not to be considered as the exclusive mechanism for overseas discovery.[912] A slip of the pen was averted. There was

---

[906]   *See* supra notes 879 - 884 and accompanying text.

[907]   482 U.S. 522 (1987).

[908]   Hague Convention on the Taking of Evidence Abroad in Civil or Commercial Matters, March 18, 1970, 23 U.S.T. 2555.

[909]   *SNIAS*, 482 U.S. at 524, 529.

[910]   *See* id. at 534-40.

[911]   *See* id. at 534 n.15 (referring to Hague Convention on the Service Abroad of Judicial and Extrajudicial Documents in Civil or Commercial Matters, Nov. 15, 1965, art. 1, 20 U.S.T. 361).

[912]   *See* id. ("the Service Convention was drafted before the Evidence Convention, and its language provided a model exclusivity provision that the drafters of the Evidence Convention could easily have followed had they been so inclined. Given this background, the drafters' election to use permissive language instead is strong evidence of their intent.").

a combined concurrence-dissent in *SNIAS*,[913] but it did not emphasize any textual argument for the obligatory character of the Evidence Convention. Instead, it relied on concerns regarding the object and purpose of the Convention,[914] and of respecting international comity,[915] in reaching its contrary conclusion.

Likewise, in *Eastern Airlines, Inc. v. Floyd*,[916] a case construing the Warsaw Convention,[917] the question was whether an airliner was liable for mental distress unaccompanied by any physical injury.[918] Article 17 of the Convention, in the original French, refers to "*lésion corporelle*," but nowhere is that term defined. Justice Marshall, writing for an unanimous Court, tried valiantly to maintain close touch with the text in making an interpretation, but to no avail. He consulted French-language law dictionaries and French law sources on contemporary understandings of the phrase.[919] Justice Marshall even attempted a structural review of the text and tried to make sense of Article 17's

---

[913]   482 U.S. at 547 (Blackmun, J., joined by Marshall and O'Connor, JJ.). The opinion is a dissent as only to the majority's "case-by-case inquiry for determining whether to use [the Evidence] Convention procedures and its failure to provide lower courts with any meaningful guidance for carrying out that inquiry." Id. at 548 (Blackmun, J., concurring in part, dissenting in part).

[914]   *See* id. at 547, 549-51.

[915]   *See* id. at 554-68.

[916]   111 S.Ct. 1489 (1991).

[917]   Convention for the Unification of Certain Rules Relating to International Transportation By Air, Oct. 12, 1929, 49 Stat. 3000, T.S. No. 876 (1934). Judging by the number of interpretive cases involving the Warsaw Convention, it is probably the most-litigated treaty in U.S. courts. *See* supra notes 810, 829, 844 and 850 with accompanying text..

[918]   111 S.Ct. at 1492.

[919]   *See* id. 1493-96.

reference to both *blessure* (wounding) and *lésion corporelle*.[920] Was this a slip of the pen? A federal Court of Appeals, ruling below,[921] decided that it was. In order to avoid making *lésion corporelle* a surplusage in relation to *blessure*, the lower court concluded that *lésion corporelle* had to include purely psychic injuries.[922] Justice Marshall chose, however, not to accord much deference to this textual canon of surplusage, despite acknowledging its relevance here.[923] Once again, a purely textual thrust for treaty interpretation was deflected into extrinsic materials. No slip of the pen, it seems, has gone unerased.

Perhaps the best-known of the "slip of the pen" cases was *United States v. Alvarez-Machain*,[924] decided in 1992. This *cause célèbre* featured the forced abduction of Humberto Alvarez-Machain from Mexico,[925] and a determination of his rights under the 1978 Extradition Treaty with that country.[926] After defeats in the lower courts,[927] the United States maintained that because the Treaty was silent as to the propriety of forced renditions of suspects (even if the

---

[920] *See* id. 1496-97.

[921] *See* 872 F.2d 1462, 1470-73 (11th Cir. 1989).

[922] *See* id. at 1472-73.

[923] *See* 111 S.Ct. at 1496. For more on this canon, *see Kungys v. United States*, 485 U.S. 759, 778 (1998) (plurality) (a "cardinal rule of statutory interpretation [is] that no provision should be construed to be entirely redundant"); *Exxon Corp. v. Hunt*, 475 U.S. 355, 369 n.14 (1986). For a clever application of this canon, *see Western Union Telegraph Co. v. Lenroot*, 323 U.S. 490 (1945).

[924] 112 S.Ct. 2188 (1992).

[925] *See* id. at 2190-91.

[926] Extradition Treaty, U.S.-Mex., May 4, 1978, 31 U.S.T. 5059.

[927] *See United States v. Verdugo-Urquidez*, 939 F.2d 1341 (9th Cir. 1991) (holding that an illegally abducted suspect had a right, under the Extradition Treaty, to be returned to Mexico if that country requested such); *United States v. Caro-Quintero*, 745 F. Supp. 599 (C.D. Cal. 1990) (same).

abduction was with the connivance of United States government officials and over the objections of the foreign country) no treaty violation transpired and the Respondent was not entitled to be released.[928] It *was* true that the Treaty was silent on this point, Alaverz conceded,[929] but there remained the small problem of Treaty Article 9 which gave Mexico the right to decline the extradition of its own nationals.[930] The government's reading of the Treaty would, Respondent suggested,[931] make that provision nugatory. Chief Justice Rehnquist, writing for the Court, disagreed.[932] With virtually no textual or contextual consideration, the Court rejected this attempt at reading an implied term into the agreement. The Chief Justice proceeded to confirm this apparently strict textual reading, however, with a review of the treaty negotiations and subsequent practice of the parties.[933]

The dissent, written by Justice Stevens, took to task the majority's handling of omissions and the insertion of implied terms.[934] The dissent would have handled the "slip of the pen" problem by relying on "'the manifest scope

---

[928]   *See* Brief of the United States, *Alvarez* (91-712) (U.S. Feb. 13, 1992).

[929]   *See Alvarez*, 112 S.Ct. at 2193-95. *See also* Respondent's Brief, *Alvarez* (91-712), at 7-21 (U.S. March 4, 1992) (although cloaking concession in terms of a search for "object and purpose" of the Treaty).

[930]   Extradition Treaty, supra note 926, art. 9, para. 1 ("Neither Contracting Party shall be bound to deliver up its own nationals, but the executive authority of the requested Party shall, if not prevented by the laws of that Party, have the power to deliver them up if, in its discretion, it be deemed proper to do so.").

[931]   *See* Respondent's Brief, *Alvarez* (91-712), at 9-12 (U.S. March 4, 1992).

[932]   *Alvarez*, 112 S.Ct. at 2194.

[933]   *See* id. at 2194-96.

[934]   *See* id. at 2199-2200 (Stevens, J., dissenting). The dissent was joined by Justices Blackmun and O'Connor.

and object of the treaty itself'."[935] Still, it seems, that the majority of the justices were persuaded by the Solicitor General's argument that, as a rule, the insertion of implied terms was to be disfavored in treaty interpretation, for fear that courts will rewrite treaties to suit their fancy.[936] That this is exactly what the government asked the Court to do with the Panama Canal Agreement in the *O'Connor* case did not appear to embarrass the United States' position in *Alvarez*. The slip of the pen cases seem to allow for a sliding scale of ambiguity. When the government is in the position of challenging the clear terms of a badly-drafted instrument, as in *O'Connor*, then the threshold of obscurity is quite low. But when presented with an omitted (but implied) term of a treaty, as in *Alvarez*, the Court then raises the threshold, or at least places additional burdens on the party taking a position contrary to that of the government.

Turning to the situational ambiguity cases, in *Volkswagenwerk Aktiengesellschaft*,[937] the issue discussed by Justice Stevens in the *SNIAS* dicta[938] was actually before the Court: were the provisions of the Hague *Service* Convention obligatory?[939] The Court reaffirmed that the relevant procedures of the Convention were mandatory.[940] The only question that remained was

---

[935] Id. at 2199 (Stevens, J., dissenting) (*quoting United States v. Rauscher*, 119 U.S. 407, 422 (1886)).

[936] *See* Brief of the United States, *Alvarez* (91-712), at 24 (U.S. Feb. 13, 1992). In its Brief, the United States relied, as support for this proposition, on *The AMIABLE ISABELLA*, 19 U.S. (6 Wheat.) 1, 71 (1821) (*quoted* at text with supra note 770), and *Maximov v. United States*, 373 U.S. 49, 54 (1963) (*see* supra notes 900 - 904 with accompanying text for Justice Scalia's critique of that case authority). *Cf.* the lower court decision, which cites *Air France v. Saks*, 470 U.S. 392, 397 (1985) for the notion that both text and context are to be used in treaty interpretation. *See* 939 F.2d at 1354-55.

[937] 486 U.S. 694 (1988).

[938] *See* supra note 911 with accompanying text.

[939] 486 U.S. at 696, 698-99.

[940] *See* id. at 699.

whether the phrase "service abroad" applied to a situation where the entity being served was an American subsidiary of a foreign corporation.[941]   On this question, the language of the Service Convention was situationally obscure. The Court seemed persuaded by the Solicitor General's argument, presented in an amicus brief,[942] that the questioned language *was* ambiguous, and proceeded to review the negotiating history of the treaty.[943]

But the Court has periodically resisted the temptation to find ambiguity where none really existed.   This happened recently in *Itel Containers International Corp. v. Huddleston*,[944] where the Court was faced with an issue akin to that in *O'Connor*: the extent of a tax exemption granted by treaty.[945] The agreements in *Itel* were the 1956 and 1972 Containers Conventions[946] and the problem was their compatibility with a state tax on leasehold interests in containers used in international commerce. The Court, Justice Kennedy writing, held that the treaty language limiting the tax exemption[947] was clear on its face, and, hence, the state tax was permissible.[948] Despite arguments that such an

---

[941]   *See* id. at 699-700.

[942]   *See* Brief Amicus Curiae for the United States, *Volkswagen* (86-1052), at screen 49 (LEXIS, Genfed Library, Briefs File) (U.S. Feb. 1, 1988).

[943]   *See* 486 U.S. at 700-06.

[944]   113 S.Ct. 1095 (1993).

[945]   *See* id. at 1098-99.

[946]   Customs Convention on Containers, Dec. 2, 1972, 988 U.N.T.S. 43; Customs Convention on Containers, May 18, 1956, 20 U.S.T. 301.

[947]   Article 1 in each of the 1956 and 1972 Conventions, supra note, gave an exemption to only those taxes "collected on, or in connexion with, the importation of goods" and those "chargeable by reason of importation." Id.

[948]   *See* 113 S.Ct. at 1099-1100.

interpretation was contrary to the views of other nations,[949] as will be discussed,[950] the majority was insistent that there was no situational ambiguity in the case. Even Justice Blackmun's dissent in *Itel*[951] does not purport to reassess the textual argument made by the taxpayers; instead, he focused on a rule of construction that would accord more with the interests and expectations of other nations — the canon of liberal construction and good faith.[952]

None of the situational ambiguity or "slip of the pen" cases really, however, advanced the debate within the Court over textualism as the first canon of treaty interpretation. Indeed, the rancor only intensified, reaching a fever pitch in *Chan v. Korean Air Lines, Ltd.*[953] Here, it seemed, Justice Scalia's pure textualism approach was vindicated. And, more importantly, the split in the Court was manifest on exactly the point at which an interpreter could break from a treaty's text. *Chan* was yet another Warsaw Convention case, and the question presented, as fairly stated by Justice Scalia in writing the majority opinion, was whether international air carriers lose the Convention's limitation of liability protection if they fail to provide passengers notice of that limitation on the ticket in 10-point type size or greater.[954] This turned on the proper construction of two parallel provisions in Article 3 of the Warsaw Convention: one requiring fair notice of limitation of liability,[955] and the other stripping the carrier of its

---

[949]   *See* id. at 1100-01.

[950]   *See* infra notes 1140 - 1145 with text.

[951]   *See* id. at 1109.

[952]   *See* id. at 1109-10 (Blackmun, J., dissenting). *See also* supra notes 818 - 836 with text.

[953]   490 U.S. 122 (1989).

[954]   490 U.S. at 123. This note is in 10-point type size.

[955]   Warsaw Convention, supra note 917, art. 3, para. 1(e) (A carrier "must deliver a passenger ticket which shall contain the following particulars ... (e) A statement that the transportation is subject to the rules relating to liability established by this convention."). The 10-point type requirement was contained in the later Montreal Agreement, *see* supra

limitation privilege if it "accepts a passenger without a passenger ticket having been delivered."[956]   A number of lower courts had equated the delivery of a deficient ticket (one lacking the clear notice of limitation) with the non-delivery of a ticket, thus denying limitation for the carrier.[957] This was the position taken by an airline passenger as Petitioner, and also by the United States as amicus.[958] The Respondent, Korean Air Lines, made a plea for textualism, suggesting that Article 3 was "neither 'difficult' nor 'ambiguous'":[959] non-delivery of a ticket was the only ground for stripping a carrier of its limited liability granted under the treaty. Each of the litigants relied extensively on evidence of *travaux* and subsequent practice in construing the Convention on this issue.[960]

Justice Scalia instead clung to the terms of the agreement and held that delivery of an irregular ticket did not strip the carrier of limited liability.[961] The textual analysis undertaken by Scalia was, in all respects, identical to Justice Marshall writing for a unanimous court in the later Warsaw Convention case, *Floyd*. There was the same rejection of an alternate reading of the treaty's terms

---

note 850, as reprinted in the *Chan* opinion, 490 U.S. at 125 n.1.

[956]   Warsaw Convention, supra note 917, art. 3, para. 2.

[957]   *See, e.g., In re Air Crash Disaster Near New Orleans*, 789 F.2d 1092 (5th Cir. 1986), *reinstated*, 821 F.2d 1147 (5th Cir. 1987) (en banc); *In re Air Crash Disaster at Warsaw*, 705 F.2d 85 (2d Cir.), *cert. denied sub nom. Polskie Linie Lotnicze v. Robles*, 464 U.S. 845 (1983); *Lisi v. Alitalia-Linee Aeree Italiane, S.p.A.*, 370 F.2d 508 (2d Cir. 1966), *aff'd by equally divided Court*, 390 U.S. 455 (1968).

[958]   *See* 490 U.S. at 123, 133. Of the ten cases reviewed here, see supra note 869, this is the only one in which the Court took a position contrary to that articulated by the United States government.

[959]   *See* Respondent's Brief, *Chan* (87-1055), at 12-19 (U.S. Aug. 19, 1988).

[960]   *See* id.; Petitioner's Brief, *Chan* (87-1055), at 29-38 (U.S. June 17, 1988).

[961]   *See* 490 U.S. at 128.

as implausible.[962] Then there was a structural engagement with the text in search of parallel provisions, in order to shed light on the questioned clause. But, again, both opinions shared the same reluctance to put much stock in such textual tools of analysis.[963] The major difference, of course, between the two opinions is that whereas Scalia stopped in *Chan* with the text (just as he promised in his *Stuart* concurrence),[964] Marshall went forward in *Floyd* to examine extrinsic sources.[965] That is probably why Marshall wrote for a unanimous Court in *Floyd*, while Justice Scalia could only manage a bare majority in *Chan*.

Justice Brennan authored the concurrence in *Chan* and believed the pure textualism approach to treaty construction to be a "self-affixed blindfold that prevents the Court from examining anything beyond the treaty language itself."[966] Brennan noted that where there is more than one possible reading of the treaty text, recourse to extrinsic evidence is appropriate to divine the "treatymakers' intent."[967] Replying to this, Justice Scalia believed that initiating a search though the relevant negotiating history was merely an "effort to depart from any possible reading of this Treaty."[968] In other words, it appeared to Justice Scalia that the concurrence had decided that the Warsaw Convention *travaux* was, in fact, inconclusive, and all that was left were yet more remote

---

[962] *Compare* 490 U.S. at 128-30 *with* 111 S.Ct. at 1496.

[963] *Compare* 490 U.S. at 130-34 *with* 111 S.Ct. at 1496-97. One text has suggested that Justice Scalia was applying the expressio unius canon. *See* William N. Eskridge, Jr. & Philip P. Frickey, CASES AND MATERIALS ON LEGISLATION 639 (2d ed. 1995). *See also* supra note 579.

[964] *See* text with supra note 899.

[965] *See* 111 S.Ct. at 1497-1502.

[966] 490 U.S. at 136 (Brennan, J., concurring). Justices Marshall, Blackmun, and Stevens joined the concurrence.

[967] Id. (Brennan, J., concurring).

[968] Id. at 130 n.3.

extrinsic sources.[969] "Even if the text were less clear," Scalia wrote, "its most natural meaning could be contradicted only by clear drafting history."[970] And only if the textual reading produces a result that is "absurd,"[971] a borrowing (without attribution) from the Vienna Convention's methodology,[972] the treaty terms can be "dismissed as an obvious drafting error"[973] or slip of the pen.

With the decision in *Sale v. Haitian Centers Council, Inc.*,[974] the Court came full-circle, finding itself in virtually the same interpretive posture as in *O'Connor*. The difference between *Haitian Centers* and *O'Connor* was that issue was joined precisely on the question of where to break from the text. The legal question to be decided in *Haitian Centers* was whether the Bush and Clinton administrations' policy of interdicting Haitian refugees on the high seas, and returning them to Haiti without any attempt to determine if any of the affected individuals were fleeing political persecution,[975] violated the 1952

---

[969]   *See* id. at 134 n.1.

[970]   Id.

[971]   Id. at 134.

[972]   *See* supra notes 859 - 862 with text.

[973]   490 U.S. at 134.

[974]   113 S.Ct. 2549 (1993).

[975]   This policy has generated both vast amounts of litigation and scholarly attention. For a sampling of the latter, *see* Abigail D. King, *Interdiction: The United States' Continuing Violation of International Law*, 68 B.U. L. REV. 773 (1988); Proposed Interdiction of Haitian Flag Vessels, 5 Op. Off. Legal Counsel 242 (1981).

Immigration and Nationality Act (as amended)[976] or Article 33 of the U.N.
Convention Relating to the Status of Refugees[977] and its 1967 Protocol.[978]

The language of article 33 was compelling in a finding that the
interdiction *did* violate the Refugees Convention, and a federal Court of Appeals
hewed closely to the treaty text in reaching this conclusion.[979] The relevant
paragraph of article 33 provided that "[n]o Contracting State shall expel or
return (*'refouler'*) a refugee in any manner whatsoever to the frontiers or
territories where his life or freedom would be threatened on account of his race,
religion, nationality, membership of a particular social group or political
opinion."[980] The government's submission throughout the litigation was that
Article 33.1 was inapplicable, by its very terms, to a situation where the putative
refugee has not reached United States territory.[981] In the alternative, the United
States maintained that since nothing in the treaty text spoke to the question of the
extraterritorial application of the non-*refoulement* obligation, an interpreting
court was free to depart from the treaty text and to establish the intent of the
parties through consultation of extrinsic sources, including negotiating and
legislative history, as well as subsequent interpretations.[982]

---

[976]   The provision in question was § 243(h)(1) of the Act, codified at 8 U.S.C.
§1253(h), as amended by § 203(e) of the Refugees Act of 1980, Pub. L. No. 96-212, 94
Stat. 107.

In *Haitian Centers* both the statute and treaty were in issue. For the Court's
handling of the statutory construction question, *see* 61 U.S.L.W. at 4688-90.

[977]   July 28, 1951, 189 U.N.T.S. 150.

[978]   Jan. 31, 1967, 19 U.S.T. 6223, T.I.A.S. No. 6577, 606 U.N.T.S. 267.

[979]   *Haitian Centers Council, Inc. v. McNary*, 969 F.2d 1350, 1361-66 (2d Cir. 1992).

[980]   Refugees Convention, supra note 977, art. 33, para. 1.

[981]   Brief for the United States, *Haitian Centers* (92-344), at pages 21-25 (LEXIS,
Genfed Library, Briefs File) (U.S. Nov. 12, 1992).

[982]   *See* id. at 25-30.

What was intriguing in *Haitian Councils* were the methods by which the government sought to make an apparently unambiguous treaty provision hopelessly vague. These methods were tried and true in the *O'Connor* case. The first was to deconstruct the very words of the treaty obligation. Article 33.1 of the Refugees Convention says a party may not "expel or return (*'refouler'*) a refugee in any manner whatsoever." The Solicitor General argued,[983] and Justice Stevens writing for the Court agreed,[984] that there was an ambiguity inherent in the disjunctive use of *both* expel *and* return. The Court noted that

> Article 33.1 uses the words "expel or return (*'refouler'*)" as an obvious parallel to the words "deport or return" in [the 1952 Immigration and Nationality Act] § 243(h)(1). There is no dispute that "expel" has the same meaning as "deport"; it refers to the deportation or expulsion of an alien who is already present in the host country. The dual reference identified and explained in our opinion in *Leng May Ma v. Barber*, suggests that the term "return (*'refouler'*)" refers to the exclusion of aliens who are merely "'on the threshold of initial entry.'"[985]

What is extraordinary in this passage is the seeming *non-sequitur* in using a provision of domestic implementing legislation as a guide to interpretation of an earlier treaty provision. The Court does not bother to say what the "obvious parallel"[986] is between the two. More significantly, Justice Steven's superimposition of a peculiar structural reading of a statute onto a treaty text violated a canon of interpretation that the words in treaties "are to be taken in their ordinary meaning, as understood in the public law of nations, and not in any artificial or special sense impressed upon them by local law...."[987]

---

[983]   Brief for the United States, *Haitian Centers* (92-344), at pages 22-24 (LEXIS, Genfed Library, Briefs File) (U.S. Nov. 12, 1992).

[984]   113 S.Ct. at 2563.

[985]   Id. (*citing* 357 U.S. at 187 (*quoting Shaugnessy v. United States ex rel. Mezei*, 345 U.S. 206, 212 (1953))).

[986]   Id.

[987]   *Geoffroy v. Riggs*, 133 U.S. 258, 271-72 (1890) (Field, J.). *See also* supra notes 818 - 821 and accompanying text.

Justice Blackmun was the sole dissenter in *Haitian Councils* and he seized on this aberrant approach by the majority: "'Return,' [the majority] claims, does not mean return, but instead has a distinctive legal meaning.   For this proposition the Court relies almost entirely on the fact that *American* law makes a general distinction between *deportation* and *exclusion.*"[988]   Justice Blackmun identified this as the fatal defect of the majority opinion's attempt at treaty interpretation.   By giving the word "return" a peculiarly American legal gloss, the Court violated one of the first principles of treaty construction, as articulated in the Vienna Convention,[989] which Justice Blackmun even quoted.[990]

Having found that "return," as used in Article 33.1, did not really mean return, the Justice Stevens then compounded his mistake by then deciding that the French word *refouler*, added into the treaty text, also did not really mean what it said.   The Court had used foreign language dictionaries in a number of earlier decisions, sometimes with success,[991] but always at least with the goal of divining the precise meaning of a foreign term.   In *Haitian Centers* the exercise seemed down-right disingenuous.   The object appeared to be to create ambiguity where none arguably existed, and this was again criticized by Justice Blackmum in his dissent.[992]

The second general technique for casting doubt on a treaty text was also employed by the United States in *Haitian Centers*: that is to create situational ambiguity by reading one treaty provision against another.   As I already

---

[988]   113 S.Ct. at 2569 (Blackmun, J., dissenting) (original emphasis).

[989]   Vienna Convention on the Law of Treaties, supra note 764, article 33, paragraph 1 (words in treaty are construed according to "ordinary meaning").   *See* supra notes 859 - 862 and accompanying text.

[990]   113 S.Ct. at 2569 (Blackmun, J., dissenting).

[991]   *See* supra notes 916 - 919 (discussing use of French language dictionary in *Eastern Airlines v. Floyd*).   *See also Air France v. Saks*, 470 U.S. 392, 400 (1985).

[992]   113 S.Ct. at 2569-70 & n.5 (Blackmun, J., dissenting).

mentioned,[993] this was used effectively in *O'Connor*. In *Haitian Centers* the government made much[994] of Article 33.2 of the Refugees Convention which said that "[t]he benefit of the present provision may not ... be claimed by a refugee whom there are reasonable grounds for regarding as a danger to the security of the country in which he is...."[995] The Supreme Court noted that any interpretation of Article 33.1 which extended the *non-refoulement* obligation to the high seas "would create an absurd anomaly"[996] with Article 33.2: "dangerous aliens on the high seas would be entitled to the benefits of 33.1 while those residing in the country that sought to expel them would not."[997]

One is at a loss, though, to identify the absurdity that gave license to the Court to break from the clear text of the Convention. Article 33.2 is simply a narrow exception to the extraordinarily broad right of non-*refoulement*, the international human right of not being returned to a country where one may be persecuted.[998] As Justice Blackmun pungently noted, "[o]ne wonders what the majority would make of an exception that removed from the Article's protection all refugees who 'constitute a danger to their families.' By the majority's logic, the inclusion of such an exception presumably would render Article 33.1 applicable only to refugees with families."[999]

---

[993]   *See* supra notes 885 - 888 with text.

[994]   Brief for the United States, *Haitian Centers* (92-344), at page 24 (LEXIS, Genfed Library, Briefs File) (U.S. Nov. 12, 1992)..

[995]   Refugees Convention, supra note 977, art. 33, para. 2.

[996]   113 S.Ct. at 2563.

[997]   Id.

[998]   *See generally* Guy Goodwin-Gill, THE REFUGEE IN INTERNATIONAL LAW (1983); Louis Sohn & Thomas Buergenthal, THE MOVEMENT OF PERSONS ACROSS BORDERS (1992); Guy Goodwin-Gill, *Non*-Refoulement *and the New Asylum Seekers*, 26 VA. J. INT'L L. 899 (1986).

[999]   113 S.Ct. at 2570 (Blackmun, J., dissenting).

Justice Stevens opinion marshals a parade of horribles in order to create ambiguity or an absurd result. Ironically, this is the threshold of ambiguity in the Vienna Convention,[1000] although the majority nowhere refers to it. The Court clearly did not like the result reached by a textual approach, and, with nary a peep from Justice Scalia, the textual analysis of the opinion segues quickly into a comprehensive review of *travaux préparatoires* and less-cogent references to legislative history. The majority did not bother to set the threshold of ambiguity. Justice Blackmun, this time citing Justice Scalia's concurrence in *Stuart*,[1001] noted in dissent "that a treaty's plain language must control absent 'extraordinarily strong contrary evidence'"[1002] and that "[r]eliance on a treaty's negotiating history ... is a disfavored alternative of last resort, appropriate only where the terms of the document are obscure or lead to 'manifestly absurd or unreasonable' results."[1003]

After *Haitian Centers* it is difficult to determine whether Justice Scalia's brand of pure textualism, as articulated in his *Stuart* concurrent and his *Chan* opinion, remains viable. The absence of any statement by Justice Scalia in *Haitian Centers* may indicate some discomfort — maybe even embarrassment — on his part. This discomfort was reflected in Justice Scalia's opinion in *Zicherman v. Korean Air Lines*,[1004] yet another in the series of cases construing the Warsaw Convention. Here, Scalia gave derisively short shrift to a textualist reading of "damage" under Article 17 of the Convention:

> It cannot seriously be maintained that Article 17 uses the term in this broadest sense, thus exploding tort liability beyond what any legal system in the world

---

[1000]   *See* supra note 854. *See also* Rogoff, supra note 869, at 576-79.

[1001]   489 U.S. at 371.

[1002]   113 S.Ct. at 2570-71 (Blackmun J., dissenting) (*quoting Sumitomo Shoji America Inc. v. Avagliano*, 457 U.S. 176, 185 (1982)).

[1003]   Id. (*quoting* Vienna Convention, supra note 764, art. 32). *See also* Brief for the U.N. High Commissioner for Refugees *Amicus Curiae* in Support of Respondent, *Haitian Centers* (92-344), at page 17 (LEXIS, Genfed Library, Briefs File) (U.S. Dec. 21, 1992).

[1004]   516 U.S. 217.

allows, to the farthest reaches of what could be denominated "harm." We therefore reject petitioner's initial proposal that we simply look to English dictionary definitions of "damage" and apply that term's "plain meaning."[1005]

The Court in *Zicherman* promptly turned to a consideration of the drafting history and subsequent interpretation of the treaty by other parties. But one form of textual clue the Court took pains to disavow: employing French legal usage as a basis for interpreting the phrase "dommage." Despite the use of such evidence in *Air France v. Saks*,[1006] and in *Eastern Airlines v. Floyd*,[1007] the Court declined a general move to incorporate wholesale French civil law into U.S. aviation and personal injury practice.[1008]

So for a Court that has become awful literalist of late, *O'Connor*, *Haitian Centers*, and *Zicherman* make for difficult cases because, at bottom, they are rejections of textualism. Even *Alvarez-Machain* (aberrant in its own right by probably being *too* literalist) is easier to reconcile with the prevailing trends in interpretation. What gives *Stuart* and *Haitian Centers* their most peculiar quality is that, in both cases, it is the government which is challenging a plain reading of the treaty.

The Supreme Court has yet to give definitive guidance on when a treaty interpreter must acknowledge that a text is vague and is thus obliged to go in search of extrinsic sources of meaning. As has already been discussed,[1009] the penchant for American courts to break away too quickly from the text is one of the most common problems of United States practice in this area. Despite the

---

[1005] Id. at 222.

[1006] 470 U.S. at 405-07.

[1007] 499 U.S. at 536-40.

[1008] *See* 516 U.S. at 222-23.

[1009] *See* supra note 808 and accompanying text.

Court's periodic tips of the hat to the first canon of textualism,[1010] and its vigorous debate on this subject (as particularly captured in the *Stuart, Chan* and *Haitian Councils* opinions), no resolution is in sight. Maybe none is to be expected. After all, it may be impossible to identify a threshold of ambiguity appropriate in all cases, and the argument has been made (particularly in the context of the Vienna Convention's strict textual approach to this matter),[1011] that it may be counterproductive to select one. Such an admission would be acceptable *if* there were principled ways to choose among extratextual materials *and* to give the proper deference to the interpretations of our treaty partners. As will shortly be seen in the Rehnquist Court jurisprudence, this happy circumstance is unlikely to occur.

ii. *Choosing Among Extratextual Materials for Interpretation.* The chief extrinsic sources for treaty interpretation have been the negotiating history (or *travaux préparatoires*) of the treaty text, the domestic record of Senate-Presidential actions in the treaty ratification process, and (last in time) the course of dealing of the treaty parties in practically construing the terms of the agreement. Each of these major sources has been featured prominently in recent judicial decisions, and the Rehnquist Court cases are no exception to the trend of resort to these extratextual materials. Indeed, in many of the cases just described, the Court has moved quickly from the text in order to consider other avenues of treaty meaning.[1012] The discussion here looks at the actual nature of

---

[1010] Virtually every one of the Rehnquist Court cases, *see* supra note 869, has cited to the now famous summation in *Air France v. Saks* that courts look first to "the text of the treaty and the context in which the written words are used." 470 U.S. at 397. *See, e.g., Itel,* 113 S.Ct. at 1099-1100; *Alvarez,* 112 S.Ct. at 2193; *Floyd,* 111 S.Ct. at 1493; *SNIAS,* 482 U.S. at 534.

Ironically, the two Scalia opinions — *Chan,* 490 U.S. 122 (1989), and *O'Connor,* 479 U.S. 27 (1986) — do not cite to any form of the *Air France* language. The only explanation might be Justice Scalia's discomfort with an interpretive test which mixes *both* text *and* context. Indeed, Scalia's pure textual approach, pressed in his *Stuart* concurrence, vindicated in *Chan,* and adopted wholesale in *Alvarez,* suggests a real dynamic tension between textual readings of words and contextual understandings of the terms of a treaty.

[1011] *See* supra notes 852 - 858 and accompanying text.

[1012] *See* supra notes 879 - 884 (on *O'Connor*), 890 - 894 (on *Stuart*), 924 - 933 (on *Alvarez*), 937 - 943 (on *Volkswagen*).

the outside sources the Court has used recently. But it is really more important to see whether there has been any consensus in selecting *among* these materials in instances where different sources lead to different interpretive outcomes.

α. *Use of* travaux préparatoires. The negotiating history of an international convention can include materials as diverse as national position papers, draft clauses, jointly-made interpretive statements, and statements made on the floor of the diplomatic conference deliberating the terms of the treaty.[1013] Sometimes the use of these materials has been quite predictable by the Supreme Court, calling for little reflection and generating little dispute. An example of this was the quick reference to United Nations materials shedding light on the phrase "well-founded fear of persecution" in the Refugees Convention,[1014] the issue in *Immigration and Naturalization Service v. Cardoza-Fonseca*.[1015] Not only did the Court consult a document contemporaneous with the drafting of the Refugees Convention,[1016] but also a manual used by the officers of the International Refugee Organization.[1017] Not much, it seemed, turned on the unexceptional use of these sources.

An instance of the Court self-consciously, and sensitively, reviewing a convention's negotiating history was in *Volkswagen*.[1018] The only problem was that *both* the majority opinion and concurrence made skillful use of the

---

[1013] *See* supra notes 841 - 844 with text.

[1014] Convention Relating to the Status of Refugees, July 28, 1951, 189 U.N.T.S. 150.

[1015] 480 U.S. 421 (1987).

[1016] *See* id. at 438 & n.20 (*citing* United Nations Economic and Social Council, Report of the Ad hoc Committee on Statelessness and Related Problems 37 (Feb. 17, 1950) (U.N. Doc. E/1618, E/AC.32/5)).

[1017] *See* id. (*citing* International Refugee Organization, Manual for Eligibility Officers No. 175, ch. IV, Annex I, Pt. 1, § C19, at 4 (undated, circulated in 1950)).

[1018] 486 U.S. 694 (1988).

extraordinarily well-documented *travaux* of the Hague Service Convention,[1019] reaching opposite conclusions. Both opinions tended to place emphasis on different parts of the negotiating record in finding meaning in the phrase "service abroad," and the consequent task of determining the scope of the Convention's mandatory requirements. The majority opinion by Justice O'Connor cleaved to traditional statutory construction techniques developed with legislative history. As a consequence, Justice O'Connor adduced great significance from changes in wording in successive draft treaty texts and from failed amendments.[1020] Justice Brennan's concurrence placed much more emphasis on a *Rapport Explicatif* issued by the Hague Conference on Private International Law shortly after the Evidence Convention was concluded.[1021] This document had been dismissed brusquely, in Justice O'Connor's opinion, as not probative of a generally-adopted interpretive statement by the treatymakers.[1022] Despite the fact that negotiating history can be contradictory in its conclusions about treaty meaning, the *Volkswagen* case can still be counted as a successful instance in which domestic techniques of handling legislative history were applied to treaties.[1023]

[1019] *See* supra note 911.

[1020] 486 U.S. at 700-02.

[1021] *See* id. at 711-13 (Brennan, J., concurring) (citing 3 [1965] Conférence de la Haye de Droit International Privé, Actes et Documents de la Dixième Session (Notification)).

[1022] *See* id. at 704.

[1023] Not surprisingly, Justice O'Connor's approach in *Volkswagen* was followed by Justice Marshall in his opinion for a unanimous Court in *Floyd*, 111 S.Ct. 1489 (1991). Justice Marshall's opinion reveals the same careful parsing of the negotiating history. *See* id. at 1497-99. But there was even an additional offering of a presumption in analyzing a treaty's negotiating history. *Volkswagen* was cited for the proposition that there is "significance [in a] change . . . from less precise term in draft to more precise term in the final treaty provision." Id. at 1497-98 (*citing Volkswagen*, 486 U.S. at 700-01). This assumption about diplomatic nature has yet to be tested in any other contexts, but, as a general statement of any exercise in divining meaning from a text, it seems sensible enough. *See also* part XII.iii.

The *O'Connor* opinion was rather less successful in its handling of *travaux*. Particularly problematic was what was *not* covered in the Court's opinion by Justice Scalia. The only real mention of negotiating history was to some various internal State Department drafts of the treaty project with Panama on the Canal Zone transfer.[1024] These were cited by the Court for the proposition that the Implementing Agreements were not intended to exempt U.S.-citizen employees of the Canal Commission from U.S. taxes, which was perfectly consonant with the Court's attempted textual reading of the treaty.[1025] What the Court nowhere mentions in its opinion is the controversy that transpired before the lower courts considering the case when the government sought to introduce affidavit testimony of the American negotiators with Panama.[1026] In essence, the government sought to manufacture a negotiating history for this bilateral treaty. This was not surprising since, unlike multilateral instruments, bilateral conventions are rarely accompanied by documented, or even publicly-released, *travaux*. A detailed analysis of the conference minutes of the American and Panamanian negotiators was undertaken by the Claims Court,[1027] but neither the Court of Appeals[1028] nor the Supreme Court had the stomach to do the same.

And for good reason: it was apparent that the negotiating history had been largely contrived by the government to further its interests in litigation.[1029] That was why the trial court gave judgment to the taxpayers, largely on the

---

[1024] *See O'Connor*, 479 U.S. at 34-35.

[1025] *See* id. *See also* supra notes 879 - 884 and accompanying text.

[1026] *See Coplin v. United States*, 6 Cl.Ct. 115, 131-32 n.16 (1984).

[1027] *See id.* at 129-31.

[1028] *See* 761 F.2d 688 (Fed. Cir. 1985), *rev'g*, 6 Cl.Ct. 115 (1984).

[1029] This is what Petitioner argued before the Court. *See* Petitioner's Brief, *O'Connor* (85-558), at 23-27 (U.S. March 22, 1986).

strength of their textual reading of the Agreement.[1030] A rather unseemly debate erupted in the Claims Court about whether *travaux*, in order to be probative of treaty meaning, had to be contemporaneous with the drafting of the instrument. Chief Judge Kozinski of the Claims Court chose not to resolve this question directly, instead noting that there could really be two classes of negotiating history at work.[1031] The first are the contemporary *travaux*, like the Hague Conference *rapport explicatif* in *Volkswagen* and the *procès verbaux* of the legal experts preparing for the Warsaw Convention signing (as used in *Floyd*).[1032] The second class of negotiating history would be the later statements of the treaty negotiators. These have been credited with some authority,[1033] because such opinions usually do reflect the views of the American negotiators — and of the United States government.[1034]

[1030] *See* 6 Cl.Ct. at 125-28.

[1031] *See* id. at 132 n.16.

[1032] *See* 111 S.Ct. at 1497-99 (using the documentation prepared by the Comité International Technique d'Experts Juridiques Aériens (CITEJA)).

[1033] *See* Samuel B. Crandall, Treaties, Their Making and Enforcement 225-27 (1904) (noting, among other instances, where Treaty of Amity, U.S.-Gr.Brit., Nov. 19, 1794, 8 Stat. 116 (1794), was later construed with help of an *aide-memoire* by one of the American negotiators). *Cf. Sumitomo Shoji America, Inc. v. Avagliano*, 457 U.S. 176, 184 n.10 (1982) (distinguishing government's official position from "evidence of the state of mind of the Treaty negotiators"). *But see Arizona v. California*, 292 U.S. 341, 359-60 (1934) (casting doubt on the use of such later opinions by negotiators, at least in the context of inter-State agreements or compacts).

[1034] It is significant, however, that the lower court opinions for *O'Connor* did consider statements by Panamanian officials in construing the treaty. *See* 6 Cl.Ct. at 131-32 n.16; 761 F.2d at 691-92. Nonetheless, the High Court declined to make any use of these sources in the *O'Connor* opinion. This was so despite the Solicitor General's attempt to introduce, in his brief, the section-by-section analysis of the Agreement, prepared by the State Department and submitted to the Senate when the main treaty was sent for advice and consent. *See* Brief of the United States, *O'Connor* (85-558, 85-559 & 85-560), at 31-35 (U.S. Sept. 30, 1986). This material had not been favorably received by one Court of Appeals which had considered the taxpayers' case. *See Harris v. United States*, 768 F.2d 1240, 1245-47 (11th Cir. 1985); *but see Rego v. United States*, 591 F. Supp. 123, 124

An exception to this occurred in *Haitian Centers*[1035] where the Respondents, representatives of the potential immigrants, sought to introduce affidavit evidence into the Supreme Court[1036] to counter the government's assertion that Article 33.1 of the Refugees Convention did not prohibit its interdiction program. The affidavit was by Professor Louis Henkin, who, in 1950 and 1951, was the United States representative to the Conference drafting the Convention.[1037] Despite its earlier attempt to introduce the same type of evidence in *O'Connor*, the Solicitor General called the Henkin affidavit an extraordinary embellishment on the record, which the "Court should neither accept nor attach any weight to...."[1038] The Court obliged by remaining inscrutably silent on the submission; not even Justice Blackmun referred to it directly in his dissent.[1039]

What Justice Stevens' majority opinion in *Haitian Centers* did graphically illustrate are the uses and abuses of negotiating history in the search for meaning in a disputed treaty text. What the Court latched-on to[1040] were two separate statements, made by the Swiss and Dutch delegates respectively on two separate days of the Plenipotentiary Conference adopting the Refugees

---

(W.D. Tenn. 1984); *Corliss v. United States*, 567 F. Supp. 162, 165-66 (W.D. Ark. 1983) (both using that material in rejecting taxpayers' case).

[1035]   113 S.Ct. 2549 (1993).

[1036]   Brief for Respondents, *Haitian Centers* (92-344), at pages 19-22 (LEXIS, Genfed Library, Briefs File) (U.S. Dec. 21, 1992).

[1037]   Id. at pages 46 (¶ 2 of the Henkin Affidavit).

[1038]   Reply Brief for the United States, *Haitian Centers* (92-344), at page 18 (LEXIS, Genfed Library, Briefs File) (U.S. Jan. 21, 1993).

[1039]   What Justice Blackmun *did* do was quote (directly from the Conference record) delegate Henkin's remarks. *See* 113 S.Ct. at 2571 n.6 (Blackmun, J., dissenting).

[1040]   113 S.Ct. at 2565. *See also* Rogoff, supra note 869, at 589-80.

Convention,[1041] which seemed to confirm the position espoused by the United States in the case: Article 33.1's non-*refoulement* obligation was not intended to apply extraterritorially. The statements were merely "placed on the record" by the Conference President,[1042] and so the decisive issue was whether the Swiss and Dutch views reflected a consensus or were merely dissenting interpretations. Justice Blackmun was quick to note this "pitfall[] on relying on the negotiating record."[1043] He marshaled evidence suggesting that the Dutch and Swiss views were, in fact, minority positions,[1044] and were, in any event, not to be given priority over the clear words of the text. "In sum," Justice Blackmun wrote, "the fragments of negotiating history upon which the majority relies are not entitled to deference, were never voted on or adopted, probably represent a minority view, and ... do not address the issue in the case."[1045]

Likewise, in *Zicherman*, the Court was obliged to distinguish between various snippets of evidence found in the *travaux*, in reaching its conclusion that the Warsaw Convention's definition of "damage" in article 17 was controlled by domestic law. The Court favorably noticed two statements made by experts at the Comite International Technique d'Experts Juridiques Aeriens (CITJEA)

[1041]   *See* Conference of Plenipotentiaries on the Status of Refugees and Stateless Persons, Summary Record of the Sixteenth Meeting, U.N. Doc. A/CONF.2/SR.16, at 2 (July 11, 1951) (statement by Mr. ZUTTER (Switzerland)); id. Summary Record of the Thirty-fifth Meeting, U.N. Doc. A/CONF.2/SR.35, at 21-22 (July 25, 1951) (statement by Baron van BOETZELAER (Netherlands)).

[1042]   *See* 113 S.Ct. at 2572.

[1043]   Id. at 2571 (Blackmun, J., dissenting).

[1044]   Justice Blackmun relied extensively on the Brief *Amicus Curiae* of the U.N. High Commissioner for Refugees, *Haitian Centers* (92-344), at 24 (U.S. Dec. 21, 1992). *See* 113 S.Ct. at 2571-72 (Blackmun, J., dissenting). Justice Blackmun was critical, too, of the majority opinion's citation to U.N. Refugee Manuals for the proposition that the non-*refoulement* obligation did not apply to refugees found on the high seas. 113 S.Ct. at 2564 n.40. Justice Blackmun noted that this conclusion was contrary to the actual position taken by the U.N. High Commissioner in the case. Id. at 2572 n.8 (Blackmun, J., dissenting).

[1045]   113 S.Ct. at 2572-73 (Blackmun, J., dissenting).

meetings in 1925 and 1928.[1046]   Justice Scalia went out of his way to reject the probity of a statement made by a French delegate at the meeting, rejecting the application of domestic law: "Not only does this remark not have the authority of submissions by the drafting committee, but it a generalization rather than a statement focused specifically upon the issue here.... And the generalization is demonstrably wrong to boot...."[1047]   So here, at long last, we have a sense that the Court recognizes that not all *travaux* is to be treated equally; statements of drafting committees are to be given greater weight than isolated remarks of other delegates at a treaty negotiation.[1048]

References to *travaux préparatoires* in the Rehnquist Court cases do not appear to follow any predictable patterns. Material is cited indiscriminately, often (as happened in *Haitian Centers*) without any real appreciation of the mechanics of international conference diplomacy, and how those dynamics differ substantially from legislative patterns. In short, negotiating history is used as arbitrarily as legislative history, oftentimes with language being cited and relied upon by both parties in the interpretive dispute. Nonetheless, the Court is prepared sometimes, as in *Volkswagen* and *Haitian Centers*, to place substantial weight on *travaux*, even if that means reaching conclusions contrary to the clear meaning of the text.

β. *"Legislative" history for treaties*. When a treaty is sent by the President to the Senate for its advice and consent under the Constitution,[1049] it sets in motion a review procedure. This process is accompanied by sufficient documentation as to allow courts to appreciate the shared understandings between the political branches regarding the meaning of an international agreement. The traditional means of communicating a treaty to the Senate includes a letter of transmittal by the President, with an attached submittal letter by the Secretary of State as well as a descriptive commentary and section-by section analysis prepared (usually) by the Legal Advisor to the State

---

[1046] *See* 516 U.S. at 226.

[1047] Id.

[1048] *See also Tseng*, 119 S.Ct. at 673-74 (for a fairly straight-forward use of *travaux*).

[1049] *See* supra notes 772 - 774 and accompanying text.

Department. If the treaty will have an impact on domestic law, the Attorney General will often add a report about the necessary legislative changes that will be needed if the international agreement receives advice and consent. The Senate Foreign Relations Committee will then consider the treaty. Hearings might be held, with members of the American negotiating team testifying. The senators might also question the Executive branch about the meaning of certain language in the treaty. The record of these proceedings, as well as a Committee Report containing the committee vote (and any reservations, understandings or declarations to be appended to the instrument), will proceed to the Senate floor. At that point further deliberation could be had, before the necessary two-thirds vote is acquired for advice and consent on the treaty and the attached reservations (if any). If successful, the President will later ratify and proclaim the treaty, sometimes making a statement at that stage. Taken together this is the "legislative history" of the treaty, and, if fully developed, can be as elaborate as any record of modern Congressional legislation.[1050] The problem, however, is that it is a rare treaty which is subject to the rigorous Senatorial review just described. As a consequence, many treaties have a very sparse legislative record.

The Panama Canal Treaty of 1977 — the subject of *O'Connor* — was, of course, an instance of a closely-scrutinized international agreement. As already indicated, however, the legislative history of that instrument did not figure prominently in the Court's decision. The Supreme Court may have wanted to avoid the confusion encountered by the lower courts in actually handling the material. This avoidance may have also revealed Justice Scalia's growing concern about the actual propriety of using the record of Presidential-Senatorial communications in gleaning the meaning of a treaty, a concern that would manifest itself in his later *Stuart* concurrence.[1051]

[1050]   The documentation of legislative history for statutes, is, of course, a modern phenomenon. *See* supra note 837. Likewise, few treaties ratified before 1930 had much in the way of a legislative record, save for floor debates.

[1051]   For more on the problem of contemporaneous interpretations of tax treaties at the time of Senate advice and consent, *see* Tax Treaty Draft Project, supra note 793, at 35-37, 46-48.

By contrast, the documentary records for Senate consideration of the Hague Evidence and Service Conventions were rather slim. But in both *SNIAS* and in *Volkswagen* substantial use of these materials were made, without so much as a peep of objection. In *SNIAS*, the Presidential letter of transmittal for the treaty was quoted at length,[1052] as well as a representation made by one of the American negotiators of the Evidence Convention, testifying before the Foreign Relations Committee.[1053] Both extracts supported the Court's conclusion that that agreement merely set out optional procedures for the conduct of overseas discovery.[1054] In *Volkswagen*, by contrast, the use of legislative history for the Service Convention was done solely by Justice Brennan in his concurrence.[1055] No mention is made of these sources by the majority, although Brennan's use of Committee testimony, transmittal and submittal letters, and delegation reports, was likely unobjectionable since the interpretive thrust of these materials accorded with the majority's own stance.[1056] Justice Brennan took exception elsewhere with the Court's holding.

[1052]   *SNIAS*, 482 U.S. at 531-32, 538.

[1053]   *See* id. at 530, 536 n.19 (quoting statement by State Department Legal Advisor and an Explanatory Report of the Convention by U.S. delegation head).

[1054]   *See* 482 U.S. at 538. One amicus party asserted the contrary, relying on other extracts of the legislative history, but this view was clearly rejected. *See* Amicus Brief of the Republic of France in Support of Petitioners, *SNIAS* (85-1695), at 4, 10-11 (U.S. Aug. 22, 1986) (citing Presidential Letter of Transmission, Secretary of State's submittal letter, and American delegation's Report, S. Exec. Doc. No. A.1 & S. Exec. Rep. No. 92-25, 92d Cong., 2d Sess. (1972), *reprinted in* 8 I.L.M. 785 (1969) and 12 I.L.M. 324 (1973)).

[1055]   *See* 486 U.S. at 713-14.

[1056]   *Compare* 486 U.S. at 704 *with* id. at 714 (Brennan, J., concurring). It should be noted, though, that Justice Brennan's selection of material from the treaty's legislative history was quite at variance with that selected by the government in its amicus brief. *See* Brief of the United States as Amicus Curiae Supporting Respondent, *Volkswagen* (86-1052), at screens 41-43 nn.24-26 (LEXIS, Genfed Library, Briefs File) (U.S. Feb. 1, 1988).

That leaves the well-publicized squabble between Justices Brennan and Scalia in *Stuart*. The engagement was short and sharp, as already recounted.[1057] All the Justices agreed that the Tax Treaty with Canada placed no conditions on the Internal Revenue Service in cooperating with their Canadian counterparts in revenue investigations.[1058]   The only question was *which* sources could be consulted to reach that conclusion. Writing for the majority, Justice Brennan used everything: textual analysis, subsequent practice by the treaty parties, Executive branch representations, and the record of Senate advice and consent.[1059] Although Justice Scalia criticized the use of *any* extrinsic material when the text is clear,[1060] he focused his ire particularly on Brennan's use of legislative history. In truth, the Senate materials that Justice Brennan consulted in the *Stuart* majority were no different than those consulted in *SNIAS* or in earlier cases. He examined the presidential letter of transmission to the Senate, a snippet of floor debate on the 1942 Tax Treaty, and the presidential Proclamation ratifying that instrument.[1061] In addition, he reviewed much the same material for the superseding convention with Canada of 1984.[1062]

Justice Scalia denounced the use of these materials as "unprecedented."[1063] He, moreover, claimed that he was "unable to discover a single case in which this Court has consulted the Senate debate, committee

---

[1057]   *See* supra notes 890 - 904 and accompanying text.

[1058]   *See* 489 U.S. at 370-71.

[1059]   *See* id. at 365-70.

[1060]   *See* id. at 371-73 (Scalia, J., concurring).

[1061]   *See* id. at 366-68 (citing S. Exec. Rep. No. 3, 77th Cong., 2d Sess. (1942) and 88 Cong. Rec. 4714 (1942)).

[1062]   *See* id. at 368-69 n.8.

[1063]   Id. at 373 (Scalia, J., concurring).

hearings, or committee reports."[1064] This is not the place to comment on this assertion, but suffice it to say that Justice Scalia may well have been extravagant in making it.[1065] The Court had used Senate materials no less than five times since 1950.[1066] Quite apart from his unsupportable claim on precedent, Justice Scalia made a number of other arguments for the impropriety of consulting a treaty's legislative history. In descending order of strength, he first noted that it is improper to give weight to the unilateral interpretations of one treaty party, namely the United States. "Whatever extratextual materials are consulted," he wrote, "must be materials that reflect the mutual agreement (for example, the negotiating history) rather than unilateral understanding."[1067] This is certainly a rhetorical plea for liberal interpretation and good faith. And the appeal has some power. Why, one might wonder, should some non-express Senate understanding of a treaty be given credence, particularly if such an interpretation is contrary to the wishes of the other parties?[1068] Indeed, this problem had been

---

[1064] Id.

[1065] For a devastating critique of Justice Scalia's claim, see Detlev F. Vagts, *Senate Materials and Treaty Interpretation: Some Research Hints for the Supreme Court*, 83 AJIL 546 (1989). Professor Vagts also provides a spirited defense of the *Restatement of Foreign Relations* sections allowing the use of Senate materials, *see* Restatement, supra note 763, at § 314, cmt. d & § 325, note 5, provisions which are intensely criticized by Justice Scalia in his concurrence. 489 U.S. at 375-77.

[1066] *See* supra note 781. For a very early instance of the Court's deference to subsequent legislative interpretations of treaties, *see* supra note 788.

[1067] 489 U.S. at 374 (Scalia, J., concurring).

[1068] *See* id. at 376 (noting that adoption of the majority's approach "reduces what hitherto has been the President's role in the interpretation of treaties, and commits the United States to a form of interpretation plainly out of step with international practice.") (Scalia, J., concurring). *See also New York Indians v. United States*, 170 U.S. 1, 23 (1898), relied upon by Justice Scalia. 489 U.S. at 374, raising concerns of the unilateral character of certain kinds of Senate declarations. See also supra note 783 (Secretary of State Hughes' admonition to Germany not to rely upon Senate debates to construe the peace treaty concluded with the United States in 1923).

For more on the Vienna Convention's disapproval of the use of domestic ratification records, *see* supra note 855 with text.

noted elsewhere in the authorities.[1069] Justice Brennan was really unable to respond to this challenge, except to note that on occasion the secret negotiating history of a treaty may be a *worse* guide to interpretation than the public Senate debates.[1070] He may well have had fresh in his mind the controversy over the negotiating history of the Panama Canal Treaties, as litigated in *O'Connor.* In any event, Justice Brennan did not — indeed, could not — answer Scalia's invocation of the good faith canon.

Justice Scalia's second argument against the use of Senate materials was his suggestion that, constitutionally, the Senate has the option only of declining to advise and consent or to attach explicit reservations or declarations as to a treaty's meaning.[1071] "[I]f Congress does not like the interpretation that has been given to a treaty by the courts or by the President, it may abrogate or amend it as a matter of internal law by simply enacting inconsistent legislation."[1072] Although he does not go so far as to say it, he raises grave separation of powers concerns in giving authoritative weight to some shared, silent "understandings" between the political branches. Regrettably, Justice Scalia did not elaborate this point,[1073] nor did Justice Brennan (in the majority) address it.

Justice Scalia was quite persuasive in his concerns regarding the unilateral character of Senate materials and the constitutional allocation of authority in the making and interpreting of treaties. His remaining criticisms of

---

[1069] *See* supra note 779 (discussing *New York Indians v. United States*, 170 U.S. 1, 23 (1898), relied upon by Justice Scalia, 489 U.S. at 374, raising concerns of the unilateral character of certain kinds of Senate declarations).

[1070] *See* 489 U.S. at 368 n.7.

[1071] *See* 489 U.S. at 374-75 (Scalia, J., concurring).

[1072] Id. at 375 (Scalia, J., concurring).

[1073] For more on the constitutional underpinnings of this problem, *see* supra note 761, 792. *See also* Malvina Halberstam, *The Use of Legislative History in Treaty Interpretation: The Dual Treaty Approach*, 12 Cardozo L. Rev. 1645 (1991); W. David Slawson, *Legislative History and the Need to Bring Statutory Interpretation under the Rule of Law*, 44 Stan. L. Rev. 383, 395 (1992).

the practice of consulting legislative history turned on their probative weight, and these concerns rang hollow. Scalia opined that "[u]sing preratification Senate materials ... is rather like determining the meaning of a bilateral contract between two corporations on the basis of what the board of directors of one of them thought it meant when authorizing the chief executive officer to conclude it."[1074] Justice Brennan pungently responded by suggesting the board room analogy was inapt. After all, Senate deliberations are open and public, he said.[1075] Moreover,

> [i]t is hornbook contract law that the proper construction of an agreement is that given by one of the parties when "that party had no reason to know of any different meaning attached by the other, and the other had reason to know the meaning attached by the first party."[1076]

In other words, if one country is affirmatively on notice of the construction of a treaty term adopted by another, and does not object, it is bound by it. Senate materials, Justice Brennan mused, might assist in ascertaining whether such notice was given and acknowledged. This observation would prove fateful in allowing the use of Senate materials in determining the intent and wishes, not of the United States government, but of our treaty partners. But Justice Brennan was certainly right in suggesting that the use of legislative history would be helpful in such an inquiry, provided, of course, it was even legitimate.

Justice Scalia saw this apparently as a backhanded way to answer his concern about the unilateral character of Senate-Presidential understandings in the treaty ratification process. But his riposte to this parry was quite curious. He wrote, "[i]t is even less clear, assuming [Justice Brennan's] position to be correct [on the general propriety of using legislative sources], that Senate understandings which are *not* the product of Executive representations in the advice-and-consent hearings should have any relevance."[1077] This was Justice

---

[1074] *Stuart*, 489 U.S. at 374 (Scalia, J., concurring).

[1075] *See* id. at 367 n.7.

[1076] Id. at 368 n.7 (*quoting* Restatement (Second) of Contracts § 201(2)(b) (1981)).

[1077] *Stuart*, 489 U.S. at 377 (Scalia, J., concurring) (original emphasis).

Scalia weighing-in on the Anti-Ballistic Missile controversy,[1078] as well as excoriating a lower court's decision, in an unrelated matter,[1079] giving substantial weight to senatorial statements which ran counter to representations made by State Department officials at the ratification hearings.[1080]

The warning language in Justice Scalia's *Stuart* concurrence had its intended effect. In the cases after 1989, the Court has just once cited to Senate materials, or purported, in any way, to rely upon legislative history.[1081] Now, it is true, that in *Chan* and *Floyd* there was simply no record of advice and consent to consult for the Warsaw Convention.[1082] Likewise, in *Alvarez* and *Itel*, pre-ratification debates were not relied upon by the parties, although they were available.[1083] So the issue remains open, although earlier case authority (and

---

[1078]   *See* supra note 780.

[1079]   *See Rainbow Navigation, Inc. v. Department of Navy*, 686 F. Supp. 354 (D.D.C. 1988) and 699 F. Supp. 339 (D.D.C. 1988). *See also* supra note 785 with text.

[1080]   *See* 688 F. Supp. at 357; 699 F. Supp. at 343.

[1081]   That was in *Haitian Councils*, 113 S.Ct. at 2562 n.34 (*citing* Exec. Rep. No. 14, 90th Cong., 2d Sess. 2, 4, 6-7, 19 (1968); S. Exec. K., 90th Cong., 2d Sess. (1968); 114 Cong. Rec. 27757, 29391 (1968) concerning the Refugees Protocol). The majority opinion's brief reference to legislative history is trivial in comparison with the extensive briefing by both parties on that evidence. *See* Brief of the United States, *Haitian Councils* (92-344), at pages 26-28 (LEXIS, Genfed Library, Briefs File) (U.S. Nov. 12, 1992) and Brief for Respondent, *Haitian Councils* (92-344), at page 21 & n.51 (LEXIS, Genfed Library, Briefs File) (U.S. Dec. 21, 1992).

[1082]   *See Chan*, 490 U.S. at 122 n.2 ("There is . . . no issue in this case as to the proper use of pre-ratification Senate materials in treaty interpretation.") (Brennan, J., concurring).

[1083]   For the legislative history on the 1956 Containers Convention, *see* S. Exec. Doc. J, 89th Cong., 2d Sess. (1966). For a sampling of the Senate ratification documents for the predecessor versions of the 1978 Extradition Treaty with Mexico, *see* S. Exec. Doc. D & S. Exec. Rep. 3, 76th Cong., 3d Sess. (1940) (Aug. 16, 1939 treaty); S. Exec. Doc. E, 69th Cong., 1st Sess. (1926) (Dec. 23, 1925 treaty); S. Exec. Doc. G, 57th Cong., 2d Sess. (1902) (June 25, 1902 treaty); S. Exec. Doc. E, 55th Cong., 3d Sess. (1899) (Feb. 22, 1899 treaty); S. Exec. Doc. R, 48th Cong., 2d Sess. (1885) & 49th Cong., 1st Sess. (1886)

Justice Brennan's majority opinion in *Stuart*) would weigh in the calculus towards using these sources. Justice Scalia's concurrence counsels caution; particularly so in cases where the Senate's informal expression of meaning ran counter either to the wishes of the administration presenting the treaty, or, as compellingly, to the expressed opinions of our treaty partners.

γ. *Evidence of subsequent practice in interpreting treaties.* In recent years, when the Court has found a treaty to be unclear, it has had "recourse to the[] [contracting parties'] own practical construction of it."[1084] Use of these sources — including later diplomatic correspondence dealing with treaty ambiguities, and the decisions of other national courts in construing an agreement — has not been without controversy. But, still, the Rehnquist Court has acknowledged the use of these materials. As the Court noted in *Cardoza-Fonseca*,[1085] the treaty interpretations made by a foreign government, court, or organization are not dispositive, but do "provide significant guidance in construing" an agreement.[1086] The weight to be accorded to such international interpretations depends, fundamentally, on their reception by U.S. courts.

If that is so, the reception given to the subsequent state practice relied upon by Respondent in *Floyd*,[1087] to establish a meaning for the term *lésion corporelle*,[1088] was positively frosty. Justice Marshall examined the same sources that the lower court did on the same issue.[1089] These materials included

---

(treaty of Feb. 20, 1885); S. Exec. Doc. 167, 37th Cong., 2d Sess. (1862) (treaty of Dec. 11, 1861); S. Exec. Doc. 18, 31st Cong., 1st Sess. (1850) & S. Exec. Doc. 10, 33d Cong., 1st Sess. (1853) (treaty of July 20, 1850).

[1084]   *Nielsen v. Johnson*, 279 U.S. 47, 52 (1929).

[1085]   480 U.S. 421 (1987).

[1086]   Id. at 439 n.22.

[1087]   111 S.Ct. 1489 (1991).

[1088]   *See* supra notes 916 - 923 with text.

[1089]   *Compare* id. at 1499-1502 *with* 872 F.2d at 1473-80.

the records of the many review conferences held to update the terms of the Warsaw Convention. The Supreme Court simply reached a different conclusion in reading these sources. There was no doubt, however, according to Justice Marshall, that the use of these sources was legitimate.[1090] The only reservation expressed by the Court in *Floyd* was the legal status of the 1971 Guatemala City Protocol to the Warsaw Convention. As an earlier Court had noted,[1091] this instrument was intended to be amendatory of the Warsaw Convention, and not interpretive. Because the United States had not ratified the Protocol (nor had many other nations), its terms were not to be given much credence.[1092]

In any event, these purely international expressions of interpretive intent for the Warsaw Convention were at least received by the Supreme Court. Hanging in the Respondent's balance was also a decision by the Israeli Supreme Court awarding damages for purely psychic injuries under Article 17 of the Warsaw Convention.[1093] Justice Marshall in *Floyd* clearly felt obliged to consider this piece of evidence, based on the Court's earlier ruling in *Air France v. Saks*,[1094] that "the opinions of our sister signatories are to be entitled to considerable weight."[1095] But he then proceeded to give rather short shrift to that foreign court decision. In essence, Justice Marshall concluded that the Israeli Supreme Court's decision was based not on an objective determination of the Warsaw Convention parties' intent, but, instead, on independent grounds of policy, grounds which the U.S. Supreme Court did not care to embrace.[1096]

[1090] *See Floyd*, 111 S.Ct. at 1499 (*citing Air France v. Saks*, 470 U.S. 392, 403 (1985) (demand that courts look to the "conduct" and "interpretation of the signatories")).

[1091] *Air France v. Saks*, 470 U.S. at 403.

[1092] *See Floyd*, 111 S.Ct. at 1501.

[1093] See id. (citing *Air France v. Teichner*, 29 Revue Française de Droit Aérien 243).

[1094] *See* 470 U.S. 392 (1985) (construing another aspect of Warsaw Convention article 17).

[1095] Id. at 404.

[1096] *See Floyd*, 111 S.Ct. at 1502.

It might be that evidence of subsequent practice by treaty parties, or by an international institution charged with the execution of the agreement (as was the case in *Cardoza-Fonseca* and *Haitian Councils*),[1097] will only be considered probative when the interpretation derived from such sources matches that put forth by the Executive branch of the U.S. government, as manifested in the relevant *travaux* or pre-ratification Senate debates.[1098] Obviously, the most effective evidence of subsequent practice in interpreting a treaty provision is that generated by the United States government itself over a long course of dealing with other countries. For example, in *Stuart*,[1099] Justice Brennan's majority opinion observed that for many years the federal government had complied with Canadian investigatory requests, pursuant to the Tax Treaty, without ever inquiring about what stage a criminal probe had reached.[1100] Such evidence of subsequent U.S. government practice is not always available. Moreover, some courts have refused to accept previous, practical constructions of treaty texts by the U.S. government if they were inconsistent or contradictory.[1101]

Despite the apparent enthusiasm of the *Saks* Court to consult the subsequent practice of treaty parties, it seems there have been strong, recent disinclinations. These were fully manifested in *Floyd*. But they also arose as

---

[1097] *See Cardoza-Fonseca*, 480 U.S. at 437-40; *Haitian Councils*, 113 S.Ct. at 2564 n.40.

[1098] In *Itel*, 113 S.Ct. 1095 (1993), the Court seemed persuaded by the Solicitor General's argument, *see* Brief of the United States as Amicus Curiae supporting Respondent, *Itel* (91-321), at screen 16 (LEXIS, Genfed Library, Briefs File) (U.S. June 25, 1992), that the subsequent practice of other signatories to the Container Conventions, supra note 946, revealed an acceptance of levies such as that imposed by Tennessee. *See* 113 S.Ct. at 1100-01. This conclusion was reached despite the intervention by Britain, in the case, to protest Tennessee's tax. *See* supra note 949 with text. *See also* Tax Treaty Draft Project, supra note 793, at 52-54 (for more on the use of subsequent practice for tax treaties).

[1099] 489 U.S. 353 (1989).

[1100] *See* id. at 369.

[1101] *See* supra note 798 and accompanying text. *See also* infra section XI.i.β (on the deference to be paid to Executive branch interpretations of treaties).

an issue in *O'Connor*, our first (and, perhaps, most troublesome) Rehnquist Court case. After the United States lost in the Claims Court as to its interpretation of the 1977 Implementing Agreement to the Panama Canal Treaty and the question of taxes,[1102] it sought to rebuild a diplomatic record in support of its view. The vehicle chosen was a diplomatic note from the Panamanian Foreign Minister, written on February 25, 1985 (just a few weeks before oral argument on appeal), in which he concurred with the interpretation taken by the United States that Article 15 of the Implementing Agreement did not insulate American nationals on the Canal Commission from U.S. income taxation.[1103] The government argued before the appeals court that this evidence of subsequent diplomatic practice was conclusive in the case, and sought a reversal of the trial court's holding. Citing a number of cases in which evidence of diplomatic correspondence on a treaty's meaning was admitted, even on the eve of litigation,[1104] the Federal Circuit Court of Appeals did reverse, despite the government's earlier protestations that it need not seek a diplomatic confirmation of its treaty interpretation from Panama.[1105]

Since the February 1985 diplomatic note was the lynchpin to the government's victory on appeal, the taxpayers extensively briefed to the Supreme Court the issue of its proper significance in the case. The Petitioners argued that post-treaty diplomatic correspondence was not an acceptable extrinsic source of meaning.[1106] The government maintained that the diplomatic note "illumined, if not conclusively determined"[1107] the treaty's meaning, although it did suggest that the text and context of the Agreement, standing

---

[1102] *See* 6 Cl. Ct. 115 (1984).

[1103] The diplomatic note is quoted at 761 F.2d at 691.

[1104] *See* id. (citing *Sumitomo Shoji America, Inc. v. Avagliano*, 457 U.S. 176, 184 n.9 (1982); *Factor v. Laubenheimer*, 290 U.S. 276, 295 (1933); *Jones v. United States*, 137 U.S. 202, 214-16 (1890); *United States v. Reynes*, 50 U.S. (9 How.) 127, 147-48 (1850)).

[1105] *See* id. at 692 (additional views of Bissell, J.).

[1106] *See* Petitioner's Brief, *O'Connor* (85-558), at 23-33 (U.S. March 22, 1986).

[1107] *O'Connor*, 479 U.S. at 33 n.2.

alone, supported its interpretation.[1108] The Court, taking the government's lead, decided not to discuss the later diplomatic note.[1109]

In two later cases, both construing the Warsaw Convention, the Court showed substantially greater enthusiasm for the use of subsequent practice. In both *Zicherman*,[1110] and in *Tseng*,[1111] the Court had recourse to the post-ratification conduct of other treaty parties, chiefly as manifested through reported court decisions construing the disputed provisions of the Warsaw Convention. The wide availability of these decisions made them an easy subject for parties to brief before the Court, so it was no surprise that this interpretive source is being increasingly recognized.[1112]

[1108]   *See* Brief of the United States, *O'Connor* (85-558, 85-559, 85-560), at 14-20 (Sept. 30, 1986).

[1109]   *See* 479 U.S. at 33 n.2. Subsequent practice by the United States and other signatories to the Refugees Convention, supra note 977, was extensively briefed in *Haitian Councils*. *See* Brief of the United States, *Haitian Councils* (92-344), at pages 28-30 (LEXIS, Genfed Library, Briefs File) (U.S. Nov. 12, 1992); Brief for Respondent, id. at pages 22-24 (U.S. Dec. 21, 1992); Brief for U.N. High Commissioner for Refugees *Amicus Curiae* for Respondent, id. at pages 10-13 (U.S. Dec. 21, 1992); Brief for the City Bar of New York, id. at 14-17 (U.S. Dec. 12, 1992); Reply Brief of the United States, id. at pages 19-21 (U.S. Jan. 21, 1993). Despite the wealth of material collected — including the actual practices of other nations, subsequent treaty projects, and later statements by Administration officials — the Court made no reference to subsequent practice in its majority opinion. Justice Blackmun does refer to some of this evidence, though, in his dissent. *See* 113 S.Ct. at 2568-69 & n.3 (*citing* 5 Op. Off. Legal Counsel 242, 248 (1981) and *United States as a Country of Mass First Asylum: Hearing Before the Subcommittee on Immigration and Refugee Policy of the Senate Committee on the Judiciary*, 97th Cong., 1st Sess. 4, 209-09 (1981)).

[1110]   516 U.S. at 227-28.

[1111]   119 S.Ct. at 675.

[1112]   *See Zicherman*, Petitioner's Reply Brief, at 4 (94-1361 & 94-1477) (July 26, 1995); *Tseng*, Petitioner's Brief, at 36-43 (97-475) (July 16, 1998).

Indeed, in *Tseng*, a thorny problem of subsequent practice arose: a later amendment to the Warsaw Convention[1113] confirmed the interpretation raised by the Petitioner. But that raised a difficulty: was the amendment an alteration, or a clarification, of the Convention's rule of exclusivity? If it was a modification, it would suggest that the Convention had not hitherto been regarded as exclusive in the respect argued by the Petitioner, and Respondent's claim (which arose before the amendment came into force) would prevail.[1114] The Court finessed this issue by simply noting that the later amendment merely confirmed the previous construction of exclusivity.[1115]

But while the *Zicherman* decision confirmed that the Rehnquist Court has "traditionally considered as aids to its interpretation the negotiation and drafting history (travaux preparatoires) and the post-ratification understanding of the contracting Parties,"[1116] the use of these sources remains controversial. A good example is *Breard v. Greene*,[1117] a case concerning the application of the Vienna Convention on Consular Relations,[1118] to require consular notification for foreign suspects arrested in the United States.[1119] Here, the Court gave only lip-service to one extrinsic source of interpretation: the views of the International Court of Justice, which had rendered an opinion on the subject in a parallel

---

[1113]   Montreal Protocol No. 4, S. Exec. Rep. No. 105-20, at 21-32 (1998).

[1114]   *See* 119 S.Ct. at 674.

[1115]   *See* id. at 674-75.

[1116]   516 U.S. at 226; *see also Tseng*, 119 S.Ct. at 671.

[1117]   118 S.Ct. 1352 (1998).

[1118]   April 24, 1963, [1970] 21 U.S.T. 77, T.I.A.S. No. 6820, 596 U.N.T.S. 261.

[1119]   For more on this case, *see Agora:* Breard, 92 AJIL 666 (1998); Curtis A. Bradley, Breard, *Our Dualist Constitution, and the Internationalist Conception*, 51 STAN. L. REV. 529 (1999); Carlos Manuel Vázquez, Breard, Printz *and the Treaty Power*, 70 U. COLO. L. REV. 1317 (1999).

proceeding brought by Paraguay on Breard's behalf.[1120] While indicating that it should give "respectful consideration to the interpretation of an international treaty rendered by an international court with jurisdiction to interpret such,"[1121] the Court proceeded to use domestic principles of procedural availability of remedies as a way to refute the interpretation that the Vienna Consular Convention gave a right of action to suspects incarcerated without consular notification.[1122]

Ironically, just a few months later the Court would eschew just such an application of domestic law to frustrate treaty rights. In *Tseng*, the Court noted that its "focus" was on "the Convention and the perspective of our treaty partners. Our home-centered preemption analysis, therefore, should not be applied, mechanically, in construing our international obligations."[1123]

δ. *Mixing and matching extratextual materials.* So as for two extrinsic sources of treaty interpretation — negotiating history and subsequent practice — the Court's views are, to say the least, incoherent. This ambivalence in the face of disputed authority says much, however, about the Court's handling of extratextual sources. When all of them support a single interpretive outcome, as in *Stuart* and *Floyd*, there is not much reason to quibble. But, as Justice Scalia foresaw in *Stuart* — and as actually occurred in *O'Connor*, *SNIAS*, *Volkswagen*, and *Chan* — recourse to extrinsic materials could easily have resulted in widely divergent meanings being attached to treaty language. The Rehnquist Court cases do not provide any objective means for selecting among these sources. Once a court moves from the treaty's text, and its immediate orbit of structural context, it is left in a void in which it is simply free to use the materials which accord with the preferred result sought.

[1120] *See* 118 S.Ct. at 1354. *See also* Case Concerning the Vienna Convention on Consular Relations (Para. v. U.S.), 1998 I.C.J. No. 99 (Order of April 9), *reprinted in*, 37 I.L.M. 810 (1998).

[1121] Id.

[1122] *See* id. at 1354-56.

[1123] 119 S.Ct. at 675.

This need not be the case. Even assuming that an interpreter moves quickly to break from an agreement's text, there should be a logical progression in checking extrinsic sources. And it would seem that the Rehnquist Court would prefer to accord greater evidentiary value to negotiating history than to either Senate ratification materials or to subsequent diplomatic and practical constructions of the treaty text. Consulting *travaux* would, after all, appear to be part and parcel of a process of establishing the context in which the words of an international agreement are being employed. The unilateral character of Senate-Presidential understandings, as well as implicit constitutional problems, tend to disqualify that source. Likewise, subsequent diplomatic interpretations of treaties are probative only insofar as there is a congruence between the current views of the Executive branch and our treaty partners. If there is a scintilla of contradiction, then that material will also be discounted.

All this means, of course, is that when all the textual and non-textual sources coincide in one authentic meaning, then no methodological hand-wringing is needed. And if some of the extrinsic materials speak at variance with the terms of the agreement, the first canon of textualism will prevail. But at the moment the threshold of ambiguity is reached, all rules favoring the use of certain materials over others are suspended. The only thing that can save the interpreter from a maddening exercise of divining the parties' intent is to tip the scales in favor either of liberal interpretation and good faith (and follow the views of our treaty partners) or of procedural deference (and accede to the expressed wishes of the Executive branch). The next two sections consider the dilemmas in these forms of deference.

iii. *Do the Views of Our Treaty Partners Matter?* The consistent rhetoric of the Rehnquist Court has been to characterize treaties as like contracts for purposes of construction. In *SNIAS*, Justice Stevens said simply that "[i]n interpreting a treaty, we are mindful that it is 'in the nature of contract between nations [to which] [g]eneral rules of construction apply'."[1124] Even more revealingly, Justice Scalia said in *O'Connor* that "[t]he course of conduct of parties to an international agreement, like the course of conduct of parties to any

---

[1124]   *SNIAS*, 482 U.S. 522 (*quoting Trans World Airlines, Inc. v. Franklin Mint Corp.*, 466 U.S. 243, 253, 262 (1984)).

contract, is evidence of its meaning."[1125]   This seemed to affirm the Appeals Court's own comment in *O'Connor* that "[w]hile possessing the force and effect of law, international agreements should be construed more like contracts than statutes."[1126] The Court's command that treaties are to be read like contracts has been applied equally to multilateral and bilateral conventions.[1127] And, if these statements were held as true by the Supreme Court, one might expect that the canon of good faith and liberal interpretation would be completely vindicated in its opinions. The reality is, alas, quite the opposite.

Now, as has already been revealed, a good faith interpretation of a treaty may not necessarily be a liberal one. And, to be explicit here, it is the good faith prong of this double canon of interpretation which most directly speaks to deference to the wishes of our treaty partners and to protecting the United States from treaty constructions which place it in violation of its international obligations. Nonetheless, liberality of construction — particularly in cases implicating individual rights (whether of American citizens or foreign nationals) — can likewise affect the interpretive expectations of treaty partners.

The Supreme Court has seemed to recognize this in a handful of recent cases in which it was easy to make a gracious bow to good faith interpretations, even at the expense of liberality. The *Stuart* case is an obvious example. There, as might be recalled,[1128] the Court decided on a meaning of the Double Taxation Convention with Canada which gave the I.R.S. unfettered freedom to cooperate with Canadian revenue authorities. Justice Brennan apparently perceived that there was a conflict between liberality and good faith in reaching this result. He noted that a liberal interpretation might suggest a finding that the treaty did, in fact, place substantive limits on binational cooperation in criminal

---

[1125] *O'Connor*, 479 U.S. at 33 (*citing Trans World Airlines*, 466 U.S. at 259-60).

[1126] 768 F.2d at 1242 (*citing Santovincenzo v. Egan*, 284 U.S. 30, 40 (1931)). The past practice of the Supreme Court seemed to indicate that treaties should be construed *more* liberally than contracts. *See* supra notes 818 - 821 with text.

[1127] The treaty in *O'Connor* was bilateral with Panama. The Evidence Convention in *SNIAS* was multilateral.

[1128] *See* supra notes 890 - 894 and accompanying text.

investigations of Canadian nationals living in the United States.[1129] But, in the same breath, Justice Brennan continued that "the evident purpose behind Articles XIX and XXI — the reduction of tax evasion by allowing signatories to demand information from each other — counsels against interpreting those provisions to limit inquiry in the manner respondents desire."[1130] In a case strikingly similar to *Tucker v. Alexandroff*,[1131] a good faith construction of a treaty prevailed over a liberal reading. The true test in choosing between the two prongs, Justice Brennan believed, was the "evident purpose" of the agreement.

Justice Brennan would later discover, however, that there were dangers in placing too much emphasis on the apparent object and purpose of a treaty. In *Volkswagen*, he found himself writing a concurrence which largely departed from Justice O'Connor's majority opinion on exactly the issue of whether the evident purpose of the Hague Service Convention was such as to require recourse to the agreement's procedures in the case.[1132] The majority opinion simply noted that they were not "persuaded that the general purposes of the Convention require a different conclusion"[1133] from the one they otherwise reached. Justice Brennan was forced to conclude that the result obtained (largely by the majority's consultation of negotiating history) was "fundamentally at odds with the Convention's primary purpose...."[1134] While certainly commendable in its attempt to consider the underlying objectives of a treaty project, the *Volkswagen* opinion does illustrate the latent dangers of such an unprincipled approach.

[1129] *See Stuart*, 489 U.S. at 368.

[1130] Id.

[1131] 183 U.S. 424 (1902). *See also* supra notes 823 - 825 with text.

[1132] The parties extensively briefed the matter, and (predictably) reached different conclusions. *See* Petitioner's Brief, *Volkswagen* (86-1052), at screen 29 (LEXIS, Genfed Library, Briefs File) (U.S. Dec. 12, 1987) and Respondent's Brief, *Volkswagen* (86-1052), at screen 29 (U.S. Feb. 1, 1988).

[1133] *Volkswagen*, 486 U.S. at 704.

[1134] Id. at 711 (Brennan, J., concurring).

These dangers quickly became manifest before the Rehnquist Court. As was already just noted, the government in the *O'Connor* case attempted to argue that the agreed interpretation of the Panama Canal Agreements, jointly made by the United States and Panama on the eve of the appeal, was conclusive on the Court.[1135] Indeed, the Solicitor General was so bold as to suggest that "when both government parties to a bilateral agreement have concurred in its interpretation, it is inappropriate for courts to chart a different course."[1136] The government noted elsewhere in its briefs that "[i]t is, after all, the Executive Branch that is charged with conducting foreign affairs."[1137]   Even more extraordinarily, the Solicitor General wrote that "deference [to the Executive branch] is the rule even when the treaty partner takes a view different from that taken by the United States."[1138] Of course, the Supreme Court was able to duck this version of the political question doctrine as applied to foreign affairs,[1139] by

---

[1135] *See O'Connor*, 279 U.S. at 33 n.2.

[1136] Brief of the United States in Support of Certiorari, *O'Connor* (85-558, 85-559, 85-560), at 10 (U.S. Dec. 3, 1985). *See also* supra note 797 with text (noting *Sumitomo Shoji America*'s discussion on this issue).

[1137] Brief of the United States, *O'Connor* (85-558, 85-559, 85-560), at 13 (U.S. Sept. 30, 1986) (*citing United States v. Curtiss-Wright Export Corp.*, 299 U.S. 304, 319-20 (1936)).

[1138] Id. For virtually an identical statement, *see* Brief of the United States Amicus Curiae in Support of Petitioner, *Chan* (87-1055), at 24 (U.S. June 17, 1988) ("Nor do we think that the contrary views of other signatories to the Warsaw Convention should be controlling.... [since] they conflict with the view expressed by the United States.") and Brief of the United States in Support of Certiorari, *O'Connor* (85-558, 85-559, 85-560), at 7 (U.S. Dec. 3, 1985). *See also* supra note 796 (discussing *Factor v. Laubenheimer*'s holding on this point).

[1139] For more on this problem, *see* Jonathan A. Bush, *How did we Get Here? Foreign Abduction After* Alvarez-Machain, 45 STAN. L. REV. 939, 956-57 (1993); Malvina Halberstam, *In Defense of the Supreme Court Decision in* Alvarez-Machain, 86 AJIL 736, 741 (1992).

simply ruling on the textual and contextual merits in favor of the government in *O'Connor*.[1140]

If this problem was evaded in *O'Connor* it roared back with a vengeance in *Itel*. In that case[1141] there was a stark disjunction between the interpretation of the 1956 and 1972 Container Conventions offered by the United States government, and that advanced by a number of foreign countries. Faced with a direct conflict between procedural deference to the Executive branch and the canon of good faith and liberal interpretation, the Solicitor General chose simply to argue that the foreign governments intervening in the case as amicus curiae were mistaken as to the character of the Tennessee tax under scrutiny.[1142] The Court grasped at this opportunity to be utterly dismissive of the views of our treaty partners,[1143] without appearing to be violating the canon of good faith. The Court indicated that it simply did not believe the eleven other nations, which had sent a diplomatic note to the State Department protesting the Tennessee tax,[1144] when those countries said that they did not "impose sales taxes (or equivalent taxes of different nomenclatures) on the lease of cargo containers that are used in international commerce among the Contracting Parties to the Convention."[1145] The Court decided there was no need to defer to a position which had no basis in fact.

[1140]   *See* 479 U.S. at 30-35.

[1141]   113 S.Ct. 1095 (1993).

[1142]   *See* Brief of the United States as Amicus Curiae Supporting Respondent, *Itel* (91-321), at screen 17 (LEXIS, Genfed Library, Briefs File) (U.S. June 25, 1992).

[1143]   *See* 113 S.Ct. at 1100-01.

[1144]   *See* id. at 1100.

[1145]   Id. at 1100-01 (citing Brief of the United Kingdom and Northern Ireland as Amicus Curiae Supporting Petitioner at 1a, *Itel* (No. 91-321). This was the same strategy used by the *Floyd* Court in rejecting the Israeli Supreme Court decision.

That leaves, of course, the *Alvarez-Machain* case[1146] as the ultimate repudiation of the canon of good faith and liberal interpretation. In truth, that decision shows that a foreign nation's wishes in the treaty interpretation process are to be utterly ignored when its interpretation conflicts with one argued by the United States government. The depth of the Court's contempt for a canon of liberal interpretation and good faith is illustrated on four different levels in the *Alvarez* decision. The first aspect is shown by the fact that the majority opinion, written by Chief Justice Rehnquist, simply ignores the express interpretation of the 1978 Extradition Treaty made by Mexico, and transmitted to the Court via diplomatic demarches and amicus briefing.[1147] Nowhere is the Mexican amicus brief mentioned or cited by the majority opinion in *Alvarez*. It is almost as if the Chief Justice was embarrassed by its presence in the judicial record. Unlike the later situation in *Itel*, when a judicial intervention by a foreign nation could at least be rationalized on the merits, this was not possible in *Alvarez*. There was simply no way to reconcile, or even to minimize, the Mexican government's interpretation of the Extradition Treaty as it applied to abductions of Mexican citizens, by American officials, on Mexican soil. So the majority pretended that the only authoritative interpretation of the treaty to be considered was the one made by the United States government, which happened to be one of the parties to the litigation.

Far more fundamental than this message that the Court was simply not interested in hearing a foreign interpretation at variance with the United States', was the corollary signal that the Court was willing to collude with the government in placing this country in violation of its international obligations under a treaty. This has sometimes been referred to as the "dual treaty approach."[1148] It simply means that the Supreme Court is free to interpret a treaty in such a way that it comes to have one meaning in domestic application, while it continues to have a different (and, presumably, authentic) meaning on the international plane. The essence of the canon of good faith and liberal

---

[1146] 112 S.Ct. 2188 (1992). *See also* Rogoff, supra note 869, at 589-92.

[1147] *See* 112 S.Ct. at 2197 n.1 (Stevens, J., dissenting).

[1148] For more background on this characterization of the problem, *see* Halberstam, supra note 780, at 51-54 (1992). *See also* supra notes 820 - 825 with text.

interpretation is precisely to avoid this problem. But in deciding *Alvarez*, Chief Justice Rehnquist was well-aware that the majority's interpretation — that a forced abduction did not violate the Extradition Treaty — would result in a diplomatic incident with Mexico. The Court as much as said that was fine, and that the Executive branch would resolve the consequent fall-out with Mexico.[1149] In doing so, Chief Justice Rehnquist mused, the President need not be worried about any judicial interference.[1150]

Perhaps the most worrisome aspect of *Alvarez*'s handling of the canon of good faith and liberal interpretation was the way the majority opinion connivingly manipulated rules of contract construction to favor the U.S. government's interpretation of the treaty. As was already discussed, contract imagery for treaties has continued to flourish in the Rehnquist Court opinions. But in *Alvarez* the rhetoric came-up hard against reality. The fighting issue was the collision between public international law's rule against exercises of sovereignty by one nation in another country and a countervailing trend in U.S. decisions allowing jurisdiction over criminal defendants even when forcibly obtained (the so-called *Ker-Frisbie* principle). This book is not the place to review the convolutions of that doctrine,[1151] but it is significant that the Court in *Alvarez* developed a novel — and utterly unsupportable — methodology for divining a treaty partner's intent in negotiating and ratifying an agreement.

Here is how the majority did it. Chief Justice Rehnquist's opinion charged to Mexico the knowledge, when negotiating the 1978 Extradition

---

[1149] *See Alvarez*, 112 S.Ct. at 2196-97 & n.16.

[1150] *See* id.

[1151] For a sampling of the vast, substantive literature about the *Ker-Frisbie* doctrine and the merits of the *Alvarez* case, *see* Charles Fairman, Ker v. Illinois *Revisited*, 47 AJIL 678 (1953); Andreas F. Lowenfeld, *U.S. Law Enforcement Abroad: The Constitution and International Law*, 83 AJIL 880 (1989); Andreas F. Lowenfeld, *U.S. Law Enforcement Abroad: The Constitution and International Law, Continued*, 84 AJIL 444 (1990); Andreas F. Lowenfeld, *Still More on Kidnapping*, 85 AJIL 655 (1991); Austin W. Scott, Jr., *Criminal Jurisdiction of a State Over a Defendant Based upon Presence by Force or Fraud*, 37 MINN. L. REV. 91 (1953); Jacqueline A. Weisman, *Extraordinary Rendition: A One-Way Ticket to the U.S. ... Or is It?*, 41 CATH. U. L. REV. 149 (1991).

Treaty, of the United States' judicial, *Ker-Frisbie* doctrine that makes forcible abductions permissible.[1152] Mexico was, according to the majority opinion,

> made aware, as early as 1906, of the *Ker* doctrine, and the United States' position that it applied to forcible abductions made outside of the terms of the United States-Mexico extradition treaty. Nonetheless, the current version of the Treaty, signed in 1978, does not attempt to establish a rule that would in any way curtail the effect of *Ker*.[1153]

This passage strangely echoed Justice Brennan's statement, in the *Stuart* majority opinion, where he cites the *Contracts Restatement* for a related proposition of construction.[1154]   What Brennan had earlier noted was that "the proper construction of an agreement is that given by one of the parties when 'that party had no reason to know of any different meaning attached by the other, and the other had reason to know the meaning attached by the first party'."[1155]   In reaching the conclusion he did, Chief Justice Rehnquist simply ignored the point that there must be a mutuality of expectation as to the meaning of a provision.[1156]

[1152] *See Alvarez*, 112 S.Ct. at 2194-95.

[1153] Id. at 2194.

[1154] *See* supra notes 1074 - 1077 and accompanying text.

[1155] *Stuart*, 489 U.S. at 368 n.7 (*quoting* Restatement (Second) of Contracts § 201(2)(b) (1981)). For more on this problem in the context of tax treaties, *see* Tax Treaty Draft Project, supra note 793, at 48-49.

[1156] The majority attempted to supply some evidence of mutuality of interpretation by relying on a diplomatic exchange from 1905 regarding the so-called "Martinez incident." Apparently Mr. Alvarez-Machain's experience had been the same as Antonio Martinez's — they had both been abducted by U.S. authorities from Mexico, and, on both occasions, Mexico protested. In response to the 1905 Mexican protest, the U.S. Secretary of State indicated that Mexico had no legal recourse under the *Ker* doctrine. Letter of Robert Bacon to Mexican Chargé, *Papers Relating to the Foreign Relations of the United States*, H.R. Doc. 1, 59th Cong., 2d Sess., pt. 2, at 1121-22 (1906). *See also* Brief of the United States, *Alvarez* (91-712), at 28 n.23 (LEXIS, Genfed Library, Briefs File) (U.S. Feb. 13, 1992). Chief Justice Rehnquist inferred from this exchange that Mexico was on notice of the *Ker* doctrine and so it was incumbent on that country to modify the later version of the Extradition Treaty. *See Alvarez*, 112 S.Ct. at 2194 n.11.

What the *Alvarez* case did was to introduce an extraordinary asymmetry into the mutual process of treaty negotiation and interpretation. Because the United States held a peculiar view as to a background principle of customary international law, that view was ascribed to Mexico in the negotiations and the burden placed on that country to, in essence, "contract out" of that rule.[1157] As anyone who is familiar with standard rules of contract construction is aware,[1158] that is an utterly unacceptable method of interpretation since it gives an unfair advantage to parties which adhere to peculiar, contrarian rules. In this case, the position held by the United States about forcible abductions manifestly contradicted public international law.[1159] Now, the majority opinion could have decided to challenge that assumption — but it chose not to. Instead, Chief Justice Rehnquist blithely noted that since the Respondent "does not argue that these sources of [customary] international law provide an independent basis for the right [he] asserts ... they should [only] inform the interpretation of the Treaty terms."[1160] But that did not change the majority's holding that the United States could embrace a treaty interpretation contrary to a background principle of international law. And, moreover, by the very act of maintaining such a view, the United States could estop a treaty partner from taking an adverse interpretation, unless that foreign nation also insisted upon the inclusion of a clause into the treaty repudiating the American position. This methodology for inferring intent from textual silence has no basis in domestic contract analogies or in the international law of treaty interpretation itself.

What Rehnquist nowhere mentions, however, is that Mexico took strong exception to the U.S. position in the Martinez correspondence, as well as in later years. *See* Brief of the United Mexican States as Amicus Curiae in Support of Respondent, *Alvarez* (91-712), at 10-13 (U.S. March 5, 1992).

[1157] Previous American decisions had indicated that U.S. courts should not honor such a particularistic gloss on customary international law. *See* supra note 821 with text.

[1158] *See, e.g., Contracts Restatement,* supra note 1076, § 201(3) ("[N]either party is bound by the meaning attached by the other...."); E. Allan Farnsworth, CONTRACTS §7.9, at 502-03 & 506-07 (2d ed. 1990).

[1159] *See Alvarez,* 113 S.Ct. at 2195-96, 2201-05 (Stevens, J., dissenting).

[1160] Id. at 2195.

At bottom, the Supreme Court sanctioned an utterly parochial reading of the Extradition Treaty in *Alvarez*. This was in defiance of that first principle of the liberal interpretation canon: that the words and meanings of treaties should be understood against the background of international, not domestic, law,[1161] as Mexico itself pointed out in its amicus brief before the Court.[1162] But Chief Justice Rehnquist was ready for this, and his riposte was the last of the four salient features of the case. For once it was clear that the Court would not entertain any deference for the views of Mexico in the case, all that could be argued was that permitting forcible abductions violated some fundamental purpose of the Extradition Treaty. As in the *Volkswagen* case, this methodology of interpretation degenerated into a debate between the majority and dissent as to what objects and purposes could be divined from the treaty.[1163]

In any event, the Court has recently shown itself to be strikingly solicitous of the "opinions of our sister signatories."[1164] while also being sharply dismissive of such views. In *Tseng*, the Court went out of its way to reject a parochial reading of the Warsaw Convention, by noting that such would be a "home-centered preemption analysis, [and] therefore should not be applied,

---

[1161] *See Geofroy v. Riggs*, 133 U.S. 258, 271-72 (1890) ("in their construction words [in a treaty] are to be taken in their ordinary meaning, as understood in the public law of nations, and not in any artificial or special sense impressed upon them by local law, unless such restricted sense is clearly intended") (Field, J.).

[1162] *See* Brief of United Mexican States as Amicus Curiae in Support of Respondent, *Alvarez* (91-712), at 11 n.4 (U.S. March 5, 1992) (*citing* Vienna Convention, supra note 764, art. 31, para. 1, for proposition that a "treaty should be interpreted in good faith in accordance with the ordinary meaning to be given to the terms of the treaty in their context and in the light of its object and purpose.").

[1163] *Compare Alvarez*, 112 S.Ct. at 2196 n.14 ("The ambitious purpose ascribed to the Treaty [safeguarding sovereignty and the rights of individuals] places a greater burden on its language and history than they can logically bear") *with* id. at 2199 (indicating that the object and scope of the treaty "plainly imply a mutual undertaking to respect the territorial integrity of the other contracting party") (Stevens, J., dissenting).

[1164] *Tseng*, 119 S.Ct. at 675 (quoting *Air France v. Saks*, 470 U.S. at 404).

mechanically, in construing our international obligations."[1165] Yet, the previous Term, in *Breard*, the Court did just that — and explicitly so — ruling "it has been recognized in international law that, absent a clear and express statement to the contrary, the procedural rules of the forum State govern the implementation of the treaty in that State."[1166]

Finally, in *Haitian Centers*, Justice Steven's majority opinion paid lip-service to the canon of good faith and liberal interpretation.[1167] At the same time, the decision made very clear that any examination of the Refugee Protocol's "broad remedial goals"[1168] and "spirit"[1169] was of absolutely no consequence in the process of interpretation. It is true that the result in *Haitian Centers* ran counter to that in *Alvarez*. After all, the Refugee Convention was not silent as to the extraterritorial application of the non-*refoulement* obligation, but seemed (at least) to be explicit on the point.[1170] Nonetheless, both opinions eschewed any attempt to look beyond textual omissions (in *Alvarez*) or exercises in deconstruction (as in *Haitian Centers*), and to see the point of the disputed provisions. Justice Blackmun, dissenting in *Haitian Councils*, must have realized this; his only reference to the "objectives and concerns of the Convention"[1171] was a tangential one.[1172] He probably realized it was pointless to bolster his dissent with teleological arguments.

[1165] 119 S.Ct. at 675.

[1166] 118 S.Ct. at 1354.

[1167] 113 S.Ct. at 2567 ("[W]e must, of course, be guided by the high purpose of . . . the treaty").

[1168] Id. at 2563.

[1169] Id. at 2565.

[1170] *See* supra notes 979 - 982 and accompanying text.

[1171] 113 S.Ct. at 2570 (Blackmun, J., dissenting).

[1172] *See* id. (discussing "absurd anomaly" noted by the majority opinion in the parallel provision of 33.2 of the Refugees Convention (*see* supra notes 993 - 997 with text)).

Perhaps these exchanges about a treaty's object and purpose were bound to fail in persuasion. Despite an internationalist belief in the positive benefits of searching for a treaty's "object and purpose," the truth is that such a exploration is standardless. It is merely an invitation for a court to superimpose its own policy values on a treaty's text and meaning.[1173] Such a teleological approach can never substitute for concrete, interpretive methods.

   iv. *Deference to Executive Branch Constructions of Treaties.* If text and context collude to obscure meaning, if there is nothing to choose among extrinsic materials, and if the canon of good faith and liberal interpretation has been exploded, that leaves just one last theory of treaty construction in our jurisprudence. Indeed, it is the single best predictor of interpretive outcomes in American treaty cases. Of the thirteen cases considered by the Rehnquist Court, *in all but one* the holding followed the express wishes of the Executive branch of the government.[1174] The deference afforded to the government — even as cast

---

[1173] For example, the mention of the Warsaw Convention's "cardinal purpose" in *Tseng*, 119 S.Ct. at 671-72, was meant to distinguish the approach taken in *Zicherman*. In *Zicherman*, the Court extolled the Warsaw Convention's emphasis on uniformity. *See* 516 U.S. at 230. But this proved embarrassing in *Tseng*, so the Court had to declare the Convention's "complementary purpose," 119 S.Ct. at 672: protecting air carriers from unexpected liabilities. Id. at 672-73.

[1174] The exception was *Chan*, as will be discussed shortly. The Rehnquist Court statistics seem to be consistent with both Warren and Burger Court case figures.

   For the Warren Court, of seven cases implicating treaty interpretation, in five the construction advanced by the United States was wholly and unambiguously embraced by the Court. *See Wilson v. Girard*, 354 U.S. 524, 529-30 (1957) (per curiam) (Status of Forces Agreement with Japan); *Kolovrat v. Oregon*, 366 U.S. 187, 194-95 (1961) (U.S. as amicus) (1881 FCN Treaty with Serbia); *Maximov v. United States*, 373 U.S. 49, 52-54 (1963) (1945 U.S.-U.K. Tax Treaty); *United States v. California*, 381 U.S. 139, 161-76 (1965) (1958 Geneva Convention on Territorial Sea and Contiguous Zone); *Zschernig v. Miller*, 389 U.S. 429 (1968) (U.S. as amicus) (1923 FCN Treaty with Germany); *United States v. Louisiana (Louisiana Boundary Case)*, 394 U.S. 11, 36-38, 48-53, 54-60, 67-73 (1969). The only exceptions are short passages in *United States v. Louisiana*, 363 U.S. 1, 62-64 (1960), in which the Court rejected the Solicitor General's interpretation of the 1848 Treaty of Guadalupe Hidalgo with Mexico, and in *United States v. Louisiana (Louisiana Boundary Case)*, 394 U.S. 11, 40-47, 60-63, where the Court disagreed with certain technical interpretations of the 1958 Geneva Convention on the Territorial Sea and Contiguous Zone.

   For the Burger Court, of the six cases involving treaty construction, in five the

in the position of litigant before the Court or as *amicus curiae* appearing in support of one party — is simply extraordinary.   What is even more phenomenal, there appear to be no limits to this deference, save one.   As already suggested, the Rehnquist Court has stopped short at saying that cases in which a government's treaty interpretation is challenged are non-justiciable.   So, for the time being, and as one commentator has mentioned,[1175] the Court plays out a dance in which it reaches the interpretive merits of a treaty case only to (invariably) comply with the Executive branch's wishes.[1176]

The Rehnquist Court, despite being chary in cloaking the government's positions with the political question doctrine,[1177] still has gone further than previous Courts in elevating deference to new heights.   As the Court noted in *Tseng*, "[r]espect is ordinarily due the reasonable views of the Executive Branch

---

interpretation made by the Solicitor General was accepted by the Supreme Court. *See United States v. Alaska*, 422 U.S. 184, 188-89 (1975) (1958 Geneva Convention on Territorial Sea); *Washington v. Washington State Commercial Passenger Fishing Vessel Ass'n*, 443 U.S. 658, 690-91 (1979) (U.S. as party) (various Indian treaties); *Sumitomo Shoji America, Inc. v. Avagliano*, 457 U.S. 176, 184-85 (1982) (U.S. as amicus) (FCN Treaty with Japan); *Immigration and Naturalization Service v. Stevic*, 467 U.S. 407, 416-18 (1984) (1968 U.N. Refugees Protocol); *Air France v. Saks*, 470 U.S. 392, 400 (1985) (U.S. as amicus) (Warsaw Convention). *But see Trans World Airlines, Inc. v. Franklin Mint Corp.*, 466 U.S. 243, 253, 257-60 (1989), where the Court appeared to act against the wishes of the Executive branch in construing the Warsaw Convention.   Some commentators have suggested that the Executive branch's desires may have been satisfied in this case. *See* Franck, supra note 769, at 75-76.

[1175]   *See* Bush, supra note 1139, at 956.

[1176]   The Court has, in effect, applied a rule of deference to agency interpretations of statutes to Executive branch interpretations of treaties. *See* supra note 577 with text. *See also* Bederman, Deference, supra note 795.

[1177]   This is so despite the government renewing a virulent form of the doctrine in the *Alvarez* case. *See* Brief of the United States, *Alvarez* (91-712), at 38 (U.S. Feb. 13, 1992). For more on the Court's wrestling with the political question doctrine, *see generally*, Franck, supra note 769.

concerning the meaning of an international treaty."[1178] In the past, there *were* substantive limits to deference. No more, it seems. This Court has not been content with merely reciting the mantra from earlier decisions that the government's proferred interpretation is "entitled to great weight."[1179] One of the essential checks on deference to the President, as detailed in earlier treaty cases,[1180] has been to check to see if the Executive branch's current interpretation squares with previous declarations. If there is a manifest contradiction, then courts have been less likely to honor a new Presidential interpretation, especially where it seems that the construction was offered only to advance the litigation interests of the United States.

But this yardstick for measuring Presidential assertions of authentic treaty interpretations has been snapped in two by the Court. It was broken in both *Alvarez-Machain* and *Itel*. In *Alvarez*, the prisoner relied on an 1881 statement, by Secretary of State James G. Blaine,[1181] that the then in force

---

[1178] 119 S.Ct. at 671 (*citing Sumitomo Shoji*, 457 U.S. at 184-85). This remark is reminiscent of the Court's holding in *Chevron U.S.A. Inc. v. Natural Resources Defense Council, Inc.*, 467 U.S. 837, 842-45 (1984), where the Court extended deference to any "permissible" statutory interpretations made by government agencies.

[1179] *See Volkswagen*, 486 U.S. at 713 (Brennan, J., concurring) (contemporaneous views of American negotiating delegation "entitled to great weight"); *SNIAS*, 482 U.S. at 535-36 n.19 ("[T]he meaning attributed to treaty provisions by the Government agencies charged with their negotiation and enforcement is entitled to great weight.") (*citing Sumitomo Shoji America, Inc. v. Avagliano*, 457 U.S. 176, 184-85 (1982)).
     No Rehnquist Court decision has, however, referred to Justice Stevens' statement in *Trans World Airlines, Inc. v. Franklin Mint Corp.*, 466 U.S. 243 (1984), that Executive agency interpretations of treaties are "not entitled to any special deference." Id. at 276 n.5. *See also* Franck, supra note 769, at 75-76; supra note 794 with text.

[1180] *See, e.g., Clark v. Allen*, 331 U.S. 503, 513 (1947); *Perkins v. Elg*, 307 U.S. 325, 347-48 (1939) (1869 Naturalization Treaty with Sweden). *But see* supra note 797 with text (discussing *Sumitomo* case and holding that where a current Executive branch interpretation squares with the views of other nations, it will be accepted even if it contradicts earlier Presidential statements).

[1181] *See* 939 F.2d at 1354 (opinion of the lower court, *citing* Secretary of State Blaine's letter to O.R. Roberts, Governor of Texas (May 3, 1881), in *Domestic Letters of the State Department, 1784-1906* (National Archives Microfilm Publication M40, Roll 93)). *See also*

Extradition Treaty with Mexico (which was substantively identical to the 1978 agreement) "did not authorize unconsented to abductions from Mexico."[1182] Chief Justice Rehnquist glibly replied that "[t]his misses the mark, however, because the Government's argument is not that the Treaty authorizes the abduction of respondent; but that the Treaty does not prohibit the abduction."[1183] The Court could have questioned the significance of this purported inconsistency of government practice in interpreting the treaty. The Solicitor General briefed this point, and made a plausible argument suggesting that there was no real contradiction.[1184] Chief Justice Rehnquist's reaction indicates that the Court was not really willing to entertain *any* evidence of prior, inconsistent statements by the government.[1185]

Itel merely made express this latent hostility to inconsistency challenges of Presidential interpretations. When the taxpayer in that case pointed out that the U.S. government had previously interpreted the 1956 Container Convention

---

Brief of Respondent, *Alvarez* (91-712), at 14 (U.S. March 4, 1992); Brief of United Mexican States as Amicus Curiae for Respondent, *Alvarez* (91-712), at 12 (U.S. March 5, 1992).

[1182]   *Alvarez*, 112 S.Ct. at 2194 n.11.

[1183]   Id.

[1184]   *See* Brief of the United States, *Alvarez* (91-712), at 29 n.24 (U.S. Feb. 13, 1992).

[1185]   As further evidence of this, the Court chose to ignore some other prior, inconsistent statements made by the Executive branch. These were relied upon by the lower court, 939 F.2d at 1354 (*citing* Contemporary Practice of the United States Relating to International Affairs, 78 AJIL 207, 208 (1984) (statement by Secretary of State George Shultz); and *Hearings on S. 1429 Before the Subcomm. on Security and Terrorism of the Senate Comm. on the Judiciary*, 99th Cong., 1st Sess. (1986) (statement by State Department Legal Advisor Abraham Sofaer)).

Likewise, in *Haitian Centers*, the Court did not credit the Respondent's assertion that its interpretation of the Refugees Convention squared with earlier practice. *See* Brief for Respondent, *Haitian Centers* (92-344), at 22-24 (LEXIS, Genfed Library, Briefs File) (U.S. Dec. 21, 1992). Justice Blackmun's dissent did discuss this evidence. *See* 113 S.Ct. at 2568-69 & n.3.

to prohibit the kind of tax Tennessee imposed,[1186] Justice Kennedy simply said that "[e]ven if this were true, the Government's current position is quite different; its *amicus* brief in this case expresses agreement with our interpretation of both the 1972 and the 1956 Container Conventions."[1187] The clear message of *Alvarez* and *Itel* is that it is pointless to challenge a treaty interpretation offered by the Executive branch, on the theory that it contradicts earlier American practice.

It is, however, still possible to dispute a Presidential interpretation of a treaty on ostensible grounds of logic. This was Respondent's arguable success in *Chan*, the only case in which the Rehnquist Court did not, in fact, esteem an Executive branch construction of a treaty. As is usually so often the case, though, the exception proves the rule. In *Chan*, the Solicitor General joined the case as amicus in favor of petitioner's position that the limit of liability in the Warsaw Convention was inapplicable when the air carrier did not give proper notice in the passenger ticket.[1188] What is extraordinary in *Chan* is that the majority really appears to be blissfully unaware that it is deciding the case contrary to the wishes of the government.[1189] The nature of the Executive branch's intervention in the case is only mentioned once, as an aside.[1190]

This extraordinary expansion in the measure of discretion given in favor of Presidential interpretations of treaties has not gone unremarked in the cases. Justice Stevens, in dissent in *Alvarez*, clearly realized that the Court's decision

---

[1186] *See* Brief of Petitioner, *Itel* (91-321), at screen 9 (LEXIS, Genfed Library, Briefs File) (U.S. Apr. 30, 1992).

[1187] *Itel*, 113 S.Ct. at 1101.

[1188] *See* supra notes 953 - 960 with text.

[1189] Justice Brennan, in his concurrence, makes just a few references to the Solicitor General's brief. *See Chan*, 490 U.S. at 140 n.6. & 145. He does note, though, some skepticism of the government's position, despite the fact that he "must owe considerable deference to [its] views . . . ." Id. at 151 n.15 (*citing Sumitomo Shoji America, Inc. v. Avagliano*, 457 U.S. 176, 184-85 (1982)).

[1190] *See Chan*, 490 U.S. at 133.

was influenced by unbridled deference. Not only did he suggest that such deference should have been constrained by the fact that the Executive branch had evidenced conflicting positions about forcible abductions abroad,[1191] but he also questioned the entire practice of giving so much credit to the litigation-inspired positions taken by the government.[1192] "That the Executive may wish to reinterpret the Treaty to allow for an action that the Treaty in no way authorizes," Justice Stevens wrote, "should not influence this Court's interpretation."[1193] The warning note sounded by Justice Stevens in *Alvarez-Machain* is not likely to be heeded. When it comes to treaty construction, U.S. courts are likely to continue masking an almost abdicationist stance in judicial review as merely gracious deference to Executive branch interpretation.

[1191] *See Alvarez*, 112 S.Ct. at 2205 & n.34.

[1192] *See* id. at 2205 n.35. *See also* the point made by the lower court on the government's fabricated position. 939 F.2d at 1353 ("Those views [of the government] appear to have been adopted only with any eye towards the current litigation."). This statement was reminiscent of Justice Stevens' observation in *Trans World Airlines, Inc. v. Franklin Mint Corp. See* supra note 1179.

[1193] Id. at 2205 (Stevens, J., dissenting).

XIII   New Canons for Treaty Construction

i. The previous section, offering an internal[1194] critique of the Rehnquist Court cases, was largely inspired by the "scholastic" debate in interpretive circles. The textualist, intentionalist, and teleological approaches to finding treaty meaning roughly match-up with the prevailing schools in statutory construction.[1195] Nothing more needs to be added here about that. But the previous discussion was also animated by a desire to see the relationship between rules and standards in treaty construction, another way to think about recourse to foundational sources as opposed to dynamic methods. At the same time, one needs to see the content of substantive and procedural doctrines which seem to actually determine interpretive outcomes. Finally, there are strong parallels between modern rules of construction for treaties and classical canons and paradigms.

As already suggested, many of the treaty cases before the Rehnquist Court have been litigated and decided as if they presented merely a slight variant on the problem of statutory construction. The Court does usually acknowledge the special quality of international agreements, usually by citation to maxims which characterize treaties as being a public-law form of a contract. But, in reality, the Court has virtually eviscerated any real content to contractual

---

[1194] By an "internal critique" I mean one that chiefly focuses on the inherent cohesion and cogency of a set of interpretive norms, as expressed by the Supreme Court. For other examples of this kind of approach, *see* Eskridge & Frickey, supra note 550, at 364-71; Popkin, supra note 555.

[1195] *See* supra note 807 and accompanying text.

methodologies in treaty interpretation. Symmetry of obligation and equivalence in negotiating parity was rejected in *Alvarez-Machain*. Recognition of foreign views and practices in treaty interpretation were expressly declined in *Floyd*, *Itel*, *Breard* and *Haitian Centers*. So while the prevailing rhetoric of interpretation is contractual, the underlying idiom and approach is clearly statutory. This is an extraordinarily mischievous development.

The fundamental fault of applying to treaties the language and methodology of the new statutory interpretation debate lies in one of the critical concerns of the interlocutors: the balance of power between judges and legislatures. This concern is simply irrelevant in the treaty sphere. As political process theorists (including the public choice school) have revealed, the fundamental model of legislation as a majoritarian process is deeply flawed. But for treaties it is simply a nonsense. The immateriality of the statutory paradigm is revealed at both stages of an international agreement's birth: its negotiation with other nations and its ratification under the Constitution.

International agreements are the product of consensus. Even those conventions with a legislative or constitutive flavor are fashioned in a contractual sense, oftentimes with the very selection of words and phrases being the result of unanimous approval by the signatory States. Because of this, it may actually make sense to search for original intent among the treaty parties, whereas to do so with domestic laws would be problematic because of the non-democratic and counter-majoritarian tendencies in the legislative process. Those in the statutory debate who denounce the use of legislative history should not be so quick, therefore, to reject the use of *travaux préparatoires*. Even more significant, though, is that the fundamental differences between the legislative and treaty-making processes should provide a warning to those (on the other side of the originalist argument) who would unwittingly use *travaux* as merely some quirky form of legislative history. Because the entire debate about intentionalism and originalism in statutory interpretation revolves around a law-making process which, at least, is *supposed* to be majoritarian, it has doubtful connection to the problem of treaty meaning.

Even more pertinent in debunking the statutory analogy are the separation of powers concerns relevant in the treaty area. Once again, treaties are a peculiar form of law. They are made on the initiative of the Executive branch, and only (and not even in all cases) requiring the advice and consent of a Senate super-majority. With treaties, it is the President who is the legislator.

Just as Presidential statements made in signing bills are accorded relatively little weight,[1196] so it has been that Senatorial actions concerning treaties are not given much credence in the interpretive process, unless such actions are framed as definitive reservations or declarations to the agreement. As has been discussed in some detail already, in treaty cases courts do not bother much in deferring to the Congress. The object of their esteem is the President.

In contrast, the debate about judicial deference to Executive branch *statutory* interpretations is really tangential to the wider concern about judicial independence *vis-à-vis* Congress. That may explain why, despite a brief flirtation with deference to agency constructions,[1197] the Supreme Court has not shown as much enthusiasm in deferring to the Executive in statutory cases.[1198] The fighting issue of statutory interpretation remains the propriety of judicial independence in construing the law. With treaties, the entire question of deference to the Executive's wishes is not really tied to originalism at all. Rather, it is the President's current desires in the application of the agreement which are accorded respect.[1199]

One last point needs to be made about the statutory analogy and balance of power concerns with treaties. Despite all of the debate regarding the allocation of interpretive power between Congress and the courts over statutes, all agree that, provided a statute is at least constitutional, Congress will always have the last word in construction. Congress can, and does, fix its drafting

---

[1196]   *See* Zeppos, *Texas*, supra note 550, at 1093, 1139.

[1197]   This was in *Chevron U.S.A. Inc. v. Natural Resources Defense Council, Inc.*, 467 U.S. 837 (1984), holding that a reviewing court must uphold an agency's interpretation of an ambiguous statute if the interpretation is reasonable. Id. at 842-45.

[1198]   For a critique of the *Chevron* holding and an account of the erosion of its rule in subsequent cases, *see* Popkin, supra note 555, at 1155-59; Stephen F. Ross, *Where have You Gone Karl Llewellyn? Should Congress Turn its Lonely Eyes to You*, 45 VAND. L. REV. 561, 569-72 (1992); Slawson, supra note 555, 1073, at 390-91, 401; Sunstein, supra note 551, at 444-46.

[1199]   *See* supra section XI.iv.

mistakes after being prompted by the courts.[1200]   The conflicting claims of textualists and intentionalists boil down to the necessity of holding Congress' feet to the fire in curing ambiguous or situationally defective laws. In large part, then, the entire constitutional debate on statutory construction is unnecessary: mistakes in interpretation can always be corrected.

With treaties, however, there is no convenient safety-valve for interpreters. After all, treaties have dual status in both international and domestic law. An American court could adopt an interpretation at variance with that of our treaty partners, but that new construction would have no force on the international plane. In such a situation, the United States could well be in default of its international obligations. To reconcile the internal and international meanings of a treaty, the United States government would be forced to renegotiate the agreement. Because any process of negotiation is consensual, there is no guarantee that a reconciliation could occur. Failing that, the United States would be obliged to terminate its obligations under the treaty. Unlike the relatively benign outcomes of separation-of-powers disputes over statutes, conflicts over treaty interpretation can have very real — and irremediable — consequences.

The dangers of the statutory analogy of treaty interpretation should be manifest from the Rehnquist Court cases. A few examples will suffice here.

ii. *Plain Meanings and Thresholds of Ambiguity*. The unifying theme of cases like *O'Connor*, *Stuart*, *Zicherman*, *Chan*, and *Haitian Centers* was the search for tolerable levels of ambiguity in legal texts. The treaty cases make one wonder why we should even care.

The truth is that a rule of plain meaning for a text means nothing unless an interpreter is prepared to live with a certain amount of vagueness. It is beyond peradventure that individual words are capable of carrying more than one meaning. Stringing words together compounds the obscurity. As was discussed in some detail in my internal critique of the recent Supreme Court treaty cases, we have many outcomes that are repudiations of textualism. These

---

[1200]   *See generally* William N. Eskridge, Jr., *Overriding Supreme Court Statutory Interpretation Decisions*, 101 YALE L. J. 331 (1991); Lawrence C. Marshall, *Let Congress Do It: The Case for an Absolute Rule of Statutory Stare Decisis*, 88 MICH. L. REV. 177 (1989).

opinions extol some sort of deferential or substantive preferences. How else can one explain *O'Connor* except as a desire to protect the public fisc from unfortunate treaty-based tax exemptions. Likewise, *Haitian Centers* is a case where the threshold of ambiguity is dropped so low that not even the most limber of limbo dancers can negotiate a plain meaning for a text. Many of the "slip of the pen" and situational obscurity cases were instances of manufactured ambiguity. The Court has consistently used its favorite techniques of verbal deconstruction, followed by structural reconstitution of the text,[1201] in order to alter the meaning of an unfortunate — but otherwise clear — provision.

What is so strange, though, is that the Court seems prepared to abide by quite a bit more vagueness in statutory cases. Why, then, despite the strong presence of Justice Scalia as the Court's leading textualist,[1202] has there been no similar adoption of a threshold of ambiguity with treaties? The truth must lie in the *sui generis* quality of international agreements. If we have a Court that consistently defers to Presidential interpretations of treaties, one must conclude that it somehow benefits the Executive branch to have a margin of discretion in challenging the textual meaning of an international agreement when one of its provisions is litigated in the courts of the United States. If courts adopt a low threshold of ambiguity, it remains in the power of the current administration to successfully challenge textual interpretations by private parties seeking benefits under treaties. This was certainly the result in *O'Connor*, *Alvarez-Machian*, and in *Haitian Centers*. And, of course, when it suits the Executive branch to adhere to a plain-meaning approach to a treaty clause, as in *Itel*, so much the better. Private litigants, in any event, have fewer resources to mount winning interpretive arguments based on *travaux*, legislative history, or the subsequent practice of treaty parties.

iii.   *Whose Intentionalism?*   Many statutory commentators have maintained that the prevailing school of legislative construction today seeks to

---

[1201]   Recall also that much of the mischief in this area can be traced to the Court's created nuance, in *Maximov v. United States*, 373 U.S. 49 (1963), between a treaty's "text" and its "terms." Id. at 54. If the terms of a treaty includes its structural context, then textualism plays little role in modern jurisprudence. *See* supra note 809 with text.

[1202]   *See* Popkin, supra note 555; Nicholas S. Zeppos, *Justice Scalia's Textualism: The "New" New Legal Process*, 12 CARDOZO L. REV. 1597 (1991).

ascertain the original intent of the law-makers in fashioning the relevant act.[1203] This methodology of interpretation certainly has its detractors,[1204] and one should also not ignore the internal schism between those that distinguish between an "original" intent and a more dynamic or evolutive design of the statute. What ever its precise theology, this school has become dominant in treaty interpretation. Its high-water mark was in *Maximov v. United States*,[1205] where the Court noted that a provision's text does not control if "application of the words of the treaty according to their obvious meaning effects a result inconsistent with the intent or expectations of its signatories."[1206] The irony is that, despite concerted attacks on intentionalism in statutory construction and a spirited attack by Justice Scalia in *Stuart*, it remains a potent force with construing international agreements.

The sad truth is that the intentionalist school of statutory interpretation has badly retarded treaty interpretation in the last half of this century.[1207] Despite whatever one might think about searching for Congress's original or dynamic intent in statutory cases, it is at least clear *who* the maker of an Act is. There is no such clarity with treaties. The problem, restated slightly here, is whether to consider authoritative the consensual process of international negotiation or the constitutional process of ratification. The Supreme Court has signaled that because of the peculiar position of treaties within the law of the land, both the negotiating history and the ratification record are to be consulted in the interpretive process. Moreover, the Court has refused to assign some order of priority to these two essential sources. Because treaties are birthed

---

[1203] *See* Eskridge & Frickey, supra note 550, at 325; Frickey, *Minnesota*, supra note 550, at 256; Zeppos, *Texas*, supra note 550, at 1077.

[1204] *See* Eskridge & Frickey, supra note 550, at 325-32.

[1205] 373 U.S. 49 (1963).

[1206] Id. at 54. The passage from *Maximov* is weirdly resonant with Justice Marshall's statement in *Citizens to Preserve Overton Park v. Volpe*, 401 U.S. 402 (1971), that when legislative history is ambiguous, the Court must only then "look primarily to statutes themselves to find the legislative intent." Id. at 413 n.29.

[1207] *See* Van Alstine, supra note 802, at 691.

twice into law, and because both the international assent and domestic ratification seem essential for an agreement to have the force of public law, the intent of both treaty-negotiators and treaty-ratifiers is credited.

The Court has yet to answer the fundamental concerns, raised by Justice Scalia in his *Stuart* concurrence,[1208] about the use of Senate ratification materials. These were, first, the propriety of giving unilateral weight to one nation's interpretation of a convention, even though that one country happens to be the United States. Second, in a constitutional sense, it was improper to elevate the Senate's passive role into that of a law-maker in the treaty field. Justice Scalia's points were likely intended as an extension of what he perceived to be the more important statutory debate. While his first point (against crediting our unilateral constructions) seems to be decisive, I believe Justice Scalia was really concerned about separation of powers matters and preserving the freedom of action and authority of the Executive branch in giving meaning and implementing international conventions. Judging by Justice Scalia's subsequent voting behavior, including votes to reverse in both *Alvarez-Machain* and *Haitian Centers*, it seems he cares more about satisfying the interpretive whims of the Executive branch than protecting the United States from default on its treaty obligations.

Nonetheless, the intentionalist paradigm in statutory construction has caused substantial mischief in confusing the issue of *whose* intent matters with a treaty. The intentionalist methodology has also failed by being virtually indiscriminate in its selection of materials for construction. Because there is an extraordinary wealth of material to be used in divining legislative meaning — all of it having equal probative value — treaty interpreters have blithely assumed the same with the sources available for negotiating history or *travaux préparatoires*. After examining the briefs and opinions in such cases as *Volkswagen*, *Floyd*, *Zicherman*, and *Haitian Councils*, one would think that the *travaux* of treaties are as extensive — and discursive — as legislative history for bills. This is simply false, but, more than that, it misleads lawyers and judges to confidently cite authority which is most certainly not authoritative.

iv. *Old Canons and New Ways to Read Treaties*. Treaty cases have, however, defied the recent trend in American statutory construction towards the

---

[1208]   *See* 489 U.S. at 374-76 (Scalia, J., concurring).

adoption of substantive canons. Apart from the Court's obligatory noises about contractual fidelity in treaty construction, no effort has been made to develop a set of interpretive norms which can stand apart from either procedural deference to the Executive branch or an utterly standardless scholastic exercise in textualism weighed against intentionalism. The irony is, however, that the Supreme Court used to embrace such a set of values. This was the double canon of good faith and liberal interpretation. It was developed by Justice Field, in *Geofroy v. Riggs*,[1209] without concern for the putative intent of the treaty parties. More than that, the value being protected was the essential benefit of treaty compliance. By conforming American treaty interpretations to those of our treaty parties, the canon of good faith solved the "dual treaty" dilemma and minimized the chances that the United States would be charged with a treaty breach. The corollary goal of liberal interpretation also served as a means, albeit a subsidiary one, of ensuring this country's compliance with its treaty obligations. It was assumed that if treaty terms were given liberal ambit, that charges of treaty breach would be reduced. And, in those isolated cases (like *Tucker v. Alexandroff*[1210] and *Stuart v. United States*[1211]) where the two prongs of the canon struck a discordant tone, well, then the greater good of good faith — of conforming American treaty interpretations with the expectations of other nations — prevailed.

My critique of the Rehnquist Court jurisprudence has charted the virtual demise of the good faith and liberal interpretation canon.[1212] And there is simply no other set of normative values to replace it. Although one could argue that deference to Executive branch views might be such a substantive canon, I believe that such pandering constitutes its own betrayal to the peculiar nature of treaties as both international and domestic law. Instead, I would propose a

---

[1209]   133 U.S. 258 (1890).

[1210]   *See* supra notes 823 - 825 and accompanying text.

[1211]   *See* supra notes 890 - 894 with text.

[1212]   In truth, the backlash against good faith and liberal interpretation did not begin with the Rehnquist Court. Its origins can be traced back to *Factor v. Laubenheimer*, 290 U.S. 276, 298 (1933) and *Charlton v. Kelly*, 229 U.S. 447, 472-73 (1913).

recipe of old, revived canons and new, substantive values or presumptions in treaty interpretation. A schematic of this methodology follows.

α. *Rule One: Begin interpretation with the treaty's text.* To the extent that the argumentation in this article has been scholastic, I acknowledge that textualism — and the textualist critique of recent judicial decisions — has been most influential in my thinking. But it is not enough, as the old canonists seemed to believe, to utter the first principle of textualism as a mantra. Rather, as I have already suggested, an interpreter must also be equipped with a realistic theory of — and threshold for — ambiguity. Vagueness will always be with us. The trick is to deal with it. The following principles might help.

A.   *Adopt the Vienna Convention's threshold of ambiguity.* In other words, a judge may only break from the text where the words of the text produce a result which is "manifestly absurd or unreasonable."[1213] This should be embraced as a high level of tolerance for ambiguity.

B.   *An interpreter should first apply the Vienna Convention test to the applicable provisions of the treaty.* This principle is intended to combat a recurring pathology in American judicial decisions to create ambiguity via structural readings of conventions in which the subject clause is made nonsensical by parallel readings with (arguably) irrelevant provisions. Of course, treaties are to be interpreted as a coherent whole, but the interpreter must fairly decide which articles are coordinate to the interpretive exercise, and which ones are not. If a treaty clause passes the Vienna Convention test, it should not be subjected to a higher level of "structural scrutiny."

Γ. *Be true to Justice Field's admonition that the words in treaties are to be "taken in their ordinary meaning, as understood in the public law of nations, and not in any artificial or special sense impressed upon them by local law."*[1214] Although courts do not usually ignore this principle, when they fail to heed it, as in *Haitian Centers*, the results are disastrous. This

---

[1213]   Vienna Convention, supra note 764, art. 32.

[1214]   *Geofroy v. Riggs*, 133 U.S. 258, 271-72 (1890) (Field, J.).

principle does not require a judge, however, to superimpose customary international law upon every treaty provision. Such would not have been required to fix the aberrant outcomes in either *Alvarez-Machain* or in *Haitian Centers*. Instead, all that was needed was for the interpreter to have sensitivity to the fact that in treaty-making no particular domestic construction of legal terms is contemplated or acceptable.

β. *Rule Two: When an interpreter is permitted to break from a treaty's text and search for extrinsic sources of meaning, it should remember that negotiating history and evidence of subsequent practice by a relevant number of treaty parties are to be vastly preferred over the legislative history of the advice and consent process or subsequent, unilateral interpretations by the Executive branch.* This rule provides the needed guidance, long absent, in choosing between extratextual sources in treaty construction. There is an explicit hierarchy of sources here: *travaux*, subsequent practice by a relevant number of treaty parties, legislative history, and, last, Executive branch statements made at the time of litigation. With this progression in mind, courts can actually weigh the probative value of evidence. Inconclusive *travaux préparatoires* may actually be bested, under this methodology, by clearly decisive statements of subsequent practice by a number of other nations (including the United States) or by clearly-documented and articulated elements of Executive-Senatorial exchanges in the treaty ratification process. But the interpreter must also keep some inherent weaknesses of these sources in mind:

A. *Treaty-making bears little relation to the legislative process.* As already discussed, the drafting of international agreements is a consensual exercise. Votes are sometimes taken at diplomatic conferences concluding treaties, but they are sometimes misleading as to the consensus that actually exists around certain provisions. Likewise, there are often struggles about the authoritative interpretations of difficult provisions. But these conflicts are rarely resolved by a vote. If an interpreter expects to find clear evidence of a provision's meaning, through *travaux*, it will most likely be disappointed, or, worse, misled (as happened in *Haitian Centers*). Instead, a court must look for a more subtle expression of consensus. This can be achieved by focusing less on statements made by individual delegates, and more on consensus explications of documents and the actual evolutive process of drafting a particular treaty clause.

B. *In order for evidence of subsequent, "practical" constructions of treaties to be relevant, they must reflect a consensus of interpretation among a relatively wide set of treaty parties.* If a practical construction of a treaty is supported only by United States' practice it should not really be considered probative within this extratextual source. Consistency in Executive branch and agency practice may, of course, build a case for a particular meaning, particularly when supported by *travaux.* Subsequent treaty constructions become probative in their own right by a consensual process similar to that found with negotiating history. A court must look for patterns of practical constructions and seek to identify broad-based agreement for the interpretation of an ambiguous provision.

Γ. *Legislative history of Senate ratification, and Executive pronouncements made in pursuance to advice and consent, are best used as a check on current interpretive positions taken by the Executive branch.* The international and constitutional law concerns of privileging implied Senatorial understandings in the treaty interpretive process will likely remain insoluble. As a consequence, this principle suggests that they be handled with extreme care. They are certainly useful in discrediting Executive branch constructions contrived for litigation, but, beyond that, have little probative weight.

γ. *Rule Three: If textual and extratextual sources fail, an interpreter should construe the treaty in such a way as to reasonably ensure that the United States will not be charged later by another country with breaching the agreement.* This is a normative restatement of the canon of good faith. No separate enunciation is made here of the corollary principle of liberal interpretation. A court must simply understand that treaties have a dual status on both the domestic and international plane and seek to reconcile the two in a single, authentic construction. This rule has particular application in cases dealing with bilateral treaties in which a foreign nation is an actual party or its wishes have been made express in diplomatic communications or in an amicus brief. If the first two rules of treaty interpretation miscarry, and a court must choose between a meaning advanced by a foreign nation and one by the Executive branch, the construction of the treaty partner is to be preferred. If a court cannot make that choice, it should take the exceptional step of declaring the cause to be non-justiciable under the political question doctrine.[1215]

v. I would hesitate to call this interpretive construct for treaties novel. It probably has much in common with practical reasoning methodologies in statutory construction. But my schematic *is* rule-based. Maybe it even errs in being too formalistic and mechanical. But I believe it fairly captures the right balance between the contractual/private character of treaties and their status as the law of the land. It also reconciles (in the only way possible) a treaty's double life in both municipal and international law.

Classical canons have unquestionably exerted their influence on modern treaty interpretation. The vector of intellectual transmission is clear: from the classical sources (particularly Cicero and Quintilian), as received by early-Modern writers (especially Grotius, Pufendorf, Rutherforth and Vattel), as adopted in parallel form in early Supreme Court jurisprudence (in such cases as *The AMIABELLE ISABELLA*,[1216] *Geofroy v. Riggs*,[1217] and *Tucker v. Alexandroff*[1218]) and by the Vienna Convention on the Law of Treaties, and as refined in today's use of new, substantive canons of interpretation for international agreements. Whether it be a grammatical or syntactical canon, or an outcome-defining rule (such as that of liberal interpretation or of construction against the drafter), or a policy-preferred canon (like one protecting sovereignty or allowing private rights of action under treaties), these modes of construction all owe their debt to classical forms and expressions.

Lastly, it must be realized that this recipe of reviving old canons and mixing them with new, and expressly substantive, principles of interpretation is intended to achieve the demystification of treaties as public law. Because both the statutory and contractual metaphors for treaties have failed to satisfy, it remains to accept international agreements as a *sui generis* species of law. In

---

[1215]   *See generally*, Franck, supra note 769.

[1216]   19 U.S. (6 Wheat.) 1 (1821).

[1217]   133 U.S. 258 (1890).

[1218]   183 U.S. 424 (1902).

welcoming this conclusion, courts can still handle treaties as something familiar and comprehensible, and not as something that is alien or inscrutable. Without that confidence in interpretive values and norms, without that sense of place for international agreements in a constitutional order and hierarchy of law, treaty interpretation will remain a frustrating, inconclusive, and, perhaps, even dangerous exercise.

Coda

XIV THE USES AND ABUSES OF CLASSICISM IN LAW

The entire complex of canons in use by our courts today is the direct intellectual product of classical rhetorical thinking. I believe this book has established at least the beginnings of a formal proof of that proposition. I wish to conclude here, however, by answering two important challenges. The first is whether my conclusion that there is an intellectual connection between classical rhetoric and modern legal interpretation is fatally flawed by a false essentialism. I thus need to consider whether I have misapprehended an historiographic sense of causation, and failed to ponder whether rules of legal interpretation might better be understood as a product of "parallel evolution" in unique legal cultures. The second inquiry I need to make is whether it is even intellectually honest to make a claim that the ideas of classical antiquity continue to play a role in our modern legal discourse. This inquiry goes to the heart of any relationship that law and the classics can have today.

i. Causation has always been a tricky subject in intellectual history. How can one know for certain whether, and how, certain ideas were transmitted from one age to another? A strict rule of causation would probably defeat most assertions of intellectual transmission. And, indeed, there are no less than three key moments in which transmission of classical rhetorical ideas had to have been made in order for those ideas to have any modern relevance for the purposes of my study: (1) the early-Modern reception by publicists like Grotius and Pufendorf; (2) the early American experience of the Framing Generation; and (3) the relatively recent attempt to codify rules of treaty interpretation and their practical application in Rehnquist Court case law.

The first moment should be the easiest inquiry. But can I say with complete certainty that Grotius or other early-Modern writers actually read — and truly appreciated — classical rhetorical theory for construing legal texts?

Sure, Grotius and Pufendorf may have cited to such writers as Cicero, Quintilian and the author of *Rhetorica ad Herennium*.[1219]   But were these serious engagements with classical material, or, instead mere examples of intellectual virtuosity and misdirection? Obviously, intellectual causation is (relatively) easy to prove when a later writer explicitly uses the ideas of a previous writer. And that is certainly the case with early-Modern publicists for the law of nations. Perhaps more speculative is the use by these writers of the raw material of classical international relations (as related in classical works by Herodotus, Thucydides, Livy, Polybius and Tacitus), as "real" examples of problems in treaty interpretation.[1220]

In any event, as time wore on in the seventeenth and eighteenth centuries, writers made fewer direct references to classical literature, and, instead, tended to cite to earlier, modern writers. Vattel, Savigny, Rutherforth, and Kent did not cite Cicero or Polybius; they referenced Grotius or Pufendorf. So, as time went on, there was a telescoping in the attribution of ideas. This was certainly so for the Framing Generation in the United States. Despite a classically-trained cadre of leaders, and strong cross-currents of Roman Republican trope and aspiration, direct references to classical rhetoric theory of interpretation for legal texts were rare.[1221] But the idea of predictable rules for construction of statutes, treaties, and of the U.S. Constitution, were prevalent. Moreover, the substance of these rules — whether intentionally or unwittingly — followed classical models. When Elbridge Gerry, in debate before the First Congress, quoted Blackstone's interpretive maxim of finding legislative intent "by the signs most natural and probable ... the words, the context, the subject matter, the effect and consequences, or the spirit and reason of the law,"[1222] he was recycling not only the structure of the classical rhetorical *status* system, but also staking a position in the *scriptum/voluntas* debate. There may not have

---

[1219]   *See* supra § VII.iv.

[1220]   *See* supra § III.

[1221]   *See* supra § VIII.iii.

[1222]   1791 House Debates, supra note 537, at 75-81 (quoting Blackstone, see supra note 514).

been a convenient or obliging citation to a classical source for these ideas, but it is unquestioned that the Framing Generation had the motive and opportunity to use them in their discourse.

Such cannot be said, of course, for those that participated in the drafting of the 1969 Vienna Convention's provisions on treaty interpretation,[1223] nor the current members of the U.S. Supreme Court.[1224] And here, I acknowledge, the lines of intellectual transmission are the most attenuated, and the connections most subtle. Part of what I have written here is the intellectual historian's version of a scavenger hunt: attempting to isolate particular instances where modern codifiers or interpreters of treaties have invoked a rule of construction that resembles — in form, structure, or content — a classical canon. This was not soul-satisfying work, but necessary, and I believe I have at least made an intelligible attempt to suggest that the drafters of the 1969 Convention and the current Rehnquist Court have at least been influenced by sources, which, in turn, borrowed from classical motifs.

But I believe there is more than an intellectual connect-the-dots exercise at work here. As a matter of historical explanation, the approach I have adopted here would probably be characterized in G. Edward White's construct of legal history as "historiographic" or even "metahistoric."[1225] Or, alternatively, in using William W. Fisher III's schematic, I would undoubtedly be rated as some combination of "textualist," "contextualist," and "New Historicist" schools.[1226] This book has largely been about texts — of received wisdoms in their interpretation. The history here has been as much about writers writing about the meaning of legal texts, as it has been about the meaning itself of such texts as treaties. By the same token, my book has been contextual, in the sense of

---

[1223] *See* supra § X.iv.

[1224] *See* supra § XII.

[1225] *See* G. Edward White, INTERVENTION AND DETACHMENT: ESSAYS IN LEGAL HISTORY AND JURISPRUDENCE 18 (1994).

[1226] *See* William W. Fisher III, *Texts and Contexts: The Application to American Legal History of the Methodologies of Intellectual History*, 49 STAN. L. REV. 1065, 1088-92 (1997).

"suggesting or refining causal explanations ... [and] showing how concepts were developed in some discursive communities and then transmitted to others."[1227] Lastly, to the extent that I have identified what may be regarded as an unexpected or counter-intuitive exemplar of legal interpretation (treaty construction), as practiced through the ages, and as seen through the prism of classical rhetorical theory, I might well be offering an "historeme" for legal culture.[1228]

Insofar as I have failed to prove the necessary causation or to establish the needed relevance of my subject, I may well be guilty of an eccentric anecdotalism in this study. As to causation, I take comfort in what I have offered here as a defense of my claim that modern legal interpretation continues to be influenced by classical rhetorical forms. Moreover, as G. Edward White has observed,

> [i]ntellectual historians often operate with a less demanding notion of causal support. According to it, if a set of beliefs is held at the time an event occurs and the justifications for the event bear some trace of those beliefs, a claimed causal connection between the beliefs and the event is supported, at least provisionally.[1229]

Indeed, even if the development of rules for interpreting legal texts is purely situational and serendipitous — and thus every new generation recreates, in an intellectual vacuum, its own canons — I am not sure that such would fatally disparage my thesis here. Assuming such consistent "parallel evolution" of canons of interpretation, one might still legitimately wonder why it is the same rules appear to be replicated over, and over, and over again. So, I am satisfied at least, that the intellectual exercise I have engaged in this volume is fully justified on grounds of causation.

[1227] Id. at 1089.

[1228] For the notion of "historemes," *see* Joel Fineman, *The History of the Anecdote: Fiction and Fiction*, in THE NEW HISTORICISM 49, 57 (H. Aram Veeser ed., 1989).

[1229] Jack Goldsmith & Steven Walt, Erie *and the Irrelevance of Legal Positivism*, 84 VA. L. REV. 673, 681 & n.32 (attributing this suggestion to G.E. White).

ii. That leaves the question of relevance, and particularly the pertinence of classicism to modern law. I have found that classicism can take many different forms in current legal scholarship.[1230] Quite a few studies continue to provide citations to, and analyze the written sources of, classical antiquity in order to expound on narrow questions of legal doctrine. An obliging citation to Justinian's *Digest* may be the beginning and end of a doctrinal writer's consideration of classical writings.[1231] Invariably, the purpose of these citations is to show some logical progression of a legal rule from Roman law, into the English common law, and thence into modern American legal practice.

The success or failure of these references — and the scholarship that is able to produce them — is, in large measure, based on fortuity: whether the nature of the legal rule analyzed lends itself to a historical analysis. It depends also, I think, on the manner of direct transmission of legal principles. The extent to which modern courts continue to cite a classical source for a legal rule may dictate the interest of academic lawyers in examining whether the provenance of the ancient source was properly appreciated by the judge or

---

[1230] My discussion here purposefully excludes the legal history of ancient law. For some of the best exemplars of current scholarship on Roman law, *see* the works of Alan Watson, cited variously in this study and such pieces as David Bogan, *Ignoring history: the liability of ship's masters, innkeepers and stablekeepers under Roman law*, 36 AJLH 326 (1992); Lambros E. Kotsiris, *An Antitrust Case in Ancient Greek Law*, 22 INT'L LAW. 451 (1988); Barry Nicholas, *Verbal Forms in Roman Law*, 66 TUL. L. REV. 1605 (1992); Martin T. Sigillito, *The* unus iudex *in Roman law and Roman legal history*, 33 ST. LOUIS U. L.J. 481 (1989); Peter Stein, *Justinian's Compilation: Classical Legacy and Legal Source*, 8 TUL. EUR. & CIV. L. FORUM 1 (1993); Peter Stein, *Judge and Jurist in the Civil Law: A Historical Interpretation*, 46 LA. L. REV. 241 (1985); Alan Watson, *Thinking Property at Rome*, 68 CHI.-KENT L. REV. 1355 (1993); John Frederick Winkler, *Roman Law in Anglo-Saxon England*, 13 J. LEG. HIST. 101 (1992).

[1231] *See, e.g.,* Michael A. Dawson, Note, *Popular Sovereignty, Double Jeopardy, and the Dual Sovereignty Problem*, 102 YALE L.J. 281 (1992); Lee Hargrave, *The Public Trust Doctrine: A Plea for Precision*, 53 LA. L. REV. 1535 (1993); Mark Peter Henriques, *Desuetude and Declaratory Judgment: A New Challenge to Obsolete Laws*, 76 VA. L. REV. 1057 (1990); Frank R. Herrmann & Bronlow M. Speer, *Facing the Accuser: Ancient and Medieval Precursors of the Confrontation Clause*, 34 VA. J. INT'L L. 481 (1994); J.H. Merryman, *The Public Interest in Cultural Property*, 77 CALIF. L. REV. 339 (1989); A.N. Yiannopoulos, *Possession*, 51 LA. L. REV. 523 (1991).

tribulal.[1232] I do not believe, however, that there are any areas of law today the doctrinal integrity of which depend on references to antiquity.[1233]

[1232] A computer-aided database search of all cases (both federal and state) decided in the United states since 1945 yielded 33 which cited directly to the Digest. (WESTLAW, Allcases database, search performed on July 28, 1999).

The Digest has been cited as authority for propositions relating to the following areas of law:

(a) *desuetude*; *Pryor v. Gainer*, 177 W.Va. 218, 351 S.E.2d 404 (1986);

(b) *double jeopardy*; *Bartkus v. People*, 359 U.S. 121 (1959); *Committee on Legal Ethics of the West Virginia State Bar v. Printz*, 187 W.Va. 182, 416 S.E.2d 720 (1992); *Commonwealth v. Bolden*, 472 Pa. 602, 373 A.2d 90 (1977);

(c) *usufruct*; *U.S. Daughters of 1812 - Chalmette Chapter v. Louisiana Dep't of Culture*, 395 So.2d 455 (La. App. 4th Cir. 1981);

(d) *preemption*; *Labruzza v. Hardware Mut. Cas. Ins. Co.*, 207 F. Supp. 789 (E.D. La. 1962);

(e) *undue influence by attorney in client's will*; *Kirschbaum v. Dillon*, 58 Ohio St.3d 58, 567 N.E.2d 1291 (1991); *In re Lobb's Will*, 177 Or. 162, 160 P.2d 295 (1945);

(f) *wills and reciprocal appointments*; *In re Stringer's Estate*, 80 Wyo. 389, 343 P.2d 508 (1959);

(g) *physician-assisted suicide*; *People v. Kevorkian*, 1993 Westlaw 603212 (Mich. Cir. Ct. Dec. 13, 1993).

Of course, it should be no surprise that the number of citations to the Digest has fallen-off in recent years. There is hardly any point to such a citation, in view of earlier American decisions holding on the relevant point, or the availability of standard legal dictionaries (such as BLACK'S LAW DICTIONARY) which provide obliging citations to Digest sections.

[1233] One possible exception may be admiralty and maritime law, in which many cases continue to cite not only to the Digest but also the Rhodian Sea Law, the first codification of maritime law in the first century B.C. The Rhodian Sea Law has been cited in 15 cases since 1945. *See* search conducted as specified in supra note. The Rhodian Sea Law has been cited in cases involving:

(a) *general average*; *Eagle Terminal Tankers, Inc. v. Insurance Co. of U.S.S.R. (Ingosstrakh), Ltd.*, 489 F. Supp. 920 (S.D.N.Y. 1980); *American African Export Co., Inc. v. S.S. Export Champion*, 442 F. Supp. 715 (S.D.N.Y. 1977); *Orient Mid-East Lines, Inc. v. Shipment of Rice on Board S.S. Orient Transporter*, 496 F.2d 1032 (5th Cir. 1974); *Cia Atlantica Pacifica, S.A., v. Humble Oil & Refining Co.*, 274 F. Supp. 884 (D. Md. 1967);

(b) *limitation of liability*; *In re Independent Towing Co.*, 242 F. Supp. 950 (E.D. La. 1965);

(c) *salvage*; *R.M.S. Titanic, Inc. v. Haver*, 171 F.3d 943 (4th Cir. 1999); *Margrate Shipping Co. v. M/V JA ORGERON*, 143 F.3d 976, 985 n.11 (5th Cir. 1998).

And, as I think can be gathered from the foregoing discussion, the rules surrounding the interpretation of legal texts are no longer dependent on classical sources. Direct citations to the *Digest* extracts on the *ius interpretandi* or to the Roman rhetoricians like Cicero and Quintilian are just not made today.[1234] There is no point, of course: both the structure and the substance of the Roman's rules of statutory interpretation have been transmitted to us by other means.

But there is a second form of legal scholarship employing the sources and methods of classical studies. There have been a handful of writers who have sought to make connections in the intellectual legal history of antiquity and today.[1235] Eschewing narrow doctrinal writing, they have sought, instead, to bridge the ancient past and today's legal world through a study of ideas. This kind of academic writing demands, as Professor Martha Nussbaum has so forcefully stated, strong scholarly qualifications in classical studies, including the ability to read Latin and Greek in the original, to understand the integrity and transmission of texts, and an appreciation of ancient history, politics, and cultures.[1236]

iii. Despite these hurdles (or, perhaps, because of them), I believe that the brand of intellectual history offers the best chance of successful discourse between the two disciplines of law and classics. I think this conclusion is largely borne out by the research I have undertaken here. Any consideration of the proper means of interpreting legal texts must, as of necessity, involve a subtle understanding of the conventions associated with meaning in any form of

---

[1234] *But see In re Lumis*, 101 Misc. 258, 265, 166 N.Y.S. 936 (Surr. New York County 1917) (construction of a will) (citation to 3 Quintilian, supra note 6, at 135-43 (passages vii. 5 & 6)).

[1235] *See, e.g.,* Paul Gewirtz, *Aeschylus' Law*, 101 HARV. L. REV. 1043 (1988) (on sexual equality in *The Orestia*); Richard Hyland, Pacta Sunt Servanda: *A Meditation*, 34 VA. J. INT'L L. 406 (1994) (on the notion of keeping promises); Martha C. Nussbaum, *Platonic Love and Colorado Law: The Relevance of Ancient Greek Norms to Modern Sexual Controversies*, 80 VA. L. REV. 1515 (1994).

[1236] *See* Nussbaum, supra note 1235, at 1607-22.

writing.[1237]   The classical rhetorician's stylized schematic of *status legalis* represents one set of these interpretive practices.

That leaves one fundamental problem to be addressed concerning the legitimacy of this branch of classical studies: should lawyers even be interested in classical rhetoric?   The answer depends, I think, on our reaction to the professional conflict which raged between orators and jurisconsults in the late Roman Republic and early Principate period. If one sides with the jurists and embraces a vision of law as an autonomous science, any association with the orators and rhetorical theory will be very disquieting. Any recognition of a continuing influence of the *constitutiones legales* in forming our understanding of statutes and other legal documents will, likewise, be dismissed.

But what if one accepts Aristotle's view that rhetoric is the art of reasoning appropriate to those things that "are such as seem to present us with alternative possibilities"?[1238] Surely one must count justice among those matters that cannot be established by demonstrative proof.[1239] With this recognition, one can see that the orators posed a double-edged — and insoluble — conundrum to the Roman jurists. The jurisconsults could persist in their claim that law was autonomously scientific, and thus perpetuate a professional identity in distinction to the classical orator's art. But, if they did so, the jurists would be forced, as Cicero demanded,[1240] to embrace a system of rules to govern their science. What the orators wanted was a system of law and not a static code of laws.[1241]

[1237]   *See* Steven Mailloux, *Rhetorical Hermeneutics*, in Levinson & Mailloux, supra note 553, at 345.

[1238]   Aristotle, Rhetoric, supra note 142, at 17-21 (passage i.2.5-10).

[1239]   *See* Max Hamburger, MORALS AND LAW: THE GROWTH OF ARISTOTLE'S LEGAL THEORY (1951).

[1240]   *See* 1 Cicero, de Oratore, supra note 5, at 259 (passage ii.19.83); Cicero, DE LEGIBUS 429-31 (Clinton W. Keyes transl. Loeb Classical Library ed. 1928) (passage ii.19.47).

[1241]   *See* Kastely, supra note 602, at 13 n.30. *See also* Miller, supra note 348, at 1183-91.

In short, the orators said that if the jurists wished to be scientists they had to adopt first principles. This the jurists would not do because it would have meant abandoning their monopoly of specialized legal knowledge achieved through casuistry and by incremental changes in legal rules.

The classical rhetoricians thus succeeded in placing the Roman jurists firmly on the horns of a fiendish dilemma. It is a predicament out of which modern lawyers have yet to extricate themselves. The ambivalence of legal academics about rhetoric and its place in legal discourse is proof enough of that discomfiture.[1242] Of course, some legal scholars have gone too far in embracing context and structuralist readings of law, emphasizing only arguments about law, and not the doctrines of law. Now that many have repudiated legal science, they find solace in rhetoric. It is a cold comfort, I believe, because the rhetoric that many legal scholars today embrace bears only the slightest resemblance to its classical progenitors.[1243]

The relationship between *status legalis* and the *ius interpretandi* lies at the heart of any modern understanding of the synergy between law and rhetoric, between classicism and modernity. Notwithstanding the legal historiography, the connection between legal science and oratory in antiquity was not overtly hostile. There was professional rivalry, for sure, and also strong ideological constraints on cooperation between jurists and orators. But the stories I have narrated here come with a clear moral that art and science are both needed in the process of legal interpretation. One is not complete without the other. The Roman lawyer's casuistry made sense only in context with the wider use of *constitutiones* and *topoi* of judicial discourse. The *rhetorica* of Cicero and

---

[1242] For some of the literature of the revival of interest in rhetoric and law, *see* the works of James Boyd White, including JUSTICE AS TRANSLATION: AN ESSAY IN CULTURAL AND LEGAL CRITICISM (1990); HERACLES' BOW: ESSAYS ON THE RHETORIC AND POETICS OF THE LAW (1985); WHEN WORDS LOSE THEIR MEANING: CONSTITUTIONS AND RECONSTITUTIONS OF LANGUAGE, CHARACTER AND COMMUNITY (1984); THE LEGAL IMAGINATION: STUDIES IN THE NATURE OF LEGAL THOUGHT AND EXPRESSION (1973). For a compendium of recent literature on legal discourse, *see* Kastely, supra note 602, at 28 n.60.

[1243] This is a point I made in David J. Bederman, *Stalking Phaedrus*, 18 GA. J. INT'L & COMP. L. 527 (1988) (reviewing David Kennedy, INTERNATIONAL LEGAL STRUCTURES (1987)).

Quintilian were the natural companions of the legal handbooks (*institutiones*) of the Roman jurists, later compiled into the *Digest*. The rhetor's use of *stasis* in legal interpretation complemented the jurist's crafting of maxims of construction.

The classical canons of legal construction were an intellectual mix of rhetoric and legal casuistry, just as today's "new" canons blend time-honored customs, linguistic sophistication, constitutional values, and policy science. Our contemporary rules of legal construction are a subtle intermixture of rhetorical *topoi* for legal discourse and casuistic, situational rules of pragmatic interpretation.[1244] Like two great rivers, law and rhetoric have meandered and mingled, running their course through time and scholarship to modernity. Classical study reminds us that every drink we take from the river both adds and diminishes the intellectual purity of the stream. This study, modeled on classical forms, has run its course, too. Part meditation, part poetic, it has sought to navigate the river. Classicism is about taking that journey. *Quam fluctus diversi, quam mare conjuncti.*[1245]

[1244] *See* Viehweg, supra note 18, at 99-107; Robert Alexy, A THEORY OF LEGAL ARGUMENTATION (Neil MacCormick & Ruth Alder transl. 1989); Bruce McLeod, *Rules and Rhetoric*, 23 OSGOODE HALL L. J. 305 (1985).

[1245] 2 Ovid, METAMORPHOSES (F.J. Miller transl. Loeb Classical Library ed. 1984) (passage xv, *Aesculapius*).

INDEX